CRITICAL ACCLAIM
FOR *TRAVELERS' TALES*

"*Travelers' Tales San Francisco* will put any tourist in the know and open the eyes of even the smuggest native."

—Margaret Weir, *San Francisco Chronicle*

"*Travelers' Tales San Francisco* is the best collection in the excellent *Travelers' Tales* series.

—John Muncie, *Los Angeles Times*

"From the grittiness of the Mission District to the overcrowded streets of Chinatown, the Victorian houses known as 'Painted Ladies' to the history of Golden Gate Park, this book is a compendium of the many faces that San Francisco presents to the world. Gay or straight, latter-day hippie or New Age roller bladers, there is literally something for everyone here."

—Everett Potter, *New York Times Syndicate*

"Like other books in the series, *Travelers' Tales San Francisco* celebrates its subject with an eclectic collection of essays and articles by a wide variety of authors. As you delve in tothe book, a richly textured and multifaceted picture of The City begins to emerge. The stories bear in at their subject from every conceivable angle…"

—John Flinn, *San Francisco Examiner*

"This is the stuff memories can be duplicated from."

—Karen Krebsbach, *Foreign Service Journal*

"A revolutionary new style of travel guidebook…."

—*New York Times News Service*

"*Travelers' Tales* is a valuable additon to any pre-departure reading list."

—Tony Wheeler, publisher, *Lonely Planet Publications*

"Like having been there, done it, seen it. If there's one thing traditional guidebooks lack, it's the really juicy travel information, the personal stories about back alley and brief encounters. The *Travelers' Tales* series fills this gap with an approach that's all anecdotes, no directions."

—Jim Gullo, *Diversion*

P9-CFQ-990

"I can't think of a better way to get comfortable with a destination than by delving into *Travelers' Tales*…before reading a guidebook, before seeing a travel agent. The series helps visitors refine their interests and readies them to communicate with the people they come in contact with."

—Paul Glassman, Society of American Travel Writers

"The essays are lyrical, magical, and evocative: some of the imges make you want to rinse your mouth out to clear the dust."

—Karen Troianello, *Yakima Herald-Republic*

T R A V E L E R S ' T A L E S

SAN FRANCISCO

TRAVELERS' TALES

SAN FRANCISCO

Collected and Edited by

JAMES O'REILLY   LARRY HABEGGER
SEAN O'REILLY

TRAVELERS' TALES, INC.
SAN FRANCISCO, CALIFORNIA

Distributed by
O'REILLY AND ASSOCIATES, INC.
101 MORRIS STREET
SEBASTOPOL, CALIFORNIA 95472

Travelers' Tales San Francisco
Collected and Edited by James O'Reilly, Larry Habegger, and Sean O'Reilly

Cover design by Judy Anderson
Cover stamp by Edie Freedman
Cover photograph: © 1995 by Shaun Heffernan
Spot illustrations by David White
Illustrations in the story "Old Growth Houses" by Wendy Wheeler
Section break illustrations by Nina Stewart
Maps by Keith Granger
Page layout by Patty Holden, using the fonts Bembo and Boulevard

Frontispiece by Ambrose Bierce, reprinted from *San Francisco Almanac: Everything You Want to Know About Everyone's Favorite City,* edited by Gladys Hansen.

Printing History

| June 1996: | First Edition |
| April 1997: | Second Printing |

ISBN: 1-885211-08-2

Careful now,
We're dealing here with a myth.
This city is a point upon a map of fog;
Lemuria in a city unknown.
Like us,
It doesn't quite exist.

—Ambrose Bierce

Table of Contents

Part One
ESSENCE

Part Two
SOME THINGS TO DO

Part Three
GOING YOUR OWN WAY

Part Four
IN THE SHADOWS

Part Five
THE LAST WORD

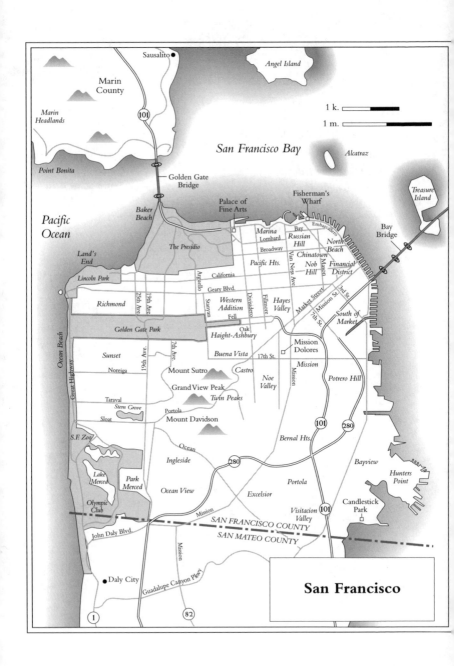

San Francisco

Preface

TRAVELERS' TALES

We are all outsiders when we travel. Whether we are traveling abroad or roaming about our own city or country, we often enter territory so unfamiliar that our frames of reference become inadequate. We need advice not just to avoid offense and danger, but to make our experiences richer, deeper, and more fun.

Traditionally, travel guides have answered the basic questions: what, when, where, how, and how much. A good guidebook is indispensable for all the practical matters that demand attention. More recently, many guidebooks have added bits of experiential insight to their standard fare, but something important is still missing: guidebooks don't really prepare *you*, the individual with feelings and fears, hopes and dreams, goals.

This kind of preparation is best achieved through travelers' tales, for we get our inner landmarks more from anecdote than information. Nothing can replace listening to the experience of others, to the war stories that come out after a few drinks, to the memories that linger and beguile. For millennia it's been this way: at watering holes and wayside inns, the experienced traveler tells those nearby what lies ahead on the ever-mysterious road. Stories stoke the imagination, inspire, frighten, and teach. In stories we see more clearly the urges that bring us to wander, whether it's hunger for change, adventure, self-knowledge, love, curiosity, sorrow, or even something as prosaic as a job assignment or two weeks off.

But travelers' accounts, while profuse, can be hard to track down. Many are simply doomed in a throwaway publishing world. And few of us have the time anyway to read more than one or two books, or the odd pearl found by chance in the Sunday travel section. Wanderers for years, we've often faced this issue. We've always told ourselves when we got home that we would prepare better for the next trip—read more, study more, talk to more people—but life always seems to interfere and we've rarely managed to do so to our satisfaction. That is one reason for this series. We needed a kind of experiential primer that guidebooks don't offer.

Another path that led us to *Travelers' Tales* has been seeing the enormous changes in travel and communication over the last two decades. It is no longer unusual to have ridden a pony across Mongolia, to have celebrated an auspicious birthday on Mt. Kilimanjaro, or honeymooned on the Loire. The one-world monoculture has risen with daunting swiftness, weaving a new cross-cultural rug: no longer is it surprising to encounter former headhunters watching *All-Star Wrestling* on their satellite feed, no longer is it shocking to find the last guy at the end of the earth wearing a Harvard t-shirt and asking if you know Michael Jordan. The global village exists in a rudimentary fashion, but it is real.

In 1980, Paul Fussell wrote in *Abroad: British Literary Traveling Between the Wars* a cranky but wonderful epitaph for travel as it was once known, in which he concluded that "we are all tourists now, and there is no escape." It has been projected by some analysts that by the year 2000, tourism will be the world's largest industry; others say it already is. In either case, this is a horrifying prospect—hordes of us hunting for places that have not been trod on by the rest of us!

Fussell's words have the painful ring of truth, but this is still our world, and it is worth seeing and will be worth seeing next year, or in 50 years, simply because it will always be worth meeting others who continue to see life in different terms than we do despite the best efforts of telecommunication and advertising talents. No amount of creeping homogeneity can quell the endless variation of humanity, and travel in the end is about people, not places. Places only provide different venues, as it were, for life, in which we are all pilgrims who need to talk to each other.

There are also many places around the world where intercultural friction and outright xenophobia are increasing. And the very fact that travel endangers cultures and pristine places more quickly than it used to calls for extraordinary care on the part of today's traveler, a keener sense of personal responsibility. The world is not our private zoo or theme park; we need to be better prepared before we go, so that we might become honored guests and not vilified intruders.

In *Travelers' Tales,* we collect useful and memorable anecdotes to produce the kind of sampler we've always wanted to read before setting out. These stories will show you some of the spectrum of experiences to be had or avoided in each country. The authors come from many walks of life: some are teachers, some are musicians, some are entrepreneurs, all are wanderers with a tale to tell. Their stories won't help you be an insider as so many travel books promise—but they will help you to deepen and enrich the experience that you will have as an outsider. Where we've excerpted books, we urge you to go out and read the full work, because no selection can ever do an author justice.

Each *Travelers' Tales* is organized into five simple parts. In the first, we've chosen stories that reflect the ephemeral yet pervasive essence of a place. Part II contains stories about places and activities that others have found worthwhile. In Part III, we've chosen stories by people who have made a special connection between their lives and interests and the people and places they visited. Part IV shows some of the struggles and challenges facing a region and its people, and Part V, "The Last Word," is just that, something of a grace note or harmonic to remind you of the book as a whole.

Our selection of stories in each *Travelers' Tales* is by no means comprehensive, but we are confident it will prime your pump, and make your use of regular guidebooks much more meaningful. *Travelers' Tales* are not meant to replace other guides, but to accompany them. No longer will you have to go to dozens of sources to map the personal side of your journey. You'll be able to reach for *Travelers' Tales*, and truly prepare yourself before you go.

JAMES O'REILLY AND LARRY HABEGGER
Series Editors

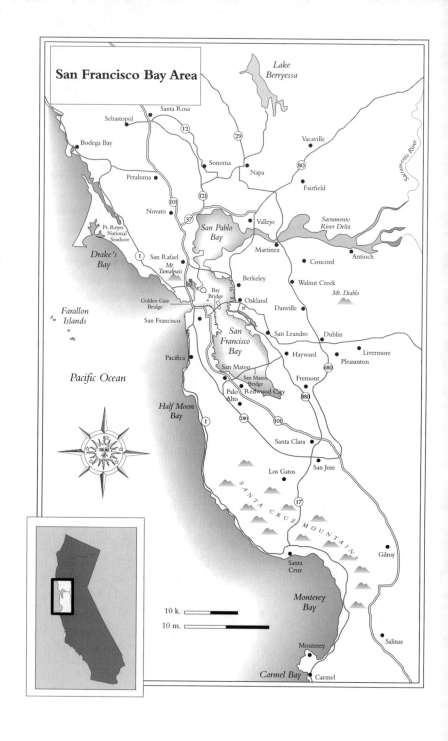

San Francisco: An Introduction

San Francisco is only 220 years old, but it is one of the world's most beloved cities, spoken of in the same breath as Paris, Venice, and Rome. To understand San Francisco one must understand that it was built by gold. In 1845 it was a hamlet of 150 people. In 1849, just after gold was discovered in the Sierra foothills but before word had spread, the population was 1,000. By the time a decade had passed, the population had swelled to 50,000—at that time one of the greatest human migrations in history.

It was a city of tremendous, instant wealth, full of miners, sailors, thieves, and vigilantes. It attracted every kind of reprobate and hard worker imaginable. Fortunes were made and lost in the blink of an eye. There were so many vessels in the harbor that residents spoke of a "forest of masts." Ships were abandoned and later buried in the landfill, or used as prisons, hotels, and warehouses. The city went up overnight, building out over the water before rising up the hills.

Gold drew adventurers and desperadoes, and they in turn drew and continue to draw spiritual desperadoes who constantly enrich the human skyline—people who aren't satisfied, who come and create new worlds for themselves and others.

San Francisco was born of immigrants and fortune seekers, and in fact attracted a new kind of immigrant to America—from China and Australia and Latin America. The city was built as a kind of international project, for despite the fact that it is near some of the world's most fertile valleys, almost everything was imported. Along with its incredibly diverse ethnic population, this dependency on the outside world gave the city from its very start a cosmopolitan flavor. The birth of San Francisco was the creation of America in miniature—a boiling cultural melting pot. As poet

Robert Hass said, "One hundred and fifty years ago, you could still throw a rock from the rickety hill-climbing boomtown and hit the Neolithic. On one day it was a sprinkling of Miwok villages among the grassy bayside hills and on the next day the Victorian novelist Anthony Trollope was walking out of a Palace Hotel in each room of which a painted garland of sunset-colored roses twined soulfully around the rim of a porcelain chamberpot."

San Francisco has survived seven major fires, the devastating 1906 earthquake and scores of others, it has been the site of pain and romance for thousands who embarked from Fort Mason on the Liberty Ships during World War II, bound for the Pacific Theater. And while the Presidio's crumbling bunkers overlooking the Pacific may bring back memories of war, the city is also full of the memories of peace, for the United Nations had its beginnings here in 1945.

San Francisco is also the heart of the Bay Area, a fertile crescent that includes Silicon Valley to the south, Berkeley—that stew of alternative thinking—to the east across the Bay, and Napa and Sonoma Valleys, America's premier wine producing regions, an hour to the north. It is also the center of the Golden Gate National Recreation Area (GGNRA), which is the largest urban national park in the world.

With only 46.6 square miles inside its borders, San Francisco is a walker's city with endless opportunities for exploration: fog-shrouded hills, shadowy Chinatown alleys, cliff-like streets that you descend with your heart in your mouth, ghostly cypresses at Land's End that moan in the wind. It is a place of endless romance. As one cab driver commented, San Francisco is "a city full of people wanting to be here."

But whatever you see and do, go somewhere near the Bay or the Pacific and sit for a while with the wind in your face. Walk Nob Hill at night with the whine of the cable beneath your feet. Think about the world and the meaning of things. For there is something in San Francisco's air, something catalytic (even the earth moves here) that will help you understand your mortality. San Francisco is America's spiritual home—a place for the rascal, the lover, the entrepreneur, the madman and the monk, in all of us.

PART ONE

ESSENCE

STEVE VAN BEEK

* * *

Pearl Necklace

An expatriate finds his way home.

A STRING OF LIGHTS DISAPPEARING INTO THE MAUVE MIST OF A pre-dawn winter sky. That's my first memory of San Francisco. It came at the end of a cramped, drowsy ride on a Greyhound bus that loped through the night down Interstate 5 from Portland.

The wheel hum, abruptly rising two octaves as the tires bit bridge bitumen, woke me. Groggily peering out the window, I saw a gray blur. It took a moment's focusing to realize that the fog was not in my brain but beyond the windowpane, big thick pillows like wet wash hanging from the bridge stanchions. Within it, smudges of light that faded with distance, faint pearls of the long necklace stretching across the Bay. I had arrived. It was Christmas vacation my senior year of university, 1965, my first trip beyond the forests of Oregon.

But then, having begun so hopefully, the picture goes blank. I think I remained awake but no further images engraved themselves in memory. Perhaps the fog was too thick to see anything except the gauzy contours of the city's towers. Then, the bus rolled into an anonymous station and my friend drove me to Stanford where we spent a week with his parents. A string of lights, vaguely re-membered. Not much to lure me back to the city decades later.

The next year, I left the United States and followed my fancy west to the East. Asia became my home and aside from short visits to Portland and two long stays in New York, I neglected to return to my homeland for 30 years. San Francisco was my natural gateway since transpacific flights called there. For my few days in the city—usually fumbling through numbing jet lag—I stayed with a friend, a juggler named Ray Jason. I'd met him in a Shinto temple hostel in Takayama at the foot of the Japanese Alps. He was traveling the world, juggling and absorbing every circus or street performance he encountered. In Bangkok, where I was living, I'd taken him to perform in the open-air Weekend Market and he'd drawn enthusiastic crowds. Every couple of years after that, I'd flop down in his Steiner Street apartment in transit to and from Portland.

Not once did I regard San Francisco as anything other than a way station. It was too... American, too fey, too smug, and too cute. It lacked the cultural viscera of New York, or the underside that might have lent it some excitement. It was fine for a stop, but not for a stay.

But then Asia began to lose its allure. Or I began to tire of naïveté, din, and chaos. The erotic exotic that had lured me to the East was being cemented

There's something about the very appropriate name San Francisco. St. Francis, the most benevolent saint in the hierarchy, was the archetypal caretaker of the wounded. His nurturing and tolerance allowed for healing and growth.

Like its namesake, San Francisco opens its arms to all sentient beings. The emotionally and spiritually wounded, in particular, have always come here looking for freedom and change, for a place to grow and be themselves.

San Francisco is headquarters of The Rainbow Nation. Here you will find all races, all orientations, all creeds coexisting far, and we mean FAR, more sanely than they do in any other American city. There isn't that nasty incessant battle for ethnic superiority one finds in the East. Other parts of the country, especially New York or Boston, seem weighted down by the legacy of their immigrant past. But San Francisco is the metropolis of possibilities. It is soft and misty. Like a dream. It seems beyond history.

—Jim Crotty, "San Francisco, What the Hell Did You Do to Your Hair?" Monk, The Mobile Magazine

over in a frantic effort to mimic the developed West. But it was an ersatz modernization. Although its gleaming facade suggested efficiency, its glass walls cloaked the same disorder that had imbued bazaars with their charm. But this concrete and anodized glass was charmless and, ultimately, soulless, concerned only with filling its pockets, not its spiritual wells. Perhaps it was my advancing age. Maybe I was merely seeking a cocoon as one does when he grows weary of traveling. I also needed to find out if I was still an American, and the only place to do it was...America. But where to start looking for myself?

I considered the heartland but I'd been away too long to link with it and its self-satisfied introversion, its celebration of itself achieved by blinkering itself to everything outside its immediate ken. I'd seen too much, knew too much, knew that in the end I knew nothing.

The Midwest, East Coast, and South were equally alien. Settling there would be like emigrating to a new country. I had spent years acquiring a new culture that in the end turned out to be nothing more than a veneer. I wanted to fit, to slide like a peg into a hole. That was possible only by returning to my roots. I'd have to find them on the West Coast.

Seattle and Portland were eternally shrouded in gray. Los Angeles mirrored Asia's anarchy and gaudy materialism. Shrill, focused on fame and dross, lacking geographic or spiritual anchors, L.A.'s burnished surfaces concealed psychoses foreign to my spirit. I needed to live somewhere willing to admit that it didn't have all the answers (or that it was even necessary to have them) but found joy in the search for them.

I wanted a city that was embedded in nature, that reached to Asia as well as Europe. I wanted to be surrounded by a few people who plunged fingers deep into soil instead of skittering across the surface, concerned only with movement across broad expanses, who were not terrified they would sink into quagmire if they paused for a moment.

San Francisco seemed to embody quietude. The reasons could be quantified, I suppose, but in the end, one's bond to a place transcends logic. It is an ineluctable tendon binding a city with a soft spot deep in one's gut. The city enveloped me, made me part of it, excused my foreignness after three decades. It held both the clear, cold light of sun and the murky uncertainty of mist. In a city of fog, there can be no certainties. Even its fog was distinctive. Contrary to Sandburg, it didn't come on little cat feet, it sloshed in like a sopping moggy slogging indoors from a storm.

In San Francisco, I could rest in the bosom of a cosmopolitan city or cross a bridge and disappear into a forest. It was the land, it was the sea, it was ponds, parks, and city streets that ran at crazy angles, horizontal and vertical. It was the scent of Asian rice and the aroma of European bread, of green tea and black coffee, of cordite from Chinese firecrackers and perfumes from Gay Freedom Day parades.

It was a city of endless options, of peoples and hues from odd pages of the atlas, speaking in tongues, blending ancient and modern cultures. It ran from the spreadsheets of the Financial District to the occultism of the Haight, through a wealth of genders and persuasions. It was individuals pursuing personal pursuits but always with an Asian tolerance that allowed great numbers of people to live in close proximity and share precious space.

It was Asia and Africa and Europe and a sprinkling of the best of America. It was a place to stretch a leg and exercise a mind, to bask in hard sunshine and shelter from rain and mist, an indoor-outdoor kind of place, a cosmos in a polity.

Ultimately, it was a string of pearly lights that began at my feet and faded with distance, disappearing into the fog, beckoning me to follow them into the unknown, just to see where they led. It was home.

Steve Van Beek is a writer, photographer, and film maker who has lived in Bangkok for the last 30 years and is now in the process of moving to San Francisco. He is the author of many books about Asia, and he has a special interest in rivers. He has explored a dozen of them, trying to understand how riparian people's perceptions of rivers affect the ways they use or abuse them. For his solo journeys, he was elected a Fellow of the Explorers Club.

"Plano del Puerto de San Francisco." So reads the formal penmanship, now two centuries old...

On August 5th, 1775, Juan Manuel de Ayala, captain of the *San Carlos*, anchored his ship outside the Golden Gate. His pilot and artist, José de Cañizares, sailed into the Bay on a launch, along with ten shipmates. During the next two months, as the *San Carlos* stood anchored off Angel Island (named by Cañizares), the pilot became the first person to map the spiny curves of our peninsula.

The following year, Cañizares returned. Now he mapped the Bay Area in detail, leading soldiers through old redwood groves and Ohlone villages. He added trees and grassy marshes to his map, and painted the landscape with blue, green, tan, and yellow watercolors. The delta area and its rivers were explored. Weights were tied to ropes and dropped into the coastal waters, sounding depth. The rocky points along San Francisco's crest were drawn as spiky promontories, jutting into the Bay like sharks' teeth.

As a pilot, Cañizares's task was straightforward. With his map the door to San Francisco would be wedged open, and Spanish conquest of the territory was assured. As an artist, though, he reflected upon more subtle goals. His map, he realized, was the very first; it had to contain everything that one needs to know at the bare beginning of things.

What is the most important at these moments of entry? What do we require from our simplest maps? Angles of approach, of course. A sense of size, certainly. An arrow pointing north, to place us among the stars. But even more essential, we need to share the explorer's vision. We must sense the land itself, sniff its air, hear the rustle of its leaves.

So Cañizares painted his map with earthy hues, peppered it with icons of vegetation, and named the islands after the birds and angels that visited him as he drew. He was able to see the land as a whole, unsullied by the industry of Man. Dividing and conquering, building and damming, sawing and dredging; these would come later.

Studying the map, we sense a kind of poised admiration: just as a cat will often watch a bird, before pouncing; or as we might admire a carefully arranged salad before tossing it into the air with tongs.

—Jeff Greenwald, "A Meditation on Maps"

⋆ ⋆ ⋆

Wild Light

Isn't it time you wore a bone in your nose?

SAN FRANCISCO HAS BEEN A CONSISTENT PROVIDER OF TRENDS TO our ever-trend-conscious nation. When I moved there in 1970, the city had just finished inventing and (simultaneously) burying the hippies. The Haight-Ashbury neighborhood sported all the scars of the hard-fought war for Love and Happiness. The winner, sad to say, was neither Love nor Happiness, but hard-core, street-toughened Addiction, which stalked the once-flowery street corners. But enough hippies still remained to give the place the dreamy air of the Love-Ins and Be-Ins, although most communes, head shops, bookstores, and cafes were crashing down hard.

In 1970, one could still wear flowers in one's hair, but it was advisable to also carry a can of Mace. There was nothing in this whole country like San Francisco one quarter of a century ago. While the war in Vietnam was growing increasingly uglier, the separate "nation" of the disaffected young had set up a world with different rules right in the heart of a major American city. If you didn't have any money—and most of the pilgrims reaching the Haight didn't—you could always eat for free at one of the many communal kitchens, or "crash" at one of the "pads" that constellated the neighborhood, or get clothes from the Diggers or from the "free boxes." There were hippies elsewhere in the world, but the prototype was formed in the city of St. Francis and, like that vegetarian, pigeon-loving saint, the Frisco hippie was filled with innocent (or naïve) delight in his magical city on the hills.

The magic of San Francisco, I always thought, was a consequence of the light. I felt blessed to wake up to a bright morning on 24th Street—near Dolores Park—with the light streaming in my bedroom window. It was as if the whole sky had just come in and surrounded the bed. Below, people walked their dogs to the park, enveloped in a golden shimmer that was both healing and forgiving. Going out for a doughnut and an espresso, I heard the word "balmy" a lot. (Croissants hadn't yet conquered the West; it was still a doughnut-and-toast world.)

Most people were really nice. They had a "sunny disposition," so to speak, even though Richard Nixon was still president, the war in Vietnam had just moved to Cambodia, and the "Zodiac" killer was loose. Some people were so nice, in fact, that, according to San Francisco's beloved wit Herb Caen, they caused a four-year drought by constantly telling everyone to "have a nice day."

On an average day, Golden Gate Park, aptly named, was home to 99 varieties of light. I counted them. I will mention a few—you can discover others: the oblique light between eucalyptus leaves at sunrise. The light in the Garden of Fragrance, which is set up as a cornucopia for every sense *but* sight. The little chunks of colored light that fall on the ground between the light-thin profusion of orchids inside the Conservatory of Flowers. The light on Hippie Hill, where the first Love-In was held (if you squint you can still see 11,000 naked hippies waving their arms hopefully). The light-turning-to-cloud in late afternoon as the Pacific breezes drive in the fog.

In San Francisco, the light changes with the clouds, from brilliant to foggy gray. When I lived there, it matched my psychic weather, from cheeriness in the morning to melancholy in the afternoon, but I was never sure if the light followed my moods or my moods followed the light.

The key, I believe, to all the novelties that sprang out of San Francisco is the light. The city itself developed because of the Gold

Rush: gold, as everyone knows, is the metal of the sun, par excellence. Gold traps light, it is light, and it gilds everything in the city, from the gates to Chinatown to the mighty bank buildings downtown. San Francisco's most famous outlaws, from Black Bart, the gentleman-poet-bandit, to Patty Hearst, the heiress-turned-bank robber, were after gold. Fire, which is "wild light," is San Francisco's most enduring specter, and firemen are among San Francisco's best-loved citizens.

Madame Coit raised a tower in honor of her favorite firemen, and today, Coit Tower is a popular emblem of the city. The Beatnik poets and artists gathered around the still extant—and thriving—City Lights Bookstore. The aforementioned hippies were also a creation of the light revealed by the ingestion of LSD-25. As for the city's relatively recent but important gay community, I only need to remind the reader that the original meaning of the word "gay" contains "light," in the sense of lightness and play. Light, and often the lack of it, influences the mood of the citizenry and civic decisions.

Given the city's foundation in light, it seems only natural that one of the great cooking trends of our time developed and flourished here: light cooking, or nouvelle cuisine. Health fads that are mainstream now have haunted the Northern California coast like a benevolent wind since the late nineteenth century, when organic

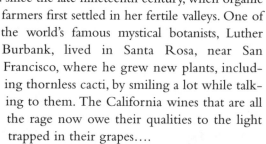

Coit Tower

farmers first settled in her fertile valleys. One of the world's famous mystical botanists, Luther Burbank, lived in Santa Rosa, near San Francisco, where he grew new plants, including thornless cacti, by smiling a lot while talking to them. The California wines that are all the rage now owe their qualities to the light trapped in their grapes....

My friend Carmen Vigil, who is a keen observer of culture and a true San Franciscan, lives in Bernal Heights, a mixed Hispanic and white neighborhood near the Mission District. Twenty-five years ago on this hill the only place to have a drink was the Ribeltadvorden, a friendly bar named by its owner after a drunken slurring of the name of his World War II ship, *Liberty and Order*. Now, Bernal Heights has a fair number of neighborhood eateries and taverns, including a Hungarian restaurant run by a bearded Magyar who makes all his own sausages and pastries.

Imre, which is his name, responded none-too-friendly when Carmen introduced me as his "Romanian" friend. As everybody but Carmen knows, there is no love lost between these two noble mini-races. Nonetheless, we soon established common ground in our mutual love for stuffed cabbage, strudel, and *palinka,* a fiery liqueur. Imre's pretty young wife nursed her baby while those dishes arrived and whistled along with the sexy *chardash* pouring out of the tape deck. Not exactly nouvelle cuisine—the stuffed cabbage and strudel were recklessly topped with sour cream and tasted exactly like my grandmother's. I filled with nostalgia like a sausage skin. I needed a nap.

On the way to the Phoenix Hotel, a lovely oasis in the seedy Tenderloin district—a neighborhood dreaded by many people since the nineteenth century—I saw some extraordinary creatures that moved dreamlike toward us. Not sure if my nap had begun or not, I asked Carmen if they were real. "They are," he confirmed gravely. "They are the neo-tribals." They sure were. The gender-nonspecific youths now nearing wore bones in their noses, brass rings in their cheeks, sticks through their lips, and discreet gold rings in their pierced eyelids.

"Excuse me," I inquired of the most decorated member of the neo-tribals, "do you wear such hardware all the time or only when you go out? And tell me, are you the latest, newest thing, the post-pierced, post-tattooed thing?"

"That's too many questions," he said, with a metallic lisp (he had a silver disk on the inside of his lower lip). "But, yeah, we're, like, way beyond piercing."

With the help of his fellow tribesmen, he gave me to understand that they didn't even talk, let alone mix, with the merely pierced (under eight holes in a row, anyway) or the slightly tattooed.

Communication was only possible when the wannabe neo-tribal-ist was pierced for bones, had more than one quarter of his or her body surface covered in tattoos, and was, hopefully, branded. Branding was a sore subject with at least one of the tribespeople who had a huge open wound on her back. It was supposed to look like a star when it healed, but she wouldn't know for sure until then. Sometimes brands took their own paths to form.

The neo-tribals were not at all shy: one of them turned around to show me the tattoo of a sun enclosing a dragon on the back of her neck. She could never see it, she explained, unless she used the mirror. The tattoo existed mainly for the pleasure of others, who regarded her from behind. The neo-tribals, I concluded, were not selfish people. And they were definitely a new—the newest—thing out of San Francisco.

Felled by Hungarian cabbage and altruistic tattoos, I fell on my futon at the Phoenix and did not rise until supper time. I wasn't exactly hungry, but I'd made a dinner date with Carmen, and he was there just before 7 p.m. The Phoenix Hotel caters to visiting musicians, so the clerks are extremely knowledgeable about things most ordinary humans don't care about. In the lobby, for instance, they rent art movies, sell massage discount coupons, re-place guitar strings, and have a complete listing of performance-art events.

"What's the hippest, newest food in San Francisco?" I asked the desk-person.

"To eat?" she said.

"No, to write about," I countered.

"Everybody's eating Caribbean right here at Miss Pearl's Jam House, and it's pretty enough to write about."

We decided to give it a try, although I live in New Orleans and Creole food is no news to me. Miss Pearl's was crowded with trendy young people, though not the latest trend. These Creole-food fanciers were barely tattooed, if at all. They were well, if conventionally, dressed, and they had credit cards. No neo-tribals here, which was too bad because I would have liked to see what they did with their bones and disks while supping.

Miss Pearl specialized in some fine "jerked chicken" with spicy mango sauce and ham-flavored greens with West Indian curry sauce, which is what Carmen had. I ordered the fish, which turned out to be a hefty mound of fillets affixed to a spicy mushroom-and-bread stuffing. It floated on an island of mustard-yellow spice. It was not New Orleans but Jamaican Creole, and too sweet for my taste. It was pretty enough to look at, but there was nothing nouvelle about it. The whole thing cried, "I'm fat! Long live pork!"

Carmen explained that the newest thing in San Francisco, not just the food, was indulgence in everything that was supposed to be bad for you. It was a funny thing: after convincing America to eat light and healthy, the capital of granola-consciousness turned the tables. The in-thing was calories. I didn't find this hard to believe. San Francisco does have a sense of humor. In fact, I think that this "let's eat and do everything bad and then die" trend has already spread to other cities, notably New York, where butter has made a spectacular culinary comeback.

A reggae band struck up in the bar adjacent to the restaurant and the calorie-saturated youth rushed onto the dance floor to do the steps of another generation.

"Is everything retro?" I wondered. "I thought that most retro already came and went. We had the Sixties last year, then it was the Seventies for about seven months—a short comeback, thank God—and now it's what, the Eighties?"

"No," Carmen said, "now it's a combination of everything: a little retro, a little ethnic, a little neo. It goes by neighborhood. The old Haight is almost all Sixties now. If you'd pulled a Rip Van Winkle in 1967, you'd think nothing changed."

Next day, I went to the Haight. It was true. Head shops and coffeehouses shined with psychedelic colors. The Cha Cha Cha was still there. Charles Manson's bus was parked at the corner of Haight and Schrader. Panhandlers perfect in every detail staffed the sidewalks. The only difference from the Sixties was that nothing was free. The psychedelic posters—especially the vintage ones—were very pricey. And the Cha Cha Cha now served, er, nouvelle

Caribbean. Charles Manson's bus was a replica. And the beggars didn't even mention change.

"Got five bucks for a croissant and a cappuccino?" one of them asked.

"What happened?" I replied. "Inflation?"

"Hey," he said huffily, "I'm not a bum, I'm homeless!"

Right.

The Haight, it seemed, was home to many neo-tribals. They squatted around their lattes in the cafes, waiting for the end of the world. The end of the world, flying saucers, divine revelations, and supernatural-beings-who-look-just-like-us seemed very popular. One store window displayed news articles and photos of aliens, as well as a large chart explicating the government conspiracy against UFOs. The New Age was well represented in the form of crystals, tarot cards, palmists, past-life regression coils, and "transporters," which looked like huge toy blenders. Some of the peddlers of these things were aliens from the Middle East. Alas.

San Francisco has always had a disproportionate share of believers in strange things. The occult has been commonplace here since the days of Sutter. In my day, people gathered regularly in Golden Gate Park to await the Apocalypse. It was fun. I am particularly fond of an episode in the mid-Seventies when I was told by a barefoot dreamer that the many agates along the beaches of California were actually precious stones washed out from the sunken palaces of Atlantis.

Dr. Weirde's Wierde Tours: A Guide to Mysterious San Francisco reports a goodly number of sites for the mystically inclined visitor. Beneath the intersection of Haight and Schrader, in addition to the Cha Cha Cha and the faux-Manson bus, is The Temple of the Sun, which we are told, is where "10,000 years ago...arose the magnificent Atlantian city of Tlamco..." Another Atlantian site in the neighborhood is Strawberry Hill, which is where the "monks of Atlantis and modern occultists commune with the heavens." The Laguna Honda reservoir just southwest of Mount Sutro was once "the lake that sup-plied the Atlantian city [Tlamco] with water via aqueducts."

Dr. Weirde holds nothing back when it comes to weirdness, so I was not surprised to learn that the fabled tunnels under Chinatown may be "locations where magical adepts could be 'channeled' or teleported from one spot to another." This is the kind of thing that makes a city fun to live in. Still, I did not want to become distracted from my goal—which was to ferret out new trends—no matter how fascinating other topics might appear to be.

It was glorious to be a teenage runner in Golden Gate Park in the heyday of the Haight-Ashbury. I ran barefoot, clad only in Jesuit-issue gym shorts, through fields of stoned half-naked dancing people who were too busy to notice the momentary interruption of their flute, guitar, and bongo playing, their embracing, fondling, screwing, their smoking this and dropping that, by a skinny boy who found them as exciting and ephemeral as the fog rolling through the trees.

—James O'Reilly,
"Declensions and Mantras"

Fisherman's Wharf might strike one as an unlikely place for innovation. A beloved tourist attraction for decades, this waterfront strip of restaurants and t-shirt shops is also home to a number of tour-boat operators and fishing-boat rentals. From here, one can get on board a boat to Alcatraz Island, its notorious prison outlined like a malignant sketch in the fog. "The Rock," as Alcatraz is called, was home to famous criminals but also to just plain criminals who became famous after they reached Alcatraz, either because they tried to escape and never made it, or because they became the subjects of movies like *The Birdman of....* I visited Alcatraz once and spent a horrifying five minutes in the haunted cell 14-D. I could barely imagine what months of confinement here could do when just five minutes brought me to the edge of a sincere scream. No, I had no desire to visit Alcatraz again but something pulled me here.

There was a drizzle in the air and there were few tourists. Bored gulls scanned the empty piers looking for the odd sourdough crust. I had just finished a shrimp cocktail and had disposed of the wrapper in a lidded trash bin. The gulls made hostile noises: two of them swooped down close to my still-shrimpy fingers and cackled their displeasure. Every fishing boat in the city seemed to be at dock. Some of these vessels were weathered veterans: unpainted, proudly rough, piled high with fishing nets, crusted with barnacles, sporting some old-fashioned gal's name, like *Lilly Marlene* and *Vivian Red*. All that was missing was the Jolly Roger flying from their masts, and I am sure that it came up as soon as their captains reached the open sea. Some of these boats displayed phone numbers on the side, being presumably for hire. I was just imagining what an adventure it might be to actually lease one of these conveyances instead of, let's say, a brand-new cabin cruiser with electronic hoists, when a gnomish gent in a peacoat approached.

"Wanna go fishing?"

"Looks like rain," I said.

He scrunched up his face just enough to produce a toothless laugh. "They bite bigger inna rain!"

"Which one's your boat?"

He pointed to the worst of the bunch, a wobbly barque with several missing sections. A kerosene-blackened cabin sat precariously in the center of it. A clothesline sporting the gnome's long johns swayed in the wind, stretched between the cabin's leaning chimney and the mast.

"Do you live on there?" I asked.

"The whole family," he said enigmatically.

I thanked him and walked on. Still, I can't help thinking that I missed something that might shortly catch on. Boarding old picturesque wrecks and taking off into the unknown with whole families of mutant fishermen might be the coming thing.

Nah.

In further pursuit of the nouveau, I took a bus to the Bohemian capital of the West, North Beach. Here, Bohemians have put their stamp on everything. Bookstores display signed books, cafe chairs have been sat on by many famous behinds, and the houses and skyline look familiar from paintings and drawings.

I went to pay my obligatory homage to City Lights Bookstore and its proprietor, the poet Lawrence Ferlinghetti. I found out, to my surprise and delight, that the city of San Francisco had named a street after the poet. What's more, I got a tour from the man him-self who walked me to Washington Square in North Beach and pointed with evident pride to the small street bearing his name: Via Ferlinghetti. This was nothing short of astonishing. No other city in the world, as far as I know, has ever named a city street after a still-living poet. Ferlinghetti himself had led a successful fight a few

years back to have some of the city streets named after distin-guished San Francisco writers. Thanks to him, now there is a Jack Kerouac Street, a Kenneth Rexroth Street, a Dashiell Hammett Street. But all those writers are dead!

The sky was very blue over our heads, and we were bathed in that special and blessed light that makes San Francisco seem the kindest burg on the planet. Ferlinghetti told me that the old Italian families who now lived on Via Ferlinghetti had no idea who he was, but when it was ex-plained to them that he was a poet, they posed no obstacle to renaming the street. Any city that names streets after poets de-serves to be saluted. I doffed my hat. This is a very new thing in-deed, and I can only hope that the rest of America follows suit.

Andrei Codrescu, a Romanian-born poet, arrived in the United States in 1966 penniless and without knowl-edge of the English language. Within

As the century closes, we are entering an exciting world of interactive multimedia, and, once again, San Francisco leads the way. No doubt you've read about or seen some of the early manifestations: men in goggles having virtual reality adventures; 500 channel interactive T.V.; video on demand; millions of people logging onto the Internet. Then there's the wild proliferation of interactive video games, kiosks, CD-ROMS, and location-based entertainment. And the techno frontier of large-scale be-ins and raves. The San Francisco Bay Area has had its hand in all of these innovations and more. Cutting edge magazines like Mondo 2000, *based at the legendary* "Mondo House" *in the Oakland Hills, and more recently,* Wired, *in the heart of SOMA's Multimedia Gulch have been covering and participating in the revolution long before most people knew what a modem was.*

—Jim Crotty, "San Francisco, What the Hell Did You Do to Your Hair?" *Monk, The Mobile Magazine*

four years he had learned to speak English well enough to publish his first poetry collection. Today, he has more than forty works to his name, including his latest novel, The Blood Countess. *He is a professor at Louisiana State University.*

★

I found myself reflecting that this city sometimes seems to have real style and a real future. We are going into the next millennium with a wonderful new Main Library, and a new Museum of Modern Art, a new Museum of Asian Art in the middle of downtown, a retrofitted and redesigned de Young with its exquisite collection of American painting, a gorgeously renewed Palace of the Legion of Honor set like a dream among pines and cypress at the Bay's mouth, and a national park in the Presidio to stroll in, and the endless pleasures of Golden Gate Park, and a waterfront you can walk on. Lots of weekends, many pleasures, and, if we make sure that we find a way to teach all our children how to read so that we can give into their hands the culture we've created, not a bad start for a new century.

—Robert Hass, "A Poet Visits the New Main Library,"
San Francisco Examiner

✦ ✱ ✦

Pacific World

San Francisco is defined by the sea.

I HAVE ALWAYS HAD A STRONG RELATIONSHIP WITH THE OCEAN. My earliest July memory is from my grandmother's beach cottage in Fair Harbor, Fire Island. Gray shingled cape, kerosene stove and lights, icebox, right on a dune overlooking the ocean, wind whistling through the screens and a plump Irish woman with white hair, housedress and black laceup shoes, love sparkling out of two very beautiful blue eyes and good pies coming out of her hands. It was wartime and we had blackout shades so that the German submarines couldn't see the shoreline. (Around this time the Coast Guard picked up five Germans off Fire Island in a rubber boat; they had debarqued from a sub and had plans and explosives to blow up the bridges around Manhattan.)

In this way, Fire Island—and the ocean—came to have a double meaning for me: deep maternal warmth and dangerous excitement. Things would wash up on shore, old military radios, empty ammunition boxes; I would look out over the ocean and try to see England and Ireland, where my grandparents had come from. Mystery and promise lie over the ocean, and the adventure begins at the sea's edge. I learned to ride the waves early. My godmother once said to my mother "My Lord, look at him ride the waves, he must be part Hawaiian."

So when I moved to San Francisco I was delighted to find out that Ocean Beach was only a ten minute breeze through Golden Gate Park from my apartment at Ashbury and Clayton. I would go to the beach at the end of the day to get the carpentry dust out of me and float in the deep blue. I would stay in 30 or 40 minutes (the water temperature is in the 50s), and when I got out I would shake so badly that I had to use both hands to get the key in the car door.

When I began to get fat, and for me changing weight is a distinct ebb and flow like a slow changing of the tides, I realized how insulating fat was—I could stay in longer and not get cold. One day after bodysurfing, I was tucking my shirt into my pants and to my shock I felt something as cold as marble or steel. It was a slab of fat above my right buttock; cold on the outside while the rest of me was toasty on the inside.

I came to a deeper appreciation of the phrase "chilled to the bone." I would drive home with the heater on full blast, then take a long hot shower but inside I still felt a deep mentholated cool. One evening while making dinner around 10 p.m. I became slightly alarmed because I began to get very warm and worried that I was developing a fever. It took me a while to realize that it was one of those rare occurrences, a hot summer San Francisco night, and it had taken me that long to warm up. I remember reading somewhere that alternating hot and cold calms the mind and opens the body. Once I had a massage after body-surfing and the masseur said, "Oh, you were in the ocean—that must be why your skin and body seems so alive!" A friend who became a surf companion for a couple of years told me he was certain that every minute he spent at Ocean Beach was a minute added to his life.

It is incredible, no two ways about it. You slide down the alley of Golden Gate Park through stands of pine and eucalyptus, past the windmill and bang—you are there at Ocean Beach with the immense Pacific before you. It is twilight, it is low tide, and the sand by the ocean has a mirror sheen from the receding waters, reflecting the undulant high fog above. I am running on sand where waves ususally break, I am running along in a twilight of reflectivity, in a sandwich of slick mirror, sand, and clouds. Where am I? I

could be ice skating, so smooth and effortless is all movement, and graceful—the dim light, the reflections, the atmospherics smooth out consciousness of body im-
perfections and running style, all in well-oiled lubricant forward. How could this be happening? It is so extraordinary, an altered state. I am running down this mirror of time and where am I going? I am suspended, zooming along (although in the reality of the other world I am running slowly) like a bee or a bird. I feel so open and spacious, yet oddly cozy and intimate before this splendor. I feel taken care of, loved by this strange and won-derful universe I inhabit. I am on this bar of sand virtually alone, the ocean is on one side and the beach is on the other and people

Ocean Beach is a hazardous beach at all times due to low water temperature and ever-shifting rip currents. (If you have the misfortune to be caught in a rip, don't panic and attempt to swim straight back to land; swim parallel to the beach until you are out of the rip.) This doesn't mean the beach can't be enjoyed—it means that the utmost respect must be conferred on the mighty and wondrous Pacific. And while a wetsuit certainly adds to the time you can spend in the water, don't let its buoyancy and warmth lull you into false confidence or bravado.

—JO'R, LH, and SO'R

are walking there but they don't want to get their sneakers wet so they won't traverse the pools of water to get to the sandy bar where all is magical. These little pools and rivulets of water are models of river erosion and formation in quick-time; like flying over ancient Arizona, watching the formation of the Grand Canyon.

Sated with this experience, I happily go back to my apartment with its white wool rug which feels so exquisite to feet newly sen-sitized by sand and water. Some red wine, my own red sauce on vermicelli and some sauteed vegetables, cooked while I dance to Mozart, round out the evening; I am ready to write thank you notes to God.

There are those days in early and late summer when it is warm, clear, no fog. I could smell such days unfolding, dry and delicious; they would wake me up at 6 a.m. If it was a weekend I would dress in worn old cotton clothes and bring along flannel sheets to the beach, an early morning bite to the air, Pacific waves rolling gently and evenly. At this time of day at the beach there is a hush, almost like a snowstorm, but here there is more brilliance to the hush, and the crunch of sand underfoot is vivid to my ears. The waves are lowly swiiiiishing (ionic pentameter) with an occasional muffled thud as one of them crashes. The beach is deserted except for one or two people walking their dogs in the distance. I take time to find the spot where I want to be, walking around, considering, pausing. When I find it I arrange the sand: a pillow for my head, a little hill on the right to cradle my body, a little hollow to make extra room for my belly, a rise to support my ankles, a depression for my feet. Down goes the flannel sheet and my body; I wrap the sheet around me and over my head. When I open my eyes the sunlight through the flannel is soft, creamy and warm. The sun is gradually toasting through the layers and reaching my skin.

The sand has a clean dusty smell with a spritz of mineral and sea salt. Have you ever noticed how clean cotton clothes being ironed smell like baking bread? Well all this bunting began to smell like that. Lulled by the low ocean and held by that wise and understanding parent, the beach sand, I fell into sleep like a babe. Gradually over the next hours people would come to the beach; a young child in squealing excitement, friends talking in low voices as their feet crunched along. Finally when I'd had my sleep and the beach became too crowded with radios, argumentative families and the seeping vibration of the repressed, I would go running into the water and KAR-CHUNG...vibrated, cold and shooting out of myself, happily rested and supercooled for hours to face the unusual heat of a San Francisco day.

There is often the added spice of seeing the board surfers (a different society altogether)—their well-kept architecture, their pride. In addition to being handsome, most of them had an artistic and color sense; you could tell it from the way they chose their boards, wetsuits, clothes, cars. Their rock and roll hardness (attitude) was partly digested by the negative ions shooting out of the tops of their heads, causing occasional outbursts of joy and play as in the beginning of heaven.

I remember one time a friend and I had come out of the water and were changing by my truck. There were three guys at the truck next to us. They were all in that talkative shiver that comes from a good time in the water. It was twilight rapidly going into dark. One guy was in the bed of the truck, jabbering away to his friends. He peeled off his wetsuit, no towel for modesty, revealing a lithe, fair-skinned body, and a lovely tool set which hung perpendicular as he leaned on the cab of the truck to pull the wetsuit off his ankles. This was exceptional—to me the genitals of most men look smelly and dirty like a sewer backwashed over them. This is especially the case at nude beaches where genitals seem plastered on à la Pin-the-Tail-on-the-Donkey, which may explain why they sometimes seem slightly misplaced on the body, overcooked meatballs and sausage.

Well, I digress. This man's genitals were as clean as laundry drying in the sun. I am reminded of Havelock Ellis quoting someone who said that young men in the farms of Central Europe smelled "like fresh-mown hay." What would this man have smelled like? What comes to mind are these Japanese pickles. They are small and cut up into little pieces; they are soft yet crunchy and make a faint squeak against your teeth; they have a strong but delicate saltiness; the plum vinegar in them has a slight smell of roses; the acid in the vinegar sends a clarifying punch through the system...

I loved the sheer variety of the weather at Ocean Beach. It could be clear and warm downtown, but at the ocean it would be cold with boiling fog, fog at times so thick that people moving in and out of it were phantasms. In the autumn twilight the sky is a deep transformative blue, a Bellini blue (see Bellini's "St. Francis in Ecstasy"). The orange yolk plasma would be flattening itself at the horizon, beginning its gullet slide into the ocean. The waves, vigorous and determined, would crest in a so-thin glasslike membrane surmounted by a bit of spumy, lacy froth through which, stained-glass like, shone the sonorous blue sky and plasma sun. The water was sharp, and vivid and cutting with the onset of colder weather. Its churning made small delicate pinging bubbles. In retrospect I would be tempted to shout for joy; but in those moments I was truly so saturated I could only let it wash over me.

In the depth of winter, after a big Pacific storm, the waves would be enormous with spume blown off the top of them like Everest in the jet stream. The water was agitated, confused; so intense that there was white froth everywhere save for occasional patches of blue. I would sometimes dream off for a moment and when I would come back for a split-second I thought I was snow skiing. But now there was a dangerous undertow. The long languid bottom slope of summer was gone. The action of the waves had cut the sand at water's edge into a sharp quarry-like drop into deep water. No surfers were out there. The waves were simply too tough with no thrust or carrying trajectory. They would simply fall down upon themselves like a building collapsing under its own weight. Or like some great enormous being, chest opening up into a big pre-sneeze breath and then bending its head downward and AAH-CHOOing all over its feet.

Imagine this scenario: you are casually walking down Market Street one sunny afternoon when a four-story hotel lifts off its foundation and hurtles toward you. You turn on your heels and run, but the hotel gathers speed and is rapidly gaining ground. In desperation, you jump feet-first on the hood of a taxi that is waiting for the light to turn green. The taxi takes off down the street as you fight to keep your balance. You're now moving 35 miles an hour, but the building is still in hot pursuit. If you lose your footing and fall, the hotel will crush you...

—David Batstone, "Secret Swell," *San Francisco Bay Guardian*

But I dearly loved these times at the ocean, even when I felt the need to keep myself as close to shore as possible because I was scared. Sometimes I would do a dead man's float, face down into the water, and would let myself be pummelled by the surf, slammed to the bottom, whipped this way and that (John Donne: "batter me, beat me, three person God..."). My body was ecstatic at being shown this new kind of fluidity. Showering at home I would find sand deep in my ears, sand in every crevice of flesh, even bits of seashell stuck in shriveled fissures of scrotum. Some hours later, over dinner, sea water stored deep in the sinus cavity would issue forth with the rapidity of cow urination, and hose down my nose onto my plate. I felt blessed that the sea was still with me.

After a while, I decided to get a wetsuit and went to Wise Surf Shop in the Sunset, which is paradoxically the most ordinary and the strangest of the many strange neighborhoods in San Francisco. Oh my goodness, how erotic it was to try these on for the first time—I felt bigger all around, both exposed and armored. I had to try on every single suit, discuss the fine points of each with the staff, who knew their stuff as they outfitted some of the most expert surfers around. Finally I bought one, black neoprene rubber with grey patches of nylon on the legs and shoulders. It had dignity and jauntiness. But above all it was amazing to have this aura of faux flesh around me. The rubber was like a new piece of bubble gum with all of the chew and none of the stick. The suit itself was like a contracting rubber band which squeezed the muscles, the result being that some muscles were easier to move, others were harder to move; it gave me a whole new relation to my muscular system.

I soon learned that the finest method of warming up the wetsuit was by peeing in it. Urinating in public was an unexpected bonus: I would say hello to people on the beach, making sure my smile did not become too broad and revealing, nor the puddle at my feet too large. But some friends didn't wash out their wetsuits after surfing. Traveling in one friend's car was like having a dead animal in the back seat.

I bought my wetsuit extra large to accommodate my ever-changing weight. Sometimes, during surfing, water would come in through the neck and give me edema legs; I looked like

*Man at his best, like water,
Serves as he goes along:
Like water he seeks his own level,
The common level of life,
Loves living close to the earth,
Living clear down in his heart,
Loves kinship with his neighbors,
The pick of words that tell the truth,
The even tenor of a well-run state,
The fair profit of able dealing,
The right timing of useful deeds,
And for blocking no one's way
No one blames him.*

—Lao Tzu, *The Way of Life*

my grandmother in her later years. Sometimes the legs would really fill up and my legs would be like spoons stirring around in large columns of water. (At one point I tried boogie boards and flippers but felt loaded down with equipment, which removed me from the closeness to the water.) Later on I bought a winter weight wetsuit. This opened up something new, for I now had a spare, and could invite friends to join me in the ocean. It was wonderful to be able to loan out this erotically charged wetsuit. Even though we wouldn't discuss it, I could feel this clean uncomplicated sharing, this erotic innocence. You didn't have to commit some god-damn sex act to see people undress. We would sometimes ride waves holding hands, or stacked one on top of the other, or one holding the other's ankles, tackle each other in the water, dive from each other's shoulders, enjoying the unworried joy of horseplay, protected from scrapes and bruises, aided in floating by the rubber, amidst the wonder and chaos of the ocean. Tankers would appear beyond the Cliff House and head into the eternal western horizon; the huge orange sun would slip into the sea. Surfing at night, something I did rarely, was a mysterious and eerie affair in which the day-friendly (yet always hazardous) waters became almost malevolent and even more unpredictable than usual. Utmost caution was required and on more than one occasion, I or a friend had a bad feeling about the conditions and we turned on our heels and went for our usual Indonesian or Japanese food.

A couple of years before I headed back east to care for my aging father, I had a singular experience which married all things wonderful about San Francisco and the Pacific. I had just finished bodysurfing; the water was spritzy and cold, cold, bluest sky, plasma sun, tops of waves like stained glass—the whole tumult I had always been in love with and returned to again and again. As I took off my wetsuit, I said to myself, "Symphony," not knowing if they were playing that night or not. I threw my wetsuit in the back of the truck, body perking with zing, and roared to Civic Center. Walking into the lobby of Davies Hall, hair full of sand, I learned that it was in fact Opening Night. In less than a minute, a man came up to me and offered me a half-price orchestra ticket he couldn't use. The journey from the dark twilight of the primeval ocean to the warm, well-lit symphony hall took only 25 minutes. Every cell of mine was wide open from the roaring surf. When the orchestra began to play Stravinsky's "Rite of Spring," I felt the roof of my head blow open and sublime energy pour out; my body was utterly receptive to the polyrythmns and syncopation that were so similar to the ocean waves I had just been immersed in.

After this divine workout, with limpid limpness I found my way home and fell into a snug sleep, adrift in the unity of art and life that only San Francisco can produce.

George Vincent Wright grew up in Bayside, Queens (New York) and graduated from the Yale School of Architecture. In addition to designing, renovating, and building houses for more than twenty years in Maine, San Francisco, and the Bay Area, he's traveled the world, ever curious about water culture, history, music, and cuisine sauvage. *He has also harbored a long interest in being president. He's back in Bayside writing and gardening after taking his 93-year-old father to France just months before his death.*

✶

More than any other American metropolis, San Francisco is a city of the sea. Other Pacific Coast cities are sheltered from the full impact of the ocean by peninsulas or islands or shoreline indentations. East Coast cities, owing to the motion of the great air masses from west to east in these latitudes, are climatically influenced far more by the continent than by the Atlantic. But in San Francisco not only are the ships of the world visible from its hills; the currents of the ocean and bay flow past it on three sides; the salt winds and fog sweep through its streets; the long Pacific combers perennially pound its western boundary.

The San Francisco experience must be in some degree an experience of the ocean. In order to know the city fully and the influences that have acted on it throughout its history, it is necessary to confront the Pacific face to face, not only at Ocean Beach south of the Golden Gate, but at representative places along the Bay Area coastline from the Russian River to Santa Cruz. It is necessary to know this shore not merely from the highway but directly, in an intimate personal relationship unavailable from the car or from the windows of buildings with an ocean view. You have to get out and explore on foot the cliffs and headlands and coves, feeling the sand between your toes and the spray of the surf on your face and even the power of the waves on your body.

—Harold Gilliam, The San Francisco Experience: The Romantic
Lore Behind the Fabulous Facade of the Bay Area

What You See
Is Who You Are

In San Francisco, the search for identity never ends.

THE OTHER DAY I WAS WAITING FOR A BUS ON FILLMORE STREET
when Dolly Parton came swaggering up. At least I thought she
might be Dolly Parton until she settled in to wait for the bus and
I got a good look at her face. Her face was not Dolly. The rest of
her was.

She wore a wide black-velvet cowboy hat over a big-big platinum wig spilling shiny ringlets all down her back. She wore a
skintight purple-velvet jumpsuit, studded black cowboy boots, two
wristfuls of jangly bracelets, blood-red Press-On Nails, an unfiltered cigarette. It was not a pretty face but she was trying hard.
Vivid Mary Kay blues and pinks and shades of dusty rose were air-
brushed under her eyes, in bold strokes across her cheekbones, her
lacquered lips. She looked tired. She gave off an aroma of Juicy
Fruit gum blended with her potent perfume, a twangy scent that
might have been called "Passion Rose" or "White Guitar."

Indeed, she was lugging a big old beat-up guitar case. The way
I had it figured, her name was Wanda June, and she came from
some desolate truck-stop town in Nevada.

That's what this city does for me. I see somebody and my mind starts spinning a story to explain *how on earth* he or she turned out looking that way. San Francisco is where you come when you want to see people looking like who they truly *are*.

I imagined that Wanda June had spent her whole life in that dead-end junction outside of Reno, strumming her guitar and waiting for her big break. On weekends she took the bus into town and hung out in the casinos, hoping for a job, an audition. One night she met the wrong man, who got her drunk and made certain promises. He talked her out of her money and onto a bus. The next thing she knew she was wandering out of an alley in Pacific Heights, hung over, trying to remember how she got here instead of Nashville. That's when I spotted her.

She dropped her cigarette to the sidewalk and ground it out with the heel of her boot.

Then she did something that amazed me and the other people waiting for the bus.

She laid the guitar case flat on the sidewalk, squatted down, and opened the lid to reveal not a guitar but an assortment of wigs and white clothing, carefully folded. A mirror was glued into the blue-velvet lining of the lid.

Wanda June shook the bracelets off her arm and tucked them in the little compartment where guitarists keep their strings and picks. Then she took off the cowboy hat and the platinum wig. Underneath, her own head of reddish-blond hair was cropped close, like a boy's.

At first I thought she might actually *be* a boy. In this town, a cursory glance does not always suffice to make that distinction—but it turned out she was a woman, after all. A different kind of woman.

She knelt on the sidewalk and selected a shoulder-length brunette wig that flipped up on the ends. She placed it on her head and adjusted it in the mirror, a more conservative look.

She shook out a white dress. No, not a dress, it was a nurse's uniform, no-wrinkle white polyester. She stepped into it, purple velvet jumpsuit and all. She kicked off her boots. She reached down the bosom of the uniform, unzipped the jumpsuit, and proceeded to wriggle out of it while everyone at the bus stop tried not to watch.

We were all smiling by now. She pretended not to notice all the attention we pretended not to be giving. I had the strong sense that she must be late for work, or she wouldn't be performing this transformation on a busy sidewalk in view of us all.

San Francisco is where people will give you a break if you need to do something a little strange.

I thought about trying to come up with something clever to say, but it was more fun just to *watch*.

She folded the jumpsuit away and managed to get herself into a pair of opaque white panty hose

I am a fine-looking woman; Still, I am running with my tears.

—Maidu song, *The Way We Lived: California Indian Reminiscences, Stories and Songs,* edited by Malcolm Margolin

without seeming particularly immodest about it. She laced on a pair of white nurse's orthopedic shoes. She shut the lid on the guitar case.

A whole new story began to spin itself out in my mind. By night she was Wanda June, singing heartbreak songs in some Tenderloin dive. By day she was Nurse Nancy with a little too much makeup, on her way to help heal the ill and infirm. Maybe on weekends she was somebody else....

The bus came. I got in line to put my dollar in the fare box. The weird little moment on the sidewalk dissolved into the familiar silence of people involved in mass transit, trying to hold onto some bit of personal space.

I took a seat three rows behind Nurse Nancy. I watched as she wiped off the makeup with a Kleenex from her purse. Her red Press-On Nails were the only remaining clue to her other identity.

She didn't know she was about to be upstaged.

An elderly woman at the front of the bus leaped up from her seat and began shouting, "Don't touch me! Don't touch me! I have the force! I have the force!" The bus driver craned around to get a look at her, and when he did the bus collided with a pickup truck trying to turn left onto Van Ness. Ka-bam! Everyone got a good jolt. The bus driver swore. The old lady kept hollering "Don't touch me!" The passengers rolled their eyes and muttered and lined up to get off the bus.

The last I saw of Nurse Nancy, she was struggling up a hill dragging the guitar case along behind her, trying to hail a taxi. She was a tiny thing. I am sure she was very late for work.

What happened next, I don't know. There's only one thing in San Francisco of which you can be absolutely sure: something always happens next.

Mark Childress is a contributor to numerous magazines, and the author of four novels and a children's book titled Joshua and Bigtooth. *He currently resides in Costa Rica.*

✳

San Francisco is famous for running a hundred-year-old operetta for the entertainment of itself, visiting sailors, and other tourists and conventioneers. The sets include North Beach (Italian jollity and cappuccino), the Tenderloin (ambisexual lower depths), Chinatown (souvenirs, restaurants, and an occasional gang rumble), Fisherman's Wharf (seafood, sea smells, and bongo players), the Haight-Ashbury (a now-gentrified counterculture), the Castro (Shangri-la for homosexuals), Nob, Russian, and Telegraph Hills (worn elegance), Pacific Heights and Union Street (spanking-bright elegance and singles shopping); the characters include beatniks, hippies, ethnics of black, brown, yellow, and pink hues, and a large supporting cast of prospering runaways from less clement climes. There are also the Old Families, who have been here more than twenty minutes and have made their money in banking, insurance, mining, railways, land, or politics. Or in the manufacture of jeans. There are the cute and the less cute crazies. San Francisco is America's Pigalle and Saint-Germain-des-Prés, if not its Paris.

—Herbert Gold, *Travels in San Francisco*

HERBERT GOLD

When San Francisco Was Cool

An ex-Beat writer takes a nostalgic look at North Beach.

THANK THE GODS THAT PROTECT WRITERS FROM THE OBLIGATION to write, the phone just rang. We bohemians in our red-lined satin capes and berets believe in mystic synchronicities. It's an old acquaintance from North Beach days whom I haven't seen since breakfast at the Caffe Trieste this morning.

Ffrank Ffollet (don't forget the extra f's, to differentiate him from the bogged-down Irish one-f Francises) is writing his own version of *Roots*—in this case, the roots of a Welshman, since Dylan Thomas just didn't have enough genius to do the job right. You need spark. You need fire. You need Ffrank Ffollet.

But now my friend's wife has been laid off from her job as a teacher's aide and the IRS says he owes $623 in taxes from four years ago when he briefly sold out to the military-industrial-bucketshop complex and took a job selling circus tickets by phone for the Firemen's Alzheimer's Benefit. Those bastards were supposed to forget to report his earnings, but you can't count on the boojwah to do it right by not doing it.

Since Ffrank owes such a small amount, the whole force of the government was coming down on him in a strike force of attack helicopters filled with auditors from the Federal Building. It makes him nervous. Even after three double espressos, his stomach is still jumpy. How can a person sing the truth of the Welsh race, their sagas, their kings in fur hats, under such pressure? As a member of an ethnic group myself, can I dig what he's saying, brother?

That's his story. And since I bought a pair of circus tickets from him, I'm partly to blame.

"OK," I said, "I'll lend you a hundred. Come and pick up the check."

"Jeez," he said, "couldn't you meet me at the Puccini? I'm pretty busy right now, got to make a couple more calls, but could take a break in an hour. Can I lay a cappuccino on you, pal?"

The Christmas Alzheimer's circus ticket salesman and Welsh epic poet knows he can count on me. He's got other trapezes to fly. And I'm a sucker for a free cappuccino.

Among my early memories of San Francisco's Old Bohemia, then bivouacked in a North Beach concentration so dense that one strategic bomb could have wiped out most of the nation's resources of unrhymed verse, are the even older bohemians of the late '50s and early '60s, complaining, "I remember the real bohemia of the '30s—Wobblies, anarchists, jug wine toters, poets, and you could get a big dollar dinner for 79 cents. There were giants in those days, young feller."

Well, when I roamed North Beach with Allen Ginsberg in 1957—he hadn't yet come to live in San Francisco, but was scouting the terrain—the *prix fixe* dinners at the Hotel du Midi (upstairs Basque), Ripley's (sort of French), the Pisa (definitely Italian) and a half-dozen other all-you-can-eat resorts cost in the neighborhood of a buck seventy-five, red wine a quarter extra. Allen preferred the New Cup Cafe (Chinese) because it was less expensive. But we are all artists here, our heads in the clouds; let's not emphasize vulgar inflation. Every young whippersnapper eventually becomes an old whippersnapper.

Surely the bohemians of the '20s and '30s ran into garrulous veterans at the Black Cat or in their studios in the Monkey Block, now buried under the Transamerica Building, who remembered

the carefree, romantic, and sexy pre-earthquake San Francisco bohemia described by Frank Norris in his novel, *Blix*. This picture of
lazy young would-bees buzzing over the seven, count 'em—well,
maybe nine hills of the Bay was published in 1899, the same year
as his better-known *McTeague*, a gritty story of Zolaesque misfortune on Polk Street. One of the miracles of my early discovery of
San Francisco was to find that Polk Street, adapted into Eric von
Stroheim's great and doomed film *Greed,* was psychically intact—
still very much as Frank Norris described it, even with the hint of
homosexuality discreetly foreshadowed nearly a hundred years ago.

When the film *Greed* was shot, von Stroheim used a corner
apartment on Columbus in North Beach to represent the Polk
Street dentist's office. When I used to visit, it was the house and
studio of a cigarette-addicted abstract expressionist painter who
moved out from New York after one of his lungs was removed. "If
I'm gonna die," he said, "might as well have some fun before I go."

It was a time of great fun in North Beach. We watched Officer
Bigaroni enter the life of poetry by rousting poets guilty of inter-
racial marijuana smoking. (A bar on upper Grant had a swinging
outdoor sign which announced: "Headquarters for Ethnics.") The
black Jewish Abominist poet, Bob Kaufman, wrote his "Notes
Found at the Tomb of the Unknown Draft Dodger." We broke
sourdough together at the old Pisa (it was called the New Pisa) and
melted with feeling as an entire visiting Japanese opera troupe arose
after the family-style dinner to express its appreciation by singing
"Oh, Susanna" in Japanese. We should have suspected, when they
took over Stephen Foster, they would move next into the automo-
bile industry.

The San Francisco Renaissance, nationally celebrated and there-
fore validated by Grove Press in a special issue of the *Evergreen
Review*, laid waste the terrain, reciting to jazz and pillaging, shoot-
ing paint onto canvas, smoking and attacking New York while
Kenneth Rexroth beamed and Zen pioneers learned how to pro-
nounce *Ommm*. (It's Ommm as in Omnipotent, not Umm as in
"Um, could you lend me a few bucks, Dad?") Heroes arrived from
Manhattan by thumb, by driveaway car, and by prop plane, as brave

in their hearts as Cortez, Richard Henry Dana, Robert Louis Stevenson, and Fatty Arbuckle, who made the trip to San Francisco a little earlier by—was it covered wagons?

Allen Ginsberg recited "Howl" with its famous results in destroying the very fabric of Western civilization.

The Circle Gallery dropped the scales from our eyes.

Michael McClure snarled, growled, snuffled, and purred his beast poems in front of my fireplace, scaring my young woman friend, who spoke only English and French, not Beast.

Ron Boise's Kamasutra instruction sculptures were arrested, jailed by the police and ultimately acquitted. I have a mug shot of a cast-iron couple caught *in flagrante* and tagged: "BOOKED. S.F.P.D." One gaunt, erotic enigma stood for years on the roof of the Anchor Steam Beer factory where it was visible from the freeway, improving the sex life of commuters until a conglomerate took over the native brew.

Katharine Ross, later to star in *The Graduate* and *Butch Cassidy and the Sundance Kid*, was a lovely young understudy in Actors Workshop productions. She lived upstairs of a grocery on Stockton near Filbert; she stood nude on stage in a daring version of Jean Genet's *The Balcony*. When I lent her my prewar Citroen gangster

*O*n October 13, 1955, nearly a hundred people packed into the Six Gallery in San Francisco to hear six new poets read. Bottles of wine were passed. At about eleven that evening, the last reader, "a horn-rimmed intellectual hepcat with wild black hair," stepped up to the front, and the crowd yelled "Go! Go! Go!" as he began chanting, his arms outstretched:

> I saw the best minds of my generation destroyed by madness, starving hysterical naked,
>
> dragging themselves through the negro streets at dawn looking for an angry fix,
>
> angelheaded hipsters burning for the ancient heavenly connection to the starry dynamo in the machinery of night.

With his poem "Howl," Allen Ginsberg had just given voice to the Beat Generation—a movement associated with bearded, bereted, and sandaled Bohemians who fueled their literary fires in the bars and coffeehouses of North Beach.

—*Sunset*, "Beat San Francisco"

getaway car—it had running boards—she wisely used the convenient parking in front of her building. When I returned from a trip to St. Germain-des-Prés, the North Beach of Paris, I found that she had collected one fire hydrant parking ticket for each day I had been obliviously dreaming at the Flore, the Deux Magots, and the Bonaparte.

She had the bedrock solidity of a true North Beach believer. Everything was for the best in the best of all possible worlds if you remembered to tuck the tickets neatly into the glove compartment—especially if you looked like Katharine Ross. The first time I was ever comp'd for a meal was at Cho-Cho, the Japanese restaurant near City Lights Bookshop, when Jimmy, the proprietor, said: "You come in with a person who looks like her, you don't ever have to pay."

I'll tell you how long ago that was. Sushi hadn't yet made it past Hawaii, crossing the Pacific. California cuisine meant Hangtown fry. Natural foods were Birdseye frozen instead of Libby's canned peas.

My excuse for moving to San Francisco—the excuse that paid my child support—was a grant to do a play at the Actors Workshop. If I took kindly, sweet-tempered, high-cheekboned Katharine Ross to dinner, you see—the logic should be clear to any other pure soul—it was only because we needed to exchange hints on success in show business. In the great tradition of noncommercial theater, my play was not performed here because I wouldn't consent to the director's wish to cast his wife in a role for which she was of the wrong generation. The play was later given an undeserved run in Los Angeles. I suppose victory over ageism and weightism means that 40-ish

A PG&E crew was working away noisily at Columbus Avenue and Jack Kerouac Alley when the guy who runs the "Psychic and Crystal Readings" studio, next to the Vesuvio, hollered from his second floor window, "Hey, when you gonna stop that noise?" At which the guy jackhammering hollered back: "You're the psychic, buddy, you tell me."

—Herb Caen, "3-Dot Journalism Lives," *San Francisco Chronicle*

mothers of several children can now enact dewy nurses just out of training.

Katharine Ross was itching to get away from Vesuvio. When she returned to Adler Alley, now called Jack Kerouac Street, it was with makeup personnel, trailer, canvas chair with her name stencilled on it, and a full crew. The ghost of Kathie Past haunted this set. I watched in the crowd of gawkers, along with Jimmy from Cho-Cho, who said, "Just as pretty. Just as pretty."

Across from City Lights and Vesuvio ("We Are Itching To Get Away From Portland, Oregon") there used to be the Bodega: flamenco dancing, can of tomato sauce over rice at night, guitar lessons during the day. A psychiatrist's ex-wife told me that her guitar would never betray her as her husband did. (He lied to her, like a banjo.) Where there is now an "adult" screening room-bookshop, there was then an art cinema and a restaurateur who liked to relax by wearing spike heels during his at-home hours. Kenneth Anger, film collagist of *Orpheus Rising,* lived upstairs with his fan magazines and his leather collection. At Vesuvio, another psychiatrist's ex-wife, author of *I'm Sorry, Darling,* the story of premature ejaculation, sat patiently for two years analyzing her divorce. She said everything many times, like a *balalaika.* The Discovery Bookshop, a treasure trove presided over by Frederick Roscoe, rhyme master, world champion in the Indoor Olympic Doggerel competition, gave employment to such clerks as David Meltzer, who now teaches poetry at New College in the Mission, and Peter Edler, a German beatnik known as the Hip Hun because he had been expelled from the Hitler Youth for talking in class. He later married a Swedish woman, ran a childcare service in Marin, and moved to Stockholm when she came into her inheritance.

Prominent vegetarians and the founder of Breatharianism, which taught people how to nourish themselves without eating, a recipe using the native chlorophyll in their skins plus a dash of the sunlight over the miracle church of Saints Peter and Paul, hung out in the Bermuda triangle of Grant, Broadway, Union, and Columbus. The geometry might suggest a rectangle to some, but at least it's not square. The prophet of Breatharianism sat at the bar of the Washington Square Bar & Grill, tossing popcorn and pretzels into his mouth while he promised to reveal the secrets of foodless feeding to anyone who bought him a brandy. "That cognac is pure sunlight, it's a known fact," he explained. A friend remembers Joan Baez crooning softly on a bench in front of the church while an admirer brushed her long, dark, glossy hair. It was a scene of peace and love until Joan said to her fan, "Get your sticky fingers the f— away from my guitar." Peace, Sister.

The spike-heeled restaurant owner on Columbus near the Hungry i entertained his patrons by singing and dancing "Tiptoe Through the Tulips." His ambition was to grow up to be Tiny Tim, but twinkletoes was stilled, due to murder by his late-night busboy. An occasional crime of passion is part of the bohemian tradition called Going Too Far.

Mort Sahl used to get his exercise sprinting to the bank when it opened to cash his paychecks from Enrico Banducci's Hungry i. Other employees were often already ahead of him in line, rubbing the sleep from their eyes and praying. Enrico was an entrepreneur with ample soul but loosely wrapped accounting skills. The one-legged hooker at his bar entertained seekers of oddness, including Alvah Bessie, the Hollywood Ten black-listed writer who came to work the nightclub's light and sound system after he was released from prison. I walked out on Barbra Streisand because she sang too loud; I blushed for Woody Allen, who panicked on stage and forgot his lines. The next day we drove to Berkeley because he said he needed to get over this trauma by viewing "girls with major hair."

When Lenny Bruce thought he was a bird and flew out a window of the Swiss-American Hotel on Broadway, near Enrico's Coffee House, which provided an outdoor office for entertainers, mobsters, financial district employees, and '60s grokkers and groovers—also Vietnam service people on R & R—Ralph Gleason, jazz and rock critic, stood by taking notes. The medical emergency crew that came to carry Lenny to the hospital taped his mouth shut because the disappointed bird was using language not in the vocabulary of your average fallen eagle. "Is there anything I can do?" I asked Gleason.

"There's nothing anyone can do now," intoned the philosopher.

The Hip Hun strolled past in his medal-bedecked caftan, which looked like a ball gown. The wife of a stage manager at The Committee offered me a fuzzy capsule from her private stash. What's this? I asked her. "A dream of truth," she said. "Try it."

The ambulance went sirening off, carrying a bird with his wing broken and his mouth taped.

Old cities are better than rapidly evolving new communities at offering enclaves and backwashes in which bohemians can set down their lightly packaged roots. In the late 19th and early 20th century, Montparnasse and Montmartre in Paris, Soho in London, Greenwich Village in New York—and the ancient inner cities of Rome, Athens, even such buttoned places as Geneva, and less-buttoned Stockholm, Copenhagen, Buenos Aires—discovered that gypsy-like strangeness could sprout in alleyways like the ailanthus tree in my native Cleveland. Sometimes a college neighborhood helped to provide the necessary cheap eats, lodging and companionship. San Francisco's street-ambling, its site as a hilly port, as destination for Latin folks, its speculative fervor, its early prosperity, its newness and oldness, gave it unique advantages. This city has studied hard how to entertain itself and others. Mark Twain came for the Gold Rush; Ambrose Bierce, Joaquin Miller, Bret Harte, and the Emperor Norton were famous beatniks and hippies before the words. The Emperor Norton wore flowers, dressed like a burn-

According to ancient tradition, the village eccentric and the village idiot are touchstones—lucky tokens, somehow; although they sometimes rave, they are to be protected. Norton I, self-proclaimed Emperor of the United States and Protector of Mexico, placed himself within this tradition.

He came to San Francisco in 1849 complete with an entourage of dogs and stayed until his death in 1880. He was a beggar—but a sovereign beggar who demanded that his title be honored. He levied taxes, and serious businessmen grinned and tithed. He issued bonds and ate free lunches. He was accorded the holy innocent's status, and honored.

—Alice Thibeau, "The Emperor's Folly," *San Francisco Magazine*

ing bush, printed his own currency. Now street poets hawk their wares in North Beach and in the Mission—still living off the yearning for distraction that a Mediterranean, forever-springtime climate helps to nurture.

Pure naughtiness has always had a central position in San Francisco bohemia, in keeping with The City's tradition of taking its frivolity seriously. The Barbary Coast and the International Settlement, archaeological remnants of which can still be found in the bidets and outdoor erotic murals not yet extirpated in the Jackson Square area, specialized in drink, sex, and the genial spending of money. This was a port, after all. The Sexual Freedom League, sponsored by the Reverend Jefferson F— Poland in the '60s and early '70s, hasn't been heard from lately. The Kerista Commune, a group marriage, men and women who share everything, used to provide me with house-cleaning service, arriving in a group marriage of three, one sanitary expert carrying a snakelike vacuum cleaner draped like a Jungian symbol about his upper body. In response to my application to visit their commune as research, they said they would take a vote. They discussed, they voted; "We've consensussed," one of them reported by telephone, and the answer came to my request: they noed.

Margo St. James started the first hookers' union, COYOTE—Call Off Your Old Tired Ethics—in North Beach. "Since I didn't find a nice old man, preferably an invalid, to support me, I went into business," she explained. "I like giving shampoos."

Another enterprising young woman, a nurse from Boston, started the Golden Gate Foundation to guide libidinous men back toward karmic tranquillity. She thrived for a few years. A receptionist used to say to the waiting clients, "The therapist will see you now, big boy."

My sons keep asking me, "Dad, were you alive before there was AIDS and herpes?"

There were giants in those days, my boys.

One of the less benign elements of the '60s flower epoch was the discovery of drugs as a shortcut to satori, nirvana, dream therapy, relief from parental nagging, aesthetic fulfillment, preparing for final exams, and foreplay. Bad drugs came into the mainstream. Thank you, Dr. Leary, Dr. Alpert, and the other Dr. Feelgoods. A poet-filmmaker-cabdriver-standup comedian named Chris preached his new discovery, chanting: "If coffee, tea, or Ovaltine don't do it, try Meth." And he had a way of injecting friends so that he would be murmuring, "Now don't you feel…" and just as the speed hit their bloodstream, he would utter the lyrical word, "…*bettah?*"

It was magic. He had a gig as standup comic at the Hungry i, he hit on my woman friend, he charmed everyone, he made a prize-winning film, and within a couple of years he gave himself a methedrine lobotomy. His IQ went from something near genius to moron and below. He became nearly blind. He wandered North Beach and panhandled and pretended he still knew me. "Chris, remember we first met at the Crystal Palace in St. Louis? Remember Gaslight Square?"

"Yeah, man. Yeah, man."

Another friend wrote a prize-winning novel on speed, but then had to relearn his telephone number and take driving lessons. Now after many years, he is trying to write another book. "My sense of nuance has come back," he says, "but it's a rough go." Wine is now his drug of choice. He hopes to nuance things again.

Bohemia promises eventual performance; not everyone fakes it very well. Ffrank Ffollet did telephone solicitation for fake charities. Another poet saw me with Allen Ginsberg on Grant a few years ago, and said, "Hey, how's it feel to be the Eastern Establishment?"

Allen looked quizzical, he looked bemused. He was worried about a friend's upset stomach and was heading for a store to buy Tums.

A hyphen and overlap between my old bohemia and the even older bohemia of a previous generation is exemplified by William Saroyan, whom I met by accident as he was boisterously touring the San Francisco Museum of Modern Art, explaining matters to his son and daughter. He came to visit my flat on Russian Hill above North Beach—Charles Reich, author of *The Greening of America,* and the sculptor who did the fakes for William Randolph Hearst's San Simeon have been my neighbors. Saroyan, a lover of Strange, adored the fresh plaster smells when newly minted Renaissance masterpieces were moved out of the studio and onto the sidewalk after the sculptor's untimely death. When I introduced Saroyan to Charles Reich, the two gentlemen stared at each other and said, like gentlemen: "Good day."

In the early '60s, since I was five or ten years younger than I am now, I had the right to a young woman friend (called "girlfriend" in those dear, dear days beyond recall). She had a roommate who admired William Saroyan. We decided to—please recall this quaint Mickey Rooney language—"double-date." The two young women arrived at my apartment and I lit a fire. Saroyan arrived and a burning crate leapt out of the fireplace, due to the draft of his entrance. "That's the tiger in the fireplace," he explained as we ran about, stifling the conflagration.

The evening had begun nicely: warm hearts and singed rug. But Saroyan decided, to her great disappointment, that his date was too young for more than avuncular attention. He gave us a tour of his North Beach bohemia, an earlier one: Barbary Coast, International Settlement. We had dinner at the Brighton Express. He asked the cook if she would like to be God in his new play. She giggled prettily, wiped her hands on her apron and said she might consider the job if it didn't conflict with her schedule for making Mud Pies, the ice cream dessert she had invented.

> *San Francisco was in my blood and bones. I knew it as a very small child and a little later as a whistling boy.*
>
> —William Saroyan

The question of the existence of God resolved, Saroyan took us to Earthquake McGoon's to hear Turk Murphy, the great Dixieland horn player, another old San Francisco bohemian from that border where North Beach fades into the waterfront, home of the longshoreman's union of Harry Bridges and the spiritual link of two raffish ports, San Francisco and New Orleans.

Late night, we said our prayers with an Irish coffee ritual on the terrace at Enrico's, where a famous pair of call girls used to cruise in their jointly owned Thunderbird. They parked in the No Parking zone reserved for taxis, callperson Thunderbirds, Zen real estate show-offs and close personal friends of Enrico Banducci, and then strolled over for an exchange of sociability in the 2 a.m. damp. The outdoor heaters sizzled. Saroyan peered with his ardent dark eyes into their faces and began to discuss their ethnic heritages, "because such things are very interesting." And when they left, he reminisced about the call girls of yore, who didn't drive Thunderbirds.

Our young women were charmed by this contact with the literature of the '30s. And then, ever courtly, Saroyan doffed his fedora to his date, the deep Saroyan scholar, said goodnight (her eyes were gleaming with pride and frustration), and began to trudge across town to his sister's house. The scholar was thankful for a glimpse of "The Daring Young Man on the Flying Trapeze," that great early story about a starving writer in San Francisco. She remembered that his Pulitzer Prize play, *The Time of Your Life,* was inspired by Izzy Gomez's saloon nearby on Pacific. "That's cool, Herb, I can make do with insight," she said, "even if he's gotten kind of lazy."

When I see my friend of 30 years ago, she still sometimes recalls that evening and says, "Poor Debbie. She thought Saroyan would be more...bohemian. But she said the same thing about a wing of the Jefferson Airplane and a vice-president of Merrill Lynch."

The working artists couldn't stay up all night, liked to tuck themselves in at closing time.

Bohemians are not what weekend visitors, bridge-and-tunnel folks, think they are. (Now I take upon myself the role of Village Explainer, pompous and patient.) Bohemians may look like outcasts and scapegoats, cultivators of private gardens, but in fact, they want to run things. Once I proposed a documentary film, *The Protocols of the Elders of Bohemia*, with the thesis that bohemians define the taste, preach the theories, support the arts, make the music, write the literature, and drink the coffee and wine which keeps society jumping, vigorous, and fun. Even bohemian dead-beats and panhandlers help give body to the soup.

A CBS producer and I strolled around North Beach, he carrying a tape recorder while I chatted with the turbulent bohemian masses, which included few actual artists, of course, but many profound lumpens living off the land. I interviewed a poetry utterer who called himself "Lawrence the Young Poet," hoping people would confuse him with Lawrence Ferlinghetti. How old are you? I asked, and he answered with fine distinction: "Five seven, because that's younger than 57."

At City Lights, Mad Alex, a handsome, tall, black street rapper, said to us by way of introduction: "I got the bucket if you got the water."

What could be a better, more mysterious, yet strangely coherent description of the marginalized performers who enact our street theater? America needs to match up the buckets and the waters. I'll drink to that.

In 1957, when Allen Ginsberg first introduced me to Mad Alex at the Co-Existence Bagel Shop on upper Grant, he acknowledged my presence with bucket-and-water riddles. The Bagel Shop, long closed, is now a video store. Alex returned from some kind of forced vacation to stand in front of City Lights, haggard, gaunt, white-haired, but still reciting his paradoxes. Bob Kaufman, our Rimbaud, our champion of doom, took a vow of silence except for harrowing, croaking demands for rent or food money. A toothless novelist and poet whose exercise consisted of hiking to City Lights to pick up his mail, whom I used to invite to Enrico's for hot chocolate—all he could chew—met a schoolteacher from Sacramento, married her and grew teeth. Henri Lenoir, cockney ballet dancer, proprietor of Vesuvio, patron of the beat painters, and Mayor of North Beach, came in his retirement to the meals offered him by Banducci. Occasionally he raised cash by selling off part of his art collection. The Hotel du Midi, *prix fixe* Basque restaurant where I met temporary true love in the early '60s, closed. Prices going up. Richard Brautigan, suddenly the rage in his Confederate general disguise, handed out free poetry:

*I give her an A+ for long blond hair...*and curtseyed winsomely when college women asked for his autograph. Later shot himself.

The hum and whir of the late '50s, early '60s mimeograph machines, churning out beat poetry, deafening me as I walked down North Beach alleys, grew still. The preeminence of rock 'n' roll slowed poetry production down to a torrent. The Reverend Pierre de Lattre, the Congregationalist minister who founded the Bread and Wine Mission to the Beats, hoping to convert them to Christianity, was instead converted himself and now lives and writes in Mexico.

The Black Cat, a link with ancient North Beach bohemia, became a gay bar and then closed. There was a dark side here, too. Bunny Simon, the stately New Orleans Creole gentleman who owned The Anxious Asp, was run out and moved his bar to Haight Street. "Some folks in North Beach didn't want a man of color doing business," he told me. Officer Bigaroni, who harassed the beats, flailing with his club, ran into his own troubles with fraud charges during his retirement. As bohemia made North Beach chic, rents became confiscatory, driving out theaters, cheap restaurants, artists and the old radicals. It's the same irony in Greenwich Village and St.-Germain-des-Prés, the iron grip of real estate speculation closing upon the graceful swan necks.

Irascible Fred Roscoe, rhyme-master with his Santa Claus beard and pinkness, closed Discovery Bookshop and moved to San Anselmo. Enrico Banducci lives with his son back east in Virginia. A few grizzled veterans still hang out at Gino & Carlo's, remembering grand old poets, grand old pool-cue fights. A few stubborn radicals like Jack Kirschman still sell their verse and their manifestos at 12 Adler Place. The countercultural physicist Jack Sarfatti, Ph.D., preaches the corkscrew shape of time to his permanent seminar at the Trieste. "Things that haven't happened yet can cause events in the past."

I know, I know, Jack.

Occasionally, I still see Lawrence the Young Poet on the bus. He's retired from seeking patronage up and down Columbus,

Broadway, and Grant. A young poet who was once five seven years old eventually gets to be eight zero.

A few cafes, bars, restaurants, bookshops still keep the faith. An occasional brave entrepreneur prevents North Beach from becoming a bohemia theme park, a kind of Beatnikworld. Recently Rumors [now the Forked Tongue], on the corner across the street from Enrico's, has been trying to put together the right ingredients—cheap food, warm hearts, a hospitable eccentric proprietor. There are blabbermouth nights, occasional fits of reggae, waitresses with metal decor pinned through haphazard parts of their lively countenances, whispered conferences among pursuers of beauty and truth, an easy layabout atmosphere, and most basic of all—cheap pasta. In North Beach today, this miracle makes a person weep with gratitude and nostalgia. The sourdough bread is baked on the premises. It's not gourmet dining; this is comfortable adequate feeding in a world of congenial loafing. Eureka, we *can* go home again. Recently I met Ffrank Ffollet there in the company of a daughter by a marriage he had forgotten. They explained that they had just happened to notice each other, found

Sunday night and Enrico's was mobbed, as in the old days that were good, because Enrico Himself was there. It was 37 years ago that Enrico opened the town's first coffeehouse and it was time to honor the founding papa. "Sometimes I wake up in the middle of the night and cry, I miss San Francisco so much," confided 73-year-old Bandooooch', who now sells hot dogs from a cart in a Richmond, Virginia, park (his son lives in Richmond).

Francis Coppola was there, looking grave. Jazz critic Phil Elwood played "Basin Street" with Mal Sharpe's Dixielanders. Bill Cosby, who once gave Enrico $100,000, no strings attached, to save the coffeehouse, ad-libbed one of those you-hadda-be-there fifteen-minute monologues about Enrico's Hungry i, a hilarious true tale of the drunken doorman who went home with all the car keys in his pocket and nobody knew where he lived.

Ms. Meredith Melville, one of the new owners of Enrico's, said to him, "Enrico, this will always be your place," and Enrico bowed, wept and whispered, "Take me home."

—Herb Caen, "The Walking Caen," San Francisco Chronicle

something familiar in their faces, and realized—"Hey, Dad? Is that you?"

"Fflorence?"

A miracle: second-generation bohemian meets second-generation beatnik.

I blessed them and found my own table under a light in the corner. A tall fellow, the ghost of Mad Alex, pale, with a fragile beard, introduced himself. "My name is Wo," he said.

"That's funny, you don't look Chinese. How'd you get that name?"

"Because Wo is me," he said. "Now will you buy one of my poems?"

Herbert Gold is the author of several books, including Lovers and Cohorts, Fathers, Family, Best Nightmare on Earth: A Life in Haiti, *and* Bohemia: Where Art, Angst, Love and Strong Coffee Meet, *from which this story was excerpted. He lives in San Francisco.*

✳

What sphinx of cement and aluminum bashed open
    their skulls and ate up their brains and imagi-
    nation?
Moloch! Solitude! Filth! Ugliness! Ashcans and un-
    obtainable dollars! Children screaming under
    the stairways! Boys sobbing in armies! Old men
    weeping in parks!
Moloch! Moloch! Nightmare of Moloch! Moloch
    the loveless! Mental Moloch! Moloch the
    heavy judger of men!
Moloch the incomprehensible prison! Moloch the
    crossbone soulless jailhouse and Congress of
    sorrows! Moloch whose buildings are judg-
    ment! Moloch the vast stone of war! Moloch
    the stunned governments!
Moloch whose mind is pure machinery! Moloch
    whose blood is running money! Moloch
    whose fingers are ten armies! Moloch whose

breast is a cannibal dynamo! Moloch whose ear is a smoking tomb!

Moloch whose eyes are a thousand blind windows! Moloch whose skyscrapers stand in the long streets like endless Jehovahs! Moloch whose factories dream and croak in the fog! Moloch whose smokestacks and antennae crown the cities!

Moloch whose love is endless oil and stone! Moloch whose soul is electricity and banks! Moloch whose poverty is the specter of genius! Moloch whose fate is a cloud of sexless hydrogen! Moloch whose name is the Mind!

—Allen Ginsberg, "Howl"

JAMES O'REILLY

I Was a Teenage Yogi

Learning to breathe takes a lifetime.

PRANA, THE ADEPTS WILL TELL YOU, IS THE LIFE FORCE OF THE breath. It is that which animates us, you and me, with each inhale, and every exhale. Now and again, over and over and over, the measure of all "time" and life.

And it was a matter of *prana* which brought me to a rocky glen near the Pacific Ocean in Marin, where finches twittered and darted and mists unfolded among shifting lattices of sunbeams. For J. M., my dear friend, had taken his last breath—prematurely, thought most of his friends who had gathered in his honor.

The high priest was another old friend, and I do mean high priest, for there was something in his demeanor of that eternal line of priests and priestesses who are simply born to their calling, which is to show us the gateways to Heaven that lie open all around us but are generally hidden by fear, self-deception, and ugly buildings. There was something, too, in his gathering of the strands of our friend's unusual life which made me do the same for my own, which made me see in this "New Age funeral" (for that is what any outsider would have called it) a brief history of San Francisco, the city of Saint Francis, as a spiritual Mecca in the late twentieth century.

The priest himself is a piece of work, Divine Artistry in full motion, a latter-day druid of sweetness and erudition, fluent in Russian, a professor of English whose hobby is Sufi dancing. As I looked at him—studied him—I couldn't help but think of the other attendees in a similar light: they were of unusual religious pedigree, had been through every practice imaginable, had consumed every drug I can name, had meditated this way and that, had been to Esalen before it existed and done zazen in Japan, Arica in Chile, est in New York, yoga in Banares, rebirthing in Santa Fe, had performed Mayan rituals at Teotihuacan and kowtowed to Sai Baba in southern India and worked with Haidakhan Babaji in Uttar Pradesh, had been to Ladakh and Bali long before they were hip, knew Fritz Perls and Ida Rolf before they died, had done Feldenkrais and Aston-Patterning before body work referred to anything but automobiles, had studied Indian dance and general semantics and neuropsychology, and dabbled at Findhorn. They read and loved Wallace Stevens, Rumi, Rilke, and Lao Tzu, and knew Freud and Jung at least as well as they knew the modern purveyors of psychological insight and panacea. They were gay and bi and hetero or weren't sure, and had been doing psychic channelling long before it became *de rigueur*.

Saint Francis's biographer Fra Tommaso da Celano wrote: "He discerned the hidden things of nature with his sensitive heart, as one who had already escaped into the freedom of the glory of the sons of God." And this is the secret of sainthood.

—Bernardino Farnetani,
Saint Francis of Assisi

These things in themselves are not so unusual these days but they haven't *ever* been unusual in San Francisco, and that is what struck me that day near the Pacific: I was the fish in the sea: how can I speak of water?

But to speak only of the past is a kind of psychological arthritis, and it's not my intention to do that. The amazing thing, looking at my fellow mourners, was that for all their collective experience, *they weren't even old yet*. To be sure, some (I shall include myself) were getting long in the tooth, a bit wrinkly, paunchy, or bald, but in general they looked good and had functioning lives.

What was it about San Francisco?

I was born and raised Irish Catholic, and the enduring legacy from my father and mother was and is an abiding knowingness about God and love with a capital L, which transcends whatever travails I may currently be enduring. The legacy of San Francisco is that God is everywhere—but particularly in San Francisco.

I say this with a smile, but why is it that I knew about chakras and mantras and mandalas before I could drive or vote? I can't blame it all on my brothers, or even take the credit for being an aberrant child, though my parents were certainly horrified by my leanings and those of my brothers—and they certainly were right about us being impressionable. But again, what *was* it about San Francisco that so impressed itself upon us? (I will never forget the day my father asked my older brother Sean what Mass he had gone to and he replied, "I didn't. I went to a Hindu temple.")

For are there not holy places in the world? Places that are, beauty aside, more unaccountably special than others? I have traveled a great deal, and have been to quite a number of these, and I count San Francisco chief among them. San Francisco nurtured the seeker in me, its light and ambience nothing less than a spiritual amniotic fluid. This is why my brothers and I were attending meditations and lectures on mysticism at the age of fourteen, why reading Aurobindo, Korzybski, Gurdjieff, and Jung were wonders equal to wandering in Golden Gate Park with hippies, smoking marijuana and listening to Country Joe and the Fish and Quicksilver Messenger Service, or dancing naked to Jimi Hendrix.

Again, like the fish in the sea, at J.M.'s funeral I realized that I had forgotten the medium I still swim in when I am here. Half of my friends are psychics of one sort or another, indeed I met my wife at a spiritual retreat at a hot spring, most of the people I am close to believe they have lived before, they use divination methods in their daily lives, ranging from the *I Ching* to dowsing rods to pendulums to taping special rocks to their heads, and most of them are successful, functioning adults, parents and grandparents. I myself have spoken to the dead and firmly believe my small daughters and certain friends visit me psychically when I am abroad. On more than one occasion I have broken the laws of physics.

So what is it about San Francisco? Is this a widespread dementia that strikes the weak-minded, the gullible, who flock to California and San Francisco like minnows or sheep or fools? I think not, though I am sure San Francisco supports more silly activities per square mile than any place in the world save Berkeley. No, I think it is that San Francisco touches the Saint Francis in each of us more than do most places. (J. M., for instance, was such a seeker, rich in love, poor in the things of this world.)

> *Satan is entrenched much more strongly than he should be in this wonderful city of God.*
>
> —Evangelist Billy Sunday

In recent years, I've been going to a body work practitioner to help work out the kinks from an old back injury (slinging huge boxes of tile from railroad cars with 300-pound Mexicans when I was a 125-pound weakling). I wasn't looking for enlightenment, euphoria, nirvana, or even an afternoon nap. I just wanted my body fixed. But it happened again—what began as physical therapy became the "venue" for the most profound spiritual experiences I have ever had. Under her hands I experienced the love of the creator through me in the swinging gate of the soul, my breath. I felt the creation of my very life with and in every breath. I learned to pray through my breath, that prayer is nothing *but* the proper attitude of one's breath towards God, and I think even the nuns who taught me at St. Cecilia's would be pleased. I know my father is, God rest his soul, just as I know he and J. M. and Saint Francis will be there when my *prana* expires, when I leave this realm as they did, as we all must.

Of course, all these things can and do happen everywhere else in the world. But for me, they happen in San Francisco as often as the fog rolls in, as readily as the tide sweeps through the Golden Gate, as constantly as the breath I take.

James O'Reilly is co-editor of the Travelers' Tales *series. He is also co-author of "World Travel Watch," a column that appears in newspapers throughout the United States.*

✳

San Francisco is like Venice and Ahens in having strange memories; she is unlike them in being lit from within by a large and luminous hope.

—Edwin Markham, quoted by Gladys Hansen in *San Francisco Almanac: Everything You Want to Know About Everyone's Favorite City*

JOHN KRICH

The Real Mission

¿Se habla español?

EACH TIME AMERICA SEALS ME IN A LAMINATE OF DEADLINES AND Dow Jones averages, bills due and bills payable, I journey to a place where urgencies fade, colors brighten and all claims on reality begin to look relative. Just a stroll down the hill—though, like a good Californian, I usually drive—leads me out of my silent, wind-scoured, chillingly pretty neighborhood into a raucous, mouldering, charmingly unscrubbed cauldron. Suddenly, the sidewalks are bordered with azure tiles and doused with the perfume of rotting mangoes; the streets are serenaded by thumping *basso* laments broadcast from souped-up Chevys; the advertisements appeal to a dozen loyalties and languages. Black-shawled Guatemalan women ply the restaurants, peddling red carnations, followed by packs of Vietnamese urchins toting bags of fresh-picked garlics, each available clapboard wall bursts with murals of naked Aztec deities and painted jungles; every sight conspires to defeat grayness and to sabotage the straight and narrow. Where thousands have sought asylum before me, I am a refugee in reverse—fleeing the benefits of the Promised Land for the immigrant hothouse and global miscellany that is San Francisco's Mission District.

If other parts of San Francisco exist to meet outside expectations of what San Francisco should be, "the Mission" is where San Francisco is San Francisco for itself. Residents know what tourists can find out only by giving up the search for postcard imagery: the most characteristic neighborhood of this city is the one with the least characteristically San Franciscan attributes. You'll find no cable cars here, and no hills for them to climb. Sourdough bread and shrimp Louis have long been replaced by corn torillas and *cangrejos a la parrilla*. Far from the ocean and close to the Bay, the Mission is also one of the sections of town least plagued by the picturesque fog.

This oblong grid that runs roughly from 14th to 30th Streets, bounded on the east by Potrero Avenue and on the west by a curtain of palms along undulating Dolores Street, contains some of San Francisco's finest Victorian-style houses. In the Mission's unfiltered light, it's easy to notice when these so-called "painted ladies" have had their makeup smeared and their rouge blown off by time, their petticoat trimmings tattered. Nonetheless, these houses have become San Francisco's own—and make the Mission's residential areas prime territory for gawking. Some of the earliest and most ornate houses in the Mission are along South Van Ness Avenue, called Howard Street when it was a millionaires' row. Another assortment of 19th-century treasures can be found on Fair Oaks and Liberty, two tree-lined streets west of Mission Street.

But the Mission's main claim to fame is its ever-multiplying ethnic diversity. The name of a popular district saloon says it all. "El Tico Nica" reads the sign, translated as "The Nicaraguan Costa Rican," or the reverse, if you choose. In recent years, the neighborhood has become a hybrid, its core Mexican and Mexican-American population supplemented with a steady stream of noncombatants from El Salvador, Guatemala, Nicaragua, and other portions of that troubled area that many travel agencies advertise as "C.A." A smattering of Cubans, Puerto Ricans, and Chileans have found a haven here, too. A stroll down Mission Street also reveals markets catering to a growing number of Chinese, Vietnamese, even Laotian tribal people. A drive farther south along the main street, leading toward the Excelsior neighborhood and beyond, is an expedition into the Pacific islands. Filipino markets sell dried fish and homemade *lumpia* rolls, but that is only the start. Find a rare green space here and you might stumble on a mass Samoan barbecue, where the charcoals are tended by formations of women in flowered muumuus.

I made my first foray into the Mission in the fall of 1968, the week Richard Nixon was elected president. I'd come to San Francisco on a break from my freshman year in college. In the days when the Bay Area laid claim to being the world capital of revolt, word reached me that the most incendiary show in town was to be found in a tiny church that then served as venue for El Teatro Campesino, the company born out of the United Farm Workers movement. I felt thoroughly conspiratorial as I searched among darkened, unfamiliar avenues. I even remember my first glimpse of the wispy palms along Mission Street. How, I wondered, did they survive so far north? Eventually, I found my way to *The Shrunken Head of Pancho Villa*, the first full-length play by Luis Valdez, who went on to write and direct *Zoot Suit* and the movie *La Bamba*.

Once I moved to the Bay Area, I was led to the Mission by

> *Living in the Mission District is like living in a tropical village. While fog erases the Golden Gate Bridge and half of San Francisco, sun streams down on the murals and graffiti in the Mission. Ranchero music blasts from taverns and radios. People gossip on their doorsteps or mill around on the street. Guys tinker with cars and whistle at women. Every spring Carnaval blows through in a flurry of feathers and drums.*
>
> *I lived in the Mission for ten years and loved being Latin by proxy. I learned to salsa at Cesar's Latin Palace, a giant dance club on Mission Street. I visited Baja California for the first time, cultivated a cactus garden, and dressed up my Victorian apartment with Mexican altars. Every Sunday morning I lit candles at the basilica next to the 18th-century Mission Dolores, the oldest intact building in San Francisco, and came to know by heart every one of the stone lambs and summer roses in its old walled cemetery, where some of the city's founding fathers are buried.*
>
> —Rebecca Bruns, "Mural, Mural on the Wall," *Travel & Leisure*

cuisine, not culture: the burrito. First at the legendary La Cumbre, on Valencia, and later at the competing El Toro, I discovered how a whole dinner could be stuffed inside one steam-heated, bargain-priced white flour wrapping. The enlargement of the burrito to humongous, Americanized proportions may be the Mission's supreme contribution to Western civilization: the story is told about a newcomer from Mexico, used to the skimpier variety back home, who ordered four burritos on his first trip to the Mission—and found his plate loaded down with ten pounds worth of these edible artillery shells.

Still, my own appreciation for the neighborhood did not flower fully until, returning from a trip to Venezuela, I wanted to replicate a fried banana dish for friends. In South America, I had sampled the delicious *manzana* bananas, tart and apple-ish as the name suggests. I assumed that they didn't exist north of the border, but one shopping trip was enough for me to discover that every store in the Mission stocked *manzanas,* as well as the over-ripe monsters the Mexicans call *machos*—and five other types besides.

But the Mission provides more than bananas. It offers a past—that rarest of commodities in the society on wheels where only right-of-way matters, epochs are but bumper stickers waiting to come unglued, history is just a rear-view mirror into which few bother to peek. That's why I pulled over the first time I spotted the freshly whitewashed adobe at Dolores and 16th Streets known officially as Misión San

A dusky Mexican señorita, magnificently dressed, entered the arena, sword in hand. For a time she parried with the bull, pricking him slightly and stepping quickly to one side whenever he ran toward her. He soon became furious, roaring and tossing his horns high into the air and making the most formidable plunges at the lady until, at a favorable opportunity, she plunged the sword to the hilt into the breast of the animal. She was sprinkled with crimson dye, and in a moment the beast lay dead at her feet. The lady was greeted with a shower of silver dollars...

—Enos Christman, 1851 diary entry, quoted by JoAnn Levy in *They Saw the Elephant: Women in the California Gold Rush*

Mission Dolores

Francisco de Asis (bestowing the name on the city) and colloquially as Mission Dolores. I don't usually brake for chapels, but this pint-sized speck of California's Spanish past, dwarfed by the accompanying basilica where Pope John Paul II, in 1987, blessed AIDS patients, stands as a singular revelation. A modest plaque tags Mission Dolores "California Historic Landmark No. 327," but it is San Francisco's building Número Uno: this schizophrenic city's single provider of psychic continuity. *Dolores,* of course, means sorrows or pains, and close by what bilingual Missionites jokingly call "Pains Park," under the mission-style turrets of Mission High, ran a stream that the Spanish christened "El Arroyo de Nuestra Señora de los Dolores." The Mission building was once the northern terminus of El Camino Reál, the Spanish road up the California coast. It was dedicated on June 29, 1776, just five days before the Declaration of Independence.

The Mission was built with 36,000 sunbaked bricks, clay walls four feet thick. Redwood trusses helped the church survive the 1906 earthquake. If you get to Mission Dolores between tour buses, you can have a moment's meditation in the oblong sanctuary under a ceiling of zigzagging earthtoned patterns reminiscent of Santa Fe. Once upon not so long a time ago, this building was the center of a vast rancho supporting 11,000 head of cattle. Bullfights were held outside the chapel, and so were ritual dances of the few surviving Costanoan Indians. The grounds of the Mission hold the unmarked remains of some 5,000 unlucky Costanoans, one of the native "digger" peoples whose gentle ways would later inspire Haight-Ashbury's hippie tribes.

The burial plot for Europeans is probably the high point of a visit to the Mission site. A proclamation in the gift shop, handed out by a local publication more known for rating purveyors of goat cheese, calzone, and Sonoma County zinfandels, dubs this the Bay Area's "Best-Looking Graveyard." Amid bursts of uncontrollable California fecundity, cacti and aloes, roses and poppies and birds of paradise, there are enough headstones of civic founders to serve the tourist as a road map. Francisco de Haro, the first *alcalde,* or mayor, of Yerba Buena, as the settlement was then called, can be found here. The street named after him is not within walking distance, but you can find members of the families who are memorialized in some of the Mission's main streets: Valencia, Guerrero, Sanchez.

Because of Mission Dolores, most people have the mistaken impression that this has always been the Hispanic section of town. But the enterprising Forty-Niners who squatted here—including one Levi Strauss, whose blue jeans factory can be viewed at the north end of Valencia—were quite efficient at wiping out the traces of prior Spanish and Mexican rule. The wealthy among them soon abandoned the area in favor of Nob Hill and its sweeping Bay views. Successive waves of poor immigrants—the Germans, the Italians and the Irish—weren't so foolish. They disdained the quest for status in favor of the Mission's sunshine. It wasn't until after World War II that Mexican immigrants to California's fields and shipyards

*D*edicated thrift-shoppers and bookstore-dwellers always face a conundrum when they are cruising up and down Valencia; where do you go to pee? You could go into a taqueria, but then you have to pretend to look at the menu, scrunching your forehead to mimic an intense decision between the super vegetarian burrito and the regular one. Then, when you think the people behind the counter have gotten used to seeing you around, you could dart for the bathroom (that is, if no one is using it), culminating in the shameful, hurtful retreat from the place once you are finished.

But fret no more; there is an alternative! Conveniently located on Valencia between 17th and 18th Streets is the brand-spanking new Mission Police Station. It's amazing how much trepidation you initially feel going into a police station, but really, this place is hassle-free. Pee without fear!

—San Francisco Bay Guardian, "Best Place to Pee in the Mission"

came flooding back to unwittingly reclaim the neighborhood's heritage.

Today, the heart of the district, the Inner Mission, is the thoroughly Mexican strip along 24th Street between South Van Ness and Potrero. While Mission Street has become an unappealing hodgepodge of cut-rate rag shops and liquor stores, doughnut stands and Foxy Lady boutiques, *La Calle Veinte-Cuatro* remains a quiet and genial stretch that simulates a visit to the downtown of a midsized Mexican farming community. Bakery windows are crammed with pink and yellow cakes; inside customers take a tray and tongs, then choose—amid hanging piñata, sacks of *frijoles*, industrial-sized cans of pickled jalapeños—from the various traditional shapes and sizes of sugary buns. For a quarter a pop, try a *novia,* shaped like a wedding dress, or a *concha*, with its icing baked in nautilus design, or the croissants that Mexicans more aptly call *cuernos,* or horns. At Casa Sanchez, one of the city's leading tortilla factories, you can get the corn cakes fresh and warm, then dip them in a variety of sauces displayed in the traditional black mortars. Or you can sit down to a full meal at the Roosevelt Tamale Parlor, a longtime neighborhood landmark. All that's missing here is a quaint plaza.

Twenty-fourth Street also houses El Nuevo Fruitlandia, which turns out to be a Puerto Rican restaurant, and Discolandia, the city's premier Latin record shop. There might be dozens of such stores in New York or Los Angeles, but San Francisco's very smallness assures that each speck of Latin culture remains distinct, a treasured resource. That is certainly the case with the Galeria de la Raza, the major showcase and patron of local Latino artists. Its Studio 24 shop next door has the city's best collection of Mexican folk objects and handicrafts, plus plenty of thick-eyebrowed icons of Frida Kahlo, the wife of Diego Rivera and the reigning goddess of every aspiring Latina artist. You can find idols to suit your fancy on the many murals that spring up on nearly every empty patch of plaster along 24th and nearby streets: from an Aztec god in a plumed headdress to Carlos Santana wielding his electric guitar. Balmy Alley, off 24th, boasts a blocklong series of murals that mix landscapes and agitprop, foliage and laundry—both real and painted.

Mission Street, which crosses 24th, is notable for its astounding heterogeneity. Each stretch of storefronts here is emblematic of the American dream and the multiethnic reality to which that dream is slowly giving rise. Just look: there is a Chinese restaurant, a Vietnamese butcher shop, a sushi café, and a Salvadoran *pupusa* stand. To this mix is added such leftovers of the Edward Hopper era as Golden Crust Pies. At this point, it's the bygone America that seems most exotic, out of place or context. All that remains of a former furniture store on 17th Street is a rooftop billboard dominating the district with its inexplicable boast: "17 Reasons Why!"

For all this, some first-time visitors to the Mission may see only the buckles in the pavement, the strewn newspapers, the gang graffiti, the broken-down *borrachos* staggering about in exaggerations of stupor so artful they border on the Chaplinesque, the abandoned Chevys and, in some unshaven faces, abandoned hopes. But they will be missing everything to use the dismissive terms "ghetto," "slum," "barrio," "low-rent." For one thing, California insures that poverty is sun-washed and diluted by space to spread out. Unlike some of its counterparts back East, the Mission is sometimes tawdry but never bleak. Its inhabitants do not give the impression of feeling trapped, just occasionally stalled. Amid the groups of sharp-eyed shoppers at the papaya stands, there is little evidence of shame and much of dignity. *La Misión* displays a world that is less busy striving to become American than showing America how to become the whole world.

The Mission illustrates the obvious paradox of travel, whether far or crosstown. For we don't go places just to expand our choice of bananas. Our quest is to reclaim a sense of the other-worldly amid mundanity. In the places where life narrows to the most basic human concerns, we glimpse a widening of our own possibilities. It's these possibilities that send me coasting down that hill more and more often.

John Krich is the author of Music in Every Room: Around the World in a Bad Mood, El Beisbol: Travels Through the Pan-American Pastime, Why Is This Country Dancing?: A No-Hope Samba Through Brazil, *and a novel about Fidel Castro entitled* A Totally Free Man. *He lives in San Francisco.*

★

The Spanish Missions of California's El Camino Real, as the many other Spanish sites in the "New World," are not just perishable historical monuments, residues of a complete past. These Missions, rather, are living voices each of which speaks with its own particular eloquence of the presence within North America of a cultural heritage that is still alive and with us. This is a heritage of values and beliefs, of saints and sinners, of Sword and Cross, of unique art forms speaking of and from two worlds, of a unique and creative religious presence, and above all of encounter of this presence with those indigenous native peoples who probably were more numerous in California than in any other area of North America. The roots of this encounter between peoples of vastly contrasting yet mutually rich cultures were planted and tended during some three centuries of Spanish presence in North America; a presence that commenced twenty-two years before the pilgrims landed at Plymouth Rock, ten years before French Quebec, and nine years before the English Jamestown. Whether we accept these earliest Spanish roots or not, they are nevertheless entwined in living manner within the many threads which constitute the fabric of what America is.

—Bruce Walter Barton, *The Tree at the Center of the World: A Story of the California Missions*

⋆ ⋆ ⋆

Circle of Gold

Two birds take flight one fine evening in San Francisco.

It was a May morning, a long time ago in Sonoma County when the population was a small fraction of what it is now. I awoke very early, easy to do in Lakeville with my bedroom window facing the low hills east of Petaluma. As I made my morning tea I could see the nearly full moon dropping into the horizon behind the long row of eucalyptus trees that always reminded me, I told Gina and Nicolle, toddlers then, of a broccoli parade. There was some pretty goldenrod print fabric on my nightstand, with some black cotton lace and a soft piece of black velvet, which by noon I had transformed into a skirt, long and flowing, and a blouse with lace trim and velvet yoke. I drove the fifteen or so miles to the university, where I found my friend Estelle waiting for me, dressed from head to toe in black and yellow, one of the many coincidences we later considered with great seriousness. With her head of thick, wild auburn curls, my long reddish-blond locks and our color-coordinated outfits, we looked like a pair of exotic birds.

Anapendulum—now known as the Commons but then intriguingly named as the companion of The Pit, the bohemian campus coffeehouse that is now part of the expanded Sonoma State University bookstore—was full to overflowing that Saturday, as a vibrant crowd of fans awaited Anaïs Nin. She dazzled us all when she appeared in her fine chiseled beauty, draped in a floor-length black cape, her signature braids crowning her head. She seemed to float on the wave of our expectations and, though I remember nothing of the content of her talk, I have a profound physical memory of its emotional impact. Her words cast a magic spell over us all, and I remember that I cried when I shook her hand, so long and delicate and frail: birdlike, as she was then.

My yellow Volkswagon had broken down on the way to campus, but the glory of the day was such that I had simply gotten out and hitched a ride from the next car to come along, refusing to speculate that car trouble might put an end to the adventure Estelle and I had planned. When I informed her of the mechanical misfortune, she offered a typically spirited response. "Let's go to San Francisco anyway," she said, and we hitchhiked back to my car to get my coat, actually a long black knit shawl, my warmest garment in those days. At the car, I decided to give it a try and when it started on the first attempt, we considered it a sign and headed off towards the Golden Gate to claim San Francisco as our own.

We walked around Union Square and as the sun began to set, decided to have dinner. The place we tried first, a new French cafe, turned us away because they had run out of food. We tried four or five different restaurants and were either turned away or, in one case, left after being seated because our waiter was a jerk. As we left the final restaurant, a cable car was passing by, no waiting behind the line, just dangerous, mid-street boarding and friendly, spirited conductors. We asked for a recommendation and the conductor said, "Just wait, I'll tell you when to get off." As the cable car groaned into its turn onto Jackson Street, he said, "Get off now, eat there," pointing to The Coachman's Bar with The Oak Tree restaurant inside.

The bar itself was a tiny, cozy place and at the entrance to the dining room we were greeted by a friendly, proper host with a charming British accent. He handed us each a carnation and seated us near the window, where every few minutes another cable car rattled by. A quick view of the menu revealed that we had ventured into a world quite unlike our own, where student budgets and the casual counterculture of Sonoma in the mid-'70s defined our diet. At that point, I don't believe I had ever ordered a glass of wine and we were suddenly confronted with choices and prices that were staggeringly out of our league. But it was a special night, we said, as we ordered mixed grill and a bottle of red wine.

We were giddy, like schoolgirls out on their own for the first time. Estelle was thoroughly in love with our waiter, a tall string-bean of an Englishman, blond and shy and obviously enjoying us thoroughly. I was in love with our meal, with the heavy silverware and the beautiful presentation, with the wine that brought an even deeper glow to my already rosy cheeks, with the tiny lamb chops, grilled kidneys, and plump, short sausages on my plate. As we lingered over dessert, the waiter brought us a complimentary after-dinner liqueur, setting it down almost apologetically and backing away from the table shyly. We paid our bill and left, insecure about having only five dollars left between us but confident, somehow, that luck was on our side. We made the short walk to North Beach and spent the night laughing and dancing and talking to strangers, who often stopped to watch us as we walked by, one of them commenting, excusing himself first for the intrusion, that he couldn't resist telling us how beautiful we were, that we lit up the street with our glow. And we were somehow both aware of it, aware of some special quality passing through us that had nothing to do with how we looked and everything to do with how we felt, how dazzled we were by the world that night, by San Francisco, by the full moon that by then hung high over the city, our golden chaperone.

As the night wound down to what we thought would be its conclusion, we made the walk up Washington Street to Powell, where we figured we would have to walk the several blocks to my car. Safety was not a concern then, in part because it was entirely safe, in most parts of San Francisco, to walk—two women, or a woman alone—at any time, and in part because we were invincible, untouchable in our charmed circle of gold. As we reached the top of the hill, we saw the last cable car of the night headed towards the barn, empty except for the driver and conductor, the same one who had started us on our journey several hours earlier. He saw us, too, and held the car until we could hop on. Instead of heading back to the barn immediately, they offered to take us to my car and in the process gave Estelle and me our own personal cable car excursion. I was sitting alone on the outside bench, soaking up all that golden moonlight, when I looked back at Estelle and our conductor. His name is Joe, I suddenly thought to myself, almost as if someone had whispered his name. I even turned, startled, but I was alone in the moonlight in the cool San Francisco night.

By the time we reached Pine Street, where my car was parked, none of us wanted the night to end. Estelle and I agreed to accompany our new friends to the cable car barn and then head back to The Coachman for a drink. "By the way," the conductor said, reaching a hand towards mine, "I'm Joe." I jumped and as our eyes met, something bright and hot arced in the air between us and I looked away, flushed and out of breath. I became quieter then, letting Estelle steer the conversation, relying on her vibrancy to carry the energy of the night.

While Joe counted his receipts and changed out of his uniform, Estelle and I played ping pong. The cable cars were tucked away in their covered ports, and never have I felt more privy to the secret inside of San Francisco. Cable cars, their image, their song, the sound of their bells, make up some of my earliest memories. I love the ride from downtown, especially the first glimpse of the bay as

The town's first literary paper of consequence was called The Golden Era; *when the rails of the Pacific Railroad were joined at Promontory in Utah in 1869, a spike of pure California gold was driven and the original can be seen in Wells Fargo's museum to this day. Women of fashion at one period sprinkled gold flakes in their hair as a footman would do with powder, and gold coin was the only medium of exchange permitted on the tables of gambling layouts in Portsmouth Square. Before the phrase "Diamond Horseshoe" was coined at New York's Metropolitan, the boxes at the opera were known in San Francisco as* The Golden Horseshoe.

—Lucius Beebe & Charles Clegg,
San Francisco's Golden Era: A Picture Story of San Francisco Before the Fire

you come over the hill. I love the creaking way they struggle up a hill, occasionally backsliding and sending a car full of terrified tourists into the oncoming traffic. And here I

Cable car

was behind the scenes, in Santa's workshop, control central, the very heartbeat of the city. We had just enough time left to make it to The Coachman and share a hot brandy before closing time. Joe's partner on the cable car was long gone, and it was clear by then that the alchemy was between the three of us. We climbed into Joe's car and headed west, where we sat and talked until the full moon sank down behind the towers of the Golden Gate Bridge and the eastern sky began to glow.

As moonlight streamed into the car like a fourth presence, Joe told Estelle to turn and look at me. "She looks like she's made out of gold, doesn't she, spun gold?" he asked, as he moved my hair out of my eyes and turned my face to the side. I was embarrassed, but I felt the glow, too, we all did; we all seemed spun out of some magical, golden fiber there in the shimmering predawn San Francisco. Reluctantly, Estelle and I said good-bye to our new friend and headed back towards the Lakeville dawn.

School was out a few weeks later and Estelle went back to Southern California for the summer. I rode the cable cars often and finally, as I knew I would, I saw Joe. I rode with him all night and when he was through counting his receipts, we went to The Coachman's Bar, this time just the two of us. When it closed, we went for a long walk down to the bay, where Joe kissed me for the first of many times and told me he loved me.

It's been a long time since I've seen Joe, longer still since I've seen or talked to Estelle. I have no idea where either of them are. At Sonoma State, there are no longer any buildings that pay homage to Edgar Allen Poe. The Coachman and The Oak Tree are both gone. The hills of Lakeville are filling with sprawling, luxury housing. It's been a long time since I wore a yellow dress and I don't remember the last time the air shimmered with so much golden possibility between me and a charming stranger. But I occasionally enjoy a good mixed grill, something I can do entirely on my own without the cooperation of the gods, and red wine still brings a soft glow to my cheeks, and for that I am very, very glad.

Michele Anna Jordan has lived within 45 minutes of San Francisco for her entire life. The author of numerous books, including the highly acclaimed Good Cook's Book of Days: A Food Lover's Journal, Good Cook's Book of Mustard, *and* Good Cook's Book of Tomatoes, *Jordan is restaurant critic and food and wine editor for San Francisco Focus Magazine. She also hosts "Mouthful with Michele Anna Jordan" on KRCB-FM, the Sonoma County NPR affiliate.*

★

Sometimes a football game was called, the women playing the men, putting up valuables and even money to bet with each other. The men kicked the ball with the foot while the women caught it with the hand and ran with it. The men hugged the woman who carried the ball. When they tickled her belly, she threw the ball to another woman.

If that woman missed, a man kicked the ball with the foot. Another woman caught it with the hands and ran with it toward their goal. Then a man hugged her again. When he threw her on the ground and rolled her around, she threw the ball. In that way another woman caught it and brought it towards their goal.

The men played with the foot, the women played with the hand: that was their playing together so that a man could hug the woman he loved. The women on their part took every opportunity to hug the men they loved; the game was like that so that this could be done.

—Nisenan legend, *The Way We Lived: California Indian Reminiscences, Stories and Songs,* edited by Malcolm Margolin

Freakin' in Frisco

Two postmodern mendicants are on the loose.

TWENTY-THREE AND ONE-HALF MILES SOUTH OF HALF MOON Bay, the three-ton Monkmobile spat another stinking strip of rubber off the back right wheel as we hit one final, jerky bump on what could have been our perfect return to The City.

But it's Frisco to me. Ever since the winter of '66 when two completely tanked Irish blokes, hands rougher than a barnacled rock, set the record straight. Rhymes with Crisco and I don't care what the sweater queens say because when you've had a hundred thousand miles of dirt under your nails and enough flat tires to fill a landfill you grab for shortcuts, and Frisco will do just fine.

It was another battle of wits between us and the God of oil. Jim noticed the smell first and we got into one of our "what's that smell…I don't smell anything," sidesplitting arguments that can only lead to a flying frying pan if we don't tear ourselves away. We could fight like pit bulls in a snake pen, teeth and nails, going for the jugular. But we're civil. We hate to argue, rip and tear, unless it smells like fire.

The piss-elegant beauty of the day betrayed our boiling melodrama. It was one of those odd, coastal mornings when the sun was actually shining. Ribbons of morning light pushed across the early swells of seaweed and a few specks of humanity were out conquering their merciless sea on designer surfboards. The Pacific slapped its sadistic waves against the shoreline without an afterthought for what the land might think. Yes the Pacific, yes Northern California, yes the wandering Monks were on their way home.

As we hugged the curves of Route 1, bound for The City, the Bounder burped a plume of blackened smoke. The flapping tire and the narcotic smell of burning oil dragged us off the road to a side-jolting stop.

I stepped out first. The back inner dual tire was shredded like a cat-o'-nine-tails, lashing out on the pavement. Smoke was billowing from far within the oil-less bowels of our treasured motor home and the hog of a gas tank was belching its last drop.

"Outta gas!"

"Yep."

"Flat tire!"

"Yep!"

"Losing oil!"

"Yep! Yep! Yep!" I was pissed as hell.

Jim got out the chicken and put on some rice in the broken pressure cooker with the holes in its side. Rice, our true companion. Rice, our lord and savior. Fried chicken our crispy revenge. I began to panic in my Virgo-rising-straitjacket sort of way and fretted over the tire, or the oil, or the empty tank, and our lack of money.

It took me back to our attempt to leave Frisco. "You must move this vehicle one eighth of a mile or one city block within 48 hours or your vehicle will be impounded."

We could see traces of the meter scooter and were convinced it was the same meter maid as the day before, judging from the heaviness of the footprints.

On the next morning Jim wanted to leave. Or I wanted to leave. We're still not sure. It's one of those endless discussions that go nowhere when we can't remember who wanted what, but I do know something changed. Jim was soon out of there, heading north. With a month's worth of rice and a box full of papers, he was off on the adventure of a lifetime. He was going to go domestic for a month, to see how the settled half lived. We bade good-bye in a surreal moment that might have looked better on film than in real life.

As he drove away with his friend I stood there, buses cruising around the corner. Every few minutes I became mesmerized by the funny electric sound, like so many gnats in your ear. The orange and white stripes reminded me of high school and the MUNI logo seemed like a good idea, sort of like a road sign announcing curves ahead, but turned on its side.

The bus picked me up near the train station and I stepped into my first ride with the eagerness of a kid going to school. I clutched my quarters so tight my knuckles were blood red. It seemed like a residential bus with several transients settled in for a long sleep. They looked as if they spent the day traveling the loop, seeing the city over and over in a dizzying circle, waiting for the driver to ask them to leave. I wondered how many times you could circle the city before that happened. I wondered if the transients all traveled the same bus every day, staking out their territory. Did that make them roommates? Did they know each other's idiosyncrasies, likes and dislikes? How did they feel about all of us short-riders invading their space?

I dropped my dollar of change in the slot and headed toward the back of the bus, pausing at the middle. It was an extra long bus with two sections joined together by a flexible midsection. As the bus lurched forward, its accordion-like joint twisted and turned with warnings not to touch the wall. I understood the warning and decided against sitting there because I knew I would, of course, have to touch the wall just because the sign said not to.

In the back of the bus were back-of-the-bus types. A broken black man in a 49ers hat was muttering to himself. Some kids in stocking caps were throwing lit matches at the floor and a large, white couple wearing matching denim crowded a seat. I sat behind them because I liked the smell of her hair: strawberry shampoo and maybe a twist of vanilla. Her deodorant smelled like raspberries and rain.

The man she was with was like every construction worker I've ever met: middle-aged, heavy in the middle, but with puffy arms and calloused hands. His thumb was black and blue and he had a dark mole on his neck in the shape of Spain. They both stared out the window for the ride to Market Street.

I felt like following them for the day.

Her hair was bleached the color of sand, dirty sand on the beach. The roots were a nice red. The tips of her nails were chewed into fragments that seem to resemble the edge of a crater. The pink fingernail polish was slightly chipped and cracked, but otherwise fine. Maybe a fresh manicure from two months ago. It was still wearing well.

The bus lunged forward and we held on for the ride as it slowly filled with Asian women. Their fingers all looked very agile and I could imagine them all sitting at sewing machines.

> "*No live animals on the bus," growled the driver to the Chinese grandmother as she pushed her way down the aisle, nodding and smiling, clutching a plastic bag with a chicken poking out its head.*
>
> "*No live animals on the bus!" he repeated. She kept moving, still smiling, still nodding.*
>
> "*No live animals!" The driver was almost shouting now as she took a seat next to a Chinese man and the bus began to fill up with people cackling in Cantonese.*
>
> *The Chinese man said something to the grandmother and suddenly her face brightened. She put both hands on the chicken and wrung its neck. Holding up the dead bird for the bus driver to see she said, "No live, no live."*
>
> —Larry Habegger,
> "Way of the Shepherd"

Their chatter doubled with every block. By the time we reached Folsom it sounded like a jungle; birdlike in fact. I expected to see Tarzan.

And a minute later I did.

Tarzan had a bleached coiffure and an admirable backside. His jeans were so strategically ripped, you could see his ass if he bent a certain way. And he was smacking gum louder than the sweet Asian women's chattering voices. Some started to laugh and their laughter rolled like a wave from one end of MUNI to the other until he carefully placed the gum on the underside of the advertisers near the ceiling. Then they stopped, but some were still snickering.

I was reading the advertisers. I was considering getting my teeth brightened with that *Hollywood Smile*, or at least going to the *Foot Doctor*. But then the two people, the denim couple in front of me, were talking.

"So what are you going to get," she said in a demanding sort of way.

"The Quarterpounder," he replied.

"That's what you ordered last time."

"No I didn't. I had the cheeseburger with fries."

"Medium or large fries?"

"Large, but it wasn't no Quarterpounder. That's what you had."

"I'm going to get the cheeseburger this time, but I want the large fries."

"You got enough money?"

"Well, then I'll forget the fries. I'll have some of yours."

"I'm not getting fries."

"You're always getting fries."

"What are you going to drink?"

"I'm having Pepsi."

"Not Sprite?"

"Oh, maybe. I don't know."

"I'm having Coke."

I was absorbed in their food preferences. I was hungrily dreaming of sitting with them at their table, wherever they were headed, and ordering the same. I decided I'd share my fries with her even if she didn't ask.

Tarzan began to jiggle the change in his pocket and I noticed a small man with dark circles under his eyes looking at the tear in Tarzan's jeans. We were both thinking the same thought. I could feel us both entering the rip in the pants and taking an unofficial tour of Tarzan's hairy terrain.

I began to dream of a miniature journey inside his pants and settling in his pocket for the day. But then I was confused, not sure if

I wanted to follow him like a miniature troll, sitting in his pocket, or stick with the denim couple. They seemed like more fun.

"Maybe I'll just order a chocolate shake and forget the cheeseburger," she said.

"Why, you think you can have some of my burger?"

"No, I just feel like a shake instead."

"Good, then I won't have to share my Quarterpounder."

"I just feel like a shake but now I feel like a Quarterpounder with Coke and fries."

"Make up your mind." He was getting impatient.

I decided on the denim couple. Their talk was making me hungry. They talked on and on about the order. It was an order they'd made countless times before. I sort of admired them for still finding ways to discuss variations on the same old Quarterpounder theme. I felt so identified in their obsession that I dreamt of a serene life, filled with just that one Quarterpounder decision. Every day would be a choice. To order the Quarterpounder. Or to *not* order the Quarterpounder. All of life could be divided by that decision. And I would be at peace.

I was so absorbed, I didn't care that the bus had filled to capacity by the time we hit Market. So many small Asian women were aboard that I wanted to be like them. I wanted to chatter in that clucky sound and not seem racist. I could feel my honorable Chinese motherhood rising to the surface. My feet felt small and my fingers felt like threading a bobbin. I could smell ginger and I began to wonder if I was on drugs.

Suddenly I noticed my dinner mates had exited. I rushed for the door, in a panic that it wouldn't open and I would have to yell "Back Door" in a loud voice with everyone watching, knowing I was a loser. But the door opened and I followed them off the bus and we walked to Burger King, with me several steps back. I was imagining us all walking arm-in-arm like old friends, discussing the finer merits of our soon to be purchased Quarterpounders.

What if all the Asian ladies had joined us? What if they had all walked out of the bus with us, chattering like parakeets, dreaming of their Quarterpounder with a Coke and large fries. All of their small-footed steps would be scurrying across the fresh vomit stains of the Civic Center sidewalk, rushing in unison to the front door of Burger King.

I could imagine Tarzan and his manly stride leading the pack. He would be stopping traffic at the street corners, allowing all of us safe passage to the other side. He would throw his head back so the light could gently lift away his wrinkles and better highlight his bleach-bottle hair.

We were all practically jogging for the door now. The big Burger in the Civic Center sky awaited us. We were like a republic of burger enthusiasts on a mission. Everyone we passed would join in our march for the door. Along Market, picking up stragglers at every doorstop, the pimps and the hustlers would hold hands, skipping behind us. The wretched winos, pissing like a fountain, prone on the concrete would jump up, carrying their limp and legless beggar dudes.

A wagonload of drag queens would come screaming out of Macy's, yelling for us to wait. Doris Fish and Tippi, and every dead queen would be flying overhead on wings partying up Market, getting kisses from Jerome. Who's Jerome?

I was feeling crowded with all these people in my mind and I didn't know who all of them were. What were they doing in my Quarterpounder fantasy? I felt like wearing a wig. A big bouffant, with maybe a center piece. Not quite a tiara. Not quite a crown. Maybe something from Piedmont up on Haight. Jerome would give me a pinch and I would walk ahead and the doors of Burger King would loom around the corner. Actually, the doors really were looming around the corner. Our pace quickened as we neared the door. A thousand clamoring hands would, if they only could, reach for the glass door and waltz past the vomit, smelling the burgers and fries. We'd file in, single line past the familiar faces. The Gay Men's Chorus would be singing from the kitchen and half of San Francisco would be blowing foghorns from their bay windows as we walked up to the counter, to the smiling clerk, and pausing for just a second, an indeterminant second…say:

"Gimme a Quarterpounder with a Coke and small fries please."

Too bad. The smell of grease woke me up from my fantasy. Then I noticed that Burger King was the home of the Whopper, not the Quarterpounder. Were my white trash friends that oblivious to the difference?

The denim man, who felt like my brother, ordered the Quarterpounder as planned with a small fries but changed his mind and had a Sprite. She ordered the Quarterpounder with large fries and a coffee. I felt somewhat empty without the thousands of Asian ladies. And I sort of missed Tarzan, but I took my cue when the denim lady looked at me quizzically. Maybe she recognized me from the bus.

I ordered the same as them and sat eating two booths away, sharing the feeling we were family at the table discussing the merits of the meal.

"So how is it?" I asked them in my mind.

"Tastes a little rare today. Would have been nice if they'd put in just a tad bit more salt with perhaps a pinch of pepper."

I watched her wolf her burger. She became absorbed in the pickle that fell out the bottom. She ate with her pinkies held out. I could see she was well trained and I thought of Alabama and charm schools for debutantes. The room felt like home with my denim couple near my side.

A wall of glass looking out on Market barely separated us from the street we'd only recently marched down. A man stood hungrily outside the Burger King. He was watching all of us eat through the glass. I could feel urgency in his eyes and we made a connection, but I wasn't sure over what. He entered Burger King and passed me by. He walked up to my friends and lunged for their remaining food. He came up with a handful of fries and the coveted pickle and stuffed it into his gnarly mouth.

She looked unfazed, as if this happened every day, and calmly clutched her coffee as if retrieving a drink from an errant child before it gets spilled. She shooed him away with her pinky as she wiped the crumbs from the corner of her lips.

But then the management got involved and the whole thing turned ugly. It was like having the police barge in on a dysfunctional family meal when you are all handling things perfectly well, despite how totally fucked things really are.

Like, what's the Gestapo doing here. He just grabbed my plate for Chrissakes.

I desperately wanted her to say this. But she let go a slight burp and the offender was dragged away, kicking and screaming and leaving a smell behind. The manager offered another Quarterpounder which the denim couple accepted, but asked for it bagged.

In a way we were all happy. We'd had our Quarterpounders, even fed a lunatic a few fries. And now had a whole other burger to our name.

I was amazed how quickly I'd bonded us together like a tribe. Just one meal together and now what was theirs was mine. I was sure I would do the same. Share my fortunes with them.

I followed them out to the

Behold Maria Elena, San Francisco belle, as she gropes across the fevered city twilight. Mongrel lady softly swaying, dangling her stuff amid the mindless rattle of some dark side avenue. Eyes cold as ice, void of wonder, she slides, all swathed in spangles, beneath the walls of rippled shadow, brushes back the panic of the darkness and smiles. San Francisco lady, city woman, slightly wasted by the rhythm of the fast beat, slightly tarnished, nonetheless still trying, still tricking through the light fantastic on the sidewalks down off Geary, grinding through the terror of another night.

—David Ogle, "San Francisco Belle," *Street Sheet*

street and across the plaza toward Polk Street. We passed Asian ladies shopping for vegetables in stalls on the plaza. Probably the same ladies as on the bus. Maybe even the same ladies who nearly ate burgers with us. If only they'd come along.

In the Tenderloin things began to get shady. Dusk was falling and the cast of street light made an interesting warmth in the cool foggy air. I could feel the fog rolling in and wondered why I didn't think to bring a coat. I split off from the denim couple and began walking home to our place by the tracks. In the night shadows I looked like a stalker. And why was I wearing my old torn jeans? I was feeling like a junkie and I needed underwear. I soon found a pair.

We'd been homeless for eight years. Homeless without a place to pull our wheels and park our smiles and dream under a familiar roof and laugh with the voice of familiar friends. We were white trailer trash vagabonds, washing our feet in the sinks of rest stops and scraping dull razors across our stubble in the metallic light of cheap roadside mirrors, scraping away the years like so many ingrown hairs.

Suddenly, the smell of chicken brought me back. Jim dug out the sports page of a week-old *Los Angeles Times* while I became absorbed in the beat of the traffic. *What the hell.* I dug out a five gallon empty gas can, sat it on the side of the highway with the nozzle pointed westward and in a fit of inspiration plucked a yellow daisy and stuffed it down the spout as far as it would go.

The rice came to a boil as Jim hollered about the Knicks and I stood outside the scraped and scarred Monkmobile making a feeble attempt to flag down motorists who seemed intent on ignoring my distress. I looked like a scarecrow with the road etched into my crooked elbows and my skin cracked like canyons, dry from a hundred thousand miles of bottom feeding.

"We're bottom feeders, Jim," I griped. "We're untouchables. Trailer trash nomads on wheels."

Night sneaks up on Haight Street with the fog from Golden Gate Park. A wraithlike post-punk with black lipstick clatters down the pavement, on her way to one of the city's nastiest dens of depravity. An obese black man sporting tricoloured hair follows her in. So do you. Hieronymus Bosch and Dante together could not have imagined the fauna animating tonight's phantasmagoria. The bouncer only lets you glimpse the throbbing, ring-in-nose action before ejecting you on to the pavement. You are too square, he says. Across the way, a clutch of crack smokers puff madly then dart off shrieking like hyenas. They jostle a tourist who is looking for signs of the Flower Children at the Anarchist Collective Bookstore. But this is the '90s. The hippies and their idealism are gone from the Haight-Ashbury neighbourhood, which is now a battleground littered with the trash of the homeless, "street people" and the champagne corks of invading yuppies.

—David Downie, "A Golden Gate to Fast Living," *The Independent*

But Jim was howling like a donkey over the week-old scores, his jolly belly quivering with excitement, fried chicken in his lap. And at that moment I realized Jim the Mad Monk was truly mad. Nothing, bar nothing, ever got him down. Nothing.

Two portly witches on the wings of a Sunday drive fueled us up and fed us a bowl of lime green artichoke soup in swinging Pescadero. We played road tag for miles until we lost them in Pacifica, honking like geese as we sped north.

Or crawled on our dripping, oily belly is more accurate. We labored up the grade, miles of traffic trailing behind. I gave up pulling over and just let them stew at our rear. Jim fell into deep reverie for the passing shoreline as he belted out an off-key warble of "California Dreaming."

"Do we know anyone there?" Jim was asking.

"I don't know who's alive. They're probably all dead by now."

So much for a triumphant return. We were rimming the city from the top of Pacifica and rows of hideous, crackerbox homes were stacked like dominoes across the barren hillside. They had that sort of grossed out, hillbilly, prefab, early-sixties suburban sprawl look; definitely a big mistake waiting for God to shake them off the hill. Our faces were glued to the front window gazing hard into the horizon looking for familiar landmarks like the Golden Gate, the Pyramid, the Condor Club, whatever. "Ugh, we're entering the city through the Sunset District. What a nightmare. This is not what I had in mind, Jim. The Sunset is like the Omaha of Frisco. I wanted a skyline, you know, with cable cars clanging and shit."

Jim got out the fried chicken again.

"I'm turning around." I contemplated doing a U-turn.

"Forget it, Mike." He snorted through the chicken, grease dripping down the walls. "Is it going to be Rotisserie Gold with the dark meat or the light meat? What's it going to be, Mike?"

"I want the white meat you greaseball. If you tell me you ate all the white meat off those bones, I'm roasting you on the end of a red hot rotisserie poker faster then you can get the chicken fat off the walls."

"God, Mike, you need to calm down. What's your problem?"

"I don't know what my problem is. I just feel anxious coming back to the city."

Like it or not, our triumphant return was about to occur through the back door of Frisco.

An envelope of fog had overtaken the neighborhood and swept over us like a tidal wave of dirty cotton underwear, smothering us in its clammy curls of moistness. Pastel pink and white, cookie-cutter Victorians with big bay windows stretched for miles to the overcast beach, looking like an old whore on Prozac wearing dime-store makeup.

"Now I remember why I left San Francisco. I hate bay windows," I moaned.

"That's sacrilegious." Jim was licking the grease off his fingers tossing the bone to Dolly Lama, our hyper-paranoid cat.

The Monkmobile came to an extremely unglamorous stop at the corner of Noriega and 19th. The Sunday bikers and baby buggy pushers were out en masse, despite the liquid sun. One ride over the hill and we were entering Golden Gate Park, former sand dunes and site of countless drug trips from the *good old days*. A quick right soon had us circling the De Young Museum looking for a place to park.

"Yo Monks, out of my way!" A severe-looking, pierced, tattooed, evil cycler from hell breezed by, pounding on the Monkmobile.

"I hate cyclers. They've got such pissy attitudes."

"Mike, that doesn't sound very p.c." Jim's eyes were closed.

The biker turned a circle and delivered a middle finger salute as he sped back toward the Monkmobile, his nostrils raging.

"Oh, I'm sure, what does this steroid queen think he's gonna do, run *me* down. I'm sorry dude I've got the bigger engine here. *Get Outta My Way* You Cheap Shit…Buy a Car." My blood pressure was boiling as I gunned the engine and bull-nosed our way toward personal contact.

His bulging biker eyes were breaking veins as he scrambled out of the way from this monster growing inside of me.

Gotta calm down. I held my breath, keeping her steady, watching the road. *Don't have to take it out on the cycler.*

Jim was surveying the park like he had found an old high school friend. "Look Mike, remember, that's where we used to do T'ai Chi, over there by the Arboretum. Hey, remember the Rose Garden?"

I pulled over at a corner, down from the Japanese Tea Gardens, just admiring the view of trees, plants, and weeds.

Another pothead biker in tie-dye shorts was lingering by the side of the Monkmobile, whispering in this obnoxious low throaty voice, "Hey, 'shrooms, you want 'shrooms?"

I was disgusted. "No, I don't want any of your stinking cow dung fungus. What do I look like, a dead-head?"

"Cool, yeah, I picked them in Marks Meadow, they're killer 'shrooms!"

"Shrooms, you got 'shrooms?" Another cycler in dreads was rolling up to the Bounder, speaking to me through the window.

"No, I don't have 'shrooms, he does," I said.

A small crowd was collecting like lint around the Monkmobile and we hadn't even found a parking spot.

Jim gracefully bounded out of the RV with his piggy trough full to the brim with brown rice and fried chicken parts and began circulating with a crowd of cyclers and strollers.

"Mike, park here!"

"You sure?"

"Just do it, park here," Jim barked.

I swung into reverse and parked the Bounder next to the curb in one easy swoop.

Kaplunk!

A crash stopped the commotion as my favorite sound of metal on metal reverberated through the melee like a good aftershock. Someone had hit us.

I turned off the key as another fart of foul black smoke trailed from the exhaust. Rushing out the door, I was followed by a contingent of cyclers. A shy girl was exiting her hippy van in a startled pot-smoking daze, having recently made intimate contact with the rear bumper of our beast.

Jim was chowing down on chicken parts, dispensing gospel to a busload of Japanese, camera-clutching tourists who swarmed the scene looking for instant Americana gratification.

The lady in the van was distressed from the sidelong swipe that ran across her V.W. I, too, was slightly stressed by the V-shaped dent in my newly replaced bumper. We were about to discuss insurance except neither of us *had* insurance so we dropped it like hot wax on foreskin.

Two dykes in leather britches and a goddess in high heels were now walking circles around us when a panting, bearded bear of a man with a forty-pound beer belly rolled up on skates. "Hey Monks, want some 'shrooms?"

"Oh god, let me tell you right now, you people smoke too much pot. That's what's going on with you!" I preached with no plan for conversion.

The crowd was getting thicker, the engine hadn't even cooled and pot was in the air.

Jim felt like selling something, anything. With this many people congregating, Jim saw potential revenue and was into it.

"Mike, do something, sell something."

But I was smiling my toothy smile, getting off on the attention, almost forgetting what a rotten mood I'd been hanging with.

San Francisco was rolling out its tie-dye carpet.

I was starting to shake hands, feeling for the veins on their arms. I like veins, the way they just pulse with desire.

A scooter was cruising us and a young dude in a bomber jacket, gripping a can of aerosol, started to paint a mural on the Monkmobile. That was the first magic of the day. Anarchy before our very eyes. *Damn right, do us with aerosol.*

A woman sprang out of the bushes holding a black, two-foot, papier-mâché head of a pony. Her vagina puckered below the bottom of her extremely short skirt and the hairs on her underarms were very prickly. She ran to give me a hug but I backed away and she was claiming we'd been neighbors many years ago. But she didn't look like any neighbor of mine. Her tongue was pierced at the end with a ring and a chain dangling down to a nipple clamp. She fastened her tongue to the Monkmobile. "I'm your Monk slave. Take me with you," she pleaded.

The Japanese tourists were recording every second.

The artist was in aerosol heaven. Jim was yelling encouragements. His name was Estria and he was painting the side of Bounder with a full mural of the Monks. Jim was smirking and fumes were flying over the crowd. We loved it.

Another face appeared. "Hey, remember me, I'm Ricky." Yes, it was Ricky, the psycho who thought he was a horse and could hear shortwave radio in his head. "How about a San Francisco handshake, I'll meet you at the windmills," he said, pulling at his groin.

"Oh my God, Jim. Old lovers, I hate that."

We snuck back toward the door of the Monkmobile just as a meter maid was ticketing the RV. "No. Wait. Stop. What are you doing? I thought we could park here."

The meter maid looked like she had pushed one too many pints of Ben and Jerry's down her throat. She stood by her three-wheeler with her helmet strapped to her head in that Gestapo sort of way that spells trouble. Miss Meter Maid wrote the ticket, crammed it on our windshield, and waddled her three hundred pounds back to her motorized tricycle to make way for another hapless victim up the street.

"Your bike looks like an ice cream cart and your mother eats poodle dung!" I yelled in retaliation. "Shit, a parking ticket, and we've only been here one hour."

"That's a San Francisco welcome," cackled my old neighbor.

Michael Lane and Jim Crotty (The Monks) are the creators of Monk, The Mobile Magazine. *They live and write about life on the road. Jointly, they are the authors of the book,* Mad Monks on the Road: A 42,000 Hour Dashboard Adventure from Paradise, California Through Royal, Arkansas, and Up the New Jersey Turnpike. *They are also the creators of the* CD-ROM, Monk's Guide to New York. *Individually, Michael Lane is the author of* Pink Highways: Tales of Queer Madness on the Open Road, *and Jim Crotty is the author of the forthcoming book,* How to Talk American: An Irreverent and Informative Guide to Our Native Tongue. *The Monks' website is http://www.monk.com.*

★

Coyote was walking down the road one day, thinking only of food. It had been several days since he had last eaten. His stomach was making noises like boiling water and his head hurt. And then, near where the sumac grows, he saw great clusters of red, delicious-looking berries! Coyote grew very excited as he ran over to grab them. Just as his hand touched the berries his mind remembered a talk he had had with the Wise Old Man. Coyote had asked, "Tell me, Old Man, where did we get this land; was it given to us by our ancestors?" And the Wise Old Man replied, "Of Course not, Coyote. We are borrowing this land from our great, great, great, great grandchildren. We must take good care of it because it belongs to them. To remind us of this, the children of the future have put bunches of red berries near where the sumac grows. These berries are theirs, so no matter how hungry you get you must never eat them. They are only to remind you that the land belongs to the children yet to come.

"What will happen to us, Old Man, if we do eat the berries?" asked Coyote. And the Wise Old Man replied, "I am sorry, Coyote, but if you eat the berries your ass will fall off."

This is what Coyote remembered as his hands touched the berries. He stopped and thought a moment. Then he said to himself, "I have always known that the Wise Old Man is a fool! What does he know? He is just trying to keep the berries for himself. Besides, how could I owe something to people who are not even here yet?" So Coyote ate the berries. He ate as fast as he could and he ate as many as he could. Coyote felt fine! He looked behind him and his ass had not fallen off. He laughed very loudly and began skipping down the road.

He had not gone far when his stomach began to hurt something awful. And then he began to get diarrhea, first a little, then a great stream. Coyote was sick, the sickest he had ever been! He thought about the children who were yet to come, and he thought about the Wise Old Man, and he was very embarrassed. Coyote walked slowly to the river where he got a drink of water and then he went to hide himself in the deep bushes. He didn't want anyone to know that he had forgotten the children yet to come, and that his ass had fallen off.

—Bruce Walter Barton, *The Tree at the Center of the World: A Story of the California Missions*

GARY KAMIYA

North Beach at Twilight

San Francisco's favorite neighborhood is a gift from Italy.

SAN FRANCISCO'S LITTLE ITALY IS NORTH BEACH. BUT TO THE innocent and discerning eye, Italy is everywhere in San Francisco. There is a secret poetic correspondence between our city and the land of olives and cypresses and warm wine-soaked earth; you have only to see and smell and remember and Italy, all at once, is here.

It is here in the Mediterranean sweep of this wind-washed seaport city as it sparkles one Sunday morning from an apartment on Jackson Street, the white and holy buildings running joyously down to the old, unknown, storytelling sea.

It is here in a dark passage through the city's secret heart on Napier Lane, on one of those rare summer nights when the air is so hot and still that the green sea-smell drifts all the way up from the piers, the muffled footfalls on the worn wooden steps, the full moon and the jasmine-scented darkness recalling the dead ends, the hidden gardens, the thousand masked and murmuring enchantments of Venice.

It is here on any city hilltop, the pale and intricate courses of the city appearing from on high through San Francisco's washed-out Tuscan light, the height and a certain shade of dark green and a distant black-clad old woman toiling up a hill bringing back sharp memories of Cortona, Gubbio, Todi, those stony hilltowns that are the most perfect places human beings have built to live in.

But if traces of Italy are everywhere in this most European of American cities, there are some *cosi Italiani* that you just can't experience unless you spring for a ticket to Rome. There's no Campari stand on the Land's End trail, for example. (Italy, a country whose every activity is governed by intelligent hedonism, would never stand for this.) Nor, when lying on Baker Beach on the hottest day of the year, will you hear the brassy "toot-de-de-toot" of the gelato man's little trumpet as he announces "*gelati…granitas…*" to the throng, making his way with his ices through the gleaming oiled-up bodies.

But there's still a lot of *Italianità* in San Francisco—and North Beach is the place to find it. It is *centro città*, ground zero, the true Latin heart of this city named after an Italian nobleman who gave away all he had and spent the rest of his life giving it away and never ran out, that summer of love eight centuries ago. If you want to listen to *bocce* players denouncing each other's shots with gesticulations so vehement and alarming that they could only be made by *Siciliani*; if you would observe espresso men who handle their gleaming Rancilio machines with truly Roman arrogance; if you are desirous of eating a *gelato* while watching, perhaps for the last time in this country, the gentlemen from Lucca in their hats and suits take their leisurely *passeggiata* as the sun dies over Washington Square—then you must be within earshot of the bells of Saints Peter and Paul. It is there that the Big Prosciutto is buried.

What is it that makes North Beach, even now in its glorious twilight, one of the greatest neighborhoods in America? It is a gift from Italy—from the Italian love of city life, from their knowledge of what makes a city work. First of all, North Beach is *dense*. Taxi drivers and artists, tourists and bums, waitresses and Gogolian clerks throng its streets day and night. It is mixed: many different kinds of businesses share its streets, not just upscale boutiques and coffee-houses but shoe stores, hardware stores, small groceries—human businesses with human faces. And it has a center: like all Italian cities, North Beach has a glorious public space, Washington Square.

Finally, and most important of all, people *live* here. Not a majority of Italians anymore: according to Marsha Garland, the head of the North Beach Chamber of Commerce, probably only 10 to 15 percent of the neighborhood's approximately 12,500 residents are of Italian descent, and most of those are elderly. Many of them sold out and moved to the Peninsula or Marin when real estate values went through the ceiling in the '70s. (Purists who are fond of decrying the "takeover" of the neighborhood by Chinese, who now represent half of North Beach's population, conveniently forget that nobody forced the Italian owners to sell.) In any case, the neighborhood has simply returned to its original ethnic confusion: where once there were Italians and Mexicans and Basques and French and Spanish and Chileans (hence North Beach's original name, the "Latin quarter"), now there are Italians and Chinese and WASP yuppies and blacks and assorted other groups. The ingredients may change; the cioppino remains.

A Genovese or a Roman walking down Little Italy's main drag, Grant Avenue (once known as DuPont) in 1910 would have felt very much at home. What a rich, chaotic, colorful scene it must have been: fruit and vegetable vendors calling out their wares in Tuscan and Venetian dialects, dozens of stores displaying yards of golden spaghetti and linguine and enticing strings of sausages. *Trattorie* everywhere, each offering its specialty. Well-dressed men and women going into the Costa Brothers' fancy grocery store or Di Grazia's fruit and vegetable store; Neapolitan fishermen in their good clothes, preparing for an evening of opera at the Washington Square Theater. Laughter, the sounds of accordion and guitar music; vociferous conversations, urchins running through the narrow alleys.

In that golden age, not so long past, families would sit in their front gardens on warm evenings, sipping the homemade wine that nearly every Italian family on Telegraph Hill made. On little Castle Alley, formerly Garibaldi Street, which runs between Green and Union, boxes of grapes would line the street in wine-making season. Family and friends would wash their feet and plunge into the wine-making bin, stomping away in the ancient ritual. Speedy's

Grocery, the landmark little store at the top of Montgomery Street, was named for the original proprietress, Emma Spediacci, whose family made wine in the basement. Every Christmas, the Spediaccis gave their regular customers Christmas packages containing a gallon of wine, gravy, and homemade ravioli. (Like many other Italian businesses in the area, the store was sold to a Chinese family in 1977.)

On top of Telegraph Hill, goats grazed on open land. They were tended by the "Goat Lady," Milanelli Cosenza, who led her bleating charges through the alleys and byways of the quarter and milked them at her customers' doors until a city ordinance forbade grazing goats on the hill in 1928.

> *Speedy's New Union Grocery remains a focal point of the neighborhood atop Telegraph Hill. Run by Chinese brothers with the unlikely names of Marshal and Art, the place has the feel of a sit-com, where every time you walk through the door you know something interesting is going to happen. The banter is often witty and hilarious, a bright spot on any given day. The Spediaccis may be missed, but the day Marshal and Art retire or sell will be another sad day for the neighborhood.*
>
> —JO'R, LH, and SO'R

At the bottom of the hill, Washington Square, which the locals affectionately called *il giardino* ("the garden"), was the social center of the neighborhood. Italian theater groups performed here; ladies and their daughters would take their *passeggiata* on Sunday here after attending Mass at St. Francis of Assisi, which celebrated its first Mass at Vallejo and Columbus in 1849. Later, subscriptions from Italian-Americans from all over the Pacific Coast financed the building, in 1924, of the magnificent Saints Peter and Paul, the twin-spired church on the edge of the square that was the spiritual center for many generations of Italians and is still the heart of the neighborhood. The great events of life—baptism, marriage, funerals—were solemnly commemorated in the soaring white building, which has the opening words of Dante's *Paradiso* inscribed in Italian on its facade.

It was, for many of the immigrants who crammed into tiny shacks and worked twelve-hour days in the store or on the Bay or the farm, a life of poverty and toil; but it was a life that was going somewhere. It was a good life, and it has left its traces. There is a joy in the neighborhood, in its very stones.

Italy is still very much present in North Beach. There are the obvious things, of course: the bakeries, the dozens of restaurants and cafes, the wonderful old shops like Figone Hardware (which has occupied its same Grant Avenue location since 1907), the *gelaterias,* the opera at the old beat Caffè Trieste on Saturday afternoons. And there are subtler manifestations: the fact that every bank in North Beach has an employee who speaks Italian, for instance, or the industrial-sized cans of Pernigotti ice cream flavorings (*pasta nocciola piemonte*) in the window of a *gelateria,* or the futuristic chrome Faema machine proudly displayed at a rakish, museum-piece tilt in the window of the Graffeo Coffee Roasting Company.

And architecture. The ornate Club Fugazi, which still provides social services to elderly Italians, is the neighborhood's most obvious example of Italianate style, but the quarter's houses have their quiet story to tell as well. The triangular, temple-like pediments and the charming balconies called "Romeos" over many North Beach entranceways recall the old country.

For me, the true Italian spirit of North Beach lives in the streets and alleys that run up and down Telegraph Hill, that quarry-sided, campanile-crowned hill that stands guard over the quarter. Wonderful accidents of topography and history govern the meandering course of these streets, not the engineer's dry logic. Walking up the twisted, tilted cobblestones of Romolo, or down Genoa or Varennes or Sonoma or Tuscany or Medau or any of the multitudinous little hidden byways and alleys and cat-crawls that course like veins through this intricate, living place, you almost expect to emerge upon the Pantheon or the Piazza Navona.

One thing seems sure to keep Italy alive forever in North Beach—food. And the quaintest place in the neighborhood is the wonderfully antiquated Liguria Bakery, across from Washington Square at 1700 Stockton. The Liguria is a storefront with mysteriously empty white shelving running up to the ceiling inside and a counter on which rest a spool of string and a roll of butcher paper. These are the implements owners George Soracco and August Azzalini use to wrap up their spectacular focaccia bread. The hours of the Liguria are posted as 8 to 5, but those are purely formal: the store closes whenever they run out of bread. A sheet of onion focaccia costs $2.00, but there is a hidden cost—"Cut up—5¢ extra." The gold-painted original phone number, "Garfield 1-3786," still adorns the window, a nice Sam Spade-era touch.

Italian delis, bakeries, restaurants, and *gelaterias* are still going strong in the Beach. There aren't as many pasta factories as there were in the old days—in 1917 there were no fewer than nineteen macaroni-ravioli factories in North Beach—but there are several still operating today. And the quarter still boasts more than its share of true Italian delis and *salumerias*—Molinari's, Panelli Brothers, and Florence, among others—where you can buy coppa, carciofi, grappa, and Barbera.

The spick-and-span Panelli Brothers, at 1419 Stockton, is one of the oldest. Bob Panelli, who runs the store with his twin brother Richard, said that it's been at its current location since 1934. "My father, uncle, and godfather were from Lucca," he said. "A lot of Italian merchants in North Beach are from northern Italy—lots from Florence." He interrupted the conversation to slice some roast beef for a regular customer. "How do you feel?" Bob asked. "*Fat,* that's how," the man replied grumpily as the meat-slicing machine whirred. "All I do is go to parties, funerals. I went to a funeral and you know where we went after? Joe's of Westlake for a full-course meal. Now, after you die, you eat and eat." He shook his head, paid for his meat, and went out.

We walked around the store. Olive oil, chianti, parmigiano, meats, pesto, and pasta. And more pasta. "I carry ten different kinds of dry pasta," Bob Panelli said. "The three biggest sellers are Del Verde, Lo Molisma, and Barilla." What percentage of his clientele is Italian? Panelli pondered. "Thirty percent," he said. "It used to be damn near ninety. The Italian community has moved out. Because of families, and high rents, and they wanted to move to the suburbs, like everyone else. I still live in the neighborhood—I'm one of the last."

The Florence Ravioli Factory, directly across the street, makes its own ravioli, gnocchi, and tortellini next door to the deli. "We were the first to manufacture tortellini—I had a Zamboni tortellini machine in 1950," said the owner, 68-year-old Louis Martinelli, also from Lucca, a beautiful walled city near Pisa famed in Italy for its olive oil. "I was the outside man. I had a 1941 Plymouth and I went around selling ravioli out of the trunk. I put a blanket over it. This was in 1955–56. I sold it to restaurants. Then business got better and I got a panel truck. Now I deliver all over the Bay Area and seven or eight states. For a single-person company, we import more pasta from Italy than almost anyone. I import three hundred containers a year of dry pasta—each container weighs 45,000 pounds. Have you heard of a pasta called De Cecco? I have the franchise for the country."

I asked him what he did for social life. "We have a Lucchese Club at the Fugazi Building. But I work so hard I go to bed at nine o'clock. Tired! I get up at four a.m. every day. I have to call Italy for business, and it's nine hours different, so if you call at six a.m. it's already three in the afternoon and nobody wants to do business." He laughed. "I've been doing it for fifty years."

A gloomy and telling milestone in North Beach history was passed recently, when the Catholic authorities, bowing to shrinking numbers, consolidated the neighborhood's three parishes, incorporating those of St. Francis of Assisi and Our Lady of Guadalupe into the expanded parish of Saints Peter and Paul. On a recent Sunday at the church, I didn't hear any Italian spoken as the churchgoers left.

There is a certain poignancy to this moment in the life of North Beach. Its day is not yet done, but the sun has set, and it will not be too many more years before even the gentle glow is gone. A living chapter of American history is coming to a close, not just in San Francisco but all across America: the saga of European immigration, a thousand hearts quickening as the great stern face of the Statue of Liberty came into view, the hopes of the poor people from Lodz and Coimbra and Galway and Salerno rising up over the crowded deck, a thousand faces silent in the mist—when the last European immigrant dies all those memories will die, too.

But life goes on in the Beach, and it would do injustice to the Italian spirit to mourn the passing of the old at the expense of the young and living.

And there is an Italian present. Most of the old Italians' children have moved out, but some are moving back to the old neighborhood. North Beach's businesses are still predominantly Italian-owned. And new blood is coming in: L'Osteria del Forno, a new charmingly *autentico osteria* on Columbus, is owned by two Italian women, and an Italian bought the Caffè Roma [now Figaro Cafe]. Walk the streets of North Beach and you will hear Italian spoken not just by the old but by the young. They are not Italian-Americans, by and large, but Italians who come here to work and live. San Francisco is probably the only American city besides New York that still draws young expatriate Italians—not enough to replace the old generation, but enough to keep the Vespas popping and the lattes foaming. In the cafés—the Puccini, the Greco, the Bohemian, Malvina's, the Trieste, the Steps of Rome, among many others—you'll find them. They may be working the bar, or just hanging out, and they will keep coming as long as San Francisco is *bellisima*.

Meanwhile, the old men sit in the park on the benches near Union Street, still arguing. They play *bocce* in the hidden little court behind the North Beach swimming pool, or smoke their cigars at Capp's Corner. If you want to know what lifelong friendship is, or how to grow old, you don't have to look any further.

Down at the edge of the Beach, on Chestnut and Columbus, 80-year-old Aurelio LaRocca sits alone in his bar, LaRocca's Corner—famous for its eye-catching sign proclaiming "This Is It!" The walls of the empty bar are covered with photographs of movie stars, boxers, showgirls. A big black-and-white photograph shows a handsome young boxer knocking somebody out with an improbably devastating punch. The picture is inscribed "To Leo LaRocca, One great guy. Thanks. Rocky Graziano."

I ask him what he remembers about early days in North Beach. He hesitates; maybe the memories don't come too easily now to the old man. Then his eyes brighten. "All the fishermen would come in here, mostly Sicilians. They'd come in here when it was too rough to go out." Were they hard drinkers? "They drank good. They'd clink their glasses, '*salute.*'"

What was it like in the old days around the neighborhood—in Washington Square, at the church? "Saints Peter and Paul," he says slowly. "I got married in Saints Peter and Paul. I think it was 1931. I was eighteen. My wife was eighteen."

He takes me around to show me a photograph of his family, posing stiffly in the style of the period. Severe black coats, earnest, hardworking faces. "This is my father," he says proudly. "And this is his mother." Then he shows me another photograph, also of his family. This one is in color. Handsome young people, a baby.

The generations come and go. Mostly, these days, they go.

I say good-bye. "Come in again," the old man says. The door closes and he shuffles over to the jukebox. I wait a minute, peering through the window, but I don't hear any music. It starts to rain. At the far end of Columbus, the spires of St. Francis of Assisi, a church without a parish, rise into the gray sky, like the masts of a beautiful ship that is sailing away.

Gary Kamiya has been in love with North Beach since at least 1971, when in a 2 a.m. state of wine-fueled exaltation he fell backwards through the Filbert Street door he had been leaning against and slid down a short flight of stairs, ending up flat on his back smiling into the darkness of an unknown basement. He has never seen the White Rabbit since then but continues to look. Formerly a film and media critic for the San Francisco Examiner, *Kamiya is now the executive editor of* Salon *Internet magazine. His work has appeared in* Art Forum, The New York Times, Sports Illustrated, Hippocrates, California, *and many other publications. He lives on Nob Hill in San Francisco.*

*

When the Gregorian Mass was offered at St. Ignatius for a final time, Father James McCauley looked out at the congregation and announced that the Latin Mass would be discontinued. He spoke slowly: "All things come to an end, so many of the things we love must come to an end—it is part of life." And then he invited Schola director Merrill Adamson to say a few words.

Adamson came forward. Softly, he said that when he first learned that the 12:30 Mass was to be cancelled he had been "angry, very angry." He admitted being puzzled by the intolerance of many priests toward the Latin liturgy. He spoke of his own love of the Gregorian Chant, how important it is for his spiritual life. But now, he said, he was reconciled to leaving St. Ignatius. The Schola would move on with gratitude for having had the privilege of singing the Latin Mass for five years. For the future, he said, God's will be done. In that spirit, he wanted to close the Mass with the "Te Deum," the great hymn of thanksgiving.

He stepped back into the choir. The singing began. Outside it was 2 o'clock on a sunny afternoon. Downtown, the big department stores were open for business. At Candlestick Park, the Giants were losing. People stood in a long, dispirited line for the *Return of the Jedi*. In Golden Gate Park, a middle-aged man, wearing only a bikini, was swaying on sparkling roller skates to music he alone heard.

—Richard Rodriguez, "The Last Chants," *San Francisco Examiner*

City Perched on a Frontier

San Francisco, the instant city: add gold and stir.

THERE WILL NEVER BE ANOTHER CITY LIKE SAN FRANCISCO. AT least not until gold or pocketable oil or some rare and delightful thing is discovered on an obscure but gorgeous asteroid and hundreds of thousands of young men—and this time, just maybe, a comparable number of women—cram into rockets and blast off to get rich and build a madcap Plexiglas metropolis. Cities like San Francisco just don't happen anymore. Greed, however happy, has grown more staid. And mass migrations of money drunkards belong to a charming but suspect past.

San Francisco claims to be unique, and it is. It is a boomtown, the very archetype of a tough, loony, and gloriously successful boomtown. And, unlike boomtowns from Alaska to the Brazilian jungle, it lasted, thanks to grace and luck. Its history is dramatic and quirky, but above all it is sudden.

On the morning of the first day of 1848 San Francisco was a boggy, flea-ridden, doubtlessly rather hung-over village. Its fewer than five hundred inhabitants were a miscellany of wanderers, wastrels, and mildly energetic pioneers. One of its leading citizens, a young Mormon named Sam Brannan, had recently written in his newspaper, the *San Francisco Star,* that the village "bid[s] fair to rival in rapidity of progress the most thriving town or city on the American continent."

Brannan's optimism was pure habit. True, the village did sit on the shores of the world's finest anchorage. The visitations of hide-and-tallow ships were becoming more frequent, and the United States of America, having grabbed California from Mexico a couple of years before, was surely looking westward. But in January 1848 San Francisco was beyond any frontier, nearly as obscure as a dim asteroid. Yet in less than 10 years it would be a world-class dream city with a population it took New York 190 years to reach and Boston 200 years.

San Francisco had a languid history before fortune pounced on it. For four or five thousand years it was the itinerant home of a tribe of gentle Indians the Spanish called Coastanoan, but which are now known as Ohlones. (The Ohlones and the other tribes of the Bay Area, the Carquins and Miwoks, much preferred the more bountiful hills of Marin, Berkeley, and the southern peninsula to the windy, barren, and deeply sandy tip of the peninsula upon which San Francisco now rests.)

The Indians' plentiful existence was ripped apart in 1776 when a Spanish expedition under the leadership of Juan Bautista de Anza encamped on a hill overlooking the Golden Gate and began the colonization of the lands around the stupendous bay. In 1579 Francis Drake had landed his *Golden Hind* somewhere north of the bay (probably at the Point Reyes Peninsula). Drake made a grand but uncharted claim to what would become Northern California. (He called it Nova Albion, and so California can claim to have given its first name to the New England of later years.) The English privateer's claim and, later, the inching of the Russians down the Pacific coast from Alaska irritated Spain, which considered Alta California (the lands north of Mexico) part of its empire.

By the time de Anza planted a cross at Fort Point and began building a presidio and, a few miles to the south, a mission, Spain's imperial energy was dissipated. The net result of its tired grasping was the discovery of the bay and the utter destruction of the

Indians. Much of the drive behind Spain's northward movement had been supplied by priests of the Franciscan order under the stewardship of Father Junípero Serra. Following the practice refined in the earlier missions along El Camino Real, the Franciscans herded their neophytes into the Mission Dolores, baptized them, and watched helplessly as they died of despair and disease.

When Mexico declared its independence of Spain in 1821, the presidio and mission were little more than empty symbols of Spanish imperialism. The new and impoverished republic attempted to develop Alta California by issuing land grants, and in the 1830s and '40s the hides and tallow produced by those giant land-grant ranches provided the bulk of commerce in and around the bay. But Mexico's hold on Alta California was as tenuous as Spain's, and on July 6, 1846, the American flag was raised over Portsmouth Plaza, the village's hub. America's conquest of California and its absorption into the Union would not take place formally for nearly two years, but the Stars and Stripes, one old settler remembered, were greeted by "the roar of cannon from the ship [the *Portsmouth*], the hurrahs of the ship's company, the vivas of the Californians, the cheers of the Dutchmen, the barking of dogs, braying of jackasses, and a general confusion of sounds from every living thing within hearing."

The doddering village over which the new flag waved was called Yerba Buena, after a "good herb" that grew on the mudflats. Within six months Lt. Washington A. Bartlett, the area's military *alcalde* (mayor), decreed a fateful name change. With an early touch of the self-promotion the city has never lacked, he discarded Yerba Buena for San Francisco, thereby linking the village with the bay. Three hundred and fifty-nine days later a "half-crazy or harebrained" man named James Marshall, poking around in a millrace in the Sierra foothills, made a discovery that would truly create San Francisco and, in the process, change the world.

The California Gold Rush was the consummation of a centuries-old prophecy. Since Columbus happened upon the New World the Spanish had been searching madly for an El Dorado, a land of gold. Other nations had watched or had looked themselves.

The English, especially, had been pleased to prey on Spain's gold-heavy ships. But there was never gold enough, and it became part of Western civilization's collective subconscious that a land littered with, bursting with, practically coated with gold, was waiting out there somewhere in the asteroid-distant reaches of the New World.

Four-time winner of the Pulitzer Prize for poetry, Robert Frost penned a few evocative lines about his western childhood in the 1870s and 1880s in "West Running Brook":

*Dust always blowing about the town,
Except when sea-fog laid it down,
And I was one of the children told
Some of the blowing dust was gold.*

—Luree Miller,
Literary Hills of San Francisco

James Marshall found El Dorado on January 24, 1848. He was the mill foreman for John Augustus Sutter, a self-inflated land baron whose "New Helvetia" included a part of the American River near present-day Coloma. The "shiny material" Marshall found at Sutter's Mill was subjected to "every test in the American Encyclopedia" and proved to be the stuff dreams and dream cities are made of. Soon Sutter, Marshall, the mill workers, and rumor-fueled settlers were picking up nuggets by the fistful. And when Sam Brannan paraded a vial of gold dust down Montgomery Street in San Francisco yelling, "Gold! Gold on the American River!" the Gold Rush was on.

It was one of history's greatest mass migrations. Word traveled with whatever speed the times allowed, and within months tens of thousands of bored clerks, lawyers, layabouts, college students, farmers, a few hard-eyed women—even a child or two—were on their way to the land of gold.

There was no easy way to get there. The voyage around Cape Horn was dangerous and long; the route via the Isthmus of Panama somewhat quicker, but sodden and unpredictable; wagon trains across the Great Basin were set upon by cholera, unamused Indians, and ill-entropy. Yet within the first three years of the Rush more than two hundred thousand Argonauts (or Forty-Niners) had arrived in the Golden State. The fabled 120-mile-long Mother Lode was speckled with five hundred or so shantytowns. The world economy was inflated with the gold wrung out of the foothills, America's westward movement was dramatically, inalterably speeded up. California was rushed into the Union, uncountable lives were enriched (by experience, if not gold dust) or cut short, and a hundred-odd miles to the west of the gold country, San Francisco was exploding.

By 1851, the city ranked fourth in foreign trade among America's ports. Its population had grown from that raggedy five hundred to forty thousand, more or less. (Who had the time or inclination to conduct a census?) San Francisco was swilling seven bottles of champagne for every one consumed in Boston. The earliest Forty-Niners had, one New York reporter wrote, "lodged in muslin rooms and canvas garrets with a philosophic lack of furniture and ate [their] simple though substantial fare from pine boards." A few months later "lofty hotels, gaudy with verandahs and balconies, were met with [everywhere], furnished with home luxury, and aristocratic restaurants presented daily their long bills of fare, rich with the choicest technicalities of Parisian cuisine."

Physical expressions of San Francisco's boomtown heritage are hard to find today. The earthquake and fire of 1906 destroyed much of the old city, and developers have forever been working their way. On Jackson Street, near the Transamerica Pyramid, some old buildings have a certain Gold

A walk in San Francisco...is a real penance....You can hardly make your way through for the throngs of carts, carriages, horsemen, and pedestrians; and where the streets are not paved with boards, you have to wade through sand a foot deep; and all the while you have no better prospect before your eyes than the naked, monotonous sand hills. Truly it is only those who place all happiness in money who could submit, for the sake of gain, to live in such a place, and forget at last that there are such things as trees, or a green carpet lovelier than that which covers the gold-laden gaming tables.

—Ida Pfeiffer, "A Lady's Visit to California, 1855," quoted by J. Kingston Pierce in *San Francisco, You're History*

Rush charm. The Mission Dolores, much rebuilt, is nonetheless a fascinating relic of the city's colonial past. Yet the tall buildings of today's downtown owe their stability to the mud, abandoned ships, and rocks piled into Yerba Buena Cove to make landfill during the Gold Rush. The very ground an important part of San Francisco rests on is a legacy of the frantic need to fill in the hill-encircled mudflats of the old village-cum-metropolis.

The Forty-Niners were young (most were in their twenties), masculine, and zestful. To most the gold rush was the grand adventure of a lifetime and, being a surprisingly educated, even civilized bunch, they self-consciously collected and burnished boomtown tales:

There was the man who cleaned up at the City Hotel barroom. He "would save the sweepings in a barrel, until full; and in washing it he obtained over two hundred dollars."

There was the man who, tea being in oversupply, dumped crates full of the stuff on the tidal flats to make land on which to build a house. By the time his house was finished, the tea in those crates, being in undersupply, was worth "more than a dozen such houses."

There were the $1 eggs, the fortunes lost at the turn of a card, and the "cellar in the earth, twelve feet square and six deep, which rented for $250 a month."

It was a "perpetual carnival" of buying, selling, speculating, getting momentarily rich and grinningly broke. Six deadly fires swept the city in the first few years of the Rush, but each time San Francisco patched itself together and raced on. Prowling gangs like the "Sydney Ducks" or the "Hounds" had to be put down by Committees of Vigilance (the West's first vigilantes). But beneath the daily tumult, the foundations of a great and permanent city were being laid.

By 1853 the river of gold was dropping in its banks. Most of the easily gotten placer gold had been taken out of the foothills. Hundreds of mining towns were collapsing, blowing away into history. But, though its boom slackened, San Francisco was already too established to follow them into obscurity. It was the Queen City of the West, commander of the magnificent bay, funnel for the riches of half a continent.

Yet if it hadn't been for a discovery eerily similar to Marshall's a decade earlier, San Francisco might have settled into something like a comfortable maturity. This time it was silver, not gold, that kindled the boom.

The scraggly denizens of the Virginia Range up near Reno, about 120 miles from San Francisco, had been looking for gold during the past ten years. There was a little up there, enough to buy beans and salt pork for men like Henry T. P. Comstock (who gave his name and little else to the silver district) and James "Old Virginny" Finny (who gave his nickname to the barren boomtown of Virginia City). But the gold was irritatingly mixed up with a dense, bluish clay. In June 1859 that clay was assayed in Grass Valley. Amidst a trace or two of gold was found $3,876 of silver per ton. The Silver Rush, upon which San Francisco would fatten, was on.

Young Samuel L. Clemens was among the first of the troops of young men to assault the Virginia Range and its monarch—the very mountain of silver—Sun Mountain. In his book *Roughing It,* Clemens (by the time he wrote it he was known as Mark Twain) confessed "without shame, that I expected to find masses of silver lying all about the ground. I was perfectly satisfied...that I was going to gather up, in a day or two...silver enough to be satisfactorily wealthy—and so my fancy was already busy with plans for spending the money."

But Twain and his fellow "almost millionaires" soon found that getting silver out of the mountains was not as simple as sitting by a handy stream while panning and whistling dance-hall tunes. For one thing, there were no streams up in those mountains; long, dangerous, frequently worthless tunnels had to be dug. For another thing, silver required expensive refining. The Silver Rush was a game for capitalists and only a very few lucky claim holders.

The capitalists and the fortunate claim holders were happily located in San Francisco. Virginia City was a "twenty-four-hour exercise in bacchanalia," but in the end it was, as Lucius Beebe wrote, "San Francisco's most solvent and essential suburb."

The city's sagging economy ballooned with the riches carried down the mountains by what Twain called an "unbroken...

writing serpent" of pack trains and stages. San Francisco's banks, notably Billy Ralston's Bank of California, became de facto owners of the Comstock district. Ralston built the gargantuan Palace Hotel with silver profits. Four of the luckiest claim holders, the fabled Bonanza Kings—James Fair (of the Fairmont), William O'Brien, John Mackay, and James Flood (his mansion now houses the Pacific Union Club across the street from the Fairmont)— began a mansion-building jamboree atop Nob Hill.

They were soon joined on the heights by the equally fabled Big Four—Leland Stanford (of the university), Charles Crocker (of the bank), Mark Hopkins, and Collis Huntington (whose eponymous hotels occupy their old mansion sites). The Big Four were the creators of what was imagined would finally ensure San Francisco and California's entry into the grand comity of American enterprise: the transcontinental railroad.

For six years the Central Pacific's laborers—many of them imported from China by Crocker—built the line across the Central Valley and over the Sierra. On May 12, 1869, the Golden Spike was driven at Promontory Point, Utah. The West was finally linked with the East, and in San Francisco it seemed that the last year of a decade had once again brought prosperity.

Instead, the railroad brought unneeded immigrants and cheaply manufactured Eastern goods. The Central Pacific's Chinese workers—Crocker's Pets, they were called—flooded what was left of

San Francisco's Chinese heritage dates back to the Gold Rush and the building of the railroads, when thousands of Chinese were brought here to perform the backbreaking labor, and the Chinese population is one of the largest outside Asia. The few square blocks of Chinatown are among the most densely populated in America, with extended families living above the shops and restaurants. As in a Chinese city, wash flutters on lines stretched across alleys. Much is said about how attractive California is to Asia—the influx of Japanese and Hong Kong investment testifies to it— but less has been written, perhaps because it is taken for granted, about how Chinese art and culture have become a significant part of the heritage of non-Chinese Northern Californians....

—Diane Johnson, "See It at Its Best," *Condé Nast Traveler*

the job market, inspiring a decades-long campaign of racism. Union organizers like Dennis Kearney, the "Cicero of the Sandlots," shook their fists at the Nob Hill bosses. When the Comstock's mines began to wilt in the mid-1870s (leading to the collapse of the Bank of California and Billy Ralston's apparent suicide), San Francisco was entrenched in depression.

San Francisco survived its first bout with labor strife and depression in its inimitable boomtown style. What Kevin Starr calls its "intensified pursuit of human happiness" has scarcely ever let up, and may have reached its greatest intensity in the decades before the earthquake and fire of 1906. Rudyard Kipling, visiting during the Gilded Age, called it "a mad city, inhabited for the most part by perfectly insane people."

The Big Four, the Bonanza Kings, and their monied chums entertained in their Nob Hill mansions, whose grand pianos and Greek statues were carried up the hill by cable cars, perfected in 1873 by Scotsman Andrew Hallidie. Those cable cars enabled the city to expand from the old, buried Yerba Buena Cove. It was in this era that the city's Victorian houses were mass-produced. It was the age of the free lunch, of Pisco Punch, and of wicked "French" restaurants. "Drinking," Kipling wrote, "is more than an institution. It is a religion."

It would never attain the ordinary, but as the century turned, San Francisco had polished up some of its frontier roughness. A solid middle class had established itself (though it wasn't until the 1880s that as much as a third of the city's population was female). It was the nation's second port for foreign goods. It had its political bosses and ethnic jostlings, and, as the dislocation brought by the railroad evened out, it linked firmly with the national economy.

San Francisco has always been a city of upheavals, though at 5:12:06 on the morning of April 18, 1906, it suffered its worst. The earthquake shattered a few buildings, broke china heirlooms, and scared the voice out of Enrico Caruso, who was appearing locally in *Carmen*. But it was the fires that almost destroyed the city. They began that morning in the city's center, destroying Billy Ralston's proud Palace, gnawing feverishly at the wooden buildings. Soon a single conflagration spread out from the business district into the neighborhoods, snapping at the heels of fleeing citizens. The fire seethed for two days and three nights until a blessed shift in the wind stopped it on the east side of Van Ness Avenue.

*C*able cars are, you see,
San Francisco's gondolas:
a ridiculously outmoded form of
transportation, but one with a
unique charm and an unbreakable
link to the history and
meaning of the city.

*And it is to Venice, I think, that
we must look for the true analogy
to this relatively small but very select portion of San Francisco and
the Bay Area. Venice, to be sure, is
much further along their common
road, but the similarities are plain.
Both once counted for more in the
great parade. Both chose to yield
their place in it to others, in return
for something they valued even
more. Both, moreover, forsook it for
the same ideal, one that Los
Angeles has never even heard of. It
is the only ideal that has ever
seemed more seductive to men than
power: a dream of charm, and grace,
and almost implausible loveliness.*

—William A. Rusher, "A City-
State of Mind," *National Review*

When it was over, more than 250,000 San Franciscans (of a population of about 400,000) were homeless. Five hundred people had been killed and four-fifths of the city's property was in ashes. But it had suffered fires before and its boom mentality ran deep; rebuilding began immediately. As the headquarters city of the West, San Francisco had no choice (and no inclination) but to rush on.

World War I provided a stimulus for San Francisco's renaissance. Just prior to America's entry into the war the city celebrated with the first of its two world's fairs: the extravagant Panama–Pacific International Exposition of 1915. Built on reclaimed land, which today is the Marina, the fair entertained millions of visitors with educational exhibits, titillating arcades, and masterfully designed "palaces" (only one of which, now the Palace of Fine Arts, remains).

Rebuilt, as sassy as ever, San Francisco enjoyed the 1920s in high style. Its bombastic, shiny, perennial mayor (he served from 1911 to 1931), "Sunny Jim" Rolph, presided over a discreetly licentious town. As his old friend Sally Stanford, the city's leading madam, said, "Sunny Jim's motto was 'Don't Stir up Muddy Waters.'" But the Great Depression stirred the waters unmercifully, of course, and once again San Francisco was wrenched with labor hostilities.

At the crucial Port of San Francisco, four thousand longshoremen competed for thirteen hundred jobs parceled out by a shameless company union. Led by Australian-born Harry Bridges, the International Longshoremen's and Warehousemen's Union (ILWU) fought scabs and union busters at the Port on "Bloody Thursday"—July 5, 1934—and then called a city-wide general strike, the largest and most successful in American history. When the strike held, union power was firmly established in San Francisco.

Despite the Depression, San Francisco managed to launch two of its (and America's) greatest building projects during the 1930s. In November 1936 the Bay Bridge was opened for traffic, and six months later the lyrical Golden Gate Bridge was completed. The city once again celebrated, this time with the gaudy Golden Gate International Exposition of 1939. The "Treasure Island Fair" (so called for the four-hundred-acre artificial island on which it was built) was gloriously ambitious and mildly scandalous, but like its predecessor, it was stalked by war.

Only the fire and the Gold Rush itself have had as great an effect on San Francisco as World War II. As the major disembarkation point for the Pacific Theater, the city couldn't help but prosper. Shipyards were built all around the bay. Torrents of war workers arrived, sunk roots, bought homes in the city and its expanding suburbs, then raised a generation of children who played prominent, pioneering roles in the tumultuous, exhilarating, postwar decades.

It was in and around San Francisco that the student protests of the 1960s and '70s were spawned; where the beatniks began that historic undermining of the country's complacency;

At the Treasure Island Fair there was a fiendish machine called the Giant Octopus, or the Flying Scooters, or Sally Rand's Nude Ranch, where a dozen young ladies dressed in cowboy hats, boots, scarves, and nothing else pretended to brand cattle and drink coffee behind large windows. [To see a photograph of the Nude Ranch, go to Pier 23 Cafe on the Embarcadero in San Francisco.]
—David Siefkin, *The City at the End of the Rainbow: San Francisco and Its Grand Hotels*

where the hippies prospered and altered America's consciousness; where the New Left flourished and the ecology movement flowered; where—and the city will accept the compliment, however left-handed—new ideas, fads, follies, delusions, and every sweet, and sometimes bitter, untempered expansion of the mind and body find a welcome home. That dim asteroid has a planetary shine, but it's still happiest perched on a frontier.

Tom Cole has lived in San Francisco before, during, and after the dawning of the Age of Aquarius. A former publisher and literary agent, his A Short History of San Francisco *is the best-selling history of the city ever written. Safe from the perils of the book world, he currently works for Geographic Expeditions, an adventure travel company, writing, marketing, and leading treks to the high mountains of Asia. He pursues his love affair with San Francisco from the quieter climes of Sonoma County's Wine Country, "about one hour and a heartbeat away from what is still and always will be one of the earth's most heart-grabbing cities."*

★

To a traveler paying his first visit, San Francisco has the interest of a new planet. It ignores the meteorological laws which govern the rest of the world.

—Fitz Hugh Ludlow

SEAN O'REILLY

Glide and the Family Church

This is one church where even the intolerant are made whole.

I KNEW THIS WAS NOT GOING TO BE A NORMAL DAY AT CHURCH when I encountered a tall transvestite in the bathroom. He was preening over the sink—the sink that I wanted to use. What should I do? If I waited maybe he would think I was interested. I could always say something like, "Could you please get the hell out of here—you make me uncomfortable." Or maybe just, "Excuse me" would do. I opted for a hasty retreat as he adjusted the fur cap on his head. I thought as I was leaving, "That was stupid, the poor guy didn't do anything to you." Nonetheless, I was relieved to join the congregation through the side door as I weaved my way through rich and poor alike.

I sat down and immersed myself in the atmosphere of expectation. Voices muted, laughter and greetings hinted at—Sunday cleanliness evident—it was definitely a Sunday crowd. What was different was the altar. There was no altar; instead there was a band setting up and the Sunday atmosphere was clarified by the overwhelming perception that I was at the theater. Three chatty lesbians sat down in front of me and a blonde with a punk haircut and a face that had seen too much of the world sat next to me. There were families with children and gay men holding hands, all mixed in with old people who were spiritual misfits or diehard leftists, yuppies seeking an inner city experience, and your average, wide-open San Francisco types of all ages. "My," I thought, "what an interesting crowd." We were all—gay, straight, crooked, and broken—waiting for the show to begin. Outside at Ellis and Taylor, the derelicts and homeless had gathered to be part of the show in their own way. They would wait for the crowds to come out of church to ask for change; beggars at the banquet, they could be counted on for color.

The music started, heavy on gospel harmonies, the lights went on and the choir started to dance and sing its way out of the back staging area. There was no cross on the stage where there used to be an altar of some sort, only a blank, curved wall twenty feet high where images from a slide projector could be seen flickering like a throwback to a 1960s dance hall.

"Praise God, here we go," I thought to myself, "the party begins." As the singing got louder and the choir emerged fully on stage, the audience jumped out of their seats and joined in, clapping hands to the powerful rhythms. The Reverend Cecil Williams walked slowly onto the stage and told us in deep and persuading tones that no one would remain dead in his church, that Glide was a church where people came *alive*. The band and the choir filled the church with praise—all of us caught up in clapping our hands and shaking to the beat—while images of soulful children and struggling women appeared on the wall. The montages of the '60s were all there on the screen and in the audience. I wouldn't have been the least bit surprised if Janis Joplin herself had jumped on stage and launched into one of her hard-core rhythms about needing a man to understand her. Vague images of Bill Graham's Winterland Arena came to mind as I watched Reverend Cecil gazing upon the crowd with a faintly avuncular air. Strobe lights flashed and the ghosts of dead rock stars seemed to haunt the hall as the music rolled in waves through the church.

Indeed, whether worship or just a good time, Glide definitely fills a social need that people have to come together and get sociable with God. This is different from the regular worship I am used to but I suspect that God enjoys all of it. The Master of galaxies and semen, oceans and dung, fools and sharks, God probably gets a bit tired of those ministers who think he is just some kind of power food. Add grace and stir—none of that stuff here.

The Reverend Cecil smoothly insinuated himself between the music and the crowd to take charge of the collective vibration that is the Glide Memorial experience. We were, he said, to express ourselves, as at Glide there would be no uninvolvement. I loved the heavy emphasis he gave to words like *involvement* and *commitment*. He said them as if they were more than mere words. Coming from his lips they were like some kind of psychic syrup designed to catch souls. I couldn't help but think that my young boys (the oldest is four) would find this kind of church very much to their liking. They would be able to jump around and shout and dance and participate in a way that is not the norm at our family's Catholic church in Arizona.

We were encouraged to hug the person next to us. This is a great place to hug someone of a different sexual persuasion than yourself. I took great pleasure in hugging lesbians and gays, a kind of contrarian perversion if you will. More singers were introduced. There were solos, some good, some not so good. Despite the exotic mix of people here, Glide is still an inner city church with a black gospel feel, whatever that is.

Reverend Cecil got up—he had been sitting—and announced that there would be no sermon as he had a special guest who would be giving her own sermon. He gave some more glowing introductions and then said, "Would you please welcome Maya Angelou." The crowd leapt to its feet as if a rock star had just been announced. The choir could hardly control its emotion. Faces radiated wonder and excitement. Lesbians gazed with reverence at Dr. Angelou and wackos of all sorts acted as if a saint was in their midst. So went my thinking.

Ah, but how surprised I was when Maya opened her mouth to do her rendition of "This Little Light of Mine." "Hey," I thought, "this woman is *good*." Maya Angelou is a wave rider except she doesn't ride waves, she rides words. I felt what she felt, got what

she got—in short, I was moved. Here I am, perhaps a tad to the
right of Newt Gingrich, and I am digging Bill Clinton's Poet
Laureate. Perhaps hell had frozen over while I wasn't looking, perhaps I had expired and people were stepping over my dead body
while pigs flew overhead in formation. Thoughts of a more irreverent nature towards the President began to fill my atavistic mind.
Sorry, I am in church, I should behave. Improper and vile thoughts
sometimes slip by. Certainly lewd ones are the music in my eleva-
tor. But what would Reverend Cecil say? I should be ashamed.

As I was engaged in my usual
diatribe with myself, a petite
Asian woman pushing the limits
of respectability in a short black
dress and power hairdo walked
onto the stage. I was intrigued.
Who was this? Reverend Cecil
said, "I would like to introduce
my wife, she is going to go over
the calendar and update you on
the church's activities." His wife
seemed to be champing at the
bit; when she opened her mouth
I knew why. This woman had

*The Glide Foundation
offers many innovative
programs and hope for Tenderloin
residents. Some 17,000 volunteers
have at one time or another lent
their hands to unique or useful
projects. Our favorite is Fathers in
the Hood. If you want to make a
big fat juicy, tax-deductible contribution or even a little one, contact:
The Glide Foundation, 330 Ellis
Street, San Francisco, CA 94102.*

—JO'R, LH, and SO'R

something to say in a big way. Within minutes I had heard how
high school dropout ratios had gone down and truancy statistics
had dropped by 30 percent in the parish's area. She lectured us, she
admonished her husband in front of the crowd, they flirted with argument, they bantered (Reverend Cecil was enjoying this), she hit
us over the head with statistics, such as Glide having 35 comprehensive programs for over 500 children. I knew then that I was in
the presence of the Empress of the Tenderloin. "How San Francisco
of them," I thought, "blacks and Asians working together. What a
combination." I later found out that the lady in question, Janice
Mirikitani, had been held in a Japanese internment camp as a child
in Arkansas, is a survivor of child abuse, and has been with Glide
for 30 years. She is a Sansei (third-generation Japanese American)

an author, poet, dancer, choreographer, and former high school teacher.

As I listened to this remarkable Japanese American president and executive director of Glide, with the choir behind her like some kind of rainbow honor guard, I felt a window open onto the past. William Leidesdorff, Mammy Pleasant, and A Toy; the names roll off the tongue with a certain melancholy. The black sailing captain and builder of San Francisco's first city hall, black madam-cum-businesswoman extraordinaire, and the Chinese madam's madam; they were among the more colorful characters out of San Francisco's past. There, thumping with the beat of the band in the ruins of Christianity, was old San Francisco.

I shook my head as the service ended and headed quickly for the door. I had to make the 12:00 Mass at St. Cecilia's.

Sean O'Reilly is a former seminarian, stockbroker, and bank slave who lives in Arizona with his wife Brenda and their four small boys. Widely traveled in Europe, he most recently spent time roaming East Africa and the Indian Ocean. He is also at work on a book called Politics and the Soul: The River of Gold, *which he describes as a "re-examination of classic Greek, Roman, and Christian philosophies as tools for moral excellence in modern society."*

✳

I don't go and study other folks. I come from where I came from, as a kid, in the little black church I grew up in. And some of the things they did I rejected, because I could see that it was a manipulation and an exaggeration. My struggle is never to fool folks; to keep it authentic—who we are and who we are becoming—rather than to mimic or to translate what others do into my own terms.

I'm not interested in being an intellectual or in being traditional, conventional. I'm not interested in having great wisdom. I'm not interested in those facets of the evangelical movement. I don't have to get stuff from them.

I got my own stuff. If it hits you, okay. That's why I've got so many different races, classes, and such a mixture of theologies and philosophies at Glide. I've got agnostics, atheists, Buddhists, Christians, Jews, Muslims—the whole spectrum....

If you got the truth, you put it out there, and everybody says, "Oh, my God. That's me." And then they improvise also. They take off, as well.

But I am noticing that we're getting more and more people—and I don't know how to handle this—who come to me saying, "Would you pray for my son? Would you pray for my daughter?" I've been saying, "Pray for them yourself." But they don't want that because they think I've got something that's greater than what they have. I keep saying, "I don't! Not really. I got the title 'minister,' but I don't want to exploit you. You do it, too." I think the way to solve it is to do it together. We're going to pray in community, you see?

—Reverend Cecil Williams, interviewed in "Sunday Morning Improv," *Psychology Today*

* * *

The Heavenly Gates

An artist-wanderer is reminded of his homeland.

SAN FRANCISCO IS KNOWN IN CHINA AS CHIU-CHIN-SHAN OR Old-Gold-Hill. In the 1860s a large group of Southern Chinese were recruited and brought over as laborers to help build the Pacific Railroad in California. They were simple peasants and worked hard to save money to send home from time to time. Eventually the place where they were working became known among their kinsfolk and neighbours as one "where they have struck gold." Immediately after the discovery of gold at Sutter's Mill in the Sierra Foothills, most of this group of Chinese went to work in the new gold-diggings and were able to send more money home. They sent for their sons and other relations to work with them. In their letters home they evidently referred to San Francisco as the Old-Gold-Hill to distinguish from the new gold field at Sutter's Mill. Since then many Chinese from southern China have come to California to find ways of making a better living. At the first glance they may have looked like those early gold-rushers from the Yankee land and Europe, but in fact they just helped to rush out the gold for others.

Although San Francisco is mentioned in a Chinese official pub-lication of the early nineteenth century, knowledge of the place at that time was confined to the Chinese living along the fringe of the South China coast, whose relations or friends had emigrated there. Even a century later, I myself, having been born in Central China, had never heard anyone talk of San Francisco till I left my native land. Certainly I never dreamt of reaching such a place.

One's birthplace is an accident, and life consists of a series of accidents which may turn out luckily or not. A single lucky accident can bring unexpected joy into one's life; that is what San Francisco has done for me.

In China there is a striking difference between the country and the city; the former is tranquil and full of fresh air, the latter noisy and dirty with dust. Many well-known passages of Chinese prose and poetry describing the serene beauty of the countryside could never have been applied to this countryside that we were travelling through now in California. There must have been quiet patches sometimes, no doubt, but the sun, glaring so brightly, beat down on my eyelids so that I had a struggle to keep them open, and drove away any tranquillity from the scene for me. The sky had been deep blue all the way, as blue as the immensely long sheets of indigo cloth that we Chinese use to make huge canopies over our courtyards to shield them from the summer sun. But the canopy that I was passing underneath was infinite, without supporting poles, and the sun blazed on. The brilliant rays seemed to have beaten up the dust from the road and scattered it round the edges of the hills, far and wide, so that it looked like a

Ask any Hong Konger. What's the second-best city in the world? Sarm Faan Si comes the instant answer. The name doesn't indicate the true esteem in which Cantonese hold the place; a literal translation of the Chinese characters comes across as "City of the Three Barbarians." But this is an interpretation based purely on the tonal intonations of the language. More apt is the common name Gow Kam Shan— Old Golden Mountain. The City by the Bay has long exerted a gilded glow that beckons brightly over the Pearl River estuary on the other side of the Pacific.

—Kevin Sinclair, "San Francisco as Seen from Hong Kong," San Francisco Magazine

sort of yellow smoke. It even made the hills and trees in their young greenery look tired and withered from being baked all the time.

The parallel lines of the highway now turned into a complicated mixture of lines, very confusing to my eyes. The activity on them seemed to be more intense than ever. There were now many houses and motels lining both sides of the highway. The neon signs, red and green, shone in the relentless sunlight like veins on a microscope slide. The scene all round became increasingly dramatic. The little faint image of the top of Mount Tamalpais was now like a huge sheet of gray-blue paint with a slanting unevenly cut line, standing upright on the flat ground to my right, while on the left were twinkling silver lines, probably of water, in the distance. Close by the foot of Mount Tamalpais, round hills with a luxuriant growth of trees, dotted with white mushroom-like houses, emerged quickly one after another. On the opposite side sprang up hills like steaming hot buns in the brilliant sun with no trees at all, but with a large number of small houses like colorful fungi scattered over them. We were now in Marin County.

My friends had planned to show me whatever they could of interest on the way, and our car now turned off the highway to follow the sign for Sausalito. Soon numerous masts appeared on a waterfront lined with warehouses. I looked over the masts to the vast expanse of water; far beyond and over on the other side where white dots and sparks gathered together San Francisco was pointed out to me. Unconsciously I wiped my face with my paw like a cat and then it was gone, for we had come to a turn in the road and left the waterfront. A unique first glimpse of a city, I thought, but what is it actually like?

My head was next completely bewildered by the sudden disappearance of the sunshine. Only a moment ago in all the sky not a wisp of cloud had been visible. Now we were confronted with masses of infinitesimal particles moving and whirling as if directed by some supernatural being to display some curious magic for us. They were not high above us as clouds usually are, but were bearing down to earth fast and were about to swallow up all the hills in front of our car. Of these, some were quickly covered without a trace, some thinly veiled, and others still stood out clearly. The scene was like a Chinese landscape in mist painted by some master of the Sung dynasty. At the same time I seemed to see the voluminous clouds and mists rotating continuously, thickening here and thinning there, so that it seemed as if all the hills were racing one another; one would appear and disappear again as another came to take its place. The whole scene was dramatically alive. It filled me with excitement. I imagined that I was back in northeastern China at Tunghai, where I taught in a school some thirty years ago and where, one Sunday morning, a colleague and I rode on horseback up a famous rocky mountain there, Yun-tai Shan, by the Yellow Sea. This mountain became famous because one of the earliest known Chinese painters, Ku K'ai-chih of the fourth century (an example of whose work, *Admonition of the Imperial Instructress,* is in the British Museum in London), wrote a treatise on how he painted it. It is a huge mountain full of grotesque and fantastic rock formations; very few trees grow on it and hardly any bushes or grass. The whole district of Tunghai is almost barren—poor country with few inhabitants. Being interested in both art and adventure I could not help wanting to pay this famous mountain a visit. "Not many people go up there," we were told, but a man who kept horses for people to ride over the mountain was introduced to us. We hired two and my friend rode off before me. It was a sunny morning and for a time we had a lovely, clear view. All of a sudden the scene in front was wiped out by massive clouds storming along. They seemed to be rushing towards us on our narrow footpath. I had fallen some distance behind my friend and watched him moving on slowly, myself filled with awe and inspiration. I felt that the following two lines from a well-known Chinese poem by Li Po described the view most appropriately:

> *The mountain rises up from the human face;*
> *The clouds grow by the side of the horse's-head.*

Gradually my friend and his horse became a faint image and then were lost. I and my horse were completely engulfed in the clouds and mists. All of a sudden a great gust of wind drove the scudding clouds over us. My friend was unprepared and was blown off his horse. He was a trained wrestler, so only his body hit the rock, and not his head. He was not really hurt and laughed as he scrambled on to his horse again. We were both young and enjoyed the thrill and beauty of the moment. We did not know where we were, nor did we care when we would reach the city again; we had been up the mountain for four hours already. We had no fear of being lost, for we had complete faith in our horses. Presently a big shaft of sunshine broke through the thick cloud-mass to reveal the formations of some of the rocks shaped with ethereal and incomparable delicacy. My friend's horse made a turn towards the sunshine and we eventually came out of the clouds and rode back along a sunny footpath, home for dinner. More than thirty years had slipped by and not once had I given this trip a thought.

What a joy it was to me now to be reminded of it, as we motored fast along this well-paved highway of America. Most of the cars ahead of us were losing their shape, and soon were visible no more. We were all engulfed in the dense clouds, or mist. There were no more hills except one sweeping flowing line slanting down on my right. At this moment, to my great surprise and delight, up there appeared in the air a distinctively Chinese vermilion-painted Gate of Heaven, though blurred by the continually rolling clouds. A glorious, heart-stirring sight indeed! I was no longer riding up the Yun-tai Shan but instead was climbing up to the Nan-tien-men, the Southern Heavenly Gate of Mount Tai in Shangtung Province, where Confucius was born more than two thousand five hundred years ago. Mount Tai is one of the most sacred mountains of China; its spirit was worshiped by the early kings and emperors even before Confucius's day. On the very top of its highest peak, a Chinese temple was built, and to approach it one must pass through the Southern Heavenly Gate, built on the gap between two enormous rocky gorges. While walking up we would see from far below the Southern Heavenly Gate as if suspended in air, either through the mist or the sunny haze. I felt that the faint gate that had appeared in the air before me now must be Chinese, for China has always preferred vermilion for her palace gates, Pailous or gateways, pillars of temples and monasteries. How could I not be moved by this unusual yet familiar sight from my own past of some thirty years ago? Indeed, it quite carried me away!

Being, however, an earthly creature I came back to earth and realized that I was being motored over a bridge—the famous Golden Gate Bridge—as Bob and Thelma told me at the same time. "But why painted in Chinese red?" My friends had no time to answer nor I to listen, for my eyes were greeted by yet another red archway, redder than the first, and also floating in air. A moment later another section of it appeared from below and the whole looked like a red ladder suspended in the air so that I could climb to Heaven. It was the second tower of the Golden Gate Bridge that we were passing. The clouds and mist became denser than ever and I could hardly see a few yards beyond our car. The noise of other cars sounded clearly but there was no visible sign of them. Tiny yellow lights on both sides made a great struggle to penetrate the mist. It was impossible to tell whether we were again in the open countryside; our whole surroundings were invisible and mysterious.

The Golden Gate Bridge virtually breathes. In a wind of 100 mph (not impossible), the mid-span can swing out twenty-one feet in either direction. Under extreme conditions of load and temperature, the towers can hoist or drop the bridge by as much as ten feet.

—Stephen Jay Hansen,
The Other Guide to San Francisco

Presently the fog grew thinner and revealed a straight street lined with houses and shops that seemed to continue endlessly. At long last we came to a halt, for me to be shown Coit Tower and a rapid view of its surroundings. We stopped again at the top of one of the Twin Peaks, but the wind was far too strong and we could hardly stand against it. Then, we had a meal in Chinatown. Finally I was installed in the house of a friend of Bob and Thelma's on Lake Street, and they departed to their hotel, for the night. What a day I had had and how my head swam with so many sights to be taken in all at once! I could hardly say a word to my friends on parting; I needed time to sort it all out.

Lying on my bed, I gathered together my first impressions of the city: surrounded by water, clean and fresh, yet mysterious and unapproachable, sprawling like numerous rattlesnakes as well as stretching out with more arms than an octopus, pioneeringly strange yet traditionally familiar, subconsciously poetic, externally indifferent yet internally human, distinctively American and unmistakably San Francisco. I let my imagination wander and looked forward to testing my dreams by reality.

Chiang Yee trained as a chemist in China and served as the Governor of his native district of Kiu-Kiang. He later turned to painting and writing on subjects such as Chinese painting, calligraphy, and family life. His observations on places and people are documented in his book series, The Silent Traveller, *which he wrote from 1938 until his death in 1977. This piece was excerpted from his 1964 book* The Silent Traveller in San Francisco.

✳

Paul Chow first learned about Angel Island nearly sixty years ago when his first-grade class was celebrating Thanksgiving. "I saw pictures of the Mayflower, Plymouth Rock, and the pilgrims," says the retired highway engineer. "I tried to find Chinese; I tried to find blacks. All I saw were white people."

Chow, who says he was a precocious child who questioned everything, asked the teacher how his people, the Chinese, got into America: "She didn't know." He asked his mother and she whispered back, "Angel Island, shhh." For years Chow thought it was one word, that he came from Angelislandshhh. "Later I understood that we came from Angel Island but we didn't talk about it." He also learned that when his father came to America at the age of 22, he remained on the island for six weeks before bribing his way off.

A section of the 740-acre island in San Francisco Bay was to be the "Ellis Island of the West," designed to process an anticipated flood of Europeans immigrating to western America via the Panama Canal. That never happened, however; the majority of the people were from Asia. And from 1910 until 1940, for 175,000 Chinese the immigration station served more as a detention and deportation center than a processing center, largely due to the Chinese Exclusion Act of 1882. The law, the first denying naturalization of a specific nationality, detained immigrants in barracks for from two weeks to as long as two years while officials conducted interrogations and checked on records, references, and relatives. Some detainees, fearing deportment, were said to have committed suicide in the barracks. The station closed in 1940 after a fire destroyed the administration building and mess hall.

That period, Chow says, is a dark chapter in this nation's treatment of Asian immigrants, a significant chapter he wants written into history books. "We Asians are never told how we came through the system," Chow says. "We came the same way as the Europeans, but the two systems were completely different. Ellis Island welcomed Europeans. Angel Island slammed the door on Asians."

Chow, however, is doing his part to shed light on that period. He lectures at schools, before social clubs, and estimates he has conducted more than 1,500 tours of the station during the past 21 years. In the men's quarters, he walks to the spot where his father's bunk had been in 1922.

Bringing his father, Chow Hing Gai, back to the station in 1974, Chow had been both touched and surprised to see the older man break down in tears. "In my whole life I had never seen my father cry," he says. "He was always this proud man, head held high, the strong man of the family." When Chow asked why he was crying, his father thoughtfully answered, "Freedom. Today I can walk in and walk out. Last time I was here I couldn't walk out so easily." Then he added, "Son, freedom is a very fragile thing. Protect it."

In 1983 Chow formed the nonprofit Immigration Station Foundation with the goal of raising $3 million to restore the two-story wooden barracks, provide more tour guides, landscape the grounds, and rebuild the pier leading to the station. Most important, he wants to interpret and preserve the Chinese characters carved on the barracks' wall—hundreds of poignant poems and messages left by anguished, angry, and homesick immigrants.

"Angel Island is our *Mayflower*, our Plymouth Rock, our Statue of Liberty; a monument to the Asian immigrants' strength, courage, and spirit," Chow says. "They shared a common dream with the immigrants who entered through Ellis Island. My dream is to make it equal to Ellis Island in people's minds."

—Nancy Hoyt Belcher, "Angel Island Beacon," *Modern Maturity*

MARY TOLARO NOYES

Dreaming of Muir Woods

Some places transcend time and space.

BACK HOME IN CALIFORNIA I MISS THE MUSIC OF THE bells...Bologna's Sunday morning concert fills the crisp autumn air. At 10:30 the kitchen window is thrown open: a glorious day—sunny, blue cloudless sky and fresh air with the promise of later warmth. Just down Strada Maggiore, toward the city's medieval center, Santa Maria dei Servi's singing campanile announces that services are beginning, that it is a day of rest, a day for the spirit to unwind itself, a day to contemplate the journey of one's soul. In the distance other bells join in and it seems Bologna is full of joy. But today I am lonely, and the pealing bells do not fill me with the usual happiness. Instead, they throw me back...

To my family and San Francisco, and Sunday mornings there. Suddenly, I am in Muir Woods. It is early, too early for the inevitable tourists who will surely arrive. I am approaching the forest gate, anxious to embrace and be embraced by a world that feeds and renews my spirit. My husband Tom is with me, and though we walk in company, each meditates in solitude, drinking in nature's splendor. I could be entering a Gothic cathedral. A powerful vertical thrust up to heaven pulls my eyes with it—everything reaching up, up to the blue patch of sky that floats serenely above my tilted-back head. In and out, in and out, the light shadows me, at times jumping ahead and shooting bright rays at my feet. The sunlight filters through the outreached arms of the giant coast red-woods, dappling the path, just as it enters cathedral windows, slashing the dark, holy space.

The profound stillness stirs my city-tired senses, shocks them into fine-tune mode. Running water from Redwood Creek cuts through and follows the trail and smoothes the jagged edges of the rocks. Its slippery splashing, slapping music untangles the knots that bunch-up the nerves, sinews, and thoughts within me. Nature's music is everywhere, a veritable symphony now unfolding around me. The rustling branches are like brooms brushing away the stress, the care, the dirt, the refuse of a life lived too much on the run, too much on the surface. The trilling wrens and squawking ravens join the wind's rustling in the branches of the trees and serenade my now expectant ears. I notice high up wind-sounds, rushing and thrashing, then up-close ones that whisk at me, flap my coattails and dislodge my hat. Sonoma chipmunks scurry busily along the ground, dipping in and out of here and there, mostly oblivious to our intrusion, not chatty like the brazen Stellar jays, whose cobalt-blueness challenges the blue of the sky itself. The sun's warmth begins to penetrate my pilgrim soul, as huge families of coast redwoods welcome me into their domain. John Muir's insistence that man assume his proper position in nature, protect it and thus enjoy its bounty, realizes itself eloquently here. I marvel that the forest flourishes so near a grand city like San Francisco. And I am grateful.

Then I think back to other visits to Muir Woods, when the sun was not shining. The famous San Francisco fog hung, settled, or just plain walked its way into the forest, and it was another kind of enchanting world, a shadowy velvet one. The tops of the majestic trees hid in its density, and I imagined them thirstily soaking in its moisture. I felt free to create my own images. I made the trees out-of-sight tall, with their highest branches full of birds and secrets I would never know, but only imagine. I liked it. I liked the luxury of imagining.

Sounds were muffled, soft. Wetness chilled the air. Sweaters and windbreakers were pulled out of backpacks and hurriedly thrown over short sleeves and goosebumps. (That is when summer visitors to San Francisco discover it can be cold and damp in California in July!) Dewy, earthy smells intensified. Shades of green and brown dominated Nature's palette in the grayness of the foggy world, even more tranquil in the absence of strong light.

I was forced to focus on the world at my feet, at arms' length. Usually overlooked Douglas firs and bay laurels, varieties of maple and oak filled in the space, as if all at once broad strokes of detail had emerged. Tangled tree trunks and distorted branches portrayed their fight for scarce light in the giants' shadows. Prolific ferns kept them company on the forest floor, especially the sword fern, brandishing its deceptively threatening fronds, as they flanked the gentle rise on the

orever is the redwoods, whose species name sempervirens *means "everlasting." Although nothing in nature lasts forever, the redwood is as close to everlasting as any living thing can get. One hundred and sixty million years ago, great forests of the tall trees grew in Europe, Asia, and North America. Redwoods towered over the tallest dinosaur. A million or two years ago, with the coming of the Ice Age, the redwoods retreated and made a last stand along the northern and central California coast. Ninety-three percent of our coast redwoods have been chopped down; of the seven percent remaining, four percent are under public ownership, hopefully forever.*

—John McKinney, *A Walk Along Land's End: Discovering California's Unknown Coast*

sides of the trail. Velvet-like moss crept on rocks and trees. Stodgy mushrooms and fungi sat placidly, having erupted from their subterranean depths following the overnight moisture. Occasional splashes of yellow and white popped up bravely, earnest wildflowers attempting to add color to the dark earth.

Redwood Creek, which can become an angry, powerful torrent during the winter storms, had slowed to a trickle during the summer drought. Nevertheless, close inspection of the trapped pools unveiled an undisturbed miniature world, busy with its day-to-day activities, unaware of my appreciative, though uneducated, probing eyes.

The huge breadth of the redwoods' trunks greeted me at my 5'2" level. The redness of their tannin-rich bark, with spongy box-like notches covering their immense surface as they shot high up into the sky...the marvelous burls allowing them to propagate by sprouting...black-lined caves in their gigantic trunks, testimony to the power of nature's lightning strikes and unforgiving storms...fallen giants, whose crash would have shattered the forest's silence...the flit of butterflies...the zip of buzzing bugs...

...then suddenly I am in Bologna again, at the kitchen table, on a lonely Sunday morning—that is not so lonely now. The bells have ceased, but the echo of their music lingers. Returning to the moment forces Muir Woods into the background, an ocean and continent away. But renewed by the comforting embrace of the familiar forest, I grab my notebook, close the door as I leave the loneliness behind and jump into the Sunday world blossoming everywhere.

Mary Tolaro Noyes is a writer living in Concord, California, with her hus-band, Tom, her sons, and Onyx, their black Lab. After years in the teaching profession, she has finally come to the writing she always meant to do. Inspired by finding her family in Sicily and, in the process, understanding her own soul, she continues to study Italian as she writes in English. Among her other projects, she is writing a book about the medieval mystery and modern charm of Bologna, a city she knows from living and studying there. Meanwhile, she dreams of San Francisco....

★

The redwood forest, the remains of a virgin sequoia forest. The interiors of certain Gothic cathedrals—Strasbourg, for example—replicate man's smallness and helplessness in this middle zone between hell and heaven, amid the columns of the primeval forests which still covered large areas of Europe when the cathedrals were built. But [Christian] Europe never had trees like the redwoods, whose life spans number over two thousand years. This forest is the idea of forest, a prototype drawn by God; no church columns attain that height, and never does a church's semi-darkness contrast so sharply with a ray slanting in from above the reach of sight. Small human figures are diminished not by the redwoods' trunks, too huge for comparisons, but by a lower level, in relation to ferns larger than a man and to the fallen, moss-covered logs which sprout new green shoots. To confirm their value as a forest symbol: the redwoods are such that the chunk of a felled tree does not die but regenerates itself in a multitude of swiftly growing sprigs.

—Czeslaw Milosz, *Visions from San Francisco Bay*

FRED SETTERBERG

✦ ✦ ✦

My Father's Jack London

Gertrude Stein said of Oakland,
"There's no there there,"
but she was wrong.

"YOU SURE YOU DON'T HAVE TO WORK TODAY?" ASKED MY FATHER. "I don't want to take you away from work."

"Really," I assured him, "I can take the day off."

"Well, work all you can," he lectured me, far from the first time, "work long and hard, because 'Life is real! Life is earnest! And the grave—'"

"I know, 'the grave is not its goal,' is it?"

"Longfellow," he pointed out.

"Right."

Morning commuters swelled behind us, scuffing their shoes upon the sandpaper footholds, clattering their briefcases against the iron handrail.

"Aren't there any working people on this boat?" my father asked incredulously, glaring down the gangplank. Dad hadn't crossed the bay on the early morning ferry since the 1930s, when he commuted from San Francisco's port to the Alameda Naval Air Base, where he was to work as a metalsmith for 37 years.

"It looks to me like they're all going to work."

I nodded toward the sleepy bevy of middle-aged men as they converged upon the boat in business suits and brash neckties, the young women dressed as their doubles in androgynous navy-blue double knits, with Nikes slipped over their nylons.

"You know damn well what I mean." Dad halted for a moment at the hatch to steal a scanning glance of the wharf. "Jack London worked right here, you realize."

"Sure, Dad."

"He was a sailor and an oyster pirate," rhapsodized my father, "and then he started arresting his oyster pirate pals when that turned out to be a better job."

"You've told me, Dad."

"He didn't take the day off whenever he felt like it."

The ferry rocked hard, broke from its moorings, and glided into the channel. It took about fifteen minutes to run the full distance through Oakland's harbor to the mouth of the bay, including one stop in Alameda. The thick and bilgy water looked like a reservoir of green ink.

"Didn't you ever take a day off?"

"Labor Day and Christmas."

We passed through a forest of masts, the harbor's small stand of yachts docked alongside the plasterboard abutment of restaurants, bars, and motels bearing Jack London's name; past the warehouse district where railroad tracks inscribed into the hot-tar streets vanished behind the port walls; alongside the navy barges and liver-green Quonset huts settled across from the shoreline's huge mechanical cranes, six-story hoists that looked like faceless white workhorses loading cargo containers aboard immense freighters bearing the names of dead presidents.

On the bow of the second deck, Dad and I lapped up the salt spray like contented spaniels nipping at the wind. The Bay Bridge slashed across the skyline, serving up San Francisco's high-rise spires upon the platter of its fourth and fifth spans. The remainder of the city was wrapped in fog.

"This is where Jack London really started out," said Dad.

"I know."

Facing the open bay, about two hundred yards from the hub of the wharf, the boat jostled atop the waves and the wind slapped our faces with calloused hands. The bay was a wild place, a tempest. Between Oakland and San Francisco, the ferry surged toward the tug of the Golden Gate, skating off toward the crazy ocean that could lead anywhere.

My father and I had been talking about Jack London for years. Oakland's most famous writer was one of our perennial subjects, and our enthusiasm had everything to do with that great American unmentionable—class.

> *You can go anywhere out through the Golden Gate—to Australia, to Africa, to the seal islands, to the North Pole, to Cape Horn...Oakland's just a place to start from, I guess.*
>
> —Jack London,
> *The Valley of the Moon*

Over time, one way or another, class showed up like a famished uncle at every family argument. It was class that Dad and I both invoked to bind us together, if only by a spider's strand, even while we used it to straight-arm each other into separate corners. As far back as I can remember, it was class that lit the fuse to our competition.

I first heard the word when my fifth-grade teacher unwisely proclaimed that America was a classless society. It was a silly, popular notion back in the early 1960s, though as school children we were then too young to trace its strands of pretzel logic. Given the ancient sorrows of class-conscious Europe—most of us were scarcely one generation away from immigrant grandparents—it must have seemed like brassy romance and patriotism to brag to a room full of ten-year-olds that our own young Republic breached no official division of wealth and status. In America, asserted our teacher, we were all middle class.

But when I passed this good news along to my parents over the evening's dinner of hot dogs, canned peas, and mashed potatoes, my father thrust his elbows upon the green Formica kitchen table-top, squared his head into his outstretched palms, and growled lowly to himself. He still wore the day's working clothes—his coffee-colored Ben Davis trousers, a bleached-bright baby-blue denim shirt rolled up to the throbbing biceps, ankle-high, steel-tipped boots.

"You don't know what you're talking about," my father informed me, scooping mounds of canned peas and mashed potatoes into his hungry mouth.

"But Teacher said."

"Teacher hasn't worked a lick in her life, and don't know what she's talking about either."

On the subject of education, my father would always be seriously divided. He was a high school graduate—but from there on, largely self-educated. He had mastered some practical science and mechanics, and he knew U.S. history very well, familiar with everything that had transpired during his lifetime. Dad was blessed with a rat-trap memory that secured squirming morsels of Kipling, Longfellow, and Shakespeare, which he had recited decades earlier at the head of his one-room country school in Oregon; but formal learning, at every level, aroused his suspicion. When it came time for me to think about college, he was full of impossible advice: *You're a fool,* he tortuously explained, *if you don't get an education so that you can live off the sweat and blood of the people who do the real work in this country!*

Books, however, were a different story.

Shortly after my fifth-grade teacher had theoretically dismantled America's class structure, I recall one Saturday morning when Dad escorted me to the public library and filled my arms with volumes of Jack London, which were, in a sense, my patrimony.

They were all the books Dad had read as a kid. *Before Adam, The Cruise of the Dazzler, Tales of the Fish Patrol.* I pored over them as I would a child's atlas of the world and then plundered the Klondike stories—"To Build a Fire," "An Odyssey of the North," and *Call of the Wild*; and then on to the sailor sagas, starting with *South Sea Tales. The Sea-Wolf* was rougher going. Captain Wolf Larsen's own shipboard bookcase was stocked with unfamiliar names and titles: Tennyson, DeQuincey, Bulfinch's *Mythology,* and *The Origin of Species.* But I plodded on, disregarding what I could not comprehend, all for the glimpse contained within those pages of boyish adventure.

What delighted me most, however, was the life behind the stories. I asked my father about Jack London, and he knew everything. London had grown up in Oakland. His mother had been a spiritualist, his father, John Chaney, who never acknowledged him, an itinerant astrologer. As a teenager, he quit school, went to sea, hit the road to join Coxey's army of the unemployed who were marching to Washington to demand jobs, landed in jail in Buffalo, and then lit out for the Yukon gold rush of 1897, only to return one year later from his Klondike stake with $4.50 worth of gold dust in his pockets. But London had also packed back to Oakland a rich trove of frontier lore, and it quickly made him one of the country's most popular and prolific writers.

Jack London wrote 50 books—Dad read them all—and shouldered assignments as a newspaper correspondent covering the Boer War in South Africa, the Russo-Japanese War, and the Mexican Revolution. He married twice, fathered two daughters, sailed the South Seas on his own yacht, and died at 40. He was the most famous American writer of his time, his own life story wrapped in a flag of self-promoting legends equaled only in our day by the Hemingway myth. To think of him now, as many people do, as the overgrown, scrappy boy of gregarious naïveté who wrote some good dog stories and then drank himself to death, is to flit over the impact he had on millions of people, and particularly the country's bright and curious workingmen, who weren't ordinarily engaged with "literature."

Jack London was their spokesman, the first great American mythmaker to insist that the hard grind of a workingman's life might contain lessons for others; that when the workingman's best instincts collided with society's boundaries, the impact could spin him off toward heroic pursuits—that *all* of history's legendary heroes, from Odysseus the sailor to Paul Bunyan the lumberjack, had been tough, thinking, workingmen. London was the model of strong hands and rough wits.

★

"Do you remember how you used to lie to me when I was a boy?" I asked my father, as we bobbed upon the San Francisco Bay on the commuter ferry.

Gulls had collected around the stern, fluttering like kites upon the tail breeze. We were gliding toward an unfettered view of the Golden Gate as the suspension beams of the Bay Bridge shivered five hundred feet above us.

"What are you talking about?"

"You told me that Treasure Island was inhabited by pirates."

Treasure Island was the U.S. naval base at the midpoint of the bridge. The island itself was manufactured from twenty million cubic yards of bay silt and landfill piled high for the 1939 San Francisco Golden Gate International Exhibition.

"You claimed," I reminded him, "that every man on Treasure Island wore a patch over his right eye and kept a parrot on his shoulder. You said that if some stranger accidentally drove onto the island, the pirates would grab him, saw off his leg, and replace it with a peg."

"I bet that made you think twice about running away from home to join the navy, didn't it?"

"I suppose it did."

"Well, then good. 'A man who calls a spade a spade should be compelled to use one.' I guess I don't have to tell you, that's Oscar Wilde."

We watched the bay waters ruffle and cream up against the ferry's hull until San Francisco was extruded from the mist. A foghorn blasted two times in the distance, and the port veered into view. The hum of the city smothered the sound of the waves splashing against our boat, and I felt sad to be so close to land.

My father and I were spending the entire day together, an event unimaginable in the past. Once, years before, when I asked Dad how he got along with his own father, he swallowed his answer hard and raised his fists to guard his face, pivoting half-circles in a boxer's defensive stance. Between us, too, it was often like that, though without blows. If we were both these days more tolerant of one another, the change was probably due to some inevitability of family geometry that neither of us had the insight or perspective to fully grasp. Fathers and sons never conform into a single shape; rather, they seem drawn from their first meeting as separate lines whose faulty parallelism is revealed only over the years as they exhibit an infinitesimal quiver toward each other arching across the page—and at some point, these two lines may intersect. Perhaps we were now at that point.

I knew that our intimacy had been rekindled by reading the right book at the right time. In this case, the book was *Martin Eden*, Jack London's autobiographical novel tracing the immense hard work of a young sailor who educated himself to become a writer.

Martin Eden is not one of the books my father pressed upon me as a kid. And it's far from London's best. But reading it for the first time this year I felt connected to all the romance and tragedy that lies at the heart of any early struggle for learning. Unlike Dad's favorite London novel—*The Star Rover*, which portrays the unshackling of a convict's imagination from Folsom solitary through some quirky means of astral projection, the dreamer loosened from his limits to experience an eternity of reincarnated adventures—*Martin Eden* doesn't promise freedom for the workingman. In the end, its disillusioned hero drowns himself.

> *A*nother young sailor *who educated himself and developed a lifelong love for the sea is Karl Kortum, former director of the National Maritime Museum. Karl almost single-handedly created the museum and was the force behind the preservation of numerous historic ships that today line the Hyde Street Pier at Aquatic Park, including the* Balclutha, Eureka, *and* C. A. Thayer.
>
> —JO'R, LH, and SO'R

And still, Martin Eden *is* Jack London—a more romantic version, surely, swollen through poetic exaggeration, though recognizable yet as a "work beast, shot through with stray flashes of divinity," the partisan of "stokeholes and forecastles, camps and beaches, jails and boozing-kens, fever-hospitals and slum streets." When Martin Eden meets the comely sister of a better-educated and far daintier young man whom Eden rescues from a street-brawling bully, he is entranced instantly by the young girl's mannered beauty *and* her volume of Swinburne on the drawing room table. It's one of literature's most unlikely seductions: the first stanzas of the decadent English poet, read aloud by the privileged young girl, ignite within Martin Eden a commitment to let learning transform him. "He had caught a glimpse," explains the author, "of the apparently illimitable vistas of knowledge."

Like Martin Eden—like my father—Jack London bore upon his back the full load of contradictory attitudes about learning and labor.

"*All my days I have worked hard with my body,*" London explained in a 1903 essay entitled "How I Became a Socialist" (which aimed to clarify why he began much of his voluminous correspondence with the salutation, "Dear Comrade," and concluded, "Yours for the Revolution"), "*and according to the number of days I have worked, by just that much am I nearer the bottom of the Pit. I shall climb out of the Pit, but not by the muscles of my body shall I climb out. I shall do no more hard work, and may God strike me dead if I do another day's hard work with my body more than I absolutely have to do. And I have been busy ever since running away from work.*"

As a young man, London ran straight to the Oakland Public Library. There he investigated William Morris, Marx, Mill, Ricardo, Adam Smith, Proudhon, Saint-Simon, Fourier—and with the inevitable crankiness of the autodidact, Madame Blavatsky and Herbert Spencer. London pored over the dictionary, adding twenty words each day to his vo-

It is true that workers, older workers in particular, have extremely naïve ideas of what white-collar people do for a living. They see them as going through life staying clean, sitting on their butts, and making a lot of money doing it. They also see them gaining a great deal of status and respect that they feel are denied them as blue-collar workers....

A lifetime of hard work and perhaps childhood memories of the depression combined to solidify the older blue-collar worker's attitude. Poverty and hard work are twin plagues; education is the vaccination against them, and, by God, his kid is going to have one.

—Reg Theriault, *How to Tell When You're Tired: A Brief Examination of Work*

cabulary. Like Caliban, he had purloined the rulers' books, leafing madly through their pages for the secrets that enslaved him. Ricocheting with giddy energy between visions of class solidarity and the bombastic pride of the self-proclaimed workingman's aristocrat—a kind of Horatio Alger Jacobin—London stood upon his soapbox in the triangular park banking Oakland's old city hall and preached revolutionary aims until he was arrested. He ran three times for mayor of Oakland under the Socialist banner—earning 245 votes in 1901; losing the election to a wealthy populist, who had once hired his stepfather, John London, as a strikebreaker.

What lay behind this drive for reconstructing his life? Not the will to power, not the winning of the girl; it was the man's ocean of curiosity. Jack London—like my father, like Martin Eden—had, in the words of his biographer Andrew Sinclair, "the vaunting ambition of the self-taught; he was always the poor boy in the public library who determines to read every book on every shelf in order to add up the whole sum of human knowledge. It was a noble and futile aspiration, and a tragic one." Tragic because it led to "an infinite dissatisfaction," the envy that knotted up Caliban's entrails—a risk borne by every young working person who dares to dip into borrowed books.

When I think of my father and *his* books, I sense curiosity's same treacherous appeal. In our family, curiosity stirred up weird and stubborn argument. When my mother's sisters would visit from the East Coast, Dad urged that their immigrant Italian family must have once marched with Garibaldi's red legions against the pope in Rome. (Nobody seemed to get it. Was their sister's husband joking, was he nuts? Who was Garibaldi?) Dad buzzed off to the living room bookshelf to select Volume G of *The World Book Encyclopedia*. Then he leafed merrily through its pages until he located Garibaldi's wizened portrait. Evidence. The world was full of histories and plots whose surface we can barely skim. Of course, while Garibaldi marched, my mother's ancestors were all fishing quietly off the coast of Calabria. But the sheer proximity of encyclopedic knowledge stirred my father; reference books containing the near-sum of human endeavor *were sitting in his living room*!

My father didn't start reading until he fell off his bicycle at the age of fourteen and broke his leg in two places below the knee. Since Dad couldn't move his leg all summer to work or play, he retreated into books. For the first time, he read Zane Grey, J. W. Schultz's Indian stories, most of Edgar Rice Burroughs, James Olivier Curwood's *Nomads of the North,* and Jack London. By the time his leg had healed, there was no place that he couldn't travel, if he could only locate the right book. Fifteen years later, Dad contracted tuberculosis and sat out World War II. He was expected to die, but stubbornly pulled through. Part of the cure was the hospital library, his one ticket beyond the terminal ward. During those three years in the TB sanatorium, my father pored over the day's newspapers and scoured the popular magazines and pulps—*Life, Collier's, Black Mask* (the last then filled with the fledgling stories of Chandler and Hammett); he read all of Upton Sinclair and Sinclair Lewis and whatever Zane Grey, Edgar Rice Burroughs, or Jack London he hadn't yet mastered—and finally, those volumes of history, social theory, and mythology crammed into Wolf Larsen's shipboard bookshelf. Like the star-roving convict of his favorite London fantasy, my father saw once again that there was a world swung open to him like a castle gate that he might enter whenever the demands of his working life temporarily receded.

But while experience showed him that reading was good for a workingman, he still had to wonder what purpose it served?

Books were finally the province of people who didn't have to work for a living, an unthinkable circumstance for him. By "work," I mean—and he meant—work hard, until you *sweat.* My father had justified his entire life through labor, working with his hands. I remember as a child touching his hands—that fleshy, familiar pair of weathered work gloves. I ran my small fingers along their cracked-dry rivulets, drawing circles around the calloused peaks. Lizard skin. Leather. Hands may not record the full measure of a life, but they contain crucial data on how each day is consumed. Hands marking time like toppled tree trunks, ring after ring. One way or another, all the men in my family earned a living with their hands.

Until I came along.

From the San Francisco side of the bay, Oakland is barely visible, a grey miniature settled upon the flat water. San Francisco has always played Emerald City to Oakland's Kansas, with the Bay Bridge spanning the distinction. But for people far from either place, the winning city is not always obvious.

After the 1906 earthquake, tent cities sprang up in every park, and hot food stations were hammered together out of canvas and boards on street corners, ladling out bowls of Irish stew, bread and tea to the refugees. A sign over one station read: "Eat, Drink and Be Merry, for Tomorrow we may have to go to Oakland." Another person asked why San Francisco had been destroyed while Oakland was intact. "There are some things even the earth won't swallow," came the reply.

—David Siefkin, The City at the End of the Rainbow: San Francisco and Its Grand Hotels

A few years ago, my friend Mitchell met some young Russians in Vienna who were fanning out through Europe at the first break of *perestroika*. When the Russians quizzed my friend about his home in America, Mitchell explained that he hailed from the nation's most beautiful city—San Francisco.

"San Francisco," pondered one Russian. "Is that anywhere near Oakland?"

"Well, yes," answered Mitchell, "it's right across the bay. But most people usually think that San Francisco is really—"

"*Oakland!*" the Russian exclaimed rapturously, "I have heard about it all my life. I would love to see Oakland some day before I die. Please," he whispered into Mitchell's ear with a hush of wonderous expectation, "*tell me all about Oakland!*"

For decades, Jack London was the most widely read American author in the Soviet Union. (Will this still be true as the cult of the worker dissolves into the vagaries of the marketplace?) Trotsky proclaimed London a prophet superior to Rosa Luxemburg. As Lenin was dying, his wife, Krupskaya, read aloud Jack London's short story "Love of Life," the terrifying tale of a lost and starving prospector who drags himself across the Arctic tundra, wrestles to the death a lone sick wolf and finally, somehow, survives.

Though often sentimental in the brooding Russian fashion, London is still the spokesman for the quintessential American port town—tough, prevailing, desperate enough to assume the risks of the indifferent ocean.

"Oakland is the best city," I proclaimed to my father, as our ferry approached San Francisco. The salt air was rank and cold, the sky rolled down like a grey curtain.

"I can't see why you even live there," said Dad, now the complete suburbanite. He had never romanticized city life, and now he read newspaper accounts daily of Oakland's crime and decay—so why try to fool him?

"Home of the Hell's Angels," I insisted, "birthplace of the Black Panthers. We've got a pretty good baseball team, too. Oakland is better than San Francisco because San Francisco is much too exceptional." It was the usual second-city argument, erected upon a bedrock of sophistry. But even as I uttered these words—Oakland as paradise, rather than as eyesore—they sounded ridiculous. It was childish comfort that I drew by arguing that I fit better than my father in Jack London's city.

"Personally," insisted Dad, a master of contrariness, "I wouldn't mind seeing the whole place burn down. Probably will."

In the nineteenth century, blacks who lived in the city center for convenience's sake often used the pastoral East Bay for excursions and picnics. As early as 1880 nearly six hundred Afro-Americans lived in Oakland, constituting the second-largest group of black city dwellers in the state. Oakland's rustic character disappeared during the economic boom of the 1890s, but the city retained a decidedly suburban atmosphere and, characteristically, a lower population density than San Francisco. The East Bay's proximity, suburban character, expanding economy, cheaper rents, and larger homes accounted for the more than 8,000 Afro-Americans in Oakland and more than 3,000 in Berkeley by World War II. The black migration to the East Bay in the 1890s also followed the rise of the white labor unions that excluded blacks from their traditional positions. Afro-Americans found jobs quite readily on the trains which terminated in Oakland; as these positions were reserved for blacks, discrimination forced them to adapt to new trends while whites stayed in San Francisco.

—Douglas Henry Daniels, *Pioneer Urbanites: A Social and Cultural History of Black San Francisco*

When I was in my early twenties, I argued with similar contrariness that I should be counted as one of my family's workingmen. I was finishing college, and, between dropping in and dropping out, I took the usual laboring jobs then available to skill-less young men, imagining that some brief tenure inside a factory or warehouse would entitle me to retain the language of my family. At Christmas we'd all gather around the dinner table, carve the turkey, drink the good bourbon, and chat up the classic working-class family concerns. There would be talk of overtime and RIF's, mandatory graveyard and swing shift, bonuses and layoffs—and then, as the best bourbon welled up and overflowed into early evening resentment, somebody would defiantly assert that the country would never be fit until working people trimmed the excesses of the rich, even if it meant plucking the rich out of their homes in the hills by the sharp creases of their starched collars. It always boiled down to what you could accomplish with your own hands.

But I didn't work with my hands. Or at least, I wouldn't be working with my hands forever, which everybody at the table except me understood.

My own home was becoming exotic. I wasn't working class. I'd only grown up there.

And although my father and I might read the same books, finding some momentary agreement in the real and imagined adventures of other men, we could never read these books in precisely the same way. This is one of the fundamental sorrows of fathers and sons whose lives must diverge once they continue past the point of intersection.

Yet how I longed to belong there, amid the comfort of hard work and bitterness—and how much more desperately I wanted to escape.

During these years—my mid-twenties, Dad's early sixties—it seemed the only books that my father and I could honestly share were the torn and grease-spattered repair manuals that governed our wheezing old automobiles. How many hours did we spend together fixing the family cars—two hundred, five hundred, one thousand? One of us would buy another clunker, and then we'd struggle to repair it in Dad's garage over the noise of sputtering engines and our own breathy curses.

"What do you think?" I'd ask my father, after pulling my old wreck of an ancient Dodge station wagon into his driveway for the ritual tune-up. "Well, I can say this. It's a heap."

"Four wheels," I argued. "Good spare in the trunk. So far, she starts right up on a cold morning."

"Well," said Dad, "we'll see."

I would pop the hood, and he'd sink his scarred hands into the heart of the machine, twisting, tightening, demanding a small tool whose name I could never remember, and with one arm jutting out from underneath the engine, he would fiddle with all of the car's hidden imperfections. When he finished, he'd glide over to the wash basin, cleaning himself by rote with a tub of lanolin soap, hand over hand over hand.

"I forget," I asked, eager to prolong the encounter. "How do you set the timing exact if the crankshaft pulley isn't marked?"

Grease and suds of creamy lanolin ran down my father's overalls and splashed across the concrete floor.

"There's always going to be some kind of mark on the crankshaft pulley," he instructed. "A notch, a light groove, something. Right?"

"Right."

"So what you do is take a tape and measure your pulley's diameter, then multiply that by the number of degrees advance setting that your service manual recommends. Does that make sense to you?"

I nodded.

"You got to know that. If you're really interested in getting it exact, you got to have some basic information. And you can't be lazy about looking it up," he insisted. "If you got the book, you got to look it up."

"And so that gives you the number of inches that you turn the crankshaft from Top Dead Center."

"Correct."

Public confidence in modern bridges was shaken when a section of San Francisco's Bay Bridge broke during the earthquake of October 17, 1989. The bridge is now solidly repaired, freshly painted, resurfaced and, to judge by the traffic jams, public confidence is ebbing back. But just to be sure—as protection against future peril from an unkind providence—the Bay Bridge now has a secret talisman: its own troll.

Welded on to the last section of steel added in the repairs, beneath the roadway in a place where only maintenance workers and pigeons can see it, is an eighteen-inch high, wrought-iron man-beast, with horned head and webbed feet. Its (his?) purpose, say the craftsmen who contrived it, is to ward off evil spirits and nature's havoc. It is an artist's bid for safety in that mysterious realm that lies beyond engineering competence.

—Economist,
"Californian Idolatry"

There is really very little that needs to be said about the malfunctioning and repair of automobiles, yet throughout these years we seemed to say it all—shoptalk being the only talk.

And then, quite suddenly, I found that my car had lost much of its usefulness—at least, I couldn't use it to get myself out of Oakland. It wasn't that the car no longer worked; we kept it running just fine. Rather, one day in my midtwenties I simply woke up stoneterrified to drive my old clunker, or anybody's car, over bridges. A great unreasonable fear, a phobia. In particular, when I crossed the Bay Bridge to San Francisco, my hands froze around the steering wheel, I flushed with cold sweat and my heart pounded like two fists beating against the inside of my chest trying to get out. It was silly, humiliating, inexplicable.

But the symbolism couldn't have been more obvious. In the San Francisco Bay Area—Oakland especially—if you don't cross bridges, there isn't any place to go. I was stuck one place, unable to cross over. It's not that I needed to give up Oakland for San Francisco (I really preferred the East Bay, I did!), but I required mobility. I was yearning for the larger world beyond my family—and yet languishing for want of the simple courage to navigate over bridges that were less concrete and iron than incomplete aspirations and misfired starts.

As a boy, Jack London found the route to his new life on the ocean. He sailed off from Oakland with the oyster pirates, through the Golden Gate as a ship's mate, prospector, and adventurer; and he returned home sufficiently swept away from his roots to remake himself into a writer. Upon the bow of his own ship—as a boy, his cherished *Dazzler*, as the wealthy author, the illustrious and doomed *Snark*—he faced the mouth of the Pacific, invigorated by its wind-snap cold and inscrutable opportunities. The Golden Gate could lead anywhere; there was no swifter, stronger, more perilous current any place between the West Coast and Japan. Like every young romantic, Jack London understood in his blood that the ocean could destroy him or fashion him into something entirely unexpected—and it did both. London was drawn to oblivion. He wanted to erase his life, wash away the past. And yet that was an impossible task. He would always cling to what he had been.

"While I cultivate new classes," London once told a friend, "I hate to be out of grip with the old."

As the ferry hitched up to the dock, Dad and I watched the passengers bumble down the gangplank, draining the boat like an empty wine bottle. Everybody was scurrying off to work, except us. Dad didn't want to get off.

"Why should we?" he demanded. "We don't have to go anywhere. We can just pay our way and go back."

"You mean you want to turn around and go home?"

"Well, we came from the ocean, didn't we? I want to see more of it."

We stood at the bow, silently inspecting the rest of the bay. To the west, Alcatraz and Angel Island were merely peaks in the fog. The ferry's engine started up again for the return trip, and Dad pointed out to me that Marin had vanished entirely.

We passed under the Bay Bridge like a dream.

It took me several years to drive fearlessly over bridges, though even now I'll occasionally feel the electric twinge of recollected

anxiety as my car rolls toward the crest of the Bay Bridge's can-
tilever, and the magnificent prospect of San Francisco breaks into
view like an ivory wave. It simply took time. By the end of my
twenties, I had fallen in love and made new friends, but most of all
I'd embarked upon life as an adult by working each day in ways that
nobody could mistake for my father's workingman's life, ways that
even—do I dare say this?—*aspired* to be middle class.

It would be attractive to say that my own working life is now at
bottom no different, certainly, no better, than my father's work history, but I know otherwise. The freedom of one generation is purchased by another's labor, and it would be a sin to disregard any
improvements, and therefore, the sacrifice. My father's life and
mine are not interchangeable, and I'll always mourn the distance
between them. But in truth, I can now only imagine the distance.

As we rode the ferry back to Oakland, lurching into a tailwind
and sailing straight into a perfect day, I felt once again the exhila-
ration of crossing the bay, and I was thankful for this watery con-
nective tissue that would always bind together our worlds. In the
distance, Oakland's downtown offices shone dully, like blocks of
chalk, and the wind roared us back home.

"Do you feel like you've seen enough of the world?" I asked my
father upon the windy bow of the ferry. Oakland's skies were sheer
blue, rippling with the rainbow effluence of its industrial breeze.

"Of course not," he said, "I hardly got started."

"Then where would you still like to go? You can go anywhere
from here," I reminded him.

"No place," he said. "You go."

San Francisco blew at our backs—and the working people of
the East Bay that Jack London had known, and my father had
labored among, and I had left, slowly drew into view. They bustled
together, swirling into the city's marvelous hodge-podge, living the
adventures that somebody else was now preparing to tell.

*Fred Setterberg was born in San Francisco, which he considers quite a big deal—
although he currently resides in Oakland. His book,* The Roads Taken: Travels
Through America's Literary Landscapes, *from which this story was excerpted,*

won the Associated Writing Program's 1992 award in creative nonfiction. When not writing about one side of the bay or the other, he spends his time reading and collecting material as the editor of the upcoming Travelers' Tales USA.

★

You ask me why I live in the grey hills.
I smile but do not answer, for my thoughts are elsewhere.
Like peach petals carried by the stream, they have gone
To other climates, to countries other than the world of men.

—Li Po

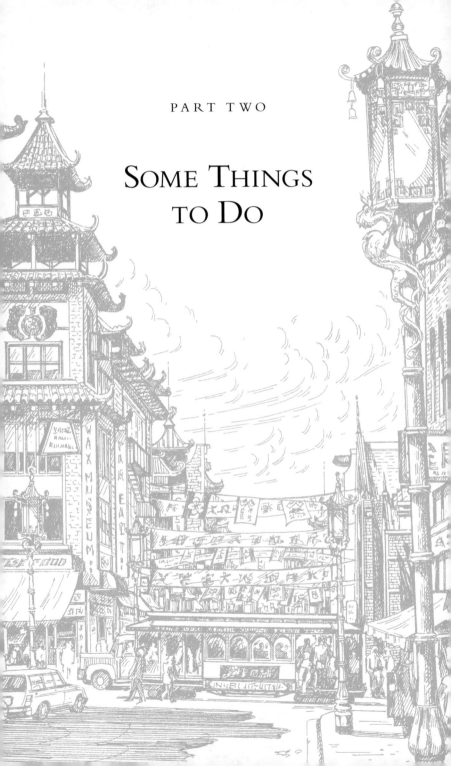

PART TWO

SOME THINGS TO DO

SUSANNA LEVIN

* * *

Night Skates

The author explores the country's premier paved ski resort.

WHEN YOU LIVE IN THE CITY, IT'S EASY TO FEEL TRAPPED: EITHER you're indoors, or you're on the street. Stepping out of an apartment building onto dirty pavement isn't usually described as "going outdoors."

This is especially true if, like me, you're the kind of person who thrives on outdoor sports, and particularly the so-called action sports, like skiing and rock climbing, where your life depends on your ability to control your body through the dimensions of time and space. The thrill-seeking city dweller has to *go to* the outdoors by car or by plane. And so the outdoors becomes a distant abstraction, a temptation, a source of self-torment.

I recently discovered that it's foolish to make such a distinction between the wild outdoors and the urban outdoors. In the process, I discovered an action sport that was made for the urban environment, for *my* urban environment—San Francisco. Now, I get my outdoor ya-yas, risking my neck and overloading my senses, in the ozone-choked air of city streets. I do it on skates, after dark.

Taking to the streets at night with an eclectic assortment of people on in-line skates (also known as Rollerblades), I experience time slowing down. I have always associated this sensation with playing in the great outdoors—dropping into a chute on skis, for example, or descending single track on a mountain bike. My ears and eyes plug directly into my motor neurons and go on high-level alert.

The night is the crucial element in this transformation. For high-speed nocturnal navigation on skates, visual processing is secondary to kinesthetics and proprioception: you rely on your body's sense of where you are and where you're going: you continuously react to terrain and gravity in an effort to remain upright and under control. Where you are on earth is much less important than where you are in space.

Of course, on earth I am in a city, yes, but it's also the country's premier paved ski resort, with an endless supply of double black-diamond runs and near-perfect conditions year-round.

Night skating didn't always strike me as a great idea. When I first started skating, I stuck to the relative safety of Golden Gate Park and broad daylight. It seemed like a winning combination. I'd heard about the night skate, and it sounded scary. The thought of contending with cars, trucks, and potholes, not to mention the hills, seemed far beyond me. Skating from Golden Gate Park to downtown was just absurd: not only was there a 300-foot elevation loss between here and there, but downtown had buses and taxis and Muni tracks and lost tourists, faking left and then turning right across three lanes of traffic. All of this, in the dark of the night.

Then one Sunday, at a local skate race in the Park, I met Jenny, a night skater who turned out to be a friend of an old friend. Jenny was a better skater than I was, but she wasn't *that* much better. Maybe it was just stupid competitiveness, but I figured if she could do the night skate, it wasn't a total impossibility. Besides, I immediately liked and trusted Jenny. She was enthusiastic and reassuring; she made the night skate sound like something fun, not some keep-up-or-die hammerfest around the city. I agreed to come out the following Tuesday night.

Of course, one better offer for Tuesday night and I would have bagged in a minute. But no excuses arose, and at seven on Tuesday I turned up at "skate central" in Golden Gate Park. It was an uncharacteristically warm, bright spring evening in San Francisco; both the fog and the wind had the night off. The days were lengthening, so it was still light when I arrived. A few skaters were already gathered and, to my enormous relief, Jenny was among them. As I rolled up, she was pulling a couple of lacrosse sticks and a ball from the back of her truck, and we started up a game of roller-lacrosse as we waited for more night riders.

I was immediately self-conscious. Roller-lacrosse was giving people the chance to demonstrate their ability to stop, turn on a dime, and jump, while I could only roll around in wide-radius arcs, at a single speed.

Skaters, on ice or pavement, are divided into only two categories: the balanced and the unbalanced. Either you are in control of your edges, and you glide with effortless, elegant grace, or you are at their mercy, prone to intermittent spastic contortions when they betray you. I was unbalanced. If I didn't try anything too tricky, I could pass, but in fact, I was too worried about looking like a dork to experiment and learn to skate backwards and do quick spin-stops. As with many sports, to gain control, you have to be willing to give it up.

Other new sports activities have cropped up in San Francisco in recent years, including an indoor roller hockey rink off 3rd Street, a golf driving range off 6th Street—both in the former industrial area south of Market Street—and an indoor cliff-climbing gym on Harrison Street in the Mission.

—JO'R, LH, and SO'R

Skaters slowly turned up. At seven-thirty, there were seven of us. I recognized most faces from around the park, but Jenny and a local racer named Mike were the only two I knew by name. Judging from the preponderance of racing skates and the sinewy legs that sprouted from them, it was a hard-core group.

The group convened. "Where should we go?" someone asked.

"Downtown," another replied.

Although this would not always be the case, on this night there was no dissent.

"Which way?"

"Let's go Golden Gate."

Helmets were adjusted (I was the only person wearing knee pads, but everyone had wrists guards and most had helmets) and a few of us turned on flashing red lights that were attached to our helmets. (I had one of these. In fact, I had every piece of protection except a condom.)

We skated out of the park and onto Fulton Street. The pack was immediately in the road and, since the sidewalk was rough and cracked, I soon joined them. As we snaked through the streets north of Fulton, I felt surprisingly safe. There were hardly any cars, and the heft of a seven-skater pack seem to justify occupying the road. Connect the dots, and we're big as a truck.

I was a little concerned that we were going *uphill*. Every additional foot of altitude we gained, we were going to have to lose. This, I supposed, was the whole point.

Within a couple of minutes, we were at the top of Golden Gate Avenue, on Lone Mountain near the University of San Francisco. From there, Golden Gate runs east, away from the park, toward the Civic Center and downtown. As is so often the case on skates, I began to appreciate nuances of this city's topography that had eluded me before. Only the Golden Gate hill isn't really a nuance: it's a fucking ski jump, plummeting over 300 feet.

As the group assembled at the crest of the first steep section of the street, I didn't really have time to think about whether or not this was a very good idea, or even possible. Had I been by myself, however, I never would have dreamed of attempting it.

Mike, a shy, somewhat awkward guy in his early twenties, had some words of advice for me. Mike looked like he wouldn't be caught dead on a dance floor, but with skates on, he was a regular Nureyev. It was the Zen master's blend of skill and brevity that made me hang on his every word. "The lights are timed," he told me. "When this next one turns red, count to ten and then go."

"All the way to the bottom?" I asked.

"All the way. But cut it loose or you won't make it."

Whatever you say, Mike. I'm putting my life in your hands. The light turned, and Mike bowed his head, giving a slow nod for each integer…nod eight,…nod nine,… "Go!" he yelled, and he went.

Then I went, lemming-like. Mike got into a tuck and so did I. A guy named Chris shot past me, a light brown blur, but then no one else. Was everybody bombing this stretch, I suddenly wondered, or was I out front with the suicides while everybody else took the pro-life route?

The first light changed a few seconds before we reached it, just as Mike predicted. Just to be on the safe side, Chris let out an authentic-sounding police siren whoop as we entered the intersection. (That sound would become the clarion call of the night skate, and my first few times out he fooled me about half the time. Every time Chris shot through an intersection, I'd turn around to see where the cops were.)

> *We closed up shop in our little Sam Spade-like office in the Sentinel Building, and wedged ourselves into the even smaller elevator. It was occupied by a handsome, exotically dressed man who looked vaguely familiar. As we assumed the posture and gaze of elevator riders everywhere, peripheral vision announced his identity: it was Nureyev! He must have been upstairs visiting Francis Ford Coppola on some movie business.*
>
> —James O'Reilly and Larry Habegger, "House of Cards on the Barbary Coast"

All my weight was in my feet. I remember looking down to see my skates tracking straight, taking comfort in their solidity. We hit that light at full speed, and then the next, and the next—with two heartbeats of apprehension verging on panic before each light blinked from red to green.

Below Divisadero, the street turns into a three-lane one-way. Mike, Chris, and I occupied the right lane leaving plenty of room in the two remaining lanes for cars. I was faintly surprised that no one honked at us, but traffic was light, and we were moving faster than they were anyway.

It wasn't quite dark as we buzzed through the projects near Buchanan Street: the air was still rich with the purple light that lingers in the San Francisco sky after sunset on a bright day. A certain part of my brain was assigned to vigilance: watching the lights, listening for cars, scanning the ground for those built-in reflective lane markers, which at that speed were like little tombstones. Most of my consciousness, however, was awash in something much more potent than adrenaline: I was having the kind of rush you only get when you're doing something really fun, really stupid, and illegal.

A Beastie Boys song came into my head. It was the perfect soundtrack: adolescent. Aggro. While screaming downhill on in-line skates at 30 miles an hour may not be an obvious time for insight, I was struck by my pleasure at behaving like an insubordinate thirteen-year-old. It was a Peter Pan thing, and I *was* flying.

We sawed old metal roller skates in half and nailed them to a two-foot piece of wood to fashion primitive skateboards. Once we learned how to use them, we plunged straight down gigantic San Francisco hills, sparks flying, having already posted friends in intersections to warn of the approach of certain death. We were amazed one day when an older surfer friend (he must have been all of sixteen) showed up with a board that actually had rubber wheels. The future was upon us.

—James, Sean, and Tim O'Reilly, "Boys in the Avenues"

We crossed six lanes of traffic on Van Ness, just beating the light, and blew by Stars, where I drink scotch in another life. As we descended into the piss of the Tenderloin, screaming past the crack dealers and prostitutes, I recognized the practical advantages of speed.

The Golden Gate roller-coaster finally bottomed out at Market Street, in the heart of downtown. Half the pack had fallen behind the lights, so we waited in silence for them to catch up. I figured out later that it had taken us five minutes, maybe less, to cover two miles: that's better than twenty-four miles per hour. It was now almost completely dark, and my self-consciousness of the roller-lacrosse game was gone. Yeah, I might not be able to skate backward, but I've always been good at speed.

We skated a mile or so to Embarcadero Center, a downtown, open-air shopping mall and office complex with numerous architectural invitations to skaters and skateboarders. One of these is a glass-walled, paved, spiral walkway in the center of a square courtyard. The walkway, which is about ten feet wide, does three rotations as it winds down from the third floor to ground level.

I had never done any trick skating, but out of sheer pack mindlessness, I followed everyone up the spiral.

Up is easy.

Down, however, calls for a series of tight turns at ever accelerating speeds and, (the hard part), the ability to stop when centrifugal force flings you out at the bottom.

A guy named Nick went first. Tall and barrel-chested, with longish black hair feathering down his neck, Nick was the only skater I suspected was older than me. But his style and his relish for radical jumps, said *pueri eternis*. Nick took the spiral fast, finishing with a skidding power-slide that stopped him just short of a group of wide-eyed tourists.

I watched a couple of other skaters do the spiral; a few zipped through it like Nick, others went more slowly; somebody grabbed the rail. It reminded me of wreaking havoc in another urban playground—lower Manhattan—when I was a kid visiting my cousin. We would slide down the escalator banisters and scale the aluminum sculptures that were Wall Street's public art.

No one was looking by the time I came down the spiral. I made it through the first loop okay, but then I got spooked by my speed. There was an opening in the railing onto the second floor, and I shot through it, only to discover I was heading straight for the plate-glass window of Ann Taylor.

I made a sharp right turn to miss the window, then applied the brake and skidded to a stop. No problem. I looked around and, comforted by the fact that no one had seen my dorky little detour, I got back on the spiral and rode the railing the rest of the way down.

We left the Embarcadero, and headed back uptown on Market Street, San Francisco's main drag. It's a strange place to be at night—so strange, in fact, that nobody really seemed to notice a pack of skaters flying down the sidewalk and leaping over benches. Now and again someone would look at me through bleary eyes, and say, "Hey…" I had the distinct feeling that they were not completely convinced I was really there.

Mike and Nick were leading, and after a few blocks they pulled up at the entrance to the Montgomery station of BART, San Francisco's subway.

"Let's do it," Chris said. Augie, a lean guy with dark skin and thick black hair, who'd been smiling since we left the park, suddenly got serious. "I'm not going," he said.

The others started down the stairs into the subway, then stopped. "C'mon man, let's go," Mike said.

Augie just skated off, saying he'd meet us at the exit. I followed down the stairs—taking them skater style: walking backward, holding the rail. I was not particularly psyched about our imminent transgression. Skaters have been banned from the streets in a few cities around the country, and this kind of sortie seemed just the thing to make trouble in this town.

It was about nine, and the BART station was empty. It didn't take long for me to see why we were here. In these quarter-mile-long underground walkways, with their linoleum smooth as butter, there's no resistance to our urethane wheels. It's like the Bonneville Speedway of skating—surreal, like the Utah salt flats, and irresistible for speed freaks. With just a few strokes I was flying through the fluorescence, whipping by ads for shoes and shopping centers.

As we neared the end of the first section of tunnel, a disembodied voice buzzed over a loudspeaker. "No skating in the station. Exit the station immediately. There is no skating in the station." The voice faded as we rolled down the next section of walkway, whizzing under a city block in about seven seconds. At the end of that stretch, a second loudspeaker hissed at us, this one a little more insistent: "No skates allowed in the station. Take off your skates or get out of the station."

There was something comical about blowing by these finger-wavers in their little booths, one after another, but I was relieved when we hopped on the escalator and headed out of the station. I didn't mind being bad, I realized, but I didn't want to get called on it.

I was trying to figure out whether skating in a BART station was a misdemeanor or not, when I understood why Augie stayed above ground. He was probably not an American citizen. Getting busted, even for a misdemeanor, could be catastrophic for him. When the rest of the group descended the stairs to skate another stretch in the next BART station, I skated the street above with Augie.

The pack emerged from the underground back at the Civic Center; from there, it's a long, steady climb on Market to Church Street, in the Castro district. The lead skaters formed a pace line, tucked in tightly one behind the other. Like cyclists, skaters can work together to cut the wind and increase their speed this way, but I hung back, unsure of my ability to stroke in synchrony.

At Church, we turned right and started zigzagging through the streets of the Lower Haight, past the slacker cafes and nightspots. The terrain suddenly got much steeper; again, we were on streets that I travel everyday but had never imagined skating. On a particularly steep stretch of Steiner Street, Augie skated up behind me and pushed me up the hill. My ego, which sometimes overvalues self-sufficiency, was tweaked, but my legs told me to be grateful.

When we turned left again, Page Street loomed monstrously between us and home. It was steep and five times the length of the stretch I'd just struggled up. All of a sudden, it felt way past my bedtime. Halfway up the first of three blocks of serious climbing, I realized how ill-suited the tools were to the purpose. When it's steep, you don't skate so much as run up the hill, in short choppy steps. In the space of three blocks, Chris and Mike had picked up about 200 yards on me; Jenny and Augie were not far behind them.

By the time we zigged back onto the relative flatness of upper Haight Street, I was sucking wind big-time. I chased the other four through the Haight-Ashbury in overdrive, never quite getting my breath back. Once at the park, the group dispersed quickly; I hardly had time to say good-bye, and thanks. I skated the short distance home by myself.

When I arrived at my house, I was still breathing hard from the chase up Haight. It was after eleven, and tired as I was, sleep was out of the question. All the brain chemicals that had me pumped up like that were a long way from quieting down. But this wasn't the kind of feeling I have after a good long run in the park or even a bike ride on Mount Tam. This was a complete release. I felt like I had been to another planet, and maybe the night is another world, as different from daytime as country is from city.

In the months that followed, I became a regular on the night skate. I eagerly looked forward to Tuesday nights. Jenny, Mike, and Augie were always there. Ingrid, a lifelong skater whom I'd always admired, started coming out again after the birth of her first child.

I looked forward to seeing all of them and to chasing them up and down hills and along the flats. More than that, though, I looked forward to being out in the night air, and visiting those parts of this city that in the daytime are sacrificed to tourists and other residents.

Our route often took us along Pier 39, where we'd stop and rest. The Golden Gate Bridge glowed in the distance, and beyond Alcatraz, the lights of Sausalito hovered just above the water. Boats floated by, and sea lions sprawled on the docks below. Big, blubbery sighs and random barks drifted up from the dark. Sometimes we'd go from there to Chinatown, where the pavement was always slick with something, maybe duck fat.

I started seeing the city differently. I began to know where it is quiet at night and where it hums; where it is cool and where the warm lingers. Parts of town that I once avoided because they were congested or boring became my favorites because there's a hill that's just the right grade or fresh pavement or timed lights.

After I started skating the streets at night, I noticed I could go for weeks without feeling that desperate urge to escape the city. I still craved the solitude, quiet and timelessness that you have to get out of the city to get. But I didn't resent the fact that 90 percent of my life was spent on asphalt, because the pavement became my medium.

In fact, when I went to the mountains, I started telling people they should come to the city and skate with me. Of course, they looked at me as if I were suggesting a new career as a crash-test dummy. But I was caught up in the wild, glorious rush of it all; I was in that state where the danger was part of the thrill, but I hadn't yet learned real respect for it.

That all changed one night, some months after my first skate, when fourteen of us set our sights on the city skater's crowning achievement: Twin Peaks, San Francisco's 900-foot apex.

We left the park and went first to the beach, making for a brutally long climb from sea level. The road to the viewing area parking lot is so steep that in some stretches our locomotion was more like duckwalking than skating.

It was a spectacularly clear night, and the view from the top is 360 degrees: from the black Pacific, identifiable only by the twinkling lights of ships in the distance, to the Golden Gate and its Bridge, to the Marin Headlands across the bay, to the pulsing lights of downtown, and east, to Oakland. That is San Francisco: an unending, glowing, buzz of life in one direction, and in the other, total darkness.

On top of Twin Peaks, I got to ask myself, again, a question I remember puzzling over when I was about six, at the top of a very tall tree. Why is it so damn easy to climb up to places from which you cannot get down?

The road that descends from the parking lot spirals around the perimeter of the mountain. As you descend the road, you start facing north, then west, south, and east. On the west side of the mountain, the air is cold, straight off the Pacific. On the city side, it's warm. Leaving aside these microclimatic oddities, the trip

I like the way the wind whips your skirts when you go by cable car up Nob Hill. I like the salt spray in your face when the surf breaks on the rocks at Fort Point. I like the white waves the ferryboats leave as they ply the bay, to the Oakland mole. I like the seals barking on the rocks at the Cliff House. I like the fog rolling over St. Francis Wood. I like the trolleys racing each other down Market Street's four tracks. I like the Irish cops and the Italian flower vendors. I just like San Francisco, I guess.

—Rita Hayworth

down this completely unlit, poorly-paved road is a virtual freefall. Compared to Twin Peaks, the spiral walkway at the Embarcadero Center was a merry-go-round. And here, there's no way to get off.

Keith, my guardian angel on this particular evening, skated with me. I kept my knees loose, to absorb unexpected ruts, and like a blind person, I followed Keith's instruction for each stretch of terrain:

"Around this bend, stand up and let the head wind slow you," he shouted. It slowed me.

Then, "Take a right at the bottom of this stretch for an uphill run-out." Worked like a charm.

With his help, I reached the bottom without incident, but as it turned out, I had precious little time to savor my accomplishment. We headed back to the park through the Sunset District, a basically flat section of town. There are a couple of big hills out there, but I didn't think we were near them. I was almost home and feeling pretty good, so I let down my guard.

I followed everyone down a block of 18th Avenue that has a slight downhill grade, but nothing major. I had a good head of steam as I entered the intersection, and I was over the lip onto the next block before I saw what lay ahead: the street suddenly got very steep—about the pitch of an escalator—and I was out of control instantly. I tried to do some slalom turns to lose speed, but I kept accelerating. In my peripheral vision, I could see houses and parked cars rushing by in blurry darkness. I went for my heel brake, but I was too late—it doesn't work at twenty miles an hour.

I looked up to see Ingrid, my skating idol, slaloming across the hill in front of me, completely in control. I shouted something, "Watch out," or "On your right," then I shot past her, almost taking her down. "Sorry!" I yelled back, feeling like the total idiot I was.

There was hardly time for self-deprecation though, as the emerging details of the next intersection revealed to me that I was in deep trouble: I had a stop sign. The cross-traffic didn't. There were headlights coming from the left. My only chance was to make a sharp right turn, going with the flow of traffic, and trying to stay close to the curb. Then I saw the streetcar tracks, lying like twin vipers in the road.

I probably could have made the turn, but my brain overloaded and I bailed, taking a semi-controlled, hard, sliding fall onto my right side. My protective gear did its job: the wrist guards absorbed the brunt of the impact, and the plastic on my knee pads grated along the pavement. I could hear the hollow scraping of plastic on blacktop as my knee pad sacrificed its outer layer to save mine. My thigh wasn't so lucky.

I hopped up and onto the sidewalk quickly, helped by my momentum, which never really stopped. Humiliated and disgusted with myself, and hoping to minimize the attention given my fall, I made a big show of being okay. In fact, I was sure I hadn't broken anything, but my right thigh felt like chopped meat.

Keith skated over to see how I was, but my quick hop up and the lack of visible blood was convincing. The rest of the pack continued on, and I limp-rolled the final half mile home. The thrill comes from the risk, but sometimes the risk turns on you and bites.

The honeymoon was over; I couldn't sit comfortably for a week. After my road rash healed, I went through a period of overly cautious skating. I enjoyed myself a lot less and mourned the loss of the ignorant's euphoria. I took a second, minor fall a few weeks later precisely because I was being too cautious: while trying unnecessarily to scrub some speed with slalom turns, I hit a patch of wet pavement and went down.

On a more practical level, though, I worked on control. I learned to carve better slalom turns and to T-stop by dragging one foot behind me, which is more effective than the heel brake. Gradually, my new and improved skating ability revived both my nerve and my pleasure.

Meanwhile, the night skate started to grow, fed by the booming popularity of in-line skates. Fourteen skaters soon became thirty; then thirty ballooned to sixty and sixty mushroomed to one hundred and forty. Dozens and dozens of skaters, not all of them very skilled, now hit the streets of San Francisco every Friday night. I join them occasionally.

For me, the allure of the skate is dimmed by sheer numbers—it's more of a parade than a sortie. What's worse is that to accommodate newcomers, the skate follows the same route every night. There's no more exploring, and to prevent massive carnage, Golden Gate Avenue and Twin Peaks are out.

Fortunately, about the same time, I discovered that if the terrain is radical enough, you can have a pretty good time in broad daylight. Jenny and Mike turned me on to the downhill terrain on

Tunnel Road, in the hills above Oakland. The area has been deserted since the great blazes of '91, so the roads are mostly empty.

What this skate lacks in nocturnal otherworldliness, it makes up for in sheer, protracted, mind-numbing speed. It's about five miles up, and then five miles full-steam downhill. It's safe because with all the trees burned down, you can see ahead for oncoming cars or cyclists around every curve. Here, in this devastated area where wildfire leveled urban habitat, I found the city skater's paradise. I went there nearly every weekend during the winter.

When ski season rolled around, I noticed an extraordinary change in myself. When I went to the mountains to ski, I didn't feel the old streak of longing, the sense that every day I spent back in the city I was missing out on the best life had to offer. As long as I had Tunnel Road, I didn't have to wake up every single morning and talk myself out of blowing off work and heading for the hills.

This is a good thing, because for now I am where I am. And for now, I'll find the thrill of the outdoors where urethane meets pavement.

Susanna Levin is an outdoor writer whose work has appeared in Outside *magazine. She lives in Portland, Oregon, where she is taking a sabbatical from writing to pursue her lifelong dream of being a middle manager at a big company. She still travels (on the company's dime) and writes in her spare time. This story was excerpted from* Another Wilderness: New Outdoor Writing by Women, *edited by Susan Fox Rogers.*

✳

After a long day at Camp Rollerblade, I pack up and head back along the two-lane highway that winds through Sonoma Valley, amongst misty hills, gnarly oaks, and immaculately laid-out vineyards. At one of the smaller wineries, I buy a glass of excellent merlot and sit outside in the slanting orange sunlight, thinking about the day's accomplishments.

I'm 44 years old and skating like a kid. In other words, I'm doing things I never dreamed of doing when I was younger. When I was growing up, in Texas and the South, sports were not for "feminine" girls. The closest I could come to sports was ballet. Now you can call me a "psycho neutron" (whatever, exactly, that is). Or you can call me a babe on blades. Or just a hell-for-leather in-line skater.

At 8:15 a.m., I'm sitting on a wooden bench in front of the vert ramp, wondering if this seeming metamorphosis is a trick of weather and light or if I've truly found my soul-sport. Over the past two-plus decades, since I've officially been a grown-up—or at least since I've shaken childhood notions of what being "feminine" means—I've tried every sport from rugby to scuba. But I've never felt my adrenaline pumping like I did yesterday.

No, I've never felt such a gut-wrenching, mind-bending rush. Not even under the ocean, dropping toward the abyss. Not even when, on the rugby field, I tackled a gal built like a freighter and scooped the ball to our wing, who scored the winning point.

The vert ramp has got to be the ultimate rush.

Odd thing is, I'm not nervous. A strange, almost Zen-like calm has settled over me. I look around at the other skaters, most of them finishing a breakfast of juice, coffee, and bagels from the big buffet table over on the ball field. My friends Sunny and Darlene have checked out, but Mike and his son are still here. So are the kids from Tokyo. Like me, the Tokyo kids are waiting for the vert ramp class to begin. And they're now addressing me as "dude." I love it. There are no age barriers any more. No cultural barriers. Not even language obstructs. It's the body that speaks, the muscles and sinews, and what it speaks of is the age-old urge to defy the laws of nature and propel the soul heavenward.

When the class begins, I study the other skaters. I watch the way they bend their knees, throw their weight forward, and pump up and down the ten-foot walls. My turn comes, and I coast onto the big contraption. Within minutes, I'm climbing and turning, inching faster toward the sheer top section where you abandon gravity and enter a world where speed meets physics and ultimately, perhaps, metaphysics. Simply put, it's the joy of finding yourself half-upside-down and completely fearless, the joy of knowing yourself in a way you've never known yourself before.

—Kathryn Marshall, "Call Me 'Dude,'"
Southwest Airlines Spirit Magazine

* * *

The Lost Roman
Baths of Adolph Sutro

Those who built San Francisco did not lack the vision thing.

SOME YEARS AGO, EXPLORING THE ROCKY SHORELINE NEAR THE Cliff House during an extraordinarily low tide, I clambered over a boulder just in time to escape an incoming breaker and found myself in a hidden cove facing what appeared to be the ruins of an ancient palace. It was Sutro Baths, for half a century one of San Francisco's prime recreation spots. Winds, waves, and vandals had broken nearly every one of the hundreds of panes of glass that faced the ocean. I walked across a beach left bare by the minus tide, scrambled up the sea wall, and peered inside.

The floor of the hangar-sized room was terraced back up the hillside, and on the lower levels were five empty swimming pools of various sizes and shapes. The long pool nearest the window was partly filled with sand where storm breakers had swept inside the building. In a sudden flashback, there came to me a recollection of the last time I had swum here many years earlier. The vast pavilion was filled with the shouts of hundreds of bathers and the music of Strauss waltzes. On the upper terraces, behind seats where thousands of spectators had once watched Duke Kahanamoku slice through the water for one hundred yards to set a new world's record, were acres of tropical vegetation, palms, big-leaved vines, exotic flowers, classic plaster statues and huge stuffed animals—all in delightful Victorian array.

The pools themselves were a wonder. You could plummet into the water from diving platforms up in the rafters; rocket into the pools down giddy slides that seemed to come down from the roof; whirl into the water from a carousel; swing out over the pools on trapeze-like rings attached to the ceiling. In memory, at least, these were pools to surpass the fabled spas of Europe and the Lucullan baths of the Roman emperors.

This aquatic magnificence was the final achievement of Adolph Sutro, an indomitable pioneer

Possibly the most obscure San Francisco song is "Holo Holo Kaa" as performed by Hawaiian entertainer Hilo Hattie, who claimed in 1965 the song was written by her grandmother after a ride in a San Francisco taxicab.

—Gladys Hansen, *San Francisco Almanac: Everything You Want to Know About Everyone's Favorite City*

and early mayor who left his mark in this vast natatorium; on the heights above, where he lived; and elsewhere in the city. In 1860, young Sutro, an immigrant from Europe, was a San Francisco storekeeper with a mighty dream. He wanted to build one of the greatest engineering projects ever attempted up to that time—a four-mile-long tunnel through a mountain to drain and provide better access to the fabulous silver mines of the Comstock Lode in Nevada.

But, to do so, he had to take on the Goliaths of the Comstock, William C. Ralston and William Sharon, whose Bank of California controlled the mines. His tunnel, they realized, would threaten their domination of the lode, and through their influence with Eastern banks they blocked his attempt to raise capital.

The turning point came when a disastrous fire swept through the mines and killed 45 men. During a two-hour oration to the embittered survivors in a mass meeting at the Virginia City Opera House, Sutro thundered his denunciation of Ralston and Sharon and their bank—"the vampires that have nearly sucked you dry."

The tunnel, he asserted, would have provided escape for the trapped miners, and he asked his audience to buy stock in the enterprise, "a cause," he roared, "which will make you the power of this land, make powerless your oppressors, and break up your arch enemy, the California Bank."

The miners shook the opera house with their roars of approval and lined up behind Sutro like the children of Israel behind Joshua at Jericho. With pledges from the miners as a beginning, later buttressed by British capital, Sutro was able to start work on the tunnel in 1869—a grueling struggle of man against mountain that culminated successfully, after innumerable setbacks, a decade later. Before he was finished, the Bank of California had collapsed; Ralston was dead; and Sutro himself was "King of the Comstock," builder of one of the engineering wonders of the age.

Then, the job done, Sutro sold his interest in the tunnel and returned to San Francisco to look for new outlets for his gargantuan energies. He invested the profits from the tunnel in land until he owned one-twelfth of the city, including the old Rancho San Miguel, around Twin Peaks. He planted thousands of trees on San Francisco's barren hills; the largest remnant is Sutro Forest on Mount Parnassus, now Mount Sutro.

His favorite piece of land was this northwest corner of the peninsula, where the Golden Gate opens into the Pacific and you can see for miles down the long white strand of Ocean Beach to the Santa Cruz Mountains rising abruptly from the sea. He bought a house on top of the headlands (now called Sutro Heights)—a cottage belonging to a settler named Tetlow—rebuilt it to suit his own purposes, and over the years indulged his lifelong penchant for tree planting by raising a forest of well-spaced Monterey pines, cypresses, and eucalyptus trees on the acres surrounding the house.

Unlike many a frontier millionaire, Sutro, a native of Aix-la-Chapelle, brought with him the traditions of a cultivated European. In the spirit of *noblesse oblige*, one of his perennial ambitions was to enlighten and elevate the masses. He opened his gardens to the public, and the families of working people could stroll on lawns under the trees and along flower-bordered paths, gaze at the ocean, and stare at the statues he erected there in the style of the gardens of Versailles—Greek gods and goddesses, heroic lions and stags, even characters from the novels of Dickens.

With the same benevolence that caused him to put the unemployed to work planting trees on his property around Mount Sutro, in the Nineties he conceived for this place at the ocean's edge a spa that would be built not for the leisure classes, like the baths of Europe, but for the masses. On the bluff below his gardens was an old resort of bad repute, the Cliff House; he bought it, converted it into a respectable restaurant-hotel, and made it San Francisco's favorite gathering place.

Adolph Sutro's appreciation for workingmen led him, in his later years, to act as patriarch to his employees, providing Comstock tunnel diggers with an early form of health insurance and sharing his dinner table with his servants. "Why should they not eat with me?" Sutro asked ingenuously. "They are as good as I, and while they work for me they must eat as well as I do."

—J. Kingston Pierce,
San Francisco, You're History

Walking over the rocks and beaches north of the Cliff House, he was fascinated by the sea life in the tidal basins and decided to construct a big pool, to be filled by spray from waves at high tide, where his patrons could find easy access to the wonders of the life of the intertidal zone. He built a stone wall across the big cove just north of the Cliff House and extended the wall seaward to an acre-sized rock, where people could fish and explore in the crevices for sea life.

In the fertile imagination of the self-taught engineer, the idea grew rapidly. If there were to be a pool, why limit the activity to passive gazing? Why shouldn't the public enjoy the health-giving benefits of bathing and swimming? (With Sutro, bathing was almost a fetish. In a time when the Saturday-night bath was an institution, he was considered somewhat eccentric for bathing daily. He took a collapsible tub on his travels and even sent portable bathtubs to his children when they went away to college.) Early designs for the baths show simply an open air "swimming pond" at the cove, next to his tide-pool "aquarium," but it soon became obvious that few swimmers would be attracted to the windy, foggy ocean front. However, the man who had built the Sutro Tunnel could not be deterred by adverse weather. He decided to create his own climate. The result was "Tropic Baths," this glass palace where the masses could bathe in a man-made tropical atmosphere under the palms.

Beneath the ruins of the Sutro Baths winds an elaborate labyrinth of caverns and tunnels. Over the years, a few intrepid explorers have ventured into these mysterious passages; whether all have ventured back out into the light of day is another question. One of the explorers who did come back out is Satanist Anton LaVey. Mr. LaVey was able to enter the tunnels via the ruins of an old dressing room. He explored deep into the maze of caverns, tunnels, and pipes, penetrating beyond the building's foundations to a region that seemed to have been untouched by human presence for decades. Coming upon a broad expanse of muddy ground, LaVey heard "guttural, moaning noises" and smelled an awful smell. A weirde, misshapen shadow moved in the blackness, and LaVey heard "the rustling or flapping of what sounded like huge wings." LaVey, a practiced explorer of occult phenomena, knew it was time to get the hell out.

—Dr. Weirde, *Dr. Weirde's Weirde Tours: A Guide to Mysterious San Francisco*

Sutro's water system was typically ingenious. Salt water from his aquarium and from another wave-filled pool below the cliffs flowed through a system of tunnels and canals into the swimming pools, so that his patrons could almost literally bathe in the waves of the Pacific in perfect comfort. Sunlight streamed through the colored-glass roof, and while swimming you could watch the waves breaking outside. In a superb gesture of fantasy, Sutro built some miniature "Sutro Tunnels" which extended back into the cliffs, where awed patrons could gaze at the churning waves in the coves and caverns below.

If the completion of the Sutro Tunnel was the triumph of Sutro's early years, the opening of the Tropic Baths in 1896 was the supreme achievement of his later life. One writer noted in rhapsodic Victorian prose:

"The baths rival in magnitude, utility and beauty the famous abluvion resorts of Titus,

Caracalla, Nero, or Diocletian…these wonderful expressions of architectural skill—airy, graceful yet substantial—are located in a wave-worn cove at the foot of the cliffs, and brought to utilitarian perfection by a triumph of engineering invention…Thus have the tides been harnessed and made subservient to the multitudes."

To provide the multitudes with inexpensive transportation to the baths, Sutro did his best to induce the Southern Pacific to reduce the rail fare to five cents on the steam line that ran out along the cliff tops to his beach resort. When the Southern Pacific refused, he was undaunted; he proceeded to build a competing electric line of his own out Clement Street and transported the multitudes for a nickel.

Meantime he had run for mayor on an anti-Southern Pacific ticket and won. But it was his last victory. The hard-driving tycoon had none of the tact required of a politician. He was past his prime; his health declined; and one year after he left office at the end of a single term, he was dead—one of the last of San Francisco's titans.

Sutro Baths continued to attract the multitudes for more than half a century after his death. Eventually part of the biggest pool was turned into an ice rink. By World War II, Tropic Baths fell into disrepair. The pools were finally closed in the early 1950s, and abandoned to the elements. For another dozen years San Franciscans and visitors were still drawn to the mammoth building to skate or wander through Sutro's museum, full of antique music boxes and other Victorian oddities. But both the rink and the museum were closed in the late 1950s when new owners decided to demolish the building for an apartment-house complex.

A short time after my last visit to the ruin, it burned to the ground, perhaps the victim of arson. A *New York Times* editorial mourned the passing of the old showplace, and quite properly chastised San Francisco for failing to preserve the historic structure. The developers were unable to carry out their plans, and little has changed.

You can still stroll through Sutro's gardens on the heights above, presented to the city as a park after his death. His house is gone, and most of the statues have been broken or hauled away. But many of his trees remain, and there are spectacular views of the surf-fringed shoreline for miles along the coast. Immediately below is the present Cliff House, which still functions as a restaurant. Its undistinguished architecture bears no resemblance to Sutro's Victorian fantasy, which burned down in 1907, ironically after having survived the earthquake and fire of 1906.

In the 1970s, this northwest corner of San Francisco, along with the rest of the city's ocean shoreline, became part of the Golden Gate National Recreation Area. Over the years since, there have been innumerable proposals for this land. Some have called for re-building the Cliff House as a modern equivalent of Sutro's palatial hostelry, but the National Park Service plans merely to upgrade the present structure. Ideas for the baths site range from removing the ruins and restoring the natural landscape to rebuilding the spa in its full glory as Sutro designed it.

In a time of diminished budgets and reduced expectations nei-ther notion seems likely to come to fruition. Meantime, you can still walk through the cove north of the Cliff House and see the crumbling remains of the pools, the stone wall, the wave-filled tide pools Sutro built, his tunnels, and his system of canals carrying ocean water into the building.

The National Park Service proposed to maintain the site as an "archeological ruin," with improved access, some natural landscap-ing around, and an intriguing added feature: on foggy nights a laser image of the original Tropic Baths would be projected onto the fog screen, a ghostly reminder of Sutro's dream of an aquatic pleasure dome for the common people, a symbol of a time when leaders dared to imagine and carry out bold visions for the public good.

Harold Gilliam is a former columnist for the San Francisco Chronicle *and author of fifteen books on the Bay Area and northern California, including* The San Francisco Experience: The Romantic Lore Behind the Fabulous Facade of the Bay Area *from which this piece was taken.*

★

The brash young Oscar Wilde was beginning to make a name for himself when he arrived a few years later on his famous lecture tour of America. (Upon arriving at New York, Wilde told the customs official, "I have nothing to declare but my genius.") Wilde saw another side of San Francisco. The English aesthete (later the author of The *Importance of Being Earnest, Lady Windermere's Fan* and *The Picture of Dorian Gray*) checked in at the Palace Hotel, seven stories of luxury lavishly bolted with iron bands to withstand earthquakes. Its immense glass-roofed central court was furnished with potted palms, rocking chairs, and spittoons and was bisected by a carriage driveway.

The young sports at the Bohemian Club and the old-timers at the Cliff House sized up this visiting tenderfoot poet in velvet knee breeches, with his dreaming eyes and languid manners, and decided to put him to the frontier tests of masculinity: drinking and poker. As night wore on at the Bohemian Club, Wilde matched his hosts drink for drink until they were all under the table, dead drunk. Then he rose, throwing his great cloak about him, to saunter back in the gray dawn to the Palace Hotel.

—Luree Miller, *Literary Hills of San Francisco*

Going In

Sometimes confronting fear is the best way out.

I SUSPECT THAT CLAUSTROPHOBIA IS THE MOST COMMON FEAR, one faced by rational beings whenever nightclubs are jammed body to body, buses are packed like sardine cans, airplane seats are the size of TV dinners, and the only way to the exit is over the backs of everyone else. How long have we known that they couldn't really evacuate the cities in eight hours?

My claustrophobia, even if rational, was a hindrance. If fear faced is fear mastered, then I had to get going on mine.

The Exploratorium is a hands-on science museum, which should top everyone's list of Where to Go in San Francisco. It is housed in what is now the Palace of Fine Arts, the remains of the 1915

Palace of Fine Arts

Panama-Pacific Exposition. Inside the museum, past the giant pin-pressions screen, the spin-it-yourself models of gas giants and tornadoes, the cow's eye dissection booth, the xylophone room, is the Tactile Dome. Advertised as "a pitch-black crawl-through tactile experience," it is open only by appointment (best made a month or so in advance for large groups).

For me the Tactile Dome provided a chance to confront my claustrophobia. Our group of six scheduled an hour inside. Ken, the Explainer, told us to remove shoes, socks, belts, earrings, dangling necklaces, rings that came off, watches, and to empty our pockets. We complied like children, rustling and giggling.

No light sources allowed inside the maze, Ken said. Liz had considered buying a glow stick in the Exploratorium Store. I'd left my flashlight, unintentionally, in the car. Just as well—no temptation.

Glasses had to be left on the desk before you went into the maze. If you wore contacts, Ken recommended that you keep your eyes closed. He said that wouldn't be a bad idea anyway.

He had a two-way radio and would check on us several times as we went along. He said that he could hear everything we say, so be careful.

"What's the worst thing you've heard?" Liz asked.

"Well..." He grinned and made his voice squeaky soft, wheedling. "This woman was saying, 'How do you like the feel of this?' and 'Do you like it when I touch that?'" In his normal tone he spoke over our laughter: "The funny part was that when she came out, she wasn't with her husband. She was really embarrassed. This guy worked with her husband, but she didn't know him *that* well."

Back to business, he said he'd let us through in groups of three, but we could go in couples or alone. We each could go through three or four times, depending on how much time we took. Who wanted to go first?

I told myself to relax. If I panicked, Ken would rescue me. It couldn't be too bad or they'd have some sort of disclaimer. I was determined. I *would* do this. If I didn't like it, I wouldn't go through a second time.

I felt better after I heard Ken check with the first group. No one had freaked out yet, but I wanted to get it over with. The dread is always the worst part. Mason and I went as the third group. As if it was a haunted house on Halloween, I asked Mason to go first to ward off the bogeymen.

Padded cylinders, swaying like punching bags, filled the first room. Light trickled in from the lobby, enough for me to see tiny flowers on the corduroy of the closest bag. We had to shove the bags out of our way, then dodge before they swung back. I fought my way to the back wall and discovered it was covered with a rubbery fabric. When I couldn't find the entrance to the next room, I felt panic rising from beneath my heart. I gritted my teeth, determined not to give up before I experienced *real* darkness.

"Found it," Mason said. "Let me have your hand."

Holding his hand steadied me. The opening was tall enough that you could walk forward on your knees, flailing with your hands. I didn't realize it on the first trip through, but some of the rooms were big enough to stand up in. Rather than risk bumping my head, I crawled all the way through on my hands and knees. Typical. I didn't test the ceiling height for fear of aggravating my claustrophobia, which caused me to suffer the claustrophobia unnecessarily.

A sudden crack of electricity. "That scared me," shouts a youngster, half in happiness. Overhead, a tesla coil, suspended from a strut, has just let fly its lightning bolt. The strut connects to other struts; the ceiling lifts and lifts into a massive roof, stretching up and outward farther than the eye can see. The Exploratorium is a vast canyon of a place, a single giant room, two and a half acres of odd contraptions, motors, lenses, artificial dust storms, amoebas squirming on a video screen, echo tubes, water waves. Experiments in progress. Shouts and laughter. Two women play with the patterns of iron filings caught in the invisible grip of a magnet, get metallic powder on their hands, and laugh. An eight-year-old concentrates on breaking the parts of a new exhibit, does not succeed. No attendant dashes over to stop him, and he glories in his freedom. There are no rules.

—Alan Lightman, "Anything Could Happen," Discover

A sharp right turn led to a ramp. Something scratchy and nubby, like fake grass, carpeted the ramp. I banged my knee on a wooden slat and wished for knee pads as I crawled up.

My friend Ron knew a group of people on Ecstasy who had been allowed through the dome naked. That sounded exciting when he told me: bodies writhing, skin against unfamiliar skin in the dark. In reality, there were too many rough, unpleasant things to brush against: Astroturf, burlap, sandpaper. Ron got a friction burn on one hand from going down a slide too fast. I was glad to have my jeans. Once I began to stand up, I wished for a helmet.

At the top of the ramp hung a long fringe of raveled plastic. Past that, the room had things attached to the walls: a muffin tin and a whisk broom, familiar and strange in the darkness. I touched a small bag with a round squishy dome inside. Ron told me later that it was a silicon breast implant.

A white web of knotted ropes crossed a shallow chasm. A green light shone beneath them. The light gave a respite from the darkness, but then I had to contend with the fear of crawling out over the abyss. Still, the distance to the next black doorway was minimal. I wrenched my thumb in my rush to climb. On a following trip, I ripped the edge of the other thumbnail. Good thing they lit the web. Otherwise you might seriously hurt yourself.

A long womb-like tunnel eased downward. I extended my legs full length, holding myself in place by my arms. Nothing yawned below my bare feet. The tunnel was a comfortable size around, upholstered in some smooth, slippery fabric. Funny how I assumed that all the rooms were draped in black because I saw no colors. I had my eyes open throughout all three trips. Somehow, keeping them open, whether I could see or not, kept the claustrophobia at bay.

Finally I decided to trust and let go, let myself slide down the gently twisting course. Without warning a drop opened beneath my feet. I couldn't sit up, couldn't be sure I'd land on my feet. I scrambled around, afraid to fall, and found no handholds.

I burst out, flopped onto my seat. The floor sank beneath me, like plopping down on a waterbed. I bounced a few times, to confirm that this was fun.

Somewhere in the darkness Mason sent waves back. We crawled together. Our bodies, familiar with each other in the dark, melded into the usual positions. His lips comforted mine. I clutched him close.

Out of nowhere, Ken asked, "How are you doing?"

"Just fine," I said. Mason and I chuckled guiltily.

I discovered I could stand. This room reminded me of playing in a Space Bubble at the county fair—only those were walled by clear plastic, lit by sunlight. I didn't jump around in here, unwilling to bash my head against an unseen ceiling or stub my toes in the soft floor of uncertain depth.

I ran my hands over the walls until I found a long thin tunnel at hip level. I shimmied inside and struggled upward. Climbing was really difficult; there were no "steps" to rest your knees on as in the earlier ramp. I had slithered partway up the tunnel when a curve seemed very familiar. Yikes! I realized I had started backwards in the maze, which Ken had told us absolutely not to do. He had stressed how dangerous it was to climb back up the slides—you couldn't get out of the way of someone coming down. I immediately slid back down at speed, anxious to get out of the way.

"I went the wrong direction," I said to the darkness.

Mason's voice was a relief. "I wondered. You disappeared."

I staggered across the air mattress to hug him.

"I found the exit." He grabbed my hand. I felt him kneel down. "Is there a body across it?" he asked.

He crawled forward. I followed. Bill had been hanging upside down in front of the entrance. No explanation for that behavior. Once he moved, we emerged into a comparatively enormous room lit by a red bulb behind safety glass. Like the perfect '60s living room, this had a circular conversation pit beneath a low, draped ceiling. Five of us fit very comfortably. I sprawled full length on some cushions. The room was an unmitigated relief.

"Now's when we need that joint," I teased. The fire hazard—trapped in a darkened maze—would've panicked me if anyone had actually pulled one out. Speaking to myself dispelled my fear.

Bill decided to move along. There were two doorways side by side. He crawled out the left. The rectangular holes seemed scarcely bigger than animal doors, but 200-pound Bill wriggled through. We waited a while to let him get ahead of us. Crowding into one of those invisible rooms was another scary proposition. I understood now why Ken insisted on small groups.

From that point on the rooms cease to have well-ordered individual identities.

The final slide seemed to go on and on, down and down, around and around. I did not worry that the tunnel would narrow—only a sadist would create such a thing. This fear was different. Without visual clues, I didn't know if Mason had gotten out of the slide ahead of me. The farther I went, the more I feared I'd kick him in the head. "Look out below," I called.

I spurted out into a sea of navy beans. I staggered to my feet. It was difficult to wade through the knee-deep morass, but I wanted away from the slide before the next person came down. I knew Ron was in the bean room. He never spoke, nor did I touch him, but I recognized the bitter smell of his sweat. It excited me to be able to recognize someone by smell. I felt closer to my mammalian roots, tracking by scent.

A woman was trying to organize a game. She wanted someone to sit in the center of the beans and guess who moved around them—sort of blindman's buff in the dark. I wanted no part of that. I struggled toward the vein of light that fell in around the curtain.

A short ramp led back into the lobby. Blinking like some nocturnal animal, I drew several deep breaths, the first in a long while. Subsequent trips proved that the air in the dome warmed as bodies passed through. A fan drew air into the resting room, so it at least stayed a little fresher.

Liz sat in the lobby. She said she'd known she was claustrophobic, but she hadn't gotten past the punching bag room. She just realized she did *not* want to get away from the exit. So she came out the way she'd come in. I told her about my claustrophobia, how the dome wasn't as bad as riding in the backseat of a small car, how Ken would rescue her if necessary, how I like to sit near an exit in a theater. My words only comforted myself. Liz wouldn't be jollied into going in again. I didn't want to make her sound cowardly, so I stopped congratulating myself.

Leora arrived, and was surprised that Liz had gotten out before her, when she'd gone in after. Liz had to rehash the whole explanation. Leora was much more understanding than I had been, despite my best efforts. It was fun, Leora said, and she was glad she'd done it, but she wouldn't go through again. She hadn't realized, before this experience, that she *was* claustrophobic.

This talk of fear stirred mine up again. The first trip hadn't been fun so much as an ordeal: uncertainty to surmount, challenges to overcome. Rather than continue to listen to their fears, I jumped at the chance to go through again, dragging Mason forward before he was rested.

"Are you sure you want to go first?" he asked.

"Yes."

Loren Rhoads came to San Francisco on her honeymoon and fell in love when she saw the sun set into the ocean for the first time. She moved to the city two years later and began Automatism Press in 1993.

★

They who built this Panama-Pacific Exposition were so wise in adopting all the good features and avoiding those which marred the preceding ones that to me it seems as near perfection as the mind and hand of man have ever wrought. This is the university of the world. It has a chair fully endowed to meet the wants and needs of each. The eye, the ear, the mind, the heart, the soul, each may have its horizon here enlarged.

—Vice President Thomas R. Marshall, quoted by Gladys Hansen
in *San Francisco Almanac: Everything You Want to Know
About Everyone's Favorite City*

JAMES ARMSTRONG

The Forest of John McLaren

America's largest city park is worth visiting time and time again.

GOLDEN GATE PARK WAS, IN MY CHILDHOOD, A VAST GREEN PLACE of flowers and wonders—and getting wet. Before outgrowing the tendency, I'd fallen into so many bodies of water there that my parents accepted their firstborn as pool prone and routinely carried towels and extra clothing to the park. At the Conservatory's fish pond, when I was seven, I reached for coins on a giant lily pad and thoroughly flustered the fat carp lurking underneath. I ruined my first suit with long pants (a white one, yet) trotting into Spreckels Lake after a toy sailboat during a junior regatta; chased a duck into Stow Lake (smelliest muck in the park); and, a year or so after that, was whisked in the nick of time from the railing of the otter pool that used to be in front of the California Academy of Sciences. (A dramatic sculpture of black stone whales by Robert Howard was later moved in to mark the spot.) And to this day, when I walk into the echoing lobby of that building and pause by the alligator pit, a ghostly parental hand seems to close down on my shoulder.

As it is for so many who have lived around San Francisco a long time, Golden Gate Park is part of my life. It's a place of escape in the midst of what I'm escaping from, a convenient, free enclave of beauty and peace in the thick of the city. It also offers culture, enlightenment, sports, and nostalgia. Especially nostalgia. When I see the August glory of the conservatory's dahlia beds in bloom, I can't help reliving my first encounter with a giant dahlia. That ruffly, purple thing was as tall as I was, and my reaction was to run up and hug it to me. It came unstuck, of course, and there was hell to pay.

The Children's Playground (one of America's first public playgrounds, completed in 1888) is also filled with memories, one of which is very much alive, for I still ride the carousel there occasionally. Now that it's been so splendidly restored—local artist Ruby Newman and her crew spent seven years repairing decades of neglect—I understand why, for me, it's always been *the* carousel. The animals (unicorns, griffins, lions, tigers) are the most storybook fantastical, gorgeously colored and bejeweled beasts I've ever seen. And the old German calliope, with the usual tiny wooden woman on the front keeping time with her silvery bell, has the sweetest voice I've ever heard. To sit and listen is to enjoy the best free concert in town.

The park has always been many things to those who use it, and this certainly is a park that people *use*. The sure marks of spring in this seasonless land are the throngs of happy people who come to see the park in bloom; we flock by the thousands for our annual swoon over acres of rhododendrons and other flowers. People use the park's facilities for picnics; for lawn bowling, golf, and archery; for practicing their fly casting; for jogging and hiking and equitation; for model-boat sailing and competitions; for playing tennis and baseball and volleyball and football and soccer. And, of course, for smooching and snoozing.

At times the park seems like the city's great backyard. Every Sunday vehicles are barred from part of Kennedy Drive, and the

> *I walked at dusk in Golden Gate Park, ambling towards the Conservatory of Flowers. A golden light was just catching the tops of the Monterey pines, and suddenly it struck me: San Francisco is a gateway to our eternal home. Nothing could be more lovely than the illumination of those trees at sunset and if such a light is not in Paradise, then I do not want to go there.*
>
> —Sean O'Reilly,
> "Lady of the Avenues"

street is left to cyclists and skaters. Every school day in the spring, shushing teachers herd busloads of shrilling children through the aquarium and the natural history museum. And most Sundays all year round there's a band concert in the Music Concourse. During opera season comes the "Opera in the Park" concert, with superstars like Luciano Pavarotti, Beverly Sills, and, on one most memorable occasion, Marilyn Horne and Montserrat Caballe singing in tandem.

Fronting the sunken concourse (clockwise from the band shell) you will find the Japanese Tea Garden, the M. H. de Young Memorial Museum, the McLaren Memorial Rhododendron Dell, and the California Academy of Sciences, which includes Steinhart Aquarium, the Natural History Museum, and Morrison Planetarium. Across the street behind the band shell is an entrance to Strybing Arboretum, a park within the park. Just west of the tea garden you come to Stow Lake, with Strawberry Hill and Huntington Falls in its midst. A short stroll east along Kennedy Drive from the de Young is the Victorian gingerbread Conservatory of Flowers. And all of these are places where San Franciscans return again and again.

An especially heavy usage of the park came after the earthquake and fire of 1906, when many thousands of suddenly homeless citizens erected a tent city there. After they were resettled, much of the park had to be re-landscaped. Less destructive, though almost as numerous, were the hippies of the sixties, who came to the park as if to Mecca. At the first "Human Be-In," held on the Polo Field in January 1967, Timothy Leary gave vent to the great motto of the

*Conservatory
of Flowers*

times: "Turn on, tune in, drop out!" And in the "Summer of Love" that year, musical groups with odd names like Jefferson Airplane and the Grateful Dead gave free concerts at Speedway Meadow. As I remember those days, every echoing underpass held at least one stoned flutist, and pot smoke hung like homemade smog in the dells and ravines. Even more exotic, the first of the Hare Krishna ceremonial processions took place in the meadow in August 1969: thousands of people, many of them robed and painted, escorted bizarre, gorgeous juggernaut carts while drums throbbed and cameras snapped amid clouds of incense.

> *The oldest building in Golden Gate Park—the Conservatory of Flowers, erected in 1879—was a posthumous (and unintentional) gift from James Lick to the city. He had intended it to be installed at his estate in San Jose, but after his death it was bought by a group of moguls, including Charles Crocker and Leland Stanford, who remanded it to the permanent care of park superintendent William Hammond Hall.*
>
> —J. Kingston Pierce,
> *San Francisco, You're History*

But those odd and carefree days were short, and as the times darkened, Golden Gate Park shared the occasional violence of the rest of the city. The seventies were tricky times in the park, and alert police surveillance was needed. (The area is safer now, but it's not wise to walk there after dark, and it is comforting to see the pairs of mounted policemen clopping along.) At the end of the decade, refugee boat people quartered nearby were discovered to be supplementing their diet by trapping ducks, geese, squirrels, raccoons, opossums, and even dogs and cats they found there. A sad sight nowadays is the occasional homeless person emerging in the morning from a makeshift den behind the sheltering trees and shrubbery.

That there are trees and shrubbery at all, much less 1,017 acres of them stretching three miles long by a half-mile wide, is a minor miracle of determination and know-how. The story began in 1870, when the city fathers purchased the property.

San Francisco actually didn't decide to have a park until all the good land in town had been taken. So it had to be located in the region known as the Outside Lands, the western half of the peninsula running from Divisadero Street to the sea—a waste of shifting dunes marked by scrub oaks, a few rocky hills and ravines, some patches of marsh, and a lot of dune grass. Transforming this swath of seaside desert into something comparable to New York's Central Park would take some doing.

Frederick Law Olmsted, designer of Central Park, was asked to come and look things over. He pronounced the project ridiculous—impossible!—and went back east where cities bought land with *soil* on it for their parks. Even so, in 1871 a civil engineer named William Hammond Hall took on the job. He laid out the roads much as they are today, resisted pressure to level everything in sight, and started finding and planting things that would grow there. He began with the Panhandle. This blockwide carpet of trees and greenery, originally designed as a carriage entrance, still ushers people into the park. Many of the monumental trees there now are the ones he established, and thus are the oldest trees in the park. They are also those most urgently in need of having young trees planted nearby, for some of them are at the end of their life span. A replacement program was begun in 1981.

The park we see today really was created by a man with a druidical passion for trees, which was apparently reciprocated.

The contrast was extreme: all morning long I studied Latin, Greek, and geometry under the gaze of black-robed Jesuits. But at noon I slipped down to the Haight and the local Krishna temple, where lunch was meager vegetarian fare, but the show was a rich pageant of characters who came for the 50 cent price and the meditation. If you didn't show the proper respect during chanting, you were thrown out. This was the fate of one wild-eyed fellow who refused to sit in a lotus position, but instead insisted on standing on his head.

—James O'Reilly, "Declensions and Mantras"

Trees grew for John McLaren as for few other people, and by the time he was 80 he'd planted a million of them overall. He started his second million with a redwood grove for the park; it was approaching 30 feet tall when he died in 1943.

For over half a century, this diminutive man from a farm in Stirlingshire, Scotland, was the astonishingly active and creative superintendent of parks for San Francisco. Uncle John, as nearly three generations of Californians knew him—and the whole state did know him—was a horticultural genius of high principles, with an unquenchable Scottish burr, a taste for his native whisky, and a mystical belief in the efficacy of manure for making things grow.

On his 93rd birthday, a passel of civic leaders got together and asked him what he'd like for a present. His response was immediate: "A hundred thousand yards of manur-r-r-e for me trees!" (Actually, he already had it, because his park had contracted for the entire local supply.)

To anyone who knows about John McLaren, the most hilariously ironic fixture in the park is the life-size (he wasn't much over five feet tall) statue of this man who detested statues. Standing solidly on a swatch of lawn, near one entrance to his rhododendron dell, the figure is examining a pinecone. It is a superb bronze, but I keep hoping that someone will do to it as he did with most of the statues foisted on him: he landscaped them with innocent seeming shrubs that slowly rose up to conceal them.

Not the least of the park's charms is its size: not too big and not too small. All major institutions are fairly close together and if you're truly determined, can be covered in a day. Still, I'd advise giving at least two days to the park and doing your farther-flung exploring—to the Dutch Windmill and Queen Wilhelmina Tulip Gardens, to the buffalo paddock (with its herd of American bison) and Spreckels Lake, to the fly casting pools, the stables, and the polo field—on rented bicycles.

Around and beyond all these things stretches the wild part of the park, hundreds of acres where structures are few, a region of small hills and unexpected ravines and glens covered with trees and bushes. No flowers except wild ones. Here the seeker of solitude can wander networks of paths or meditate by small lakes, observed only by the ubiquitous mallards. If you stay in your car, you'll never know about this part of Golden Gate Park. You must walk. In the midst of all the bustle and hustle of this densely populated city, here are places to get away. These wilder areas perform a valuable public service.

And Golden Gate Park is not just a fair-weather place. Go there when a really dense fog rolls in and see the trees melt into the mist, as in a Chinese scroll painting; savor the muting of colors and the softening of outlines to bare essential. Stow Lake has a special magic then, as the whiter gulls wheel through silver air, flying above pewter water patterned by the dark wakes of ducks.

Museums, of course, are just *made* for drab days. And the sound of rain on the Conservatory's near-acre of glass is…well, you must hear it for yourself.

James Armstrong is a writer and photographer who in the '70s and '80s was principal photographer for the San Francisco Ballet and the Bay Area representative for After Dark *magazine. His imagery has figured in numerous magazines, calendars, and on greeting cards, and his travel writing has appeared in* National Geographic Traveler, Islands, Motorland, *and national newspapers. Presently, he is collecting rejection slips on a children's book about a family of operatic toads and a comic novel based on his years trying to write movies in Hollywood in the '60s. He lives in El Sobrante, California.*

*

In Golden Gate Park that day
            a man and his wife were coming along
     thru the enormous meadow
           which was the meadow of the world
He was wearing green suspenders
            and carrying an old beat-up flute
                 in one hand
    while his wife had a bunch of grapes
       which she kept handing out
            individually
         to various squirrels
           as if each
        were a little joke

    And then the two of them came on
           thru the enormous meadow

which was the meadow of the world
and then
at a very still spot where the trees dreamed
and seemed to have been waiting thru all time
for them
they sat down together on the grass
without looking at each other

—Lawrence Ferlinghetti, "In Golden Gate Park That Day…,"
A Coney Island of the Mind

Sam Spade's San Francisco

Real and imaginary characters haunt the streets.

As the late-afternoon fog settles over San Francisco with its usual stealthy grace, a man wearing a trench coat and a rakish fedora stands in front of a plaque under a street sign. "Burritt," the sign proclaims. And beneath it a bronze plaque reads as follows: "On approximately this spot, Miles Archer, partner of Sam Spade, was done in by Brigid O'Shaughnessy."

And at once a delicious shiver of recognition runs unbridled through the group of men and women—fourteen in all—that a San Francisco author, historian, and tour guide named Don Herron (he is the man in raincoat and fedora) is leading on one of San Francisco's ambulatory delights. It's called the Dashiell Hammett Tour and this moment, when those evocative words are first seen plainly, is a time inevitably cherished by all the Hammett buffs. By extension that includes the fans of Sam Spade, Hammett's sterling fictional detective, and that intricately woven big-city adventure of his, first a highly acclaimed novel and then a movie that so frequently graces the television screen: *The Maltese Falcon.*

Those named on the plaque are, of course, characters in *The Maltese Falcon*—Miles Archer, the first murder victim in the tale, and Sam Spade and Brigid O'Shaughnessy. Don Herron explains—

185

for those few on this tour who can't easily recite from memory the dialogue from *The Maltese Falcon*—how Brigid, the lovely, mysterious, treacherous yet beguiling Brigid, had said to Sam Spade in his office soon after the story's beginning: "Help me. I've no right to ask you to help me blindly, but I do ask you. Be generous, Mr. Spade. You can help me. Help me." And Spade rivets her with his cold eyes and says: "You won't need much of anybody's help. You're good. You're very good."

Typically Hammett, those cynical, trip-hammer lines. Samuel Dashiell Hammett wrote stories that were lean and spare and crackling and hard as flint and as intense as fire. He wrote with his bare knuckles, and he gave us not only *The Maltese Falcon* but also *The Thin Man, The Dain Curse*, and a number of others. He created a new school of detective fiction and with it that quintessential private eye, Sam Spade of San Francisco, and the mean alleyways of a life bruised to the bone.

Spade turned from the parapet and walked up Bush Street to the alley where men were grouped. A uniformed policeman chewing gum under an enameled sign that said BURRITT ST. in white against dark blue put out an arm and asked: "What do you want here?"

"I'm Sam Spade. Tom Polhaus phoned me."

"Sure you are." The policeman's arm went down. "I didn't know you at first. Well, they're back there." He jerked a thumb over his shoulder. "Bad business."

—Dashiell Hammett,
The Maltese Falcon

Hammett wrote about what he knew, which was the bleak, shadowy world of the private investigator and the unsavory people he encounters in his line of work. After coming out of the ambulance corps in World War I and failing in a variety of pursuits, Hammett, who had grown up in Baltimore, worked for a time as a Pinkerton detective and learned about violence and human frailty. Settling in San Francisco, where he began to write, he would in time know success and then would look as a famous author should—handsome, well-tailored, as trim as a reed, with a mustache and a dashing manner that fit his times, the '20s and '30s.

The city where Hammett derived his inspiration and gave life to Sam Spade was the San Francisco of old. It is the Baghdad-by-the-Bay memorialized by the ultimate San Franciscan, Herb Caen, the *Chronicle* columnist. Dashiell Hammett was a part of the city's fog.

And now here is that fog and the Burritt Street plaque, put up by the city's Hammett admirers in 1977, and Don Herron leading the Sam Spade buffs. The group includes Hammett literati, Humphrey Bogart fans (Bogie played Spade in the film), and those who merely enjoy walking the streets of San Francisco. Herron is telling them in entertaining fashion about the sites that hold significance in Hammett fact and Hammett fiction. This walking tour is an education and high theater, too. It's a flavorful, four-hour entertainment that sticks to the ribs.

Since 1977, Herron, in addition to lecturing, writing books, and driving a cab, has conducted literary walking tours that cover sites associated not only with Dashiell Hammett but also Robert Louis Stevenson, Mark Twain, Ambrose Bierce, and the Beat Generation writers of the '50s. But Dashiell Hammett is perhaps closest to his heart.

The tour begins at noon on a summer Saturday at the San Francisco Main Public Library, just a few blocks down Larkin Street from the apartment on Eddy Street that Hammett shared with his wife, the former Josephine Dolan. They had been married July 6, 1921, in St. Mary's Cathedral on Van Ness Avenue. "Hammett came regularly to this library," Herron tells the group. "He was working at Samuels Jewelers downtown in the advertising department. For a while he worked again as a detective for the Pinkerton agency. In the library he would read the magazines and the books and one day after reading several detective yarns he said, 'I can do that.' The truth is, he could. And he did. He wrote for *The Black Mask,* a pulp detective magazine, and then as his skills increased he began to write novels. It was in this library that Dashiell Hammett saw his future."

As the walk continues, reality and fiction blend. Near the Main Library stands the City Hall where in *The Maltese Falcon* Sam Spade is called into the district attorney's office for questioning. Here is where Spade enjoys telling off the district attorney, talking swiftly, pausing only for one sarcastic aside to the stenographer: "Getting this all right, son? Or am I going too fast for you?" Over there on McAllister Street is where the shoot-out occurred in another hard-boiled Hammett tale, *The Whosis Kid.* On Post Street at the Charing Cross Apartments is where Hammett had the notion of a new detective he elected to name Sam Spade. Obviously he borrowed the first name as a shortened version of his own, Samuel. As for Spade, presumably it's taken from the tedious spadework that a private detective must engage in. Whatever its derivation, the name has echoed through the years: Sam Spade, a hard-bitten name that speaks of late nights and muted trumpets and beautiful women.

About his conception of this particular gumshoe, Hammett would write: "Spade had no original. He is a dream man in the sense that he is what most of the private detectives I worked with would like to have been and what quite a few of them in their cockier moments thought they approached…"

Now the group is walking—and Herron sets a fast pace—up and down the hilly streets, from the tip of the Tenderloin to Nob Hill. The tour ventures through streets with names such as Hyde and Leavenworth and Post and California and Monroe and Powell and Sutter, names with a distinct San Francisco tang, and all of them serve as wellsprings of the illuminating Hammett stories that tumble out of Herron's crisp narrative. The building at 130–150 Sutter, for instance, is where the office of Samuel Spade and Miles

The interior of the new Main Library is a marvel, so deeply delicious you forget your previous ideas of what a library is. The eccentric skylight in the atrium pours down light. The catwalk-like bridges that get you there are delicious, the transition from Sierra granite to creamy French limestone is delicious. The wood paneling—some sycamore to pick up on the trees outside, wavery maple and lacewood—is delicious. The sense of space and openness is delicious. It's a building to be inside of simply for the pleasure of being there.

—Robert Hass, "A Poet Visits the New Main Library," *San Francisco Examiner*

Archer was located. At Spade's apartment on Post Street, he says through clenched teeth to Brigid O'Shaughnessy: "I won't play the sap for you"—which is pure Sam Spade, and pure Bogart.

The group learns that in the first paragraph of *The Maltese Falcon,* Hammett describes his Sam Spade, who bears little resemblance to the small-featured, narrow-shouldered, dark-haired Humphrey Bogart. "He looked rather pleasantly like a blond satan," Hammett wrote about Spade. From Herron the intriguing details flow concerning the real-life derivation of Hammett's evil characters, including Wilmer, the rotten gunsel who threatens to "fog" Spade if he doesn't "lay off." And there are the San Francisco hotels whose names punctuate Herron's recitation: the Clift and the St. Francis and the Sir Francis Drake; all of them figured in the life of Dashiell Hammett or in the fictional lives of the characters that emerged from his fertile imagination. Although the hotels have different names in the Hammett stories, their origins are no mystery to fathom. Walking through the rear entrance of the James Flood Building on Ellis Street to the doors on Market Street, one treads the very same marble that Hammett walked on his way to work at Samuels Jewelers—and it is in that building that Hammett set the locale for his fictional Continental Detective Agency.

And now, after the group has absorbed so much fact and lore, contentedly swamped by literate oddments, the tour has gone full circle and ends downtown at John's Grill, a wonderfully old San Francisco chophouse. There, at John's, Hammett dined and did some of his writing. In contrast to the hotels cited in *The Maltese Falcon*, John's Grill is known in the book's pages by its rightful name. After the lengthy walk through San Francisco's past, the group finds pleasure in John's Grill where the San Francisco sourdough bread seems particularly crunchy, the calamari tantalizing to the taste buds, the wine a perfect complement. And one wonders: perhaps at this very table Dashiell Hammett once wrote about Sam Spade and Brigid and Nick and Nora Charles. On the cover of the menu, which may be purchased, is an art deco painting of Dashiell Hammett, a sporty figure in his snap-brim fedora, standing in front of the restaurant's door. A special drink for the Hammett fans to relish is called the Bloody Brigid. One may order a "Sam Spade's Chops" dinner—a rack of lamb, baked potato, and sliced tomato. In _The Maltese Falcon_ the detective orders "chops, baked potato, and sliced tomatoes."

John's Grill is also called "The House of the Maltese Falcon," since it abounds in genuine Hammett memorabilia. Upstairs is the Dashiell Hammett Room where the walls are decorated with pictures of Hammett and photos from the films made from his novels. Below the still pictures from _The Maltese Falcon_ are dialogue captions—so many of them, the pictures and the well-remembered spoken lines, that at once the perennial movie springs again to rich, abundant life.

Dashiell Hammett enjoyed his fame, particularly when the big money was rolling in from Hollywood. In World War II, too old for the draft, he enlisted in the Army and edited a GI newspaper in the Aleutians. Later, he taught mystery writing at the Jefferson School of Social Science in New York. His health, never robust, began to fail; he died of cancer in a New York hospital in 1961. He was 66. He had stopped writing at 39. His eulogy was delivered by the woman with whom he had shared his life for years—playwright Lillian Hellman, who called him "a man of simple honor and great bravery." He was buried at Arlington National Cemetery.

His fellow detective story writer Raymond Chandler once said that Hammett should be credited with "taking murder out of the parlor and throwing it into the alley where it belongs."

Into the alley and into the streets of a San Francisco that no longer exists. But some of it does, on the Dashiell Hammett Tour, and it is there to see. It is there to savor.

Don Freeman has been a critic-at-large columnist for the San Diego Union-Tribune _since 1992. Before that, for many years, he was a TV editor/columnist for the_ San Diego Union. _He has won a number of San Diego Press Club awards and is an emeritus judge for the prestigious Peabody Awards. He has written more than 300 articles for magazines such as_ The Saturday Evening Post, TV Guide, Travel & Leisure, Sport, _and_ Emmy. _San Francisco is his favorite city and Dashiell Hammett one of his favorite authors._

✳

Of all the pyrotechnic personalities who blazed across the skies of San Francisco in the early years of the century—Jack London, George Sterling, Gelett Burgess, Bruce Porter, Arnold Genthe—none was more brilliant, eccentric, or talented than architect Willis Polk. And none made a more enduring contribution to American culture. Just as Jack London overturned the tables in the literary world, so Polk did in the field of architecture. His most significant work was a structure of revolutionary design that was at least forty years ahead of its time—the progenitor of all modern glass-and-steel skyscrapers.

You can see it on Sutter Street near Montgomery—a shining jewel of a building to delight the eye amid the humdrum structures of the downtown district. It is hard to believe now that Polk's building was originally greeted with shock, incredulity, and disapproval.

He designed it for a piece of income property then owned by the University of California—a site the university originally intended for a hotel. When the building was completed in 1918, it hit the city with the impact of an architectural explosion—as the irreverent designer doubtless intended. The front "curtain wall" is glass, reflecting the sky, nearby buildings, clouds, and wraiths of fog like a seven-story mirror framed in elaborate ironwork.

The building was named for another San Francisco innovator—Andrew Hallidie, a regent of the university and the inventor of the cable car. Subsequent owners, however, apparently unaware of the building's historic value, dropped the name, referring to it only as "150 Sutter," and permitted considerable violence to Polk's design in remodeling the first floor for a clothing store.

The glass curtain wall was a radical innovation in an era when walls were supposed to be solid and substantial. A few other American architects had experimented with glass but none had gone this far. Theoretically the glass wall had been possible ever since the Eiffel Tower in 1889 had demonstrated that a steel framework could rise to great heights and that heavy bearing walls were no longer necessary. But tradition dictated that the walls still should be massive, as if they, and not the steel frame, were holding up the building. With this structure, Polk opened the door to new and imaginative designs not bound to stone and masonry.

Yet no one went through the door. The concept was too advanced. The building was regarded as a freak, and several decades passed before architects began to catch up with it.

—Harold Gilliam, *The San Francisco Experience: The Romatic Lore Behind the Fabulous Facade of the Bay Area*

JAY STULLER

* * *

The Rock

Only tourists remember this place fondly.

IT TAKES JUST A GENTLE PULL ON A LEVER TO CLOSE FOURTEEN of the prison's cells at a single time. In a mere three seconds each door, 250 pounds of hardened steel bars, comes shut and locked with an explosive crack of metal thunder. Perhaps the most intimidating sound in the history of American justice, the very definition of "slammer," it's a signature of the U.S. Penitentiary, Alcatraz.

From 1934 to 1963, Alcatraz housed gangsters, kidnappers, and killers, reputedly the toughest, most hardened, and most incorrigible federal convicts in America. Used as a threat against convicts in other federal pens, it took only criminals who couldn't follow rules elsewhere. Alcatraz subjected them to a regimen meant to control rebellious ways and crush their very souls.

On a Saturday night in early March, the prison's population is composed of twenty rather unhardened Boy Scouts and their seven adult guardians; they have earned the chance to serve a little time thanks to volunteer work on the island. Now part of the Golden Gate National Recreation Area, Alcatraz is managed by the National Park Service. The penitentiary's worldwide notoriety attracts more than a million tourists annually.

Ostensibly escape-proof—it was once known as "Uncle Sam's Devil's Island" and "Hellcatraz" for convicts—the concrete-and-steel cages of "the Rock" were hell on earth. The sublime views of San Francisco and a bay full of ships and sailboats only added to inmate despair. More than 33 years have passed since the last real convicts shuffled off the island in shackles. And despite spooky stories gleefully told by Ranger Lori Thomsen—the Park Service "warden" who's leading this adventure—there's not a single sign of ghosts.

While sitting in cell C-109, however, on a thin and narrow mattress that rests atop the bed frame's interwoven steel slats, one is given serious pause. At five-by-nine feet, less room than many animal shelters allow a dog, the cell seems even smaller. Painted in white and two shades of putrid green, the concrete feels cold against one's back. A bare bulb saturates the space with harsh light.

It's obvious that a man would have come to know every bump on these horribly intimate walls, that patterns in the ceiling would remain in the mind's eye long after the lights went out. In the darkness of the Alcatraz that was, an inmate is alone. Yet the night is not still.

Restless bodies turn in other cells. The muffled engine from a passing boat crescendos and fades. Dancing across the water on gusts of wind are the taunts of San Francisco: horns, sirens, and even female laughter from the St. Francis Yacht Club just a mile away. And then there are the birds.

A seasoned con might sleep through the periodic outbursts of roosting gulls and herons. But for a new "fish" on Alcatraz, the sudden squawks would rudely break an uneasy slumber. And while no spectral shades of deceased convicts are floating about, at 2 a.m. in a tiny cell the Rock sure has a way of giving one the unholy creeps.

With 22 acres of windswept sandstone and no fresh water, the barren island simply wasn't suited for settlement. Alcatraz was left untouched until the early 1850s, after the United States acquired California from Mexico. American military engineers figured the island would make a fine fortress for guarding the strategic harbor through which passed so much gold. Armed to the teeth during

the Civil War, the garrison fired only once in earnest, at an uniden-
tified ship. They missed.

Pressed into double-duty as a makeshift military prison, Alcatraz
held soldiers guilty of desertion or other crimes. Later, the prison
even housed American Indians, including one of Geronimo's men.
At the turn of the century, overwhelmed by U.S. Army prisoners
and convalescents from the war in the Philippines, the military decided to build a new cellhouse. Completed in 1912, the three-story
structure of reinforced concrete is still—next to the Alcatraz light-
house—the island's most prominent building. By 1933, however,
the military took a look at the high cost of maintaining Alcatraz
and prepared to close it.

J. Edgar Hoover, the aggressive
young director of the FBI, had
other ideas. A crime wave in the
1930s changed public attitudes
toward the treatment of law-
breakers. A master at raising the
FBI's profile, Hoover did little to
quell the celebrity surrounding
"public enemies," such as Al
Capone and George (Machine
Gun) Kelly, even as his G-men
tracked them down. Yet the
gangsters had caused problems

> *The Miwok Indians have
> always considered Alcatraz,
> the barren sandstone rock in San
> Francisco Bay, to be inhabited by
> evil spirits. They must have been
> petrified with fear when the
> U.S. Army brought them to the
> rock in chains and shackles in
> 1859, the first year Alcatraz
> was used as a prison.*
>
> —Dr. Weirde, *Dr. Weirde's
> Weirde Tours: A Guide to
> Mysterious San Francisco*

for federal prison wardens. Pushed by Hoover, U.S. Attorney
General Homer Cummings agreed on the need for a "super
prison." They chose Alcatraz, and James A. Johnston to run it.

A lawyer, banker, and civic leader, the 60-year-old Johnston
seemed an odd choice. Yet he had experience; two decades before,
California's governor had asked him to take over the barbaric
Folsom Prison. By abolishing striped uniforms and corporal pun-
ishment, Johnston earned a reputation as a humanitarian reformer.
But the times—and the man—had changed.

Under Johnston, Alcatraz bore the imprint of Frederick Winslow
Taylor, the so-called "father of scientific management," whose

time-and-motion studies made American factories models of efficiency. Prisons had always been places of rules and rote procedure,
but Johnston pushed penology into the realm of mad science.

Each day began at 6:30 with a loud clang from the cellhouse
alarm, followed by the day's first official count. Convicts had
twenty minutes to brush their teeth, make their beds, and get
dressed. Marched down the 300-foot-long corridor that inmates
called "Broadway," the men entered the dining hall.

Given twenty minutes to eat, convicts stood at the shriek of
a whistle. Their utensils were counted, and the men were
marched back to their cells for another official count. The same
drill prevailed at lunch and dinner. Walks to the workshops—
where convicts made gloves and pallets, and washed laundry—
meant passing through metal detectors, or "snitch boxes;" strip
searches and shakedowns were random and frequent. At 5:30
the cell doors closed a man in for the next thirteen hours. The
lights went out promptly at 9:30. On foggy days—when the
tower guards did not have a clear line of fire—the men weren't
let out except for meals.

"An hour, a week, a month meant nothing," says former Alcatraz
convict Nathan Glenn Williams. "A year only served to indicate
you were 365 days closer to release. For those who were serving
interminably long sentences—such as 150 years plus natural life—
even the calendar lost its meaning." Another ex-convict called the
machine-like routine "an exquisite form of torture."

On three of the prison's quartet of freestanding, three-tiered
cellblocks, Johnston replaced the key-opened doors of soft strap
iron with bars of tool-proof steel. He installed the then novel locking system. The heavy-metal slam was indeed intended to intimi-
date, to remind prisoners that the guards were in total control.

With 336 remodeled cells available, most convicts were kept in
B and C Blocks, split by Broadway. D Block, the "Treatment Unit,"
was used for segregation. Six cells in D Block had solid-metal
doors; doing time in "the Hole" meant as much as nineteen days
spent in solitary confinement in one of these six cells, often in total
darkness.

Johnston built elevated gun galleries at each end of the cell-house. From behind bars on the narrow walkway, guards could see the prisoners at all times. A series of electronically controlled gates and doors secured the cellhouse entrance. In the ceiling of the dining hall were tear-gas canisters. Barbed wire topped a cyclone fence that encircled the prison. Signs went up warning boats to stay at least 200 yards from the island.

Most penitentiaries had one guard for every ten convicts; Johnston hired one for every three Alcatraz prisoners. He ordered twelve official "counts" per day, but random and unofficial tallies could push the daily total past thirty. Even if a man got past the guards and man-made obstructions, he still faced a formidable natural barrier—the cold waters and swift currents of the bay.

No man was directly sentenced to the island. He "earned" his way there if he was disruptive, threatening, or posed a security risk at another federal pen. A convict also earned his way off, but only back to another federal prison. The idea was that no one would be paroled directly from Alcatraz. A prisoner could depart by way of the morgue, but it was said that even dead men left the Rock in handcuffs and shackles.

In the early years, new arrivals were showered and strip-searched, the first step in deflating egos. "I never saw a naked man

For Al Capone, the move to Alcatraz was like checking out of the Waldorf into a cave. No Corona Coronas; only roll-your-own, and he had fat thumbs. No old cronies to visit him; only Mae, his blonde wife, once a month for 40 minutes, the time limit then; and she would squeeze in two visits on each trip from Florida, by arriving in San Francisco toward the end of a month. None of those niceties that $20,000,000 could buy. Stanford Bates, then federal prison director, called Warden Johnston one day: What was this he heard on the radio?—Capone ordering silk underwear from a London haberdasher. "That's funny," said Johnston. "I just left Capone and I distinctly remember he was wearing regulation long johns because they were held up with a safety pin."

—J. Campbell Bruce, *Escape from Alcatraz: A Farewell to the Rock*

yet," Johnston later said, "who could maintain any sort of dignity."
At their cells, prisoners were issued plain overalls. "You are entitled
to food, clothing, shelter, and medical attention," Johnston told the
prisoners. "Anything else you get is a privilege."

Books and magazines were censored, vetted of any item relating
to crime. An inmate could write and receive letters, yet these too
were heavily censored and sometimes not even delivered. Time in
the recreation yard—where inmates played softball, chess, and
dominoes—was limited to a couple of hours on weekends.
Convicts could work in the kitchen or in one of the prison shops,
but Alcatraz had no commissary in which the men could spend
their paltry wages.

With good behavior, convicts were allowed a single one-hour
visit per month. This offered small comfort, for the inmate and visitor could see each other only through a thick plate of glass and
were forced to talk through a telephone. Guards monitored conversations and quickly cut off discussions of current events, prison
conditions, and criminal activities.

Any and all "privileges" could be taken away for the most
minor transgression. In the first few years of Warden Johnston's
reign, that included talking to other inmates. Take a swing at a
guard and you might get three weeks in the Hole. Legend has it
that some convicts were confined to the cellar of the old military
fort, in spaces as dank and dark as any medieval dungeon.

The most fabled Alcatraz getaway involved Frank Lee Morris
and brothers John and Clarence Anglin. In 1962, using pilfered
tools, they chipped through vents in their cells and replaced the
grates with cardboard replicas. With lifelike dummy heads placed
in their bunks—to fool the guards during nighttime counts—they
climbed into a utility corridor in the middle of B Block, went up
to the ceiling and painstakingly cut through the bars of a vent.
They made an inflatable raft from stolen raincoats. The preparations took six months.

On the night of June 11, the trio exited through the roof,
climbed down a drainpipe and got away. Prison officials found per-

sonal effects belonging to the convicts floating in the bay, but no bodies. If the three made it, they apparently never pulled another crime. Television accounts of the break and movies such as Clint Eastwood's *Escape From Alcatraz* keep speculation on their fate fresh. The Bureau declared them dead. Others think—or want to believe—that the Anglins and Morris are still alive and free. It's part of the Alcatraz legend.

Popular perceptions of the Rock's most legendary prisoner are a mismatch with reality. At the federal pen in Leavenworth, Kansas, where he was sent for murdering a man in Alaska, Robert Stroud turned himself into an expert and writer on bird diseases. Many considered him a genius—and a psychopath. Transferred to Alcatraz in 1942 for killing a prison guard, Stroud was disliked by guards and inmates alike. He spent seventeen years segregated in D Block or in an isolated cell in the prison's hospital. At Alcatraz, he wasn't allowed to keep birds.

But Stroud's biographers figured that a book called *The Bird Doctor of Leavenworth* didn't have much marketing zing. *The Birdman of Alcatraz*, made into a 1962 film starring Burt Lancaster, captured the public's imagination. To the chagrin of guards at Alcatraz, Lancaster portrayed Stroud as a gentle man.

The pressure of dealing with such men proved hard on correctional officers. Cold winds ripping through the Golden Gate made a night in a tower most unpleasant. The same went for an eight-hour shift in a gun gallery; the narrow corridor between a solid wall and a row of bars was as confining as a cell. There was high turnover among the officers.

Yet for some it was their most interesting assignment, particularly those who lived in island apartments and cottages with their families. In her book *Eyewitness on Alcatraz,* Jolene Babyak, the daughter of an associate warden, describes her childhood as delightful. "Islanders quickly saw advantages to their lives," she writes. "Children were safely tucked away from busy streets, in a neighborhood where everyone knew everyone else."

The children commuted to school on the boat *Warden Johnston,* which made dozens of trips to San Francisco daily. They played on the old Army parade ground, and mothers often didn't even lock the doors at night. No burglar in his right mind would hit a house on Alcatraz.

Yet Morris and the Anglin brothers—among 36 men who risked their lives in fourteen separate attempts—had shown that Alcatraz was not really escape-proof. Nor was it cost-effective. The prison's 336 cells held an average of 260 convicts at a time; during its history the prison housed a total of only 1,576 inmates. By the early 1960s, the $13 a day it took to keep an inmate on Alcatraz made it the most expensive prison in the federal system. To fix the crumbling buildings would cost $5 million. Attorney General Robert Kennedy ordered the Rock closed.

On the morning of March 21, 1963, Olin G. Blackwell, a languid Texan who'd spent two years as warden, had only 27 convicts left. Alcatraz served its final breakfast: dry cereal, bowls of steamed whole wheat, scrambled eggs, fruit, toast, butter, and coffee. Afterward, convicts were released from their cells for the last time. In handcuffs, leg irons, and waist chains, they were led down Broadway, single file.

The last inmate to enter Alcatraz, No. 1576, now had the dubious honor of being the final convict to leave. Blond and lean, 29-year-old Frank Weatherman hobbled down the gangplank, then turned to the media. "All of us are glad to get off," he muttered. "Alcatraz was never no good for nobody."

Maybe so. But among the media contingent was a newsreel photographer named Les Thomsen. Like other newsmen, he was intrigued with Alcatraz. It was an interest he passed on to his daughter. Lori Thomsen has spent her eight-year Park Service career on the island. She's interviewed fifteen former inmates and numerous guards, and even tours other prisons while on vacation. "I guess I'm just fascinated by them," she says.

While visitors typically are interested in the prison, the rangers treat all periods of the island's history as equally important. The Civil War era is given display space, as is the nineteen-month occupation by Native Americans that began in 1969 when protesters sought to establish a school and a cultural center on the island.

When Alcatraz opened for public tours in 1973, the Park Service figured the interest would last only a couple of years. Today, in the summers, tour boat operators turn away about a thousand would-be visitors per day; 4,500 visitors is the maximum permitted. "The million we get each year is about all the resource can bear and as many as the staff can manage safely," says Thomsen.

It's tough to beat a Thomsen-guided night on the island. After the last boat has departed, she leads the Boy Scouts through the tunnels under the exercise yard, into the gun galleries and through the prison's hospital. Next comes a collection of shivs confiscated in another federal pen. For the wide-eyed boys she pantomimes how convicts stuck

I was surprised to see sunlight shining in the morgue.... I was thinking how I would feel if I were a prisoner, especially in the room in the dark with the stinking toilet. It would be painful to be here for years and years if you were sorry for what you did.

—Noelle O'Reilly, age 9

them into the livers of other inmates marked for death. She also takes the group to the cellhouse roof to see the vent through which the Anglins and Morris escaped.

On the Sunday morning after Thomsen's tour, an Alcatraz celebrity ambles off the first boat. White-haired, Nathan Glenn Williams certainly doesn't look like a bank robber. But from the late 1930s through the early '50s he was an accomplished practitioner. From an affluent family in eastern Washington State, Williams knocked over banks throughout the United States. Caught, convicted, and sentenced to a state prison in Washington, he got out thanks to connections. Williams married and had a daughter but couldn't stay straight. Caught once more, he landed at McNeil Island Federal Penitentiary near Tacoma and in 1953 earned his way to the Rock.

Eventually he lost his wife and his daughter, who was adopted by a family member. Williams spent six long years on Alcatraz, where he witnessed two of the island's eight murders and a brutal stabbing.

But Williams did not change his life because of Alcatraz. "I really don't have anything good at all to say about this awful, awful place," he explains. Yet after his release from prison in 1963, Williams created a volunteer agency to drive the families of prisoners to visit inmates at McNeil Island. He embraced his past, gave lectures to youth and civic groups, and was reunited with his daughter. In 1980 he was given a Presidential pardon by Jimmy Carter. Several years later he was honored for his volunteer work by President Ronald Reagan and had lunch with him. And Williams, like ex-inmates Leon (Whitey) Thompson and Jim Quillen, wrote a book about his experiences; his is aptly titled *From Alcatraz to the White House*. Once a month he makes the trip down from Seattle to the Rock, where he enjoys talking with tourists and leading tours.

When asked about the sounds that give one the unholy creeps, Williams recalls, "Well, at first the old foghorns would drive you crazy. But you got used to 'em. The same goes for the noises from other convicts." And the seagulls? "Jeez, I haven't thought of them in years," says inmate No. 1103. "There was a lot to despise about the place. But I really hated those damn birds."

He no longer hates his former guards. "There was a time when I would have killed any one of them in an instant," he says. "We have such different perspectives. They went home, had a drink, and got to enjoy their families, while us convicts were locked in a small cell. But some of those men are now my closest friends. They eat dinner at my house and stay the night. Way back when, I'd have never dreamed of such a thing."

Jay Stuller is a senior editor in Chevron Corporation's communications group. His freelance work has appeared in magazines such as Smithsonian, Reader's Digest, Playboy, Travel & Leisure, *and* Audubon, *among others. His most recent endeavor is* How to Love a PMSing Woman.

★

Walking up the road to the cell house on Alcatraz, with birds twittering and vines growing through a retaining wall, a sense of blue sky and bay on the periphery of vision, it occurred to me what a wonderful monastery could be built here. There was something in the cold air which reminded me of Mont St. Michel with its compelling mix of gloom, aspiration, and loneliness. After my boat ride back to the city, I met G.K., who told me that (despite being a-religious) he had always thought that a cathedral should be built on the island in place of the prison. And I had to agree— it would be perfect. I can see the rose window with light pouring in from the Golden Gate, inflaming the very air; I can see the Zen monks and Catholic nuns and Tibetan lamas and even the Sisters of Perpetual Indulgence wandering in prayer, singing in praise of God or Gaia—and I couldn't resist the thought that somehow this would build on all the suffering and evil that dwelled here. Of course, in today's determinedly secular world, convincing any government body to build such a monument to the spirit (whether of man or God) would be tantamount to a backyard scientist successfully mounting a mission to Mars. Yet nevertheless, it would be perfect, it would be *right*, and when it was built it would be acclaimed as one of the wonders of the world, indeed destined—and how could anyone at the end of the twentieth century have ever been so short-sighted as to resist it?

—James O'Reilly, "San Francisco 2020"

✶ ✶ ✶

Javacrawl

A group of friends practices the art of going nowhere fast.

I'VE ALWAYS BEEN CURIOUS ABOUT THE POTENTIAL FOR MEETING someone at a coffeehouse. You know, someone *special*. Is this what's going on at coffeehouses at night? I don't know, I'm usually there while there's daylight. I mention this to a handful of friends at a party, and they don't know either. So I ask if anyone would be up for doing a coffeehouse crawl with me some night. "YESSSSS!" they all say. Boy, I wasn't ready for *that*…So I enlist my good friend Nancy and our sports buddies George (billiards) and Marty (softball). We'll check out the coffee thing after dark. I make a list of a nice cross-section of coffeehouses and tell them the ground rules. Number one: Nancy and I do not sit with George and Marty at these cafes. Hey, we already *know* these guys. The idea is to see if we can meet someone new. George seems a bit nervous at the prospect. Nancy looks excited. She knows my chatty personality will equal fun for us. Number two: We have to make an effort to meet someone. Take the initiative, start a conversation, be friendly. Everyone looks nervous except me. What am I to conclude from this? That I've been in a lot of coffeehouses. Actually, my three friends spend very little time in coffeehouses. I tell them they are very friendly places. Eyebrows start to arch. These folks need some java. We're off.

I try to start easy, the Marina district. Lots of singles here. Chestnut Street from Fillmore to Divisadero is filled with hot spots. The Grove is a relatively new coffeehouse and already very popular. We split up according to plan. Nancy orders tea and I quiz the guy behind the counter about the various desserts. He's funny and friendly. I immediately wish he was on the other side of the counter. I settle on the apple pie and a latte and look around the room for some guys sitting alone. Three possibilities. The guys I really want to talk to are wedged so tight into a corner table that it would seem foolish to ask to share their table. Certainly obvious. I approach another table with two guys and ask if we can share their table. They tell me the other two chairs are taken. By whom, Casper the ghost? I go to my third choice. The two guys at this table agree to share, *reluctantly*. I start talking to one of them. Turns out he used to live in the same town right outside of Boston as I did. We start right in on the neighborhood, lousy winters, and Bostonians. He seems very pleasant. Nancy is chatting up his friend. These fellas are both doctors and have lived in San Francisco less than a year. I tell them who my doctor is and they know him. My new friend wants us to guess who his friend looks like. "He's a dead ringer for someone really famous!" Really? I'm stuck. The guy looks familiar, but not as familiar as, say, Tom Cruise. He gives us a clue. "It's a famous comedian." The comedian look-alike is not enjoying this game. My light bulb clicks on. "Jerry Seinfeld" I say. My friend concurs. We keep talking about life in the city, coffee-houses, and other seemingly relevant things. Suddenly the doctors look at each other in that knowing way and tell us they have to leave. They get up, walk around us and leave. Almost in mid-sentence, Nancy and I look at each other. Oh well, my pie was delicious and the coffee is good, too. Nancy lets me taste her tea, the Love blend. Not very effective in this case.

I look over at George and Marty. They chose to sit at a large table in the center of the room that seats about eight. They don't seem to be talking to anyone. Nancy and I walk over. "George and I had a great conversation," Marty tells me. I tell Marty about our experience. "They must be gay," Marty says. Guys have such simple explanations for everything. I insist they're straight, just not ready for my brand of coffeehouse friendliness. George notices that a lot of people seem coupled, or grouped, together. "I feel like I'm imposing on these people," he tells me. Marty agrees, and reminds me that Saturday night is still date night. I thought that went out years ago. "It's an amiable place, though, very Marina," Marty adds. Nancy sums it up best: "Hey, where else could we get a tea called Love?"

I had been wanting to check out The Brain Wash for some time, and since SOMA usually means nighttime in my mind, this is the perfect opportunity. There is a lot going on in here. The place is bigger than I expected, especially the laundry room. A sea of washers and dryers, and it's so *clean*. I have my own washer and dryer at home, but this looks like it would be fun. You can play pinball while you do the laundry. The cafe is crowded, and a band is setting up at one end of the room. The chairs catch my eye. They're hand painted with various well-known consumer product logos. Nancy and I canvas all the chairs in the room. Then we canvas the crowd. It's a young crowd. *Real* young. I quickly realize that Marty is the oldest person in here, and he's not even that old. Most of the people at the long counter are ordering beers. There is a large table in the center of the room filled with people. Actually they've pushed together about three or four tables. They're all drinking beer and yelling and screaming. Nancy tells me they're playing a college drinking game called quarters. You flip a quarter into the glass and drink beer, or something like that. I've been out of college for a while. Not these folks. They all look 21. Nancy gets some fruit juice and I order another latte. We sit along the wall so we can get a view of the entire cafe. The guy seated next to us is waiting for a neighborhood club to open. We've never heard of it. He looks about 22. Nancy points out that there are no lights on in the kitchen. They are cooking in the dark. This seems to have Nancy worried. I'm much more preoccupied with the fact that our group is the oldest one in here. George and Marty are chatting up a young gal across the room. For only a few minutes. Then she leaves. I feel like I'm in a college bar. Most of the folks in here are drinking liquor, not coffee. Why is it called Brain Wash *Cafe*?

Nancy and I collect George and Marty and move to the other side of the cafe, where the band is about to start playing. We listen to a couple of songs and conclude that the band is good. My pals think this place is a winner. They think it's friendly, easygoing, fun. Me, I'm ready for the Steps of Rome at this point. Soon.

I had to include one grunge coffeehouse on our tour, it's only fair. We all seem a bit apprehensive. There aren't a lot of people in The Coffee Zone, which surprises me. It's the Haight on a Saturday night. I guess there are a lot of options in this neighborhood, so everyone is spread out. Nancy and I step up to the counter. I notice that there is a troll doll affixed to a large tip jar. He has a lot of wires and straps around him. This troll is in bondage. I mention this to the guy behind the counter. "Hey, he used to have more leather than *that!*" he tells me. I order straight coffee in this place. Nancy has more tea. We take a look around. The folks in here seem to be seated fairly spaced apart from each other, and no one seems to be talking. It's eerily quiet. Two guys are playing chess, one guy is writing in a notebook, another couple is sipping

History class is now in session: In 1890, San Francisco had 3,117 saloons, one for every ninety-six residents, which made it the true golden age; it has been downhill ever since to the present one for six hundred. Cocaine and morphine were easily available for a dime to fifteen cents a fix, and opium was a drug on the market. Same year, there was a bar with topless waitresses at Kearny and California; the police eventually made the Glamazons put on blouses, but didn't specify that they had to be buttoned so they weren't. On June 14, 1876, a local ordinance was passed that "the hair of every male imprisoned in County Jail be cut or clipped to a uniform length of one inch from the scalp." Shortly thereafter, the U.S. Circuit Court declared that unconstitutional, especially after finding out that the ordinance was aimed at and enforced only against the Chinese and their pigtails. It was quite a town, quite a time.

—Herb Caen, *One Man's San Francisco: A Continuing Love Affair with The City*

their drinks. A guy walks in with something wrapped around his head, just a lot of rags done pirate style. It does not work. Another guy walks in who looks like Jerry Garcia, but hairier. Okay, so no one looks really approachable. Everyone looks *dazed*. I notice the SF Net computer, and it looks inviting for the first time. Nancy and I pull up a chair. We've never tried this, but Nancy works with computers for a living so I'm confident. A quarter for six minutes so we pool our quarters. We have four. Our first twelve minutes are spent trying to figure the thing out. Finally we're in the chat group. This is live chat. And fast. Our handle is Simbacat, which is my cat's name. Lots of good names in here—Miss Anthrope, Ruby Tuesday, Calvin. And Hobbes, of course. Our name proves androgynous enough, because Calvin and Hobbes are quickly trying to find out if Simbacat is male or female. We spend the next twelve minutes being mysterious and trying to keep up with this fast-paced cyberchatter. A guy comes up behind us and watches. He tells us he's a regular on SF Net and has actually met some of the people he's talked to on-line. I'm a softie so I tell Calvin and Hobbes that Simbacat is a sex kitten right before I sign off with "ciao, meow." This net stuff is fun. But it's a Saturday night and we're talking to a *machine*? Bad sign. We round up Marty and George, who are starting to get that dazed look on their faces. On the way to the car I get an earful. "I just picked up a newspaper and pretended I wasn't there," Marty tells me. "Everyone smelled," says George. Maybe they were just jealous that we got to the computer first.

The Steps of Rome wasn't on my original itinerary, but it didn't take me long to realize that it should have been. My group is starting to wilt, so I encourage them on the drive over to North Beach. "This place is really cool, lots of good-looking guys and gals. It just oozes sex. Eurosex." George wants to know if he can have a beer yet. I decide to drop the liquor ban. When we get to Steps, Nancy tells her favorite story about this cafe. She actually heard about this cafe while visiting Rome. On the Spanish Steps, no less. A Roman (or should I say Romeo?) started chatting her up, and when he learned that she was from San Francisco, told her that a friend of his had just opened a cafe in North Beach called The Steps of Rome. Apparently he had wanted to name it The Spanish Steps, but someone had already taken that name. Or so he said. Anyway, this little episode has always made Nancy feel like an insider at Steps, and that's okay. We trade stories about our experiences in Rome. You get lots of material in Rome.

At this point we're a bit coffeed out, so Nancy and I order gelato. The place is packed. It's after midnight in North Beach. The crowd is spilling onto the sidewalk. Talking at Steps would be impossible at this point. The music is cranked way up and the din is deafening. Good thing the windows are open to let some of the noise out. It's the usual Euromix on this particular night. They're nice-looking *and* cool. I can't see a single available seat inside so I step outside and notice an empty table right out front. Prime real estate. I grab it. Nancy follows, and we enjoy our gelato among the beautiful people. Four guys are seated next to us. One of them is very drunk. The other three are having fun with him. The drunk fellow gets up and walks away. The three remaining Romeos are from Brazil, Spain, and England. They're smoking and drinking. Like most everyone else in the place. They start telling us stories and are laughing throughout. We start laughing, too. *Everyone* appears to be having a hoot of a time here. It's infectious. It's like being in Rome.

I could stay much longer but we have one more spot to check out, so I look for George and Marty. Nancy and I don't see

We do not wish to say, or even imply, that San Francisco is the wickedest and most immoral city in the world; that her men are all libertines and her women all fallen; that she has no noble sons and pure daughters. This is only a single chapter on her wickedest ways—the deepest shade among many brilliant lights. But we would say to the parents of San Francisco to look closer to their daughters, for they know not the many dangers to which they are exposed—know their associates, guard their virtue—and to mildly counsel their sons, for when upon the streets of this gay city they are wandering amid many temptations.

—B. E. Lloyd, *Lights and Shades in San Francisco* (1876)

them anywhere. We wade through the crowd and finally spot them on the mezzanine. They're reading a newspaper and drinking a beer. Not what I expected. The music is getting *louder*. One of the guys behind the counter is dancing up a storm. "Every place has to have its own Fabio," George tells me. Okay by me. People continue to pour in. George spots a trend. "These guys go to the counter while the girls wait at the table." That's very European, I tell him. We're near the back door, so we make our way out. I wave to Fabio. I think he sees me.

Savoy Tivoli on Grant was a must-do on this coffeehouse crawl. Hey, it's been around in one form or another since 1907. *Something* is working if it's been around that long. It's 1:15 a.m. and this place is packed, too. I walk in and a guy at the bar immediately makes eye contact with me. Laser beams. He won't take his eyes off me. I don't kid myself. It's almost closing time and he's by himself. He's hoping I'm *it*. Boy. I keep walking. It's a long bar and I get to the other end, where there's a little more elbow room. I ask for a cup of coffee and am told that they already stopped serving coffee. Huh? Looks like the Savoy is more of a bar than a coffeehouse these days. The fact that many of the patrons are drunk reinforces that notion. I order cranberry juice. Nancy gets a beer. We look for a table on the front patio, which is one of the nicest features of the Savoy. It opens out onto the street, so you're inside and outside at the same time. Guys all around us. Empty beer bottles litter the small tables. I'm too sober for this. The noise is intense. Suddenly the bouncer starts yelling at everyone to move into the other room. "This section is closed! Grab your drinks and move next door. Now!!" He doesn't sound nice about it at all. Most of the crowd staggers into the next room. So now we have two roomfuls of people packed into one room. I start looking for George and Marty. Once I find them, I wave and motion in my direction. I'm not about to move. By the time they make it over to Nancy and me, the bouncer starts telling everyone to *leave*. We've barely touched our drinks. It's 1:45 a.m. I'm not about to argue with Mr. Personality, so we leave.

Our little group is very animated on the drive back home. I think we had fun. Yes, we definitely had fun. We're already recounting incidents that took place just a few hours earlier. And laughing. Which means we'd surely do it again.

Elaine Sosa is a former stockbroker who grew weary of going to work at 6 a.m. In 1994 she left Wall Street behind and started "Javawalk," a coffee-walking tour in the heart of San Francisco, as a way to legitimize her coffeehouse addiction. To her pleasant surprise, Javawalk has become a bona fide business.

*

The Diana the Huntress Café, which also sold Diana the Huntress Café sweatshirts, was a women's café. There were Amazon symbols, arrows, spears, shields, and a sun-dried copy of a book by Kate Millett in the window....

A serving person in granny glasses, an ankle-length skirt, and a flowing purple blouse brought juice to other patrons. To Laura and Tim she brought nothing, not even conversation. "Why doesn't she serve us?" Laura asked.

"She can't see me," said Tim.

"I don't understand. You're not filmy or gauzy or transparent like some bug's wings, are you?"

"To her I am. It's the Diana the Huntress *Society* Café. It's like a club. I'm not a member."

"Pardon?"

"But you are. But since legally, you know, civil rights, they can't legally keep me out, they just keep me invisible."

A little indignation brought the roses back to Laura's cheeks. This was the ticket: get her out of herself.

"Should we make a fuss?" she asked.

He gazed soulfully down at the women warriors on his placemat. He averted his eyes. He cleared his throat delicately. "We don't want the pretty femme doing anything, uh, doing anything in my sparkling apple cider," he said.

"You seem to know," she said. "Then why'd you bring us here? Me, I understand, but why both of us?"

"I brought another woman here once in her deep distress. She had a sadness about a guy. It seemed to console her. You know, distraction tends to console. Smile, okay?"

She considered it. She wasn't sure she wanted to be consoled. She wasn't even amused yet. But she was just a tiny bit *interested*. "Let me try," she said.

She waved at the attractive and slender young creature who was serving others, not serving them. The waitperson in her long skirt seemed blind; yet she was wearing her glasses. She was blind in her glasses, blinkered in her assumptions, blind to the interlopers. "She doesn't even see me," Laura said.

"Let me explain. You're with a man. My invisibility seems to be contagious."

"I could starve here."

"Right. We could die of thirst. Too bad for us."

It wasn't apple juice or date walnut bread sandwiches with cream cheese, that were the issue in this territory. It wasn't even cream soda. It was politics.

Perhaps it was good for Timothy as it was good for Laura. He tasted what it was like to be on the losing side. And then they headed for a Winchell's Donuts, where the orange plastic seats fit like spoons over the behinds of male and female alike, for they were all God's creatures.

—Herbert Gold, *Travels in San Francisco*

STEPHEN HARRIGAN

⋆ ⋆ ⋆

Fort at the End of the World

The Presidio, which used to be the nation's oldest,
continuously functioning military post, is now a national park.

IMAGINE THE BAY OF SAN FRANCISCO IN 1776, ITS SURFACE glittering against a windswept wilderness of chaparral and serpentine grasslands and wooded streams. Vast tracts of cordgrass marsh soften the bay's shorelines; the rocks and islands that rise from its waters are white with pelican droppings or obscured beneath a twitching blanket of sea lions. Past the islands and the distant margins of the bay the Marin Headlands rear up into a sky pulsing with shorebirds and migrating hawks. And from the summits of the dunes an observer can see the mouth of the bay, the narrow, elusive, fog-shrouded passage that has been hidden to European exploring ships for more than 200 years. On a grassy vale above the bay, a handful of leather-jacketed soldiers, Franciscan friars, and civilian colonists have built a rude adobe fort, a presidio, to enforce their claim that California belongs to Spain. They have journeyed from Sonora, across 1,800 miles of desert and freezing mountain passes, losing only one traveler to death. Now, planted among a nervous population of Ohlone Indians, they constitute the northernmost permanent settlement of the Spanish Empire.

The Presidio that we know today took its name from that original forlorn outpost. What began as a mud fort became, several centuries and empires later, a sprawling military complex of 1,480 acres, incorporating two distinct infantry posts, an airfield, several hospitals, a national cemetery, cavalry barracks, a mammoth brick fortress guarding the harbor mouth, a golf course, a pet cemetery, and a network of coastal-defense batteries spanning the eras between the Civil War and World War II, to defend the bay.

Before the coming of the Spaniards, Central California had the densest Indian population anywhere north of Mexico. Over 10,000 people lived in the coastal area between Point Sur and the San Francisco Bay. These people belonged to about forty different groups, each with its own territory and its own chief. Among them they spoke eight to twelve different languages— languages that were closely related but still so distinct that oftentimes people living twenty miles apart could hardly understand each other. The average size of a group (or tribelet, as it is often called) was only about 250 people. Each language had an average of no more than 1,000 speakers.

—Malcolm Margolin, *The Ohlone Way: Indian Life in the San Francisco-Monterey Bay Area*

On a map of San Francisco, the Presidio is that commanding blank space you see at the foot of the Golden Gate Bridge, an area roughly the size of the Financial District, Nob Hill, Chinatown, North Beach, Russian Hill, and the Tenderloin combined. As you drive into the city across the bridge, the Presidio is what greets you—a luxuriant green headland in which occasional clusters of buildings are visible through the trees, bordered on one side by miles of bay shore and on the other by the Pacific. This enchanted location was considered by generations of military personnel to be the prime duty station in the United States. An army officer of the last century, the story goes, had only three wishes: to make colonel, to die and go to heaven, and then to be posted at the Presidio.

But it is park rangers, not soldiers, who will be posted at the Presidio from now on. Targeted by the Congressional Base Closure Commission in 1989, the Presidio officially went out of business as a military installation in the fall of 1994. It is now a key component of the Bay Area's Golden Gate National Recreation Area, which includes the Marin Headlands, Muir Woods, the Sutro Baths, Mount Tamalpais, and Alcatraz.

As a public space, the Presidio is a rather awkward bonanza. How do you turn a vast piece of real estate containing 870 buildings—ranging from Civil War barracks to bowling alleys, fast-food restaurants, and maintenance sheds—into a national park? The various government prospectuses I read on the subject are bursting with irrepressible 21st-century jargon. We taxpayers are promised not only a "threshold to sustainability" but a "synergy for success." It will be a center for "global linkages" and "unparalleled public outreach," whose former barracks buildings and airplane hangars will be thrumming with think tanks and task forces studying fuel-cell technologies and waterborne diseases. The only problem is that, at least for the present, the Presidio is something of a white elephant, an immensely costly addition to an already beleaguered national parks system. Once these buildings are generating revenue as bed-and-breakfasts and headquarters for farsighted policy groups, the Presidio can begin to control its huge operating deficit. Interpretive signs have been erected at the park's historical sites and along its hiking trails. Visitors to the Presidio in this troubled transitional time are likely to find it an uncrowded and even ghostly place. The soldiers are gone and tourists have not yet swarmed in to replace them. Most of the activity at the Presidio seems to be centered at its golf course, which—for years a perk for soldiers—is now open to the public.

But perhaps I received that impression of emptiness only because I arrived in San Francisco during the waning days of a January of solid rain. My bike tour of the Presidio had been canceled, and so I retired to the Burger King near the post headquarters to drink an iced tea and ponder my itinerary. The Presidio Burger King, I noticed incidentally, has one of the greatest views that any restaurant in America can boast. Sitting in a plastic booth, I looked out upon the panoply of the Golden Gate, the spires and cables of the bridge glowing orange against the swirling gray clouds.

The sky refused to clear, but at least the rain diminished enough for me to contemplate a leisurely walking tour of the Main Post, the richly historic centerpiece of the Presidio. The Main Post had been recommended to me by Stephen A. Haller, the park historian, as the ideal spot from which to get a good impression of the Presidio's long and ever more complex tenure.

"The Presidio has been called a layer cake of history," Haller said. "Actually, layer cake is not the right image. It's more as if someone threw a coin in the water and you're watching the ripples go outward as time expands."

The Main Post is where the first coin was tossed. When I left the Burger King and walked over to the Officers' Club, I was standing in the heart of the old Presidio. Though the bay was less than a mile away, it was hidden by clouds and fog and by the towering greenery of the Monterey pine and cypress and eucalyptus that were planted with military efficiency in the 1880s.

The Officers' Club, built in 1934 as a Spanish Colonial Revival showpiece, was erected over the ruins of the original presidio's chapel and *commandancia*. I had the opportunity to visit the main dining room, which is no longer open to the general public. There a small pane of glass is set into one of the walls. This curious little window is dark until you press a button next to it, which turns on a light that allows a peek at the crumbling adobe wall still residing within the newer building.

Except for that one tantalizing glimpse, the old presidio is nowhere to be seen, buried and absorbed as it has been by succeeding waves of military history. The garrison was vital in securing the Spanish presence in Northern California. But even in its salad days the Spanish presidio was undersupplied and undermanned, and after Mexico's overthrow of Spanish rule, in 1821, it continued to go to seed, until it was abandoned altogether fourteen years later.

It was soon reoccupied by American forces, after California was seized from Mexico during the Bear Flag Revolt of 1846, and for well over a century it remained a critical defensive bastion and deployment center for U.S. troops. The many wars, incursions, invasions, and police actions in which the United States Army has taken part are cataloged in the architecture at the Main Post. Here are the Victorian Gothic cottages built during the Civil War to provide housing for officers and their families; here is a row of barracks built of indomitable red bricks during the expansionist fervor of the Spanish-American War; here are the thick concrete edifices, with graceful Mission flourishes, that were the headquarters of the Western Defense Command during the Second World War, and here, by the flagpole at Pershing Square, is the site where General John J. Pershing's house stood before it was consumed in a fire that killed the general's wife and daughters while he was in Mexico chasing Pancho Villa.

All this conflated history was visible to me in a single glance as I stood beneath the awning at the entrance to the Officer's Club, sheltered from a new episode of rain. Flanking the entrance were two ancient cannons that were once part of a gun battery, named the Castillo de San Joaquin, that the Spanish had established on a rocky bluff miles away, at the entrance to the bay, in order to guard against Russian or English warships, whichever might enter.

It is often said that the native people of the Bay Area lived lightly upon the land, without altering it in any way. This is not quite true. They didn't destroy, but they did alter. Like native people throughout much of California they regularly burnt their meadowlands to clear the brush, create good game habitat, and encourage the growth of certain annual grasses and flowers from which they could more easily harvest grain and seed. They tended to confine their digging of bulbs and roots to certain areas, thus keeping the soil loosened in those areas and encouraging the growth of larger bulbs and straighter basketry roots. Their continual pruning of willow and hazel fostered the growth of long, straight shoots, ideal for basket making, and they planted tobacco along the margins of the streams. At the time the Spaniards arrived, in short, the Bay Area was not a "virgin wilderness" over which tribes of "wild" people roamed. The Bay Area was a deeply inhabited environment, and its landscape bore the cultural imprint of its people as surely as did the farmlands of Europe or New England.

—Malcolm Margolin, Historical Introduction to *Berkeley Inside/Out*, by Don Pitcher

I strolled in the rain down Funston Avenue, named for Frederick Funston, the hero of America's Philippines adventure. The long row of Civil War cottages that lined the street here faced east, though when they were built they faced in the opposite direction, toward the old parade ground. They were reoriented between 1874 and 1878 to greet the new forest the army had planted.

In time the Civil War cottages will be leased out as bed-and-breakfasts. For now, they appeared mostly vacant, though a few of them had curtains in the windows and cats snoozing on the porches and signs indicating that a lingering captain or lieutenant was still in residence.

The homes of higher-grade officers were more imposing: two-story residences reflecting the architectural enthusiasms of their eras, from fish-scale shingles to mansard roofs. A walkway behind these houses led across an old brick footbridge, past rows of family housing for enlisted men dating from the 1930s and on into that strangely perfect forest decreed into existence by the U.S. Army. The walkway, a concrete path with cobblestone borders, led straight uphill to the Presidio's boundary at Pacific Avenue. The walkway was littered in places with sickle-shaped eucalyptus leaves, and the light fell in moody swaths through the branches overhead. The path was called Lovers' Lane, a name that conjured up images of couples walking here on moonlit nights, the foghorns lowing plaintively across the bay, on the eve of a separation that would carry a soldier to Cuba or France or some deadly atoll far across the Pacific Ocean.

Lovers' Lane followed the track of the original Spanish path that led from the adobe presidio to Mission San Francisco de Asis, more commonly known as Mission Dolores, which the friars built for the salvation and subjugation of the local Ohlone tribes. Today the trail would lead through what is now Pacific Heights and the Haight-Ashbury, but the route I took veered off on what was billed as an "ecology trail." After the incessant rains the dominant ecological feature of the trail was mud, and under the sodden pine boughs I slid and skittered my way to a little picnic area known as Tennessee Hollow, named for the First Tennessee Volunteer

Infantry Regiment, which camped here during the Spanish-American War. At the far end of the hollow were more nondescript NCO housing units, but in its center a rock wall encircled El Polin spring. This was the spring from which the Spanish soldiers and colonists drew their water. A plaque beside it repeated an Ohlone legend: "All maidens who drank from the spring during the full of the moon were assured of many babies and eternal bliss."

I climbed out of the hollow, followed the road back to my car, at the Main Post, and then cruised down to the waterfront, to a vast landfill stretching below the green bluffs of the Presidio.

At one time, in the days of the Ohlones, this was a lush marshland, and the anchorage for Spanish ships calling on the Presidio lay just offshore. But the marsh was destroyed in order to create a space for San Francisco's picture-book world's fair, the 1915 Panama-Pacific International Exposition. After the fair closed, Crissy Field took over the site. This was an early army airfield with a grass runway, home to barnstormers, balloon squadrons, and the homing pigeons that were sometimes used as pilot-to-ground messengers in the days before radio made a trustworthy form of communication.

Today it is an expanse of concrete and chain-link fence and empty buildings, the most poignant structure being the lackluster hangar where World War II Nisei soldiers were trained—young men of Japanese-American descent whose mission it was to serve as battlefield translators at places like Attu and Guadalcanal. They rehearsed for this perilous duty while their families were being rounded up as security risks and sent to internment camps.

In time, the old hangar will be turned into an interpretive center honoring the Nisei soldiers. The grass airfield dating from the days of biplanes will be restored as well, and marshland will be reintroduced along the fringes of the bay. A walking trail, which already exists as a part of the Golden Gate Promenade, follows the water's edge all the way to Fort Point, at the base of the Golden Gate Bridge.

Fort Point is the Presidio's most spectacular historical site, a pristine relic from the Civil War constructed more or less on the site of the abandoned Spanish Castillo. The fort faces the turbulent waters of the bay entrance, and overhead the Golden Gate Bridge rises above the open quadrangle in stunning proximity, a vaulting roofline of shining girders that rumbles with traffic both day and night.

The fort, a three-story building of granite and red brick, is faceless and utilitarian. It has the smooth, closed-up completeness of a clamshell. There is only one entrance, a low passageway known as a sally port, and when you walk inside and look up at the three tiers of arched gun casements you have the feeling you are looking at an immense man-made beehive. Each one of these casements, along with the open barbettes on the roof, was home to a cannon that was capable of hurling a 32-pound cannonball two miles into the bay. Now they are virtually empty.

Fort Point was built to protect against a Confederate invasion that never came. None of its ordnance was ever fired in anger—a circumstance it shares with the rest of the batteries strung along the seaward margins of the Presidio. It was my intention to hike the next morning from Fort Point along the coastal bluffs on the Pacific, inspecting those batteries as I went.

I planned to walk four or five miles, to follow the trail down to Baker Beach and then out of the Presidio all the way around to Land's End, arriving at the Cliff House in time for lunch. But I hadn't counted on the fascination I would feel for these secretive fortifications. Most of the batteries date from the turn of the century, when they were built to accommodate the mighty breech-loading guns that replaced the muzzle-loading cannons of Fort Point. The batteries had names like Cranston, Boutelle, and Godfrey, but those names appeared only on the map of seacoast fortifications I had picked up at the Presidio museum. The miniature fortresses had yet to be restored or interpreted in the manner to which national park visitors are accustomed, and so they seemed hidden away and inscrutable, with no information to impart to a casual hiker except their own, blank presence.

The iron and wood doors that led into the interiors of the batteries were closed and locked, sometimes rusted into place and overgrown with vegetation. It was frustrating not to be able to enter those concrete-reinforced burrows, to visit those sleeping quarters and observation posts of long ago. Some of the batteries were set so deeply into the bluffs that all I could see of them were their gun slits, peering out at the Pacific like the patient eyes of alligators.

The most commodious of them was Battery Chamberlain, armed in 1904 and active until 1948. It was ensconced in a point above Baker Beach, near where Lobos Creek filters down from the heights of the Presidio to the Pacific. Most of Battery Chamberlain's guns have long since been taken away, a broad sloping apron of blank concrete left in their place. I climbed up a ladder to what I supposed was an observation platform and looked out over the ocean, watching the gulls and cormorants, the waves slamming into the rocks below, the dune grasses and cypress boughs surging in the sea wind. Overcast as it was, I could easily make out the two pincerlike points—Land's End to the south, Point Bonita across the channel to the north—that marked the entrance to the storied bay of San Francisco. These batteries were here and the Spaniards had built a presidio in the first place to guard this bay against an invasion by sea. For over 200 years, this presidio had been vigilantly watching, but no enemy—no militant Russian fur traders, no English armadas, no Confederate gunships, no Japanese aircraft carriers—had ever bothered to come.

The imminent arrival of swarms of Communist troops posed special problems for small boys growing up in sight of the Pacific during the Cold War. We knew we were a scant two miles from the beach, and therefore in grave danger—but we knew also that early views of landing craft would give us time to get ready with weapons in the backyard. We prepared our arsenal in earnest: giant three-foot-long wooden scissors with nails on the blades to close around Russian and Chinese necks, bows and arrows, home-made lances and formica shields, blowguns, and of course, flame throwers fashioned from copper pipe and hairspray. It's a marvel we didn't kill ourselves, an even greater blessing that Khrushchev and Mao saw the folly of a maritime assault on San Francisco.

—James, Sean, and Tim O'Reilly, "Boys in the Avenues"

After several hours of poking around the batteries I set aside my ambitious plans to reach the Cliff House for lunch and instead

walked back to my car and drove to the San Francisco National
Military Cemetery, which commands a gentle hill just west of the
Main Post. The cemetery covers 28 acres. Originally the post
cemetery, it was opened to military personnel from all over the
country when it was declared a national cemetery, in 1884. Many
soldiers were dug up and replanted here; they gained in death the
coveted posting that might have eluded them in their earthly careers. I walked aimlessly uphill through the rows of tombstones,
most of them simple upright slabs so white and bleached they
seemed to be made of salt, the birth and death dates incised in the
quaint calligraphy of distant eras. There were casualties from Korea,
from World War II and the Vietnam War; there were inscriptions
honoring soldiers who had drowned in some unknown place or
succumbed to disease in the Philippines or been killed in the
California Lava Beds during the army's bitter and heartless campaign against the Modoc Indians.

As I climbed the hill the sky grew lighter, until enough sun had
leaked through the clouds to spotlight a field of tombstones near
the summit, making those bone white markers gleam strangely, like
silver. I stood behind the grave of Julius Gron, whose tombstone
said that he was a corporal of Company E of the 13th Regiment
of Wisconsin infantry. A veteran of the Spanish-American War, he
died on July 6, 1934. It seemed to me that Corporal Gron, buried
at the crest of this hill, high enough to see over the trees to the waters of the bay, had the best spot in the cemetery. From this spot I
could see sailboats thronging the waters around Alcatraz; I could
see the Marin Headlands and Sausalito and Tiburon and the red-
tiled roofs of the old airfield and finally the great bridge, hovering
golden in the sky above the trees, looking like some sort of celestial visitation.

There had been some hard feelings here and there among some
military people when it became apparent that the Presidio's history
had come to an end and the army was going to have to give it up.
And who can blame them? Who would want to give up the dream
of serving out one's career in this Valhalla at the edge of San
Francisco Bay, sipping drinks in the Officers' Club, playing golf

amid the eucalyptus, strolling down the same paths used by Spanish *soldados*? As a civilian standing in my new national park, I felt reluctant to take possession of this paradise post, feeling that it still belonged more to Corporal Gron than it did to me.

Stephen Harrigan is a novelist who makes a living as a journalist. His writings include Arkansas *and* Jacob's Well. *He is the senior editor for* Texas Monthly *and contributes to* The Atlantic Monthly, Esquire, *and* Outside. *He lives in Austin, Texas.*

✳

The last time I saw Rob he took me to the pet cemetery in the Presidio. Our relationship had ended, but we hadn't officially said goodbye, face to face. Rob's suggestion to include an offbeat cemetery in the ritual didn't surprise me; he's a man fond of mischief and games and magic tricks.

Above the cemetery and to one side, rising like a giant red canopy, was the overpass of Doyle Drive, the approach to the Golden Gate Bridge. The sign on the fence around the cemetery warned us away from the sacred pet ground: "toxic danger." But Rob said it was merely because the soil had become leaded when paint from the overpass dripped into it. We'd be OK as long as we didn't squat down and start eating dirt. I pictured red paint covering that ground, soaking into the soil where dead pets lay, some already bloodied, surely, having met their fates trying to cross the street.

Inside the gate, past the danger sign, graves of beloved pets lay. The place had the strange quality of being both poignant and kitsch. Homemade crosses bore photos wrapped in cellophane of a beloved Fido or Ralph or Terrance. Favorite squeaky toys and bones were taped or stapled or nailed to the tombs of others. Some graves included tributes to a pet's short life in elaborate poetic verse.

We each thought of favorite pets we'd lost in childhood. Mine was a puppy who was hit by a car in front of our house. I wouldn't believe he was dead because his tail continued to wag spasmodically for a full minute after the accident. When my parents finally convinced me, I cried inconsolably for an entire day. Rob remembered his dog Brownie who ran away, and how the family decided it was just as well; the dog couldn't even learn to sit on command. But one year later the local paper featured a photo of the dog, a "stray" found by a deaf woman. Brownie had become a highly trained dog for the hearing-impaired, and he'd even saved his owner's life on one occasion.

Rob and I told each other our stories, laughed together in that toxic pet cemetery before saying our good-byes. Somehow the setting felt appropriate. Quirky but poignant. A place of final farewell, with a twist.

—Lucy McCauley, "Pet Cemetery"

LINDA WATANABE MCFERRIN

Gulf of the Farallones

A place of profound wildness lies 32 miles out to sea.

THE PASSENGERS WERE ALL STANDING ON DECK IN THEIR THREE-point stances (legs slightly apart, one hand on the boat rail), staring into a glass-green sea where the football-shaped head of a turtle appeared and disappeared like a magician's rabbit. Roger and Meryl, the naturalist guides, were excited. This was a leatherback turtle. Leatherback turtles are rarely seen. The drone of the Ranger 88's engine was hypnotic. The boat circumscribed slow, sickening circles. Moments later, my friend Margo was folded over the railing of the stern, succumbing to seasickness. A few minutes more and I was doing the same thing. We were having a fabulous time!

Clearly, the Oceanic Society Expeditions tour of the Farallon Islands is not for the lily-livered or the weak-stomached. Not at all. When a wind rank with the guano of thousands of curlews and puffins rises up over the islands, we of the intrepid spirit throw out our chests and inhale deeply, filling our lungs—"ah, the sweet smell of nature!" we say, and mean it.

This was not supposed to be a luxury cruise. My friends and I had deduced this at once when we looked through the briefing packet, provided in advance by the Oceanic Society. "Dress warmly," it warned. "Even on the sunniest day, it is cold. Bring waterproof rain gear. Be prepared."

As we waited with the others in the grey dawn of the San Francisco Yacht Harbor, it was already apparent who was in the know and who wasn't. Our naturalist leaders, Roger and Meryl, cast appraising eyes over the crowd. They reminded us that it would be cold out on the Gulf of the Farallones. I thought, "They can see right through us. They're picking out the environmental imposters."

Roger summarized what we could expect to see on our trip to the Farallones: an island covered with wildlife, a glimpse of the pristine past before our species became the dominant one on earth. One half of all the seabirds in California congregate on the Farallones. We would see western gulls, tufted puffins, storm petrels, and auklets. We would see fin-footed and flipper-footed animals—harbor seals, elephant seals, orcas, and porpoise, and because of "El Nino," a warm current that follows a four-to-five-year cycle, we might even see some generally more southern species like blue sharks "about the size of Meryl." He finished his short lecture, and we all turned to witness the eagerly awaited arrival of our vessel.

If the heavy socks, rainboots, and seasickness precautions had not already signaled that this was no balmy pleasure voyage, the dark, equipment-crowded cabin and short-order fare of the Ranger 88's galley would have. On deck, our naturalists' instructions made it perfectly clear that we were setting forth with a purpose. They demonstrated the three-point stance, which one uses for balance, and indicating the pertinent parts of the boat, taught us the terminology we were to use to directionally indicate sightings: bow (front of the boat)—"12 o'clock;" stern (back of the boat)—"6 o'clock;" port (left side)—"9 o'clock;" and starboard (right side)—"3 o'clock." Then we were heading out to sea, our passage trumpeted by the foghorn's hoarse and relentless cry.

Three-foot seas, six-foot swells, wind 15-25 knots in the Bay—north to northwest, southwest winds 10 knots at the Gate—a lacy froth uncurled beneath the cut we made in the waters' cloudy green. The wind shifted when we got out past the land. This translated into a gentle rocking that I handled expertly with my three-point stance. As we neared the Gate, Meryl pointed out the light-house and Point Bonita, mistranslated from the Spanish, "Point Bonnetes," named for the hooded monks who were its early occupants. Upon that lonely point, the cliffs were crowned in fog, the surf gnawing away at their foot. Murres stood, soldier-like, all along the shore, their torpedo-shaped bird bodies at military attention. A black albatross flew past us on some part of its eight-year sojourn at sea.

murre

We were on the continental shelf, where ice had once been trapped in a long-lost glacial age. On the pancake-flat horizon, every change was magnified, as if in a concave lens. A host of ragged-winged pelicans swooped by, looking vaguely prehistoric, with their entourage of ever-hopeful, klepto-parasitic Herman's gulls. The great seven-foot wingspans of these pelicans makes them the second largest California bird. Pelicans live for thirty years, their heads turning a skeletal white if they manage to survive beyond the fifth, but for the pelican, too, survival has become more and more difficult. Like the largest California bird, the condor, the pelican is endangered by a pesticide-induced lack of calcium in its eggs.

Our boat dipped and climbed. We were in the shipping chan-nel, the borders marked with buoys. Before us, in the commercial party boats that dotted the waters, fishermen angled for pink salmon. Behind us, the shearwater—a kind of oceangoing or "pelagic" bird—trawled our wake. Human and animal, all were busily mining the briny deep, beaks and poles poised. The sea rose and fell beneath us, and suddenly we felt as if we weren't moving at all, the ocean strangely calm. Far across its vitreous surface, the Farallones quavered, swathed in cottony fog. It was dangerous, at this point, to look over the side of the boat—like trying to read a book on the bus. But, at the same time, it was irresistible. Sea lions sported alongside the vessel. Beautiful jellyfish tents glistened around us, their long tentacles streaming like marine kite tails. A

large sunfish, big and flat as a shiny satellite dish, inscribed circles
first to starboard then to port, occasionally breaking the waters' surface with a clumsy but spirited leap. A great connoisseur of jellyfish, it was obviously celebrating a windfall. Then someone sighted
the leatherback turtle, its enormous ridged shell arcing above the
glycerin-smooth waters and disappearing again, and the boat motored slowly around and around, and soon the recumbent forms of
sea-sickened passengers were draped all over the deck.

We smelled the Farallones before we saw them closely. First
"discovered" in the Euro-sense of history in 1542, the Farallones
are a cluster of islands comprised of two larger land masses and several small ones just 32 miles west of San Francisco. According to
Roger and Meryl, Sir Francis Drake was the first historical person-
age to set foot on them. It was evident as we drew closer to the island that we were looking at a great wildlife resort—the Hilton
Head Island of western pelagic wanderers. The census was high.
Over a quarter of a million birds swarm over the island each year,
and we saw many of them that day—nesting on rocks, strutting
along the shoreline, craning their necks along the high ridges, or
watching us with a diffident air. Sea lions lolled on the sandy
shelves, occasionally diving over the deep end in search of abalone
or sea urchin. It all bore an uncanny resemblance to Rio or Cancun
or any popular resort, except for an undeniably animal smell that
reached out and seemed to say, "Do not enter. No humans allowed." This smell made it particularly easy to comply with the
Oceanic Society's noninvasive approach to wildlife encounters. We
were not permitted to land on the islands, which was fine with us.
The heavy fence of scent that surrounded them was unbreachable.

By this time, our naturalists, Roger and Meryl, were deep in a
kind of eco-orgasm. Smiling to themselves, their talk had deterio-
rated to whispers, whistles, and low crooning sounds. Occasionally,
we'd catch a bird name like "pink-footed shearwater," "pigeon
guillemot," or "Cassin's auklet." Every so often they'd remember us
and point out an exciting island inhabitant like the petrels, adding
that these birds were sometimes called "little Peters," because
they're so light they appear to walk on the water.

We circumnavigated the islands. Sugarloaf, the island so named because of the white crust of guano that coats it, seemed to rise like a warning finger, a great "Do Not Disturb." But a disturbance from any of us was highly unlikely. We had worn our sunscreen, our stomachs were upset, lips blistered, eyelids sunburned, noses running, skin breaking out in strange rashes. And strangest of all, because of the wind and the sun, there emanated from many of us the salty perfume of our outdoor adventure—a faintly animal smell. It seemed to work an odd magic on our normally stressed-out personas. A curious contentment—or was it exhaustion?—imbued us.

The trip back to port was deliciously relaxing, a time for reflection upon the nature of humanity, meditation upon our place in the great chain of life, or more simply, a snooze. By the time we were back at the Yacht Harbor and the Marina Green, a ragged but satisfied group, we were already missing the seabirds' cry, the limitless vistas, the rare opportunity to be, for a change, an unobtrusive observer. We staggered wearily off the boat; suddenly unaccustomed to a foundation without pitch and roll; reluctant to readjust to the old expectations, the limitations and the demands of our terribly linear lives; very, very grudgingly giving up our sea legs.

Linda Watanabe McFerrin is a poet, travel writer, and fashion merchandiser. She has been a contributor to over 40 literary journals, newspapers, and magazines including the San Francisco Examiner, The Washington Post, *and* Modern Bride. *She is the author of two poetry collections and has just completed a novel set in Japan. When she is not on the road, she directs art and consults on communications and product development for apparel manufacturers. She lives in Oakland, California.*

*

One of the world's greatest (cheapest) water-borne thrills is the San Francisco-Sausalito ferry. As soon as you pass through the ticket wicket at the San Francisco ferry terminal, you are in another world. The sun sparkles off the water. A smell mixed of salty sea and diesel fuel entwines you. Seagulls screech and soar.

I board the Golden Gate Ferry and ascend to the topmost deck, where about twenty other passengers, most toting guidebooks, are already savoring the sun and the splendid sight of pastel-colored houses climbing to Coit Tower. Looking through their eyes, I am reminded once again just how scenic San Francisco is.

Suddenly, with a toot and a puff of black smoke, the ferry sets off, turns around and begins to churn through the water. On the enclosed deck below, half a dozen people sit at tables reading or chatting. But the real action is on top, where a chilly breeze is whipping and passengers are pulling on sweaters and coats, and all around us gulls are crying, sailboats are skimming, tugboats are plowing, and the Transamerica Pyramid, the Bay Bridge and Alcatraz are all being veiled in a thin gray mist. As we approach Alcatraz, the lighthouse beams its forlorn, steadfast light and the water tower and prison buildings stand out as stark symbols of that island's grim history.

Rounding Alcatraz, the boat begins to sway with the waves; then the elegant span of the Golden Gate Bridge reveals the full grandeur of its design and the awesomeness of its construction. A tanker appears, steaming slowly toward the ocean; then a sleek and sinister gray warship crosses our path.

For a few moments I feel close to the wild heart of the bay—the wind tears at my hair and clothes, gulls plunge and wheel around bobbing fishing boats, the sun trails a blinding gilded cape on the water, the bridge turns spectral in the onrushing brume, stray flecks of water salt my lips.

Then the scene gentles again. Sausalito's Mediterranean visage—pale blue, cream and terra-cotta houses set among clumps of green trees—comes into view; the weathered waterfront buildings and compact town green approach. Soon I will be walking down Bridgeway, past the cafes and galleries, the t-shirt shops and *haute couture* shops.

But for now I close my eyes and relish those wild moments a few minutes before: the wind-tossed, all-too-brief taste of the seductive sea beyond.

—Donald W. George, "Cruising to Sausalito," *San Francisco Examiner*

K. M. KOSTYAL

West Coast Orient

*For generations of Chinese, this was
the gateway to Gold Mountain.*

BETWEEN THE HIGH-RISE GLITTER OF SAN FRANCISCO'S
Financial district and the elegant bristle of the city's Nob Hill
mansions lies another culture altogether, a culture of only 24 square
blocks, unique unto itself. A Chinese town with an American
dream. A paradox.

If paradox inspires you, then you will enjoy the exact moment
when you step out of the refined Occidental hum of San Francisco
and into the cacophonous Orientalism of Chinatown. The street
sounds now become as intrusive as honking horns and shrieking
deliverymen, as subtle as the click of mah-jongg tiles or whispered
chanting to gilded Buddhas. Pay attention to the exotica in the
stores, the smells of roast duck and pork hanging in meat shop windows, the heady perfume of incense. Catch the intonations of sunlight that splay out among the dark shadows of the buildings,
splashing Chinatown with gold.

It's morning, and with the cadence of ritual, shopkeepers begin
their preparations for the day. Along Stockton Street merchants set
out crates of fresh vegetables in front of their stores, methodically
turning the sidewalks into vegetable bazaars. The crates hold no

231

heads of lettuce, no rotund cabbages or russet potatoes. Instead, there are slender versions of broccoli with tiny white flowerets, smooth green-white stalks of bok choy, tender crescents of snow peas.

By midmorning a soft Chinese chatter overhangs the crates, as women gossip together while patiently picking out their produce. They feel each pea within its pod to see that its firmness and full-ness meet their expectations. The women come here often, even daily, to buy fresh. Some live in overcrowded tenements in the overcrowded heart of Chinatown; others make a pilgrimage here from outlying districts, taking the cable car or the bus officially called the 30 Stockton but known to all as the Orient Express.

But however and from wherever they come, the troubles they take are worthwhile. For here they can get ingredients with which to conjure up the old culture, the tastes and textures of the Orient. There are silky plum sauces, tangy soy and chili sauces, packages of dried herbs and fruits, catfish and turtles gliding around shadowy tanks that make the seafood stores look like aquariums. And noo-dles, an infinite variety of noodles: wheat noodles, glass noodles, arrowroot noodles, rice noodles.

To the non-Asian such foodstuffs seem arcane, if not downright unidentifiable. If you ask the passing deliveryman with the pig car-cass slung over his shoulder what, for example, the charred black lumps in that bin are, he may answer with a puzzled shrug, indi-cating that he doesn't understand your strange foreign tongue. But someone nearby may take pity on you, the benighted foreigner, and explain in broken English that the lumps are called thousand-year-old eggs. "Very good for your liver functioning."

In a celebrated novel about life in Chinatown—Maxine Hong Kingston's *The Woman Warrior*—a recent immigrant, the elderly Moon Orchid, takes her first walk through the streets and alleyways of Chinatown. She remarks to her sister, Brave Orchid, who has lived here since childhood, "So this is United States. It certainly looks different from China." But she adds, "I'm glad to see the Americans talk like us."

They still speak Moon Orchid's language in Chinatown—Cantonese, the dialect of that first Chinatown, neighborhood of the "China Boys," as they were called in the 1840s with condescending affection. Sadly, affection dissipated and condescension turned to resentment as a wave of immigrants, leaving behind droughts, floods, and civil unrest in China, poured into California during the Gold Rush. A second wave, coming in the 1860s to work on the transcontinental railroad, was met with harsh discrimination, to the point of physical violence.

In 1882 Congress approved the first of the infamous Chinese Exclusion Acts, effectively banning the entrance of new Chinese immigrants—even, in some cases, the wives and children of men already in this country. The acts also denied Chinese immigrants the right to gain U.S. citizenship. The China Boys who had come here with the high hopes of all new immigrants found themselves doomed to live out their days in "bachelor society" enclaves.

Not until 1943 were the exclusion acts repealed. Since then, San Francisco's Chinatown has grown into one of the largest Chinese communities outside Asia. But vestiges of the old bachelor society sill linger around the benches and tables in Portsmouth Square, where aged men huddle over games of Chinese chess while others pass the day watching them.

Yet a vigorous hopefulness also infuses the square. Young people often come here before and during the Chinese New Year to

ℬeyond the Chinatown gate we heard the jabbering tones of Cantonese coming from all directions, shops were stocked with everything from breathtaking ivory carvings to cheap plastic ninja figures and knockoffs of Frederic Remington bronzes. In a seafood market a tubful of dying fish thrashed in an inch of water, next to a pile of huge clams whose foul-looking siphons stretched forth from their shells like turkey necks.

We had dim sum at the restaurant next door, the kids gamely trying everything that appeared at our table.

"What's this, Dad?" our ten-year-old asked, prying at a mound of tofu with chopsticks.

"Bean curd," I said, with my mouth full.

"Beef turd?" she gasped. We calmed her down and soon meandered on.

—Stephen Harrigan, "Four Days and Three Girls and One Bay," *Condé Nast Traveler*

celebrate themselves and their traditions. Early in the morning, long before the old men shuffle out to set up their chess game, young men monopolize the square. In a prideful, leaping show, they practice kung fu, a martial art with precise, controlled movements of dance.

It is recorded that on April 5, 1874, a gigantic mass meeting, attended by more than twenty thousand persons, took place in San Francisco, at which various city and state officials delivered violent harangues against Chinese. Copies of the resolutions of the meeting and also of the speeches were sent to Congress and President Grant by a special committee. The following were some of the accusations:

That not one virtuous Chinawoman had been brought to America, and here the Chinese had no wives or children.

That the Chinese had purchased no real estate.

That the Chinese ate rice, fish, and vegetables, and that otherwise their diet differed from that of white men.

That the Chinese were of no benefit to the country.

—Chiang Yee, *The Silent Traveller in San Francisco*

Dancing, too, brings the young men to the square. Not teen-style American dancing, but a type as intense as kung fu. Each year in February, young Chinese go from place to place in the neighborhood in groups of five or six, performing the celestial art of Lion Dancing, giving an auspicious greeting to the Chinese New Year.

Chinatown is at its festive best at this time of year. Beginning on New Year's Eve (whose date is based on a lunar calendar), the sidewalks bloom with a profusion of quince blossoms and fragrant narcissus and peonies. Alongside the flower stalls stand crates of still more color—red tangerines, giant orange treats to be taken home and enjoyed during the family gatherings that mark the start of the eight-day New Year's celebration.

On the second weekend of the holiday the festivities go public, and spectators pour through the lintel gateway on Grant Avenue to watch Chinatown celebrate. The rat-a-tat report of firecrackers heralds the lion dancers, making their way down the street. The lead dancer holds a huge, ferociously expressioned lion head over his own. With practiced feline leaps, the lion roars, crouches, and hops around the popping firecrackers, all to the accompaniment of gongs, cymbals, and drums.

The sight of such displays seems quite reasonable in this neighborhood, with its aura of a street bazaar. As you watch the lion and listen to the mesmerizing beat of the drum, the city skyscrapers hovering on the horizon and the Bay Bridge glimmering in the background may seem mere mirages, while Chinatown's squat brick buildings crowned with pagoda roofs become the only reality.

The upwardly inclined roofs are believed to keep away prankish spirits, who apparently find the angled surfaces hard to alight on. The skyscrapers, by contrast, are intended to withstand seismic vicissitudes. Who can say which of the two designs will, over time, prove the more propitious?

As Chinatown's pagodas go, the most appealing may be the emerald-and-ruby-colored jewel at 743 Washington Street, just east of Grant Avenue. It now houses a branch of the Bank of Canton, but before World War II it was the very nerve center of Chinatown—the Chinese Telephone Exchange building. In the era before in-home dialing, the Chinese operators in the exchange were said to "know the name, address, and telephone numbers of every one of the 2,477 subscribers…and could locate a person at any time of day or night, so well did they know the habits of their subscribers."

Chinatown is no longer the homogeneous community it was in the days of the exchange. Today it is attracting new immigrants—not only Southeast Asian refugees but also newcomers from Hong Kong, who are resettling here. Chinatown's Cantonese old-boy network, traditionally headed by the power brokers of the Chinese Six Companies (a communal organization led originally by immigrants representing each of China's six regions), is losing ground to this new influx of immigrants, who now rent many of the storefronts and are living, as the earlier immigrants once did, above their businesses.

Though many San Francisco Bay Area Chinese now lead a suburban life outside the boundaries of Chinatown, they still consider the old community their spiritual home. On Sundays they make a

weekly pilgrimage to Chinatown to stroll its streets and eat at one
of its nearly 100 restaurants.

Many of their children come every afternoon, after "American
school," to attend Chinese school. You can see them toting backpacks, their t-shirts bright with slogans of American youth, going
through the gates of such institutions as the St. Mary's Chinese
Language School or the Nam Kue School. There, for two hours a
day, they are imprinted with the Cantonese language and the race
memories of their heritage. Perhaps, too, their minds broaden
enough to absorb the duality, the paradox of their Chinese-
Americanism.

The densest concentration of purely Chinese wares in
Chinatown is encountered along the side streets running between
Grant and Stockton. Here you will find the herb shops, their
show windows featuring intricately curled and twisted roots of
ginseng. The smaller, cheaper varieties of ginseng are boxed and
covered in cellophane wrappers, like boxes of chocolates; large
pieces are displayed, and priced, as though they were precious
jewels. Sundry other herbal esoterica—sliced antlers, bits of horn,
unmentionable parts of walruses—are also available in the tidy,
narrow little shops. Or, if you have an ailment that needs attending and the herbalist knows enough English to understand you,
he will carefully weigh and measure the powdered ingredients for
a curative potion, then tally up your bill on an abacus. The herb
shops are definitely worth venturing into, no matter the initial in-
timidation they may engender.

Another imposing but no less worthwhile stop is at one of the
Buddhist or Taoist temples up and down Waverly Place. Waverly,
along with Spofford and Ross Alleys, is a narrow street that recalls
the intriguing, sinister Chinatowns of 1940s detective films, where
fierce Chinese gangs called tongs warred with each other for control of concrete turf.

No longer sinister, these alleyways are still intriguing, Waverly
especially so for its series of painted balconies and a popular restaurant called the Pot Sticker. Paradoxically, the Pot Sticker's interior

is pure oak-and-fern California-ness, but right beside it is a door that opens onto a narrow, dilapidated flight of stairs. At the top on the left is another door, usually locked. But a knock will admit you to a world that is incarnations away from the Pot Sticker.

This is Jeng Sen, a Taoist and Buddhist temple done in red, the color of happiness and good fortune. Fruits and flowers are placed in homage before the golden statuary in the simple altar area, and small red altar lanterns jangle overhead. If you believe in the power of Taoist alchemy to "transform spontaneously," you might allow the intoxicating smell of the temple's incense to transport you in spirit to the Orient of your imaginings.

That is the way of the Tao. The way of modern commercialism is found on Grant Avenue. Here shop after shop is filled with the gewgaw sameness of souvenirs: rough-cut figurines; Chinese rice porcelain; quilted, raw-silk jackets; slinky *cheongsams*—the traditional high-necked tight-fitting brocade dresses whose design is intended to "conceal yet reveal."

But there are fine import shops on Grant as well, especially jewelry shops, bright with the glitter of diamonds and emeralds warm with the glow of fine jade (a stone whose qualities Chinese sages liken to virtue). Most jewelers also display a sampling of *netsuke* (pronounced NET-ski)—minute, intricately carved ivory fig-

In the 1920s, Inspector Jack Manion won the nickname Mau Yee, the Cat, because of his cunning and apparent knowledge of everything that went on in Chinatown. The last of the hatchet men were convinced that he not only had eyes in the back of his head but that he never slept. He used to fool them by standing in a crowd, reading the Chinese newspapers posted on the walls, apparently studying and digesting the calligraphic information. Actually he could read hardly a word of Chinese, but the highbinders did not know this. All of his psychology was simple but effective. When a show of force was needed he had only to march into a tong headquarters, listen silently and intently to what was but gibberish to him (though never showing this), then violently whip out his handcuffs and slam them on the table in front of the startled tong officers.

—Richard H. Dillon, *The Hatchet Men: The Story of the Tong Wars in San Francisco's Chinatown*

urines in the shapes of animals and saints and mendicant Buddhas who have eschewed worldly desires for ascetic lives. But look closely at any *netsuke* collection and you are sure to find a few examples of naughty *netsuke* as well—entwined ivory couples engaged in the most worldly of pleasures.

Before darkness falls and the neon marquees of Chinese theaters and restaurants turn Chinatown ablaze with nightlife, there is one more place belonging to the daylight hours that is worth visiting: the Golden Gate Fortune Cookie Factory in Ross Alley. Not a labor-intensive operation, the one-room factory seems to require the efforts of only one or two people to run it. The one worker visible at all times is the woman operating the factory's heavy equipment—a small Rube Goldbergesque device that rotates tiny hot griddles. She fills each griddle with batter as it comes toward her, then removes the small cooked pancakes as they come back within reach and crimps them into crescent shapes after deftly inserting a paper fortune.

Fortune, too, is a handmaiden of paradox. A hundred years ago the Chinese were the ghettoized outcasts of San Francisco. Today they are cheered, at least on the one night a year when they stage the city's largest party—the annual Golden Dragon Parade, a finale to Chinese New Year.

Long and lavish, the parade attracts about half a million spectators. As night comes on they line the streets, waiting expectantly for the sounds of gongs and cymbals that echo through the high-rise corridors as the parade's many lion dancers make their way through downtown, then into Chinatown itself. Interspersed among the celestial dancers are

> *Another street spectacle is the Bay to Breakers footrace, held every May, in which upwards of 100,000 people run and walk from San Francisco Bay to Ocean Beach, many dressed in wild costumes and in some cases only their birthday suits. My three girls and I walked in this year's race. We were fascinated at the social panorama of San Francisco as it unfolded, gays, transvestites, drunks, and criminals who would have probably robbed people if there weren't police on every corner…it was wonderful. Great live bands every few blocks.*
>
> —James O'Reilly,
> "San Francisco 2020"

cadres of small children marching in parade step, dressed in the robes of their particular martial arts school; the *de rigueur* beauty pageant floats, including one for the parade's queen, Miss Chinatown USA; and marching bands, decidedly American in character.

Also decidedly American are carloads of waving city and state politicians, who seem like miniatures beside the solemn figures of the Eight Immortals. These papier-mâché god-men tower over all else, their stilt-legged walk and ten-foot-tall presence lending a dignity to the whole proceeding. But, for all their imposing character, they are not the centerpiece of the parade. That honor belongs to Gum Lung—the 125-foot-long Golden Dragon.

It takes eleven men at a time (three teams change off every few blocks) to support the serpentine evanescence of the silk dragon as it curls and roars through downtown, claiming the streets as its own. Chinese tradition says that Gum Lung is a divine creature. Wherever it appears, "it dispels gloom, drives off evil spirits, spreads good fortune, and radiates the happy spirit of the New Year."

The faces of the parade-goers attest to its powers. As the dragon draws near, their expressions melt into delight. Dragon magic apparently bends not to the limitations of time or space or ethnicity.

Confucius once said: "The dragon's ascent into heaven on the wind and the clouds is something which is beyond my knowledge." But you needn't understand magic to enjoy it. Such is paradox, and such is the joy of being in Chinatown.

A contributing editor to National Geographic Traveler, *K. M. Kostyal has a particular affinity for Asian marketplaces. Her travels have taken her from the Arctic to the Antarctic and to most of the continents on the globe. Her articles have appeared in American and European magazines and her books include* Field of Battle: The Civil War Letters of Major Thomas J. Halsey, National Geographic's Driving Guide to America: Washington D.C., Virginia, West Virginia, Maryland, and Delaware, *and* Compass America Guide to Virginia. *She lives in Alexandria, Virginia.*

★

Many traditional Chinese worship gods, goddesses, and their ancestors on a daily basis. One of my favorites is the Kitchen God. This tiny statue of a god resides in the kitchen by the stove throughout the year. Although there is no general agreement regarding his identity and origin, he is worshiped by both Buddhists and Taoists. He is worshiped and burned at the end of the year when he returns to Heaven to report on the family's good and bad deeds. A replacement Kitchen God assumes his duties for the new year. I hope he presides over my dinner parties.

Kuan Yin is the Goddess of Mercy, the symbol of love, tenderness, forgiveness, and pity. Kuan Yin is very popular in Chinatown because we see statues of her throughout shops and businesses here. Kuan Yin represents kindness and tenderness toward mankind.

Tien Hau is a busy goddess, known as the Goddess of Heaven and Sea. She also watches over and protects travelers, writers, actors, sailors, and prostitutes. According to legend, she was a courageous woman of great strength, who fought against evil and human suffering.

—Shirley Fong-Torres, *San Francisco Chinatown: A Walking Tour*

Into the Sunset

*An autumn evening sets the mood
for exploring San Francisco Bay.*

ALL SUMMER I WORKED LONG HOURS WITH LITTLE CHANCE OF escape. Weeks of freeway commuting sucked away my energy, until October, when a surprise created ideal conditions for a backyard adventure. An invitation had arrived from a kayak tour outfitter to paddle San Francisco Bay. A gaggle of kayakers would leave from the U.C. Berkeley sailboarding dock, paddle west toward the San Francisco skyline, enjoy an *al fresco* dinner, and return to port after moonrise.

The Berkeley Marina that Friday afternoon glowed with Indian Summer. I drove past sailboats, parks, skaters, waterfront businesses, and seafood restaurants. A kitchen crew relaxed outside on a wrap-around deck designed to take advantage of bay views. Nearly a dozen puffed souffle hats bobbed as chefs and sous-chefs chatted next to a wooden railing, blue sky and water forming a cool contrast to starched white uniforms. You couldn't set up a movie scene more picturesque.

Our group was impossible to miss with its trailer layered with sea kayaks. We introduced ourselves—a mix of experienced trippers needing a quick aquatic fix and first-time paddlers. Kayaks, paddles, and life vests were unpacked and soon surrounded us in an impressive radius. We taped small green and orange "glow sticks" (similar to the things that glow inside a trick-or-treater's plastic pumpkin) to each boat to serve as running lights. After getting our gear—along with tide information and safety precautions—we helped each other into the doddering boats and snapped our waterproof spray skirts in place.

Too bad I can't brag about my kayaking skills. I have a hard time even getting in. But once ensconced with my center of gravity low and balanced, I feel cradled by the water. It's like swimming without getting wet. My partner and I pushed away from the dock in a two-person kayak. I reacquainted myself with the fantastic sensation, pulling my way along with a light, double-sided paddle. Sunshine gilded the water inches away.

We began paddling toward Alcatraz—opposite the flow of whatever traffic might once have been generated by escape attempts. South of the island, to our left, modern day escapees fled city jobs for the weekend via the Bay Bridge; their suburban counterparts rushed equally fast on the upper level to reach the night life scene. Beyond Alcatraz, Fisherman's Wharf, and the Golden Gate, the sun began to spill an Orangina sunset around us. It was late in the day for commercial shipping traffic, and winds were too calm for pleasure craft. We were, in fact, the only boats out on the water, an exclusive group of not-so-rare sea birds.

My partner, a congenial woman, sat in the front compartment. I sat in back, watching her paddling style and roughly matching her paddling stroke for stroke. We maneuvered and traded stories, all without seeing each other's faces, establishing a working and social relationship as shadows began to trail us.

The nugget of Yerba Buena Island loomed larger as dusk fell, a heavy contrast to the erector-set latticework of the Bay span. Traffic noise droned over the water to us, where our paddles scooped minute quantities of bay water. Still far ahead, lined in color, were the hills and towers of San Francisco, including Telegraph, Russian, Nob, Coit, Transamerica, and Sutro. The Golden Gate Bridge took on a succession of shades: coral, fuchsia, mauve, and deep purple. From our vantage point, the San Francisco skyline was nothing less than a sculpted sand castle surrounded by a great moat of darkening water.

Surrounded by civilization, our kayaks enjoyed a calm, even isolated expanse of sea. I imagined myself a crew member on an explorer's ship from Spain, seeing the Bay for the first time: no buildings, no bridge linking the Marin headlands with the San Francisco peninsula, and nary another schooner for many leagues.

The lights on the Bay Bridge emerged slowly from a still-bright sky. Car headlights joined the light show, and then, building by building, the lights of offices and apartments winked on. Whenever I pulled my attention back to the land from a glance at my paddle or a look at a bird overhead, the lights were multiplied until it seemed as if all were in readiness for that singular moment when the postcard photographers line up for The Perfect Shot of San Francisco at twilight. We sophisticated Bay Area folk *oohed* and *aahed* as if we had just been bused in from the prairie.

A few more paddle strokes, a few more blinks, and it was dark. Swags of light rose and fell on the cables of the Bay Bridge, forming the outline of a row of Christmas trees suspended far above us. The water became a dark blanket, an old pier, a two-mile guideline of pilings and planks to our right. We followed its dark shapes and reached the

She has distinction, beauty, charm, and many lovers. One must envy the good fortune of those who are yet to come under her spell. When such a one comes for the first time to this glamorous city, he will learn to love her cool, gray beauty; he will delight in seeing her rise ghostlike on her high hills—an uneven, sawtoothed Whistler silhouette, dimly outlined against an indefinable sky. And sometime he will watch from a ferry at sunset these startling color-changes which turn the sky from flaming apricot to blue and then to that cool, compassionate, all-encompassing gray which lays its mask over the city like a visible hush. At the Golden Gate he will see the sun lie low in a bed of cherry coals, flaming between black headlands. And then, suddenly, the city will be swallowed up in darkness, and all will vanish save the flashing jewel of Alcatraz, fantastic island castle of a pastry-cook's dream.

—Glenn C. Quiett,
They Built the West (1934)

last decrepit pilings to raft up for dinner. From the stowage areas of our boats came a potluck picnic; cheeses, crackers, fruit, and cookies passed from hand to hand across the bows of our kayaks. Now in deeper and less protected waters, the wind picked up slightly, and the boats bounced sociably against each other as we ate and drank. A helicopter chopped overhead. A single yacht, out for a Friday evening cruise, motored by half a mile away, its wake a mere riffle by the time it nudged our boats.

The tide had turned. We stowed our gear and started eastward again toward the dock. The lights still drew our gazes backward. You don't see crowds, crime, or heavy construction at that distance, just the mystic twinkle of lights across a cushion of darkness.

My arms were warm with the exercise, my face cool with damp air. An ocean-scented breeze followed. Our party spread out according to rhythms of conversation and paddling. A younger woman in a single kayak paddled next to us; the rest of the group followed in twos and threes. The running lights glowed as faint beacons to keep us in visual touch. And then, in front of us, the eastern sky brightened behind a dark ridge and a hint of silver turned into a white moon platter that gleamed above the Berkeley Hills. My paddle plied moonlight as I neared the marina.

We passed a bay view restaurant dressed in candlelight and linen. As we paddled by, each section of picture window filled with diners who had stood up and leaned into the glass to watch us. Some sketched silent greetings with upraised arms. We waved our paddles. A few more strokes, and we were landlubbers again.

The jewel of San Francisco continually turns new facets my way—even when I haven't stepped ashore. On that outing, poised between day and night, summer and autumn, sea and sky, I learned that the city can rekindle a traveler's spirit—something I can pack on every journey.

Native Californian Lynn Narlesky writes for travel, business, and family publications such as Frommer's America on Wheels Travel Guide, Sunset, Country America, Continental Profiles, *and others. She is currently writing a book about the Golden State's eco-tourism treasures, but interrupts her work at every opportunity to swim, sail, kayak, canoe, and windsurf California's magnificent waterways.*

★

Often, as I gazed out my window, I wanted to peel back that human skin to see what it had been once. I tried to imagine the thoughts of those first European sailors who chanced to come through the fog bank always masking the estuary, through the Golden Gate into the sun-swept, glistening bay. Were they not stunned? Were they not seduced by the land, realizing itself forever eastward? Did it not come to mind that this was a new Eden, a new chance to start the human story all over again? That, too, is part of the American myth, and we have at each new landfall dreamed the dream again.

—Nathan Irvin Higgins, from the Foreward of *Pioneer Urbanites: A Social and Cultural History of Black San Francisco*, edited by Douglas Henry Daniels

CATHLEEN MILLER

✦ ✦ ✦

Locomotion

Public transit can be a San Francisco treat.

AFTER GIVING MY FRIEND MARY THE THREE-DAY WHIRLWIND tour on her first visit to San Francisco, my heartbreakingly beautiful city, I wanted to know the highlight of her trip. I admit I expected her response to be one of the many world-famous tourist attractions we'd visited, but she thought for a minute and smiled. "I'd have to say the bus ride from your house to the Financial District and back."

This trip with Mary, one I took daily, was in my memory just like any other: stand on the corner amidst the candy-colored Victorians and board the No. 1 California, wind through Pacific Heights, and start climbing up, up, up Nob Hill. Stand on the crowded bus (rather like riding a bucking bronco as the electric beast jerks down the narrow corridor of Clay Street), crest the hill, and suddenly glimpse the brilliant aquamarine waters of San Francisco Bay shimmering beyond the Marina. Then we glide back down the east side of the hill headlong into the Pyramid building. Along the way the experience is shared with a panoply of the city's bus riders, ranging from the grande dames of society heading downtown to Union Square, to the pierced, tattooed, black-leather coffee-shop kids.

On the return trip there's the pandemonium of stopping in Chinatown where the tiny old Chinese ladies wait anxiously, ready to charge the door. Lugging bok choy and an occasional plastic bag bulging with a very nervous live fish suspended in a teacup full of water, they elbow on. All the while they're discussing in a sing-song dialect the successes of the day's shopping.

Sadly I realized the ravages of familiarity had worn away the thrill I felt from these experiences, and I thought back to some of my earlier days in San Francisco, when I was a stranger to the city, a visitor agape with wonder at every new postcard panorama and quirky encounter. I began to think of all the fun I'd had aboard San Francisco's many diverse methods of public transportation and realized that some of my liveliest adventures in the city had begun before I reached my destination. And largely because this communal mode of travel brought me into sudden contact with a cornucopia of colorful personalities, one of the town's greatest riches since the days of the Barbary Coast.

One of my earliest visits was New Year's Eve, when I was a tourist standing at Union Square knee-deep in 1984 calendar pages. I turned toward the sound of the clanging bell and saw a scene from a movie: against a blue-violet sky, a crowded cable car poised briefly on Powell Street, the patrons wearing evening gowns, jewels, tuxedos, and party hats, clutching the handrails with one hand and using the other to toot, "Buh-BRRRR" into noise-makers. Aboard the cable car, a cassette playing Tony Bennett crooned, "Where little cable cars, go halfway to the stars...." With a grinding of wheels, they slid away into the new year, and I stood transfixed on the spot wondering what kind of magical rabbit hole I'd fallen into.

This memory, like one good thing, led to another: another trip to San Francisco, with another friend, Marty. We bought all-day transit passes and rode the streetcars to parts of the city I haven't seen since. First we took the J-Church all the way out to the end of the line, and were surprised to find the type of family neighborhoods with little white frame cottages that would exist in almost any small town. Then we came back and changed cars just to see where the new one would take us. We'd pop out of the station like moles, walk around for a few blocks, and then pop back in and do it all over again. It was during this afternoon that I began to realize that San Francisco *was* a small town masquerading as a big city; it was a sprinkling of treasures from every type of society, simply crammed into the confines of a seven-by-seven-mile peninsula.

Growing up in rural Missouri, I had always been part of the car culture of America. Things were too spread out to walk, so we sequestered ourselves in our separate automobiles and headed on our journeys isolated and untouched by other travelers along the road. So it was not until I visited San Francisco that I discovered public transit, and one of my favorite things about it quickly became the opportunity to eavesdrop on lives very different from my own. It became the urban counterpart to one of our forbidden pastimes from back home: listening in on the party line.

On yet another trip to the city, I boarded a MUNI bus on Haight Street and sat in front of a rather odd looking woman, about thirty-five years old. She was wearing an early sixties thrift-shop coat in a sickly shade of green with buttons the size of silver dollars. Her head sported a shoulder-length blonde wig with a little flip at the ends (I remember thinking she looked like a Midge doll, Barbie's long-forgotten friend.) She also had a rather dazed look in her eyes.

At the next stop another woman boarded wearing a turban, lots of gold gypsy jewelry, and flowing flowered pants. "Hello there! Oh, my gosh, I haven't seen you in years!!" she gushed to Midge. "I barely recognized you with your hair like this!" The two of them sat together in the seat right behind me.

Midge asked if Gypsy Woman was still singing. "Oh, yes, I'm still singing in clubs, sometimes in the Haight, mostly South of Market. I get around."

"Well, you look like Gracie Slick in that outfit."

"Yuck! I hate the way she looks. Although Paul Kantner must think I look like her. He keeps trying to hit on me every time I see him. When did you do your hair like this?" I smothered a laugh.

"This isn't my hair, it's a wig. I have cancer and I'm going through chemo; all my hair fell out."

"Oh…gosh, that's terrible. I'm sorry to hear that."

"It's okay; I'm doing much better now. The doctor says I'm going to be fine. But here's the good part. They give me this amazing pot to fight the sickness. You get really queasy when they give you treatments, and I bake brownies and put the pot in them. I just finished a couple and I'm higher than a kite right now."

"Wow. Well, all right! Do you have any more?" At this moment I exited with regret, as I was meeting an ever-punctual friend. I considered riding on for a few more stops, but when I imagined apologizing for my tardiness, explaining that I was listening to a conversation on the bus and couldn't tear myself away, the imagined look of reproach from Miss On Time set me moving.

A much different bus trip came later after I had moved to San Francisco and lived in Pacific Heights. At 5:30 in the morning I was bouncing along sleepily with the stockbrokers on the No. 1 California, heading down to the Financial District in silence. Since the market opened in New York at nine, they all had to be at their desks by six. The young brokers stepped down the aisle in their Italian wool suits, their hair still damp from the shower, faces glowing pink from an early-morning encounter with a razor. By the dismal bus lamps, the ambitious ones scanned the *Wall Street Journal*; some of the more light-hearted caught up on the Giants scores in the *Chronicle*. And the rest of us just tried to stay awake so we wouldn't miss our stops. Soon we became rather more alert when the bus pulled over at Hyde Street and a Chinese man staggered on board carrying a large dead pig. He maneuvered it through the door, collapsed onto one of the handicapped seats, and rode a few blocks to Chinatown, where he and his pig left us. I, and the rest of the newly aroused passengers (newspapers forgotten), watched in fascination as the man entered a small hole-in-the-wall Chinese restaurant. The yellowish-green light from its windows cast a harsh contrast onto him, the delivery men, the trash trucks, and the blue pre-dawn activity of the awakening city. I thought about this man for the rest of the day. Where did the pig come from? Was that his wife waiting inside the restaurant—the woman who opened the door for him? Had they agreed last night that she would come down early to start the pot stickers and he would come later when the buses started running? Did the driver charge full fare for the pig?

San Francisco's Barbary Coast origins go back to the 1850s and the waterfront hangouts of Sydney Town. It was an area rife with low dives and grog shops, populated by muggers, thieves, and murderers. Typical of the sort of joint found there were The Boar's Head, a "dance hall" whose main stage attraction consisted of a woman having sex with a boar, and a bar called The Fierce Grizzly, so named because a live grizzly bear was chained beside the door.

Another attraction of the time was a character known as "Dirty Tom" McAlear, a filthy beggar who never bathed and who earned his living by charging a few cents and then eating or drinking any object or liquid offered, no matter how foul. This behavior was too much for even the usually tolerant San Franciscans: Dirty Tom's career came to an end when he was arrested and jailed for "making a beast of himself."

—Rand Richards, *Historic San Francisco: A Concise History and Guide*

Then there are the cab rides. Many adventures come to mind in this category, but one stands out. Yet another friend, Bruce, was visiting my husband and me on his first trip to San Francisco, trying to recover from a freshly-shattered romance. We had also given him the standard three-day whirlwind tour, working hard to cheer him up, but nothing could lift him out of his funk. He responded to views of the Golden Gate Bridge and strolls through North Beach with the enthusiasm of a man due to face the firing squad at dawn.

On Saturday night we went to a party in Hayes Valley, close to the Civic Center, hoping that the proximity of exotic city women and liberal doses of our host's home-brewed ale would cheer him up. Bruce stood glumly in the corner all night and finally at two in the morning, we called a taxi. The three of us crowded into the back seat and my husband gave our address to the driver, a very short man wearing thick glasses. He could barely see over the dashboard, and I wondered for the umpteenth time about the strange life of a cab driver on the graveyard shift. He had some

1930s music playing that reminded me of the scene from the *Wizard of Oz* where Dorothy and the gang are being spruced up in Emerald City and they're singing, "...come out of the dark and into the light." As the cab moved forward the wisps of mousy brown hair floating around the shining dome of the driver's bald head began to float with the motion of the car. Involuntarily, in the back seat, we all started swaying in unison and I asked the driver who was singing. "It's the Boswell Sisters. They're my favorite."

The taxi was speeding up Fell Street and as we crested a hill we left the ground, producing a sinking sensation that sent my stomach through the floorboard. I screamed and the guys laughed. I guess this was the cab driver's cue that we were game for a good time, so he floored it. On top of the next hill we jumped into the night sky; then coming back to earth, the car smacked the pavement and we thrashed around the back seat as if we were on some amusement park ride out of control. I saw mutilation and sudden death looming, but worshiper of the serendipitous moment, I was willing to risk it. Charged by this latest thrill, the driver hit the gas and the engine of the cab roared like a plane ready to lift off the runway; now we were truly airborne. As we approached the Pacific Ocean at Mach I, we all hunkered down in the back seat, breathless to see what would happen next. The demon driver rolled down his window, and while we laughed hysterically, he screamed "Yeeeehhhhh-haaahh!!!! I used to rides hosses, now I drives me a cab!!!" In the rear view mirror I could see a wild look of ecstasy emanating from behind the coke-bottle-bottom glasses. By the time we landed, Bruce was positively giddy. He staggered around on the sidewalk while my husband tipped the driver.

"Hey, now, *that* was fun," Bruce pronounced. And I would have to agree. There have been many other San Francisco moments when the journey was at least as exciting as the destination: a golden sunny ferry boat ride to Sausalito where I drank a beer on the deck as a sea breeze blew through the Golden Gate, and a jazz band played in the cabin. The commuters mingled as if at a cocktail party with the aquamarine bay for a backdrop. Then there was a BART trip returning from a Prince concert at the Oakland

Coliseum; the subway train crammed full of fans singing Prince songs in unison. It seemed as if dozens of sardines were belting out "LIT-tle red Corvette, baby, you're much too faaasst…" as we stood shoulder to shoulder, laughing and swaying, hurtling through the nighttime tunnel underneath the bay—the rabbit hole—toward San Francisco.

As visitors to this unique city soon learn, the adventure lies in navigating from Point A to Point B in a town precariously perched on top of the world and surrounded by water; where parking takes longer than driving; and where you meet some amazing characters traveling in your direction who agree that Getting There can be as much fun as Being There.

Cathleen Miller's travel stories have appeared in the San Francisco Examiner, Denver Post, *and* New Orleans Times-Picayune. *She and her husband, Kerby Macrae, recently moved from a Victorian in Pacific Heights to an old farmhouse in an Amish corn patch near Zion, Pennsylvania. Her hobbies are moving, changing careers, applying for credit cards, skunk siting, and tempting the Amish with liquor. Currently, she teaches writing at Penn State.*

★

I sit atop the U.C. Medical Center parking garage and look out, a lesser god surveying her domain. Sutro Tower, Twin Peaks, and seven floors of the medical center rise behind me. The ocean is a murky shadow spread out to the left, downtown is almost invisible to the right, and St. Ignatius Church and the Golden Gate Bridge waver ghostlike before me. The screeching wail of brakes echoes through the fog as the narrow-nosed N-Judah trolley turns toward me on its tracks below. The section of track here runs in a lazy "S" from Cole Valley's Carl to the Sunset's Irving Street, the joint of the two neighborhoods where Golden Gate Park and the trolley begin their trek out to the ocean.

The trolley's hairy claws reach up crookedly, gripping the wires, its rear car swinging around the tracks as the first accordioned section of the front car screeches around the bend to complete the "S". It is a roller coaster ride when you're just starting to hold your breath, preparing for the real excitement as you head west—where lies California's eternal claim to superiority over the rest of the country—the ocean sunset. The sun rises over the ocean in the east, of course, but how many are awake to see it or have time to watch?

The Sunset, the whole long neighborhood named for this event, begins right here at my street and stretches out fifty straight flat blocks in preparation for the once-an-evening performance. I come up here obsessively, constantly checking to make sure that San Francisco is real and I'm really here.

—Lisa Meltzer, "Inner Sunset"

JOHN BRANT

Brooding at Ocean Beach

Is it the end of the world or the beginning?
San Francisco's biggest beach can help you figure it out.

THE BEST WAY TO THE BEACH IS THE STREETCAR, THE N-JUDAH line, starting way downtown below Market Street, rising to daylight to the Haight-Ashbury, then beeping and sliding west along the Avenues and Golden Gate Park to the end of the line on the Great Highway. Something about the streetcar—its ponderous swing and rhythms—settles the mind to reverie, to the prospect of the activity for which Ocean Beach seems tailor-made: brooding.

Ocean Beach fronts the Pacific for three miles along San Francisco's western edge. Long and flat and relatively featureless, it tends to get overlooked by tourists, which suits the residents just fine. The people living here don't mind that Ocean Beach is too cold for swimming and too foggy for sunbathing, that the prevailing winds pile the waves unceremoniously along the sand, that the squat dunes blot out most views of the lovely city.

These folks *want* the obvious beauty eclipsed; they *want* the city to disappear; they *want* to be alone and shivering with the wind and fog and waves, watching the huge container ships slide in and out of the Golden Gate with the stateliness of melancholy. And they want—though they don't necessarily celebrate—to see the t-shirted tourists get blasted by midsummer gales that send them diving back to the shelter of their rented cars.

All this leaves the knowing beach walker free to brood. When I first came to San Francisco, I was young and bumptious and eternally at sixes and sevens. Ocean Beach then took the place of a patient friend. I would take every dream and heartache there, and, walking south at low tide, my hands buried deep in my coat pockets, I would fondle and burnish my troubles. But the great thing about the beach was its scale. For the first mile my worries seemed huge and tragic, during the second mile they were forgotten, and by the third mile they had assumed their proper weight and importance. After an hour's walking and brooding, I would be ready to take the streetcar back to my life.

Such was my self-absorption that I thought I was the only serious brooder on Ocean Beach. But then I read in the sports pages about how Dave Kingman, then a young slugger for the Giants, tramped the sand in a similar manner. Interviewed after a game in which he'd repeatedly struck out, Kingman said, "Guess I'll be down at Ocean Beach at dawn, trying to figure it out."

Sluggers, lovers, drifters, dreamers; partiers ending their nights and dog walkers starting their days; the flotsam and jetsam and cream of San Francisco all eventually land at Ocean Beach. They walk a cold, foggy edge between the city and the sea. Depending on the shade of their thoughts, the quality of their brooding, they may cast their lot in either direction. Should they struggle over their lives behind them, or the Pacific before them? At Ocean Beach, either can seem imaginary, both can seem true.

John Brant is a contributing editor for Outside *magazine and a senior writer for* Runner's World. *His articles have also appeared in* The New York Times Magazine *and* Wort. *He lives in Portland, Oregon.*

∗

Beyond San Francisco's coast was another civilization—the Chinese. I exclaimed how wonderful it was to think that we were sitting right on *the edge of Western civilization!* At the same time I felt nostalgic, for I had passed over the Pacific some twenty-seven years ago and had not crossed it since. Confucius once remarked: "Well, the principle of Tao, the Correct Way, is not prevailing; I shall set myself adrift on a raft on the sea!" Confucius was born at a time when China was in a chaotic state with the feudal lords vying for power with one another. He went to them one by one and tried to persuade them to adopt his principles of government, but none paid him any heed. So he sighed and wished he could drift away from his ungrateful country. Of course he did not go away but instead taught and compiled the famous Chinese classics. If he had carried out his threat and managed to drift on a raft out to sea, he would probably have landed on the coast of Japan, for his birthplace was on the Shangtung peninsula in the North China Sea. Suppose again an *if*, only an *if*, his raft had not stopped at the Japanese coast but had drifted on and westward, he could have landed in this very bay. Then he might have started his teaching here and promoted Chinese civilization in Western America as he had done in North China. San Francisco would then have become the beginning point of Eastern civilization instead of the edge of the Western.

—Chiang Yee, *The Silent Traveller in San Francisco*

Lotusland

Bacchus charms a reluctant acolyte.

A FEW DAYS SIPPING WINE IN THE CALIFORNIA SUNSHINE—HOW bad could it be?" coaxed my husband. I let myself be persuaded. For years we'd heard glowing reports from visitors who'd been enticed by Napa Valley's siren song. But, as I discovered on a brief visit last summer, not everyone is vulnerable to this particular enchantment. For my husband, the valley's soft sell of the good life was innocent fun, for me, a hard-core East Coast urbanite, it was insidiously creepy.

My husband is a wine buff: learning about it, collecting it, and tasting it is one of his hobbies. I, on the other hand, while happy to drink wine, am also happy to leave the subtle discriminating to him. I am an unrepentant Philistine, a vinous ignoramus. Blindfolded, I can just about tell a red from a white. And what is worse, a skeptic to the bone, I'm convinced that I'm not alone. In a room full of tasters sniffing bouquet, I always think I detect more than a hint of pretension.

Agreeing to the trip in a spirit of marital compromise, I hoped I'd be able to leave my jaundiced views at home and enjoy myself. After all, as my husband pointed out, Napa offers much more than wine tasting. He was sure I'd have a good time.

In hindsight, our reading material on the plane might have given me cause for concern. My husband buried himself in *Napa: The Story of an American Eden,* a 500-page history of the intrigues, familial and corporate, of the region's land grab and viniculture; I was reading (for the third time) *Howard's End,* the story of a man of commerce foundering in moral darkness until saved by a sensitive woman.

The owner of our Napa Valley bed-and-breakfast had offered to arrange everything: private tours of vineyards, dinner reservations, and a date for a mud bath. Her voice on the phone, trilling with enthusiasm, had made me nervous. I prefer to do things myself, but our cheery, eager hostess sounded so genuinely warmhearted it had seemed perverse to resist. We'd put ourselves in her hands. Now our trip lay before us like a *prix fixe* menu, promising pleasure but without the satisfaction of initiative.

We arrived at the San Francisco airport to find the baby-blue convertible she had ordered waiting. My husband, looking jaunty behind the wheel, happily tucked himself into the new self-image the hipmobile bestowed. Perhaps this would be the first of a string of sports cars in our future, he suggested.

We flowed across the Golden Gate Bridge and aimed for an electric blue sky. Our "private hideaway in the wine country" was easy to find. The innkeeper was at the front door. "Welcome! Welcome! You must be so stressed out. But not to worry, we've got just what you need!" Two splits of Champagne were waiting in an ice bucket in the middle of our brass bed in "The Brass Room." My husband steered us straight to the hot tub for the prescribed cocktail-cum-soak before we changed for dinner.

The valley couldn't have been more scenic, the restaurants more trendy, or the atmosphere more determinedly convivial. As we walked around St. Helena the first evening, the Napa Valley Wine Train, restored to evoke the Orient Express, chugged slowly through the center of town. Through the velvet-draped windows we glimpsed happy tourists enjoying a facsimile of bygone luxury as they sipped the local product. Standing on the caboose deck others raised their glasses to strolling pedestrians in a toast to Bacchus, as they passed clinking and clacking into the distance.

In the morning my husband generously offered to go alone on his first wine tour, a three-hour seminar at Mondavi Winery. He returned ecstatic over the in-depth explanations of vine-pruning techniques and malolactic fermentation. He was also somewhat drunk. As the day wore on and I joined him on other wine tours, I found myself in a constant state of slight inebriation.

The fact that these tours were a vast promotional effort had somehow not dawned on me back home, where I had worried about the level of appreciation that would be expected. At every winery we were escorted by a member of the professional hospitality staff, invariably an attractive young woman, who shared her personal wine preferences with us and referred to the proprietor of the vineyard in awed tones. We seemed to be at a party given by an absentee lord of the manor whose ghostly presence was felt in the family photos and vintage car collections on display. The guides, who tasted whatever they poured for us, spoke knowingly and glowingly about *balance*, *suppleness* and *the light floral finish*.

We tasters nodded apprecia-

The Napa Valley Wine Train has stirred up controversy since it started taking passengers for a slow ride up and down the Napa Valley six years ago. Some Napa Valley residents oppose the train, maintaining that it brings the agricultural community a step closer to becoming an amusement park. But it would be hard to fashion a less intrusive way to tour the valley.

On each trip, the train allows as many as 220 people to gaze at the lush, vine-filled valley rimmed in the background by velvety foothills, while they drink Napa Valley wine and eat a three- or four-course meal. The 36-mile trip from downtown Napa to St. Helena and back takes three hours. Though I have driven the same route along Highway 29 a hundred times, I have never seen the valley unfold so magically. If anything, the train probably keeps hundreds of touring cars out of the valley.

—Patricia Unterman, "Napa Valley Wine Train," *San Francisco Chronicle*

tively and dropped references to cabs (as in Cabernet Sauvignon) and the subtle taste of aged oak. I figured at least some of us must know what we were talking about. We certainly all tried to appear serious as we swirled and sniffed and sometimes spat like true aficionados. Wine tours are free, but perhaps *this* was the price of entry: appearing to be there in the service of our wine cellars instead of just on line for a free nip.

The settings for these tastings seemed as self-conscious as I was. Although the wine-making buildings were in fact just glorified warehouses, as much market-conscious planning seemed to have gone into their design as into the making of the wine. The winery building was usually the icon of the vineyard and frequently appeared on the label.

The vintners had dressed their plants in every imaginable disguise: a Victorian mansion, a French chateau, a scaled-down copy of Monticello (in tribute to Jefferson the oenophile). The valley, 3 miles wide and 30 miles long with over 200 wineries, seemed to me like one giant outdoor mall—each winery and sales outlet decked out in its unique image, a monastery from Mykonos next to a palace from Tuscany—a mall merchandising just one product.

Our last afternoon in Napa was spent most fittingly in Calistoga at a spa that promised "the ultimate realm of relaxation." The spa, in a '50s-era motel, was decidedly seedy. I had negotiated my husband down from the "Ultimate" to the mere "Deluxe Pamper Package," agreeing to reserve the full herbal facial and foot reflexology for a future visit. After undressing and storing our valuables in a plastic satchel that we carried unceremoniously from room to room, we were led, towel wrapped, into a private treatment room for two—a large tiled space with a sunken hot tub in one corner, some pegs on one wall and a shower head on another. In the middle were two concrete sarcophagi filled with the therapeutic sludge. Our attendant instructed us before leaving to lower ourselves in so that we were just under the surface.

The mud, mixed with sphagnum moss, was buoyant and repulsively squishy. Associations with primal ooze and worse were inescapable, and I found it took considerable concentration not to panic. What might be earth to a Californian was to me just fancy dirt. I obsessively replayed in my mind the attendant's dubious claim that merely hosing down the top surface of the mud with boiling water was sufficient to sterilize it.

My husband, unlike me, seemed to be having no trouble relaxing. A beatific smile on his face, he hummed quietly to himself as his cares fled his body along with his cellular impurities. My relief on finally emerging and showering off was tremendous.

After some time in the scalding tub trying hard not to faint, we lay on stretchers in an adjacent room, wrapped in layers of sheets and blankets, listening to canned sounds of the wind and sea, as ice-soaked compresses were mercifully applied to our foreheads. Finally we had massages during which our muscles were kneaded and tenderized to a state of total flaccidity. I left on noodle legs, wilted and numb.

But, although my muscles had been beaten into submission, my brain was still fighting back. With my corporeal self in first gear and my psychic self still in fourth, I felt as though I was engaged in a sort of medieval struggle of the soul. Napa's soft sell of sybaritic pleasure, its seductive invitation to a collective euphoria, had met implacable resistance.

Boarding the plane to fly home, I felt that I was escaping from the Land of the Lotus-Eaters. To be honest, the trip was not without pleasure, but I have to be careful about acknowledging that to my husband. With the slightest encouragement, he would change careers and buy a vineyard.

Elizabeth Roper Marcus was an architect in a former life. Now she travels to see what she hasn't yet seen and writes to figure out where it is that she's been.

*

Vineyards thrived in Southern California as early as 1818. Wine was made from grapes called Mission, or Criolla, brought north by the Franciscan monks and generally ascribed to Father Junípero Serra. George Calvert Yount, a trapper from North Carolina and the first white settler in Napa Valley, planted Mission vines bought from General Mariano Vallejo in Sonoma in 1838, but by midcentury the Mission was being replaced throughout California by better European varieties.

California enjoys unblinkered sunlight many months of the year; all along the North Coast, gaps in the mountains admit cooling fogs from the Pacific. These qualities were recognized by Agoston Haraszthy, a Balkan immigrant who started a winery in Sonoma, called Buena Vista, in 1856. Haraszthy traveled to Europe in search of good wine-grape varieties and brought back thousands of vine cuttings, possibly including Zinfandel, and claimed the state of California owed him money for the effort. The state disagreed. Controversy hung about Haraszthy, but he is commonly recognized as the inspiration behind California's early enological successes. Haraszthy's sparkling wine, Eclipse, was the toast of San Francisco for a time. His Sonoma winery eventually failed and the flamboyant, questing Haraszthy perished in pursuit of other prospects, in Nicaragua.

—James Conaway, *Napa: The Story of an American Eden*

⋆

Parts Unknown

Watch out for those Watsu sharks!

AS A TRANSPLANTED, HYPHENATED HIBERNO-BRIT OF MIXED extraction in California, I can prove Darwin's theories about adaptation of the species and protective coloration at any second's notice. Leather vests and belts with giant buckles, S & M boots with jaunty spurs—I've worn 'em all. Shorts and bulging t-shirt? Sure. Never again will I own a navy suit. I've given up coats, gloves, and Office Drag forever, and my wardrobe consists of leggings, cut-offs, and a handful of dresses, mostly black.

So you wouldn't think the question of what to pack for a trip to California's hot springs would loom too large, would you? The spas are all "clothing optional," which at first I thought meant you could get into the warm, smelly pools of therapeutic mineral properties in your swimming togs, or "me batheners" as we used to call them in Dublin when we went swimming in the Tara Baths.

Which is why I checked what to bring with Wally and Louisa. The owners of Passion Flower, a sensual aids shop in Oakland, they were most helpful. "Heck—nothing!" said Wally, a short man with a ginger handlebar who looks as if he'd be at home with an oil can and a greasy rag in a Jiffy Lube autoshop. I was misunderstanding the phrase "clothing optional," Wally explained. It just means you get naked. Louisa, who's much taller, with hippy hair, added help-fully, "We climb into the car while still in our bathrobes and we drive straight to Harbin, drop' em and jump into the pool." Nonetheless, I packed my regulation black, the one I swim laps in at the YMCA.

Turn that into *swam*; I haven't seen it since. That was three years ago and I've now been to many hot springs with friends. On two embarrassing occasions, I even encountered a current business con-tact, locking eye contact firmly in order not to let my gaze drift down. I've also spotted a lot of naked men practising yoga *asanas* and the crane position "in the naughty," as we used to say. But I don't think I've ever spotted a piece of lycra or shirred elastic, ex-cept upon one lone nappy-wearing one-year-old in Harbin, which is near Middletown in Northern California, and is the best-known and most famous of all the hot springs.

Well okay, make that "notorious." You could say that Harbin—unfairly—is saddled with a name for its cruisin' vibes, despite al-lowing neither alcohol nor smoking. But it's also the sort of place where you might easily bump into some marketing manager you know from the corporate world and wind up saying "Oh sorry, Bob, I didn't recognize you," as he flits rapidly behind the nearest bush, hands clutching his rights and entitlements. Lawyers and computer programmers also frequent Harbin, not just free female spirits called Seagull and Sensitive New Age Guys in pigtails.

More or less the first thing you see in the carpark is a little bench, with a California-style notice explaining this micro-gulag near the hated car fumes is the only place you can smoke. This refers to cigarettes, not to marijuana, and is a reliable indication as any that heavy Camel smokers will not be happy here, as indeed they never are anywhere in California. The next thing you notice, after a short trudge uphill to the bathing area of warm and hot and plunge pools, is that everyone is in an extremely good mood and nobody is wearing a stitch.

Clearly, any "batheners" are *de trop*. It's impossible not to just frankly stare. Deprived of the chance to see naked bodies on a daily basis in our city lives, we are easily stunned by the, um, sheer diversity of our wobbly bits. I tried in vain to repress a tendency to gape and point. My friend lost the battle and boldly engaged a Generation X-er twenty years her junior in jolly banter, while a rabbinical gentlemen tried to flirt with her from the other side of the pool.

It's just not that easy to strip off in front of a small swimming pool of men and women when you've never been introduced. But letting boldness be my friend, I dropped the towel and plunged right in, with one smooth movement and an almighty splash, only to find that nobody was noticing anyway. They're mostly pretty wrapped up in themselves and intent on getting more into that state—aside from an occasional insect being lovingly rescued from the waters and dried upon the pool edge next to a tiny Buddhist shrine. But a nearby notice says "No diving or sexual behavior in the bathing area."

I leave it to your imagination to picture the scene: Sensitive New Age Guys (also known as SNAG) and veg-head babes, sometimes calling themselves Star and aged from 18 to 70, dunk their limbs in a chin-high, 100-degree Fahrenheit pool that holds twenty or more, while nearby there is a little heartshaped paddling pool for lying in and reading. Only whispering is allowed. Many are lovey-dovey couples, of which a healthy proportion—at least one quarter, say—are same-sex gay couples, girls or boys. Garbo types are wearing a wooden bead on a leather lace around their necks, signifying the desire to be left alone; but they are few. Clearly, couples come here on their second or even fiftieth date. Shortly thereafter, a bearded man who said his

> *As I sank gratefully into the roasting hot water at Harbin, my gaze came to rest on the crude statue of a deity adorned with flowers. A pagan shrine for the naked water worshippers? My thinking was interrupted by the aging biker who was soaking with obvious satisfaction. "Are we blissed yet?" he asked. Suddenly everything was as it should be. There were no more questions to be asked, no troubling moral issues to be resolved. We were blissed—no need to know anything else.*
>
> —Sean O'Reilly,
> "Lady of the Avenues"

name is Jeff asked me if he can "Watsu" me. Confused and un-
comprehending, I said "Okay, sure," and it turned out that "Watsu"
is a kind of underwater New Age massage. The idea is to emulate
the secure feeling of the baby back in the womb, simulated through
a rocking motion. Jeff grabbed a-hold of me, aided by the anti-
gravitational properties of the mineral-heavy spa water, and rocked
me in his arms, twirling our limbs around in a trancelike ballet. I
shut my eyes in silent horror and dread as various parts of me
heaved out of the water in full public view. Luckily my ears were
full of water, so I missed any comments; but I noticed my friend
rejecting the skinny rabbi's efforts to "Watsu" her, a pity since *this*
we'd really like to see.

I afterwards learnt that Jeff is what's known in Harbin as a
"Watsu Shark" from Hawaii. But, later protesting that he is actually
a "Watsu Tuna," Jeff convinced me to learn Watsu too, which I did,
nervously, upon a fragile German tourist girl with an equine nose
and Princess Anne overbite.

My Watsu teacher was a tanned, fiftysomething naked woman
called some long Indian name who advised me to stare deeply into
my partner's face and try to "visualize her as a little child" so that
I could keep her nose out of water and conquer "inappropriate energies" as I rocked her. Me, I wasn't aware of anything "inappropriate"—other than the fact that we were two completely naked women
who didn't know each other from Eve rocking each other around this
smelly pool full of strangers; but I didn't dare to contradict her.

Talking of "inappropriate energy," however, I'd have to mention
Ricardo, the Mexican truck-driver who nibbled my big toe after
darkness fell (well, he'd hardly want to do it if he could see it in
daylight, let's face it). Thinking this might be another "Watsu" exercise, and that Ricardo might be a "Watsu Anchovy," I waited
before asking him to desist, for fear of hurting his feelings. That's
your classic, Harbin-style misunderstanding. One lucky thing about
Harbin, though (or unlucky, if you prefer) is that for many people,
there's nowhere to go to be "inappropriate" unless you break into
the massage hut or the bushes, where rattlesnakes, bobcats, scorpi-
ons, and brown recluse spiders are not totally unrecorded.

The accommodation is a series of public "dormitories" in the woods and an old converted Victorian spa hotel. Also available is a sleeping deck where you can plonk your sleeping bag, which is where I slept with several dozen other snoring people beneath the shooting comets (there's a wonderfully visible stream of stars in August and September).

A cinema shows nightly movies (but Scorsese's *The Last Temptation of Christ* conflicted with the "Intimacy and Relationships" workshop while I was there); and Thai massage by an Italian SNAG called Gabriel, whom I had mistakenly thought said "thigh massage." There's a vegetarian dining room and a campsite. Good value for someone intrepid or fancy free, or who just wishes they were.

Not far away, beyond Winters on Route 20 in an equally wild and unspoilt landscape, is Wilbur Hot Springs, which boasts a really sumptuous Victorian stage coach hotel and highly sulfurous springs: one as hot as 115 degrees and guaranteed to turn your jewelry a weird colour. They have dormitories, as well as private rooms of considerable comfort and seclusion. Unlike Harbin, it has a private feel; this is where people who've had enough or too much of the real world come to recover. Coming here with another girlfriend who was recovering from a problem, I learnt that everyone is undergoing recovery in the hot springs world—marriage or work or the Sixties, which were too good to them (grass and beer), or the Seventies, ditto, (cocaine, poppers), or the Eighties (Jane Fonda, jogging, Chardonnay) because they *might* have been at Woodstock since they sure as hell don't remember being there. (Alas, I was in Dublin for most of this era and I remember all of it only too vividly; we had a deprived adolescence, indeed.)

Most celebrated of the spas is the Esalen Institute, where the hot springs dramatically teeter on the summit of rocky, craggy cliffs and you steam above a crashing Pacific ocean far below; however, unless you volunteer as a pool cleaner, it's probably too expensive for the likes of us. In the other direction, my favorite hot spring of the lot is Orr Hot Springs off Route 101, past the teeny-tiny microbrewery of Hopland (Red Tail lager and cheesecake) and down a serpentine track through Orr's ancient stand of coastal Redwoods.

Because it's smaller and farther away, Orr is the friendliest and least "cruise-y." Alcohol is allowed, but only in plastic mugs. You push your sleeping bag, bathrobe, and food supplies down in a sort of trolley ("This sorta reminds me of my grandparents fleeing the czar's pogrom," said my friend as she put her *zaftig* shoulder to the wheel) and you take your choice of accommodation: cabin or sleeping bag in a dorm. You share the big kitchen and you hang out in a shallow, warm pool, or else a deep but very hot pool, with instant therapeutic effects on your aches and pains. There are also small and old-fashioned bath tubs, into one of which my friend and I squeezed but got stuck as she related bracingly indiscreet memories of past trips to Orr to me, or another excitingly cold plunge pool.

All have rather rocky bottoms and we quickly developed a condition known as "Orr Burn" or sandpapered bum. We lay in the warm pool for most of 36 hours one recent weekend, rejoicing in the way our cares and woes floated away as we chatted unselfconsciously about Harbin versus Orr, and whether either were good for picking people up, with: a) a short salmon fisherman from Half Moon Bay ("I never try it without my cowboy boots," he maintained); and b) a school teacher from Ukiah, who said he always got lucky in Harbin, but never in Orr; and c) a couple of embarrassed gay British women tourists; and d) a 14-year-old boy, who was too overcome with shyness to strip off himself for traditional adolescent reasons, but was very, very friendly indeed. Reluctantly dressing to go back to Real Life, I felt as though my limbs were made of rubber bands and my skin had been polished with a chamois buffer.

This is pretty much what people have done to relax throughout the ages—the Romans and Greeks, for instance, did it. The Turks do it. The Hungarians do it. The Germans do it. In Lisdoonvarna, farmers do it. Birds and bees don't, as a rule. But we could do with a re-introduction to its therapeutic benefits. Or is "Recovering Californian" the only personality description needed here?

One thing I want to know, Who took my bathrobe? It was the only thing I brought to Orr last weekend and it's hanging somewhere on a peg in the Redwoods. Hey, let's go back.

Elgy Gillespie is an Anglo-Irish travel writer who currently shares her home in San Francisco with numerous cats and roommates. She is a writer for Worldview *and formerly the editor of the* San Francisco Review of Books. *She has written several books about Ireland and freelances for Irish and British magazines.*

★

We were relaxing in the warm pool at dusk, feeling the stress of the city lifting from our bodies, when we noticed that the place was getting crowded. Bathers kept coming down the steps into the pool until flesh was pressing against flesh whether you wanted it to or not. Then a masked woman in flowing robes paraded around the pool deck with a candle, and before we knew it everybody was moaning and wailing and moving around the pool in opposing circles. There was nothing to do but take part, and when the moon rose huge and round above the hill I realized what was happening: unknowingly we'd come to Harbin on the night of the full moon, a big deal here.

—Larry Habegger, "Way of the Shepherd"

PART THREE

GOING YOUR OWN WAY

LUCY MCCAULEY

Step by Step

She put on her sneakers and climbed halfway to the stars.

I DISCOVERED HILLS IN SAN FRANCISCO. STEEP, 90-DEGREE inclines, or so it seemed, hills with grooves in the sidewalks to help you keep your footing. And so it was that I also discovered walking in San Francisco. I had always been a runner back home in Boston, but for me, hills and running didn't mix.

It was January, and for a solid month the rain came down cold and pelting. I was visiting San Francisco for the winter, considering a permanent move. Everyone said I would fall in love with the city. But that year, with the rain coming down, the place didn't seem too attractive. The house I was staying in leaked, and I spent my days racing from room to room with buckets. I missed my friends and I even missed the snow, which I told myself I liked better than rain because at least you can make snow angels.

To keep up my spirits, I started to walk the hills of Noe Valley, where I was staying. Every few days, I'd put on my windbreaker and a baseball cap and head out the door. Up hills and down, each time I tried to walk a little farther.

Gradually, with each walk, the city began to change for me; a new terrain waited on every block. A set of narrow cement stairs that snaked up a hillside overgrown with vines. Soggy acorn caps that crunched out a soft percussion beneath my feet. The scent of moist dirt and pungent, bracing eucalyptus that accompanied me through almost every block.

Some hills were so steep I had to stay on tiptoe all the way up. On those streets, cars parked perpendicular to the hill, side by side in rows, defying gravity, precarious as dominos lined up on their edges. Downhill, I bent my knees in a two-step jog, my toes thrusting through the small holes I'd worn in my running shoes. By my second week on the hills, I traded them in for a good pair of walking shoes.

I walked streets named Sanchez, Eureka, Alvarado. I liked their colorful names, so different from the staid, bricked streets of Boston, with names like Beacon, Charles, and Exeter. I started looking forward to what I'd find on the next street up and over— walks past the kinds of things I'd never had time to notice on fly-by runs: sweet rosemary in violet-blossoming shrubs that peeled almost decadently onto sidewalks. Low, bare sycamores with wet, stumpy fists twisting skyward. And the famous "painted ladies," Victorian houses that are even more astonishing than the photographs I'd seen. Vibrant turquoises, fuchsias, oranges, golds, somehow all mingling beautifully on the façade of a single house. Another with a yellow sun bursting from the crown of its roof. A house with whimsical purple hares hopping across its face.

My walks became little adventures. Each day, I'd pick out a different hilltop in the distance and head for it, mapless, dead reckoning in the general direction. Years ago, I once spent half an hour attempting to drive a car to the end of a rainbow I'd spotted in the distance. That's how those walks felt, like heading toward some treasure on the horizon.

Some days I'd find myself walking through the salsa-samba sounds of the nearby Mission District. There, women stood on sidewalks firing off rapid Spanish, and the spicy scent of Salvadoran *pupusas* wafted through the air.

Just beyond the Mission, I once found Bernal Heights, where a lush green mound rose in the air like an oasis. I climbed the streets that wound toward it, the occasional staircases, until I reached the dirt path to the top of the mound. There, above the city, everything looked hazy and undulating. I could see the ocean and the bridges—Bay Bridge in one direction, Golden Gate in another. I could see planes taking off like great galumphing birds from San Francisco International. The city seemed to rise up as if from a cloud, with me in the heavens.

One afternoon, when the rain at last was ending, becoming a pleasant, misty spray, I aimed my feet toward the highest hills I could see from Noe Valley: Twin Peaks. Surreal, windmill-like telegraph poles perched on top of it, red lights winking through the mist. This, I knew, would be my biggest challenge yet by foot; it would take several hours, maybe half the day.

I walked up hills and down, up flights of steps and down. With each street I forged, I felt my anticipation rising like those towering telegraph poles. Suddenly, I came upon a stair half-hidden by white blossoms and shrubs. A single stream of sunlight warmed it. A white-haired man stood on the adjacent street corner, leaning on a cane and staring at the sunbeam-covered stairs as if at an apparition. I walked swiftly past him, heady with the sense that my goal was near. I began the climb up the sunbeam, feeling the old man's eyes on my footsteps, feeling him willing me up the streaming light. Eucalyptus hit me like a hallucinogenic. I began a purposeful jog, bounding from stair to stair all the way to the top: an opening through the bushes onto a schoolyard of screeching children.

I rounded one corner and then another, and the long forked horns of the tower creatures grew larger. Soon I was climbing the sloping dirt trail to the top of the main hill of Twin Peaks. I stood sweating and blinking up at the telegraph pole with its red lights. I'd walked more than two hours, almost all the way straight uphill.

There is something about reaching the highest place on a particular landscape. It offers you perspective and a view, of course, but also vision within. A view to the spirit. I found a rock and rested. Below, row houses wound like train cars around hillsides. The wind whipped long grass, clouds above flowed in and out of their rabbit and dog imitations. The mist turned to blue-gray fog, and from where I sat I could see it billow through the magnificent red shoulders of the Golden Gate.

Sitting there on Twin Peaks, I felt satisfied in a way I hadn't since leaving Boston. Like I'd taken on something and reckoned with it, overcome something. Something like the fear and sadness that had come with the change of coasts. I sat there unmoving on that rock, looking out at the day as it changed into early evening, and I thought how I could come to love this city, just as everyone had said.

Lucy McCauley is a writer and editor living in Cambridge, Massachusetts, whose essays have appeared in such publications as the Harvard Review *and the* International Quarterly. *She is the editor of* Travelers' Tales Spain.

★

My first job in the big city was not the exciting news-reporting one I'd imagined. I had to settle on a plebeian job answering phones at a radio station. Our station offices were on Maiden Lane, just off Union Square. I'd read that this promenade had attracted the rough crowd during the Barbary Coast days and had been named for the belles who would ply their wares, themselves, by leaning over the wrought iron balconies and beckoning the sailors below.

Despite the cultural surroundings, I was not content. To me, this most beautiful of cities was a lonely place. Armed with a youthful shyness, it took a small miracle for me to be drawn into conversation, and those dreams of becoming a broadcast whiz started to fade as the months went by. It was hard to have any sense of community feeling when the rent was high, my salary and savings were low, and I had to sober up to tough grown-up realities.

My sole Midwestern image of San Francisco had been shaped by Rice-A-Roni ads—the clanging cable cars making a steep trip toward the blue sliver of a bay. For years before and after my arrival, those gilded relics had been removed for repair. Only tourists, I surmised, would find rolling down the tracks on Powell Street a thrill. The only transport for me was the bus or subway and the passengers wore the blank expressions of commuters.

After what I thought was too much media attention, the cable cars were to be rededicated, but I didn't realize that Union Square was the site.

I found thousands swarming to my normally peaceful lunch spot, trying to catch a glimpse of the proceedings, lining the streets in front of the St. Francis Hotel, Neiman Marcus, Macy's, and Saks. A raised platform held the civic leaders who gave their requisite snippets about how much these vehicles had been missed.

I jumped up on the edge of a marble planter which afforded a view of Tony Bennett climbing onto the stage. After the cheering died down, he asked that we join him in a song. There was no question as to what song. A stillness suddenly settled on the crowd, the only movement came from swaying palm trees and the sun's glint on the surrounding buildings. It was a moment of reverence. Without musical accompaniment, Bennett's clear tone filled the Square…"I left my heart in San Francisco…." As the crowd joined in, I looked around. There was a spirit which no anthem I'd heard before had inspired. Without a tinkling piano underlining the simple song, it became a love song—but to a city? The City. As Bennett led us through "when I come home to you, San Francisco, your golden sun will shine for me," the crowd drew silent, then the yells went up and the ceremony was over.

I realized that the cable cars were only a small element to this celebration. It was an image which people proudly proclaimed as *theirs*. Suddenly, I felt a new love for this place, despite the disappointments which the city had nothing to do with. I've seen those cable cars hundreds of times since and will always remember the day San Francisco became my home.

—Kay Schaber, "Tony and a Song in the Square"

✦ ✦ ✦

El Matador Lives

A former bullfighter plays a trick on old man time.

WHEN I CREATED EL MATADOR, I WAS LIVING IN A LITTLE HOUSE at 844 Bay Street. As my family grew, we moved to a bigger house on Pacific and then to a house we built across the bay on the lagoon in Belvedere. For years I maintained a ludicrous schedule: I would set forth from home at eight in the morning for the twenty-five-minute trip across the bridge to my studio on Telegraph Hill, write and paint until five, go home to play with my kids and have dinner with my wife, and then return to San Francisco at nine and stay until midnight. It was crazy, but if one had to commute, what a lovely one that was. Every day I looked forward to crossing the bridge and seeing San Francisco shining in the morning light....

Jack Kerouac wrote—so long ago and so well—in *Desolation Angels*:

> It's the bridge that counts, the coming-into San Francisco...
> over waters which are faintly ruffled by ocean-going Orient
> ships and ferries, over waters that are like taking you to some
> other shore.... It's seeing the rooftops of Frisco that makes
> you excited and believe, the big downtown hulk of buildings,
> Standard Oil's flying red horse, Montgomery Street high-

buildings, Hotel St. Francis, the hills, magic Telegraph with her Coit-top, magic Russian, magic Nob, and magic Mission beyond with the cross of all sorrows I'd seen long ago in a purple sunset with Cody on a little railroad bridge—San Francisco, North Beach, Chinatown, Market Street, the bars, the Bay-Oom, the Bell Hotel, the wine, the alleys, the poorboys, Third Street, poets, painters, Buddhists, bums, junkies, girls, millionaires, MGs, the whole fabulous movie of San Francisco...the tug at your heart.

In 1947, Jack Kerouac came from Lowell, Massachusetts, to the Bay Area and fell in love with San Francisco. He and Allen Ginsberg, Alan Watts, Gregory Corso, Michael McClure, and Lawrence Ferlinghetti helped make North Beach the mecca for the Beat Generation in the mid-1950s.

And, of course, Rexroth. Kenneth Rexroth would hold forth at the Matador reciting poem after poem, sometimes in Japanese, not caring whether we understood or not. Like Rexroth, the novelist Herb Gold straddled the worlds of both the Beats and the Establishment, but offbeat writers like Kerouac and the others usually preferred the atmosphere of, say, the Coffee Gallery, the Co-Existence Bagel Shop, and The Place, all around the corner on Grant Avenue.

Jack Kerouac came into the Matador only one time, and he was already a star. He had an aura about him. His 1957 book, *On the Road*, written, it was claimed, in twenty days, had made a big impression all over America but especially in San Francisco, home of flower children and beatniks (a word, incidentally, coined by columnist Herb Caen). *On the Road* is the wild saga of a group of pals wandering across the continent, boozing, whoring, and "digging the scene." It catalogues the postwar search for meaning with live-for-the-moment intensity, absolute honesty, and a fascination with ethnic subcultures.

I walked with every muscle aching among the lights of 27th and Welton in the Denver colored section, wishing I were a Negro, feeling that the best the white world had offered was

not enough ecstasy for me, not enough life, joy, kicks, darkness, music, not enough night….

It was about Kerouac, incidentally, that Truman Capote made his
famous and unjustified remark, "That's not writing, that's typing."

Kerouac came into the bar that night with Larry Ferlinghetti, the
celebrated poet and owner of City Lights Bookstore. I'd never met
the author of *On the Road* before, and actually, I was reluctant to
meet him since I'd just written an
unfavorable review of his latest
book, *Dharma Bums*, which had
appeared in the *Saturday Review*.
He was tanned, good-looking,
and a little drunk, but intriguing.
I thought he was older than me,
and he was, by thirteen days.

"I'm sorry I had to write that
review," I said to the beatnik god.
"I liked *On the Road* a lot, but I
just didn't understand this one."

"You will," he said affably. "In
about ten years, you will."

Then his mood changed. He
stared sadly into his bourbon, as
though the answer to the mystery
of life lay among the ice cubes.

"Been readin' Freud," he said.
"No man can believe in his own
death, Freud says, and when he
tries to imagine it, he perceives that he really survives as a spectator. But then, Freud's a fraud. Say that three times fast—Freud's a
fraud, Freud's a fraud, Frood's a fried. See, I can't do it."

Then he brightened and clapped me on the shoulder. "You
know, life's like a sewer—you get out of it what you put into it."

Without another word, he lurched out into the night, on the
road again.

> *My interest in
> Martinis probably
> began in childhood. During the
> fifties and sixties my father owned
> a saloon in San Francisco called El
> Matador, a swank place frequented
> by David Niven, Eva Gabor, and
> Tyrone Power who came for good
> jazz and cold Martinis. Though I
> drank ginger ale when I first sat at
> the bar as a ten-year-old, I heard
> magic in the gravel-like hiss of the
> Martini shaker. It went well with
> the jazz piano, the low lighting,
> and the conversational secrets of
> adult life. I wasn't cool then, but
> I knew Martinis were cool, and
> eventually I would drink them.*
>
> —Barnaby Conrad III,
> *The Martini: An Illustrated
> History of an American Classic*

*

In the fifties, Barbary Coast and North Beach saloon keepers, nightclub owners, and restaurateurs used to visit cordially back and forth. Even ex-madame Sally Stanford would come over from her Sausalito restaurant, Valhalla, with her beloved parrot, Loretta, on her shoulder. We were all friends, Coke Infante of the Condor, Henri Lenoir of Vesuvio, Enrico Banducci of the Hungry i, and others would make the rounds of each other's places—we didn't mind the store *all* the time. I'd take in the wonderful singing waiters and waitresses at the Bocce Ball at least once a week, and when Mike Nichols and Elaine May did their comedy and improv act at the Hungry i for a month, I was there every night. On Sundays, the Black Cat served brunch with opera and fizzes, and the tenor, José, dressed in jeans and high-heeled red shoes, would sing the parts of Carmen, Mini, and Tosca. (Quipped a customer: "He can also handle men's parts.")

Performers from nearby clubs and shows would come into the Mat between or after performances. Flamboyant Inez Torres would undulate by after dancing at the Sinaloa. Walter Hart, the queen of Finnochio's next door, was a regular, as was Wing, the inscrutable Chinese artist, who was a walking fortune cookie ("Wise is the ax that sharpens itself," and so on). Eartha Kitt, Ronny Graham, Paul Lynde, and their producer, Leonard Silliman, came in nearly every night of the long, long run of their show, *New Faces*.

One evening I said to Leonard, who was preparing a new show, "You really should go down a block to Ann's 440 Club and catch the singer—a kid just out of high school with the damnedest voice you ever heard. Nobody ever sang "Flamingo" quite like that. Going to be a big star, and they're selling his contract for only five hundred dollars."

Leonard, always looking for new talent, scurried out of the Matador. He came back in an hour looking elated.

"Got him!" he exclaimed.

"You got Johnny Mathis?"

"Naw," said Leonard, "couldn't stand his weird voice. But I signed up the female impersonator on the program, T. C. Jones—going to put him on Broadway next season in a one-man show that I guarantee will be a huge hit!"

He did, and it was.

Another performer from down the street, Lenny Bruce, spent a lot of time at the Matador. I remember that one night he was at the bar nursing a Coke when he saw the flamenco dancer José Greco and his group come in.

"Those flamingo dancers knock me out," he said in his Long Island accent. "The guys always stand there clapping their hands over their heads, lookin' down over one shoulder as though they're applaudin' their own ass."

Labeling Lenny Bruce "irreverent" would be like calling Lizzie Borden unfilial. Steve Allen, another visitor to the Mat, wrote in his book *Funny People*: "There are few people to whom I would apply the word *genius*, but Lenny Bruce is one such. He was certainly a great deal more than just a successful nightclub comedian; he was, in fact, a comic philosopher." One night Lenny and Jonathan Winters came in at the same time. After a brief nod they sat at tables across the room from each other. They were a study in contrasts: Midwestern Jonathan—stocky, jowly, jolly; and New Yorker Lenny—lean, swarthy, and good-looking in a ferrety, furtive way. I'm not sure just how it happened, who started it, but all of a sudden they were both on their feet doing comic routines at each other like dueling banjos while the lucky customers who happened to witness it clutched their sides in helpless laughter. Oh, to have had a tape recorder!

I don't remember everything that happened that night, but Jonathan did a wild reenactment of what Babe Ruth's dressing room might have been like after he hit his sixtieth home run. Something like this, with Jonathan alternately doing the Babe and his manager:

"Babe, there are a lot of kids outside waiting for autographs."

"Screw the kids—where're the broads, the booze?"

"They've been waiting a long time, Babe. Here's some baseballs to autograph for them."

"Oh shit, all right. Hand me the rubber stamp and open the door." (Stamping the balls.) "This is for the skinny little Eye-Italian here—what's your name, boy?"

"Joe, sir, Joe DiMaggio."

"There you go, you little fag. And what's that little kid's name next to you?"

"Jackie, sir, Jackie Robinson."

"Well, here's one for you, you little runt."

And so forth, growing more outrageous all the time. Then Lenny would try to top whatever Jonathan had done. One bit of Lenny's involved Oral Roberts getting a collect call from Rome from the newly elected Pope John:

"Hello, Johnny, what's shakin', baby? Yeah, the puff of smoke knocked me out.... Got an eight-page layout with Viceroy: 'The New Pope Is a Thinking Man.' ...Hey, listen, Billy wants to know if you can get him a deal on one of them dago sports cars....When you comin' to the coast? I can get you the Steve Allen show the nineteenth.... Wear the big ring.... Yeah, sweetie, you cool it, too...No, nobody knows you're Jewish!"

Jonathan countered with Maud Frickert's tale of her brother Maynard's attempt to fly with 146 pigeons scotch-taped to his arms: "Got airborne, did all right, till those bad boys threw the popcorn on the ground in the quarry..." Word began to spread up and down the street about this impromptu comic windfall. People hurried in to catch what they could of the happening.

It was a night to remember, and Lenny was a person to remember. Dustin Hoffman in the film *Lenny,* while relentlessly earnest, failed to show how very funny Lenny was; he wasn't just a dirty-talking civil rights crusader. Of course, he did shock San Francisco at the time—this was in the Eisenhower years when even using the word "virgin" in a movie, which happened in *The Moon Is Blue*, could shake up Hollywood and the nation. People on the stage didn't use such language as a ten-letter word for an oral copulator, nor did they mock formal religion or discuss racial discrimination. But Lenny inspired belly-laugh humor when he discussed serious and controversial matters. One night a Texas redneck in the audience was giving him a bad time about a racial issue. Lenny pointed a finger at him.

"Sir, let me put something to you. You're on a desert island, and you have your choice of marrying a black woman or a white woman, right? Now, before you answer with your choice, I feel obliged to tell you that the black woman is Lena Horne and the white woman is Kate Smith."

Even the victim laughed.

Another time he said, "Look, I don't talk dirty. It's you people who have the dirty minds. For example, give me a four letter word ending in unt meaning a woman." (Pause) "See what I mean? I was thinking of aunt."

Off stage Lenny was shy, gentle, and loving, with a delightful naughty-little-boyness about him. The only time I ever saw him irritated was once when I thoughtlessly telephoned him at eight in the morning.

"I hope I didn't wake you up," I said.

"Oh shit no," came the mumbled growl. "I always get up thirteen hours before I go to work!"

It was terrible to see him shrivel up and lose his health, his humor, and his career after the ordeal of his obscenity trials in San Francisco, Los Angeles, and New York. The New York trial alone lasted almost six months. He always thought he would be found innocent—he believed passionately in the First Amendment—but he was found guilty and faced a long term in jail.

While his case was being appealed, his drug use increased. One night in his room in the Swiss-American Hotel, across the street from the Matador, he ran around his room flapping his arms and shouting, "I'm Super-Jew!" He then leapt from the second-floor window and crashed to the sidewalk. Miraculously, he was not killed, and when the medical emergency crew came to take him to the hospital, they first taped his mouth shut to silence the obscenities he was screaming.

On August 6, 1966, he was found in a hotel bathroom dead of an overdose at the age of 40. Ironically, after his death all his obscenity convictions were reversed.

Toward the end he had told his mother, "I failed at what I tried. I thought I could show them a way to care; instead of feeling hatred, I wanted to wipe out all the hypocrisy. But it's like opera, not everyone likes opera...."

As writer Paul Krassner eulogized him: "He fought for the right to say on the nightclub stage what he had the right to say in his own living room." And Joe Morgenstern wrote in a very perceptive article on him in *Playboy,* "Comics always fail. Failure is written into their contract with a tumultuous world that has more pressing things to do than laugh."

Lenny is still funny, not in print perhaps, but on the few recordings one can still find—comedic classics like "Comic at the Palladium" and "Thank You, Masked Man," his portrait of the Lone Ranger as an insufferable Jewish moralizer. But he left a larger legacy. Very few comics are happy offstage; mixing high ethics and belly laughs is tough on a man's soul, as the sad saga of Lenny Bruce showed us. But in San Francisco, he also demonstrated that someone who dares to speak out, using humor as a scalpel, can change the way we look at ourselves forever....

For the record, the Matador is still there. Sort of. The bullfighting motif and artifacts disappeared. The big mural I worked so hard on has been covered up with puce material, there are pool tables, and there is no trace of *la fiesta brava* around the electronic pinball machines. Decorators' shops line the Barbary Coast, and Lenny Bruce's ghost cackles around where the Hungry i used to be. From time to time at places like Moose's, I see my longtime bass player, Vernon Alley, who is now a respected member of the prestigious Bohemian Club and former arts commissioner. We get together to reminisce about that golden time and the golden folk in that golden city of yesteryear. And maybe it *was* as good as we think it was. As novelist L. B. Hartley wrote, "The past is a foreign country; they do things differently there."

Or as a character on *The Mary Tyler Moore Show* said, "I didn't like nostalgia then and I don't like it now."

One evening in February, 1994, I drove by the Matador and saw that the sign was down. I peered through a window, and though it was dark, I could see that the place was gutted, piles of lumber indicating that an extensive remodeling job was in progress. Nothing about the place indicated that there had ever been a place called El Matador.

Except! Except the beautiful six-foot mat across the double-door entrance, which announced to the world in black with big white letters, "El Matador." It was the only tangible proof left that there had ever been a place of that name, but it was firmly cemented to the sidewalk. My resolve was instant; dammit, the Mat's mat mattered! That was my mat, and I must have it forever.

I stationed my wife at the corner to keep an eye out for the fuzz—it would be terribly embarrassing to go to the slammer for vandalism at my time of life. Then I pressed my son, Barny, who was born about the same time as the nightclub, into vigorous action. With one eye cocked for policemen or the new owner, we pulled, yanked, and pried. After ten minutes, the great mat was ripped away from its bed and, like a giant manta ray, was flopped into the trunk of the car. Feeling as though we'd pulled off a monstrous college prank, we drove away jubilantly.

"Just think," I panted. "That mat was trod upon by Ingrid Bergman, Ava Gardner, Rita Hayworth, Marilyn Monroe, Hedy Lamarr, and Vivien Leigh. Plus three Gabors and their mother."

My more literate son added, "And Caldwell, Steinbeck, Capote, and Kerouac."

"Well, it was fun while it lasted," I said.

"I hate that expression," said Mary, "the fun's not over 'till it's over. There's plenty of fun left."

Barnaby Conrad is the author of 25 books of fiction and nonfiction, including Hemingway's Spain, How to Fight a Bull, *and* Matador, *which has sold more than three million copies. He is an artist, former bullfighter and American vice-consul in Spain, founder and co-director of the Santa Barbara Writers Conference, and a native San Franciscan. From 1953 to 1964 he owned and presided over El Matador, his famous San Francisco club. This story was excerpted from his memoir of those days,* Name Dropping: Tales from My Barbary Coast Saloon.

*

The rain was getting good Sunday night as I coaxed The White Rat through the Broadway Tunnel into North Beach. I brake for ghosts, and there were too many: Don Sherwood, John Huston and Howard Gossage at Enrico's. Barnaby presiding over El Matador, Joe Vanessi throwing Paul Robeson out of his restaurant. Coke Infante and Billie Rich hanging out at New Joe's (they called it No Jews), Frankie Lupo on his knees at Lupo's as he implored you to try his latest pizza, Dizzy Gillespie doing the 2 a.m. breakfast show at Basin St. West, where the illegal booze came in coffee mugs....

—Herb Caen, "The Walking Caen," *San Francisco Chronicle*

★ ★ ★

Looking for Mr. Big

The author and some fellow lunatics
want to mess with the food chain.

IN THE DEPTHS OF SLEEP, I WAS DREAMING THAT I HAD FALLEN IN the ocean and giant Great White sharks were attacking me. I was punching them, trying to fight them off.

Then I awoke in a sudden fury, sweating, my arms and legs twitching. It was 2 a.m. An hour later, still wide awake, I got up and headed for the boat. You see, we were going fishing for Great Whites. As I cruised down the empty highway, I couldn't get that dream out of my mind.

At the dock, Ski Ratto and his brother, Robert, had already arrived, also an hour early. "I slept about an hour," Ski Ratto said. "This is getting to me. I keep thinking about how big they are."

A few minutes later, up drives Abe Cuanang, also ready for the trip. "Couldn't sleep," he said. Great White sharks have a way of doing that to you. Every one of us, faced with the prospect of tangling with a man-eater, not only could not sleep, but found ourselves at the dock in the middle of the night, consumed by the passion of the adventure.

It wasn't long before our two skiffs, seventeen-foot Boston Whalers, were whipping across San Francisco Bay, heading out to sea. After passing the orange glow of the Golden Gate Bridge, the Pacific Ocean was as dark as the sockets of a skull.

I had been fishing for Great White sharks for several years, but lately I had teamed up with the brothers Cuanang, two of the finest saltwater anglers and boatmen in the country. They were Abe and Angelo, anglers extraordinaire. It was the Cuanangs who developed a system of trolling a hoochie baited with pork rind for lingcod and rockfish, a rare but effective way to fill a boat with fish. Fishing in separate skiffs, they had been catching 700 to 1,000 pounds of fish per trip in a week, then selling the fish on the commercial market. Together we hoped to catch something a little more elusive.

If there was ever a day when a fisherman might hook and fight a 17-foot, 4,000-pound Great White with rod and reel, this was it. We knew the huge fish was there, waiting, eating whatever it wanted. One that big has never been caught by rod and reel in history, not anywhere and not by anybody. We didn't plan on trying to kill a fish like that, but to go one-on-one with it, then cut it free. Man versus man-eater.

The chances never seemed better. Just the day before, Ski Ratto had been fishing for rockfish and lingcod, and when he turned on his depth finder, the bottom registered 120 feet deep. But suddenly, on the screen, the bottom of the ocean appeared to be rising to 80 feet, then 50 feet, then 40 feet. But the boat had not moved. Impossible? A malfunction? No: it was a shark under the boat, a fish so gigantic that the electronic sonar impulses sent by the depth finder were bouncing off the shark and reading it as the ocean bottom.

Later, just as Ratto was bringing a small rockfish aboard, he looked down and saw it. A Great White four feet across at the head was looking right at him, just two feet from the boat, about a foot below the surface.

"He had a giant eye that looked right at me," Ratto said. "A strange feeling went through me like nothing I have ever felt. I panicked and gave the boat full throttle and got the hell out of there."

It was the seventh Great White episode experienced among Ratto, Abe Cuanang, and me in a 10-day span, including twice watching 600-pound sea lions get annihilated in less than two minutes. So we were back, this time prepared.

We arrived at our secret spot just as daylight peeked out from the east. First we had to catch our "bait."

We dangled 16-ounce chrome jigs along the ocean bottom, yanking the rods now and then to make the lures flutter. Bang! A hit! It wasn't long before a 12-pound lingcod came aboard. Just about the right size for bait. In less than half an hour, we had caught several.

We moved the boats to the prime area, then hooked the live lingcod through the back with a hook about ten inches long and four-and-a-half inches wide. Clamped to the hook was three feet of chain, then twelve feet of four separate 1,000-pound test strand wire for leader. We had heavy big-game tuna rods with roller guides, and for reels, Penn Internationals with five hundred yards of 130-pound test line.

We set two lines out at 70 feet deep, the chain providing all the weight necessary to get it there, and let the live lingcod swim about. We set two other lines about 40 yards off the boat, about 30 feet deep, with large red balloons tied on as "bobbers." Kind of like fishing at a pond for bluegills,

Indian summer, when days are mild and bay waters calm and flat, is a fine time to try shark fishing. You don't need to take a long, seasickness-inducing boat trip. Staying inside the Golden Gate, you get good fishing action; a high probability of success (even for neophytes); and lots of delicate, unfishy-tasting meat (cook it like swordfish).

Using light saltwater tackle (20- to 30-pound test), you can catch dogfish (actually a small shark; they run 5 to 30 pounds) and leopard sharks (to about 25 pounds). With heavier gear and 40- to 60-pound test, go for soupfins (50 to 70 pounds, fine eating, and capable of long, frenzied runs full of wild fight) or cow sharks (100 pounds and up). Use 6-foot wire leaders: sharks have teeth. Bait with squid or midshipman fish.

—*Sunset,* "Shark Fishing: Lots of Sport, Beginners Welcome"

right? Well, not quite. One "bait" we used was a 60-pound bat ray Abe Cuanang had caught in San Francisco Bay and saved for the Big Day.

There were no other boats in view for miles. The ocean had just the slightest roll to it and our only companions were passing gulls, murres, and shearwaters. Occasionally a few sea lions would cruise by, then start hopping across the sea like trained porpoises, then jump like penguins out of the water and onto an island. We all saw this and immediately knew why.

"The big guy is down there," said Cuanang. "There's no other reason for them to hop like that." You see, when a Great White is cruising around, even sea lions are smart enough to get the heck out of the water.

We were all quite tense, but after years of planning and testing various rigs, it seemed we had everything in order. The two boats were tied together with a quick release. From below, their shadow would appear to be a large square platform, not an elephant seal or anything else a shark might want to eat. That is why surfers get mistaken for shark food.

shearwater

We were going over our plans one last time. If there was a pickup on a bait, the boats would be released, and after setting the hook, the boat would be gunned 75 yards to get immediate distance between us and the shark. "Got it?" asked Abe.

Before anyone could answer, there was a violent jerk on one of the rods, the one hooked with a three-and-a-half-foot lingcod swimming 60 feet deep. For the flash of an instant, we all froze.

Then Abe Cuanang, who was closest, grabbed it. His eyes looked as if they were going to pop out of his head. Later, Ratto said I had the same look.

"I can feel his head jerking side to side with the bait," Cuanang shouted. "He's eating it!"

He put the reel on free-spool and the shark started to swim off, straight ahead of the boat. The line peeled off the revolving spool. I was just about to shout "Strike!" when Cuanang put the reel in gear to do exactly that. But nothing happened.

"Something weird's happening," Cuanang said. Then it hit him. "He's swimming for the boat! He's swimming for the boat!"

Cuanang reeled with ferocity to pick up the slack. But when the line tightened, the shark was gone, and so was the bait.

We all looked at the bare hook. The only sound was a seal barking in the distance.

"He robbed our bait," Ratto said.

Well, somewhere out there in the briny deep was a Great White shark with a lingcod in its belly.

How big was he? Likely bigger than anyone can imagine.

A day before one of our shark hunts, one of the biggest Great White sharks ever documented washed up at Año Nuevo State Park on the San Mateo County coastline. The shark was 18 feet long, weighed an estimated 4,500 pounds, and had a mouth big enough to eat a man in one bite and two gulps.

It may have been the same Great White that was responsible for two deadly attacks in the same area. At nearby Pigeon Point, an abalone diver was nearly bitten in half and killed by a shark, and in Monterey Bay, a surfer was ripped right off his board and killed.

"We hypothesized that a twenty-foot killed the kid in Monterey," said John McCosker of Steinhart Aquarium in San Francisco, one of the world's leading shark experts. He had a look of awe in his eyes.

"How did you estimate the size?" I ask him.

"We compared the tooth marks on the surfboard to shark jaws in the museum (at Steinhart), jaws of known length, comparing the space between the teeth. On that basis, we figured it was an 18-, 19-, or 20-footer."

When the Great White's massive corpse washed up at Año Nuevo, park rangers first thought it was an elephant seal, since they breed in the area, until they got a closer look. The shark was measured, photographed, and filmed—Steinhart's McCosker was contacted. He immediately arranged a scientific study and autopsy of the creature.

"But when we arrived the next morning, the shark was gone," McCosker said. "The high tide at night washed it back out to sea. It was the big one that got away."

When shown photographs and videotape of the shark, McCosker and other experts were astounded by the size of the fish. The only people I know who have looked eye-to-eye with 4,000-pound sharks are McCosker and Al Giddings of Ocean Quest.

"We estimated it at 4,500 to 5,000 pounds, a huge female," Giddings told me. "Imagine that." Giddings is a world-renowned underwater photographer who has swum unprotected with eighteen-footers and returned with amazing photographs.

One of the few people who documented the shark was Año Nuevo Park Ranger Chuck Scimeca. "I came over a rise and saw it on Cascade Beach," Scimeca said. "I got out there and couldn't believe it. The bulk—I'll never forget it. Its head was four feet wide."

The documentation that sharks of this size roam so near the Bay Area should shock the public into realizing that danger quietly inhabits such nearby waters. There have been more shark attacks off the Bay Area coast than anywhere else in the world. McCosker tries to keep track of each one.

Scientists call the area bordered by Año Nuevo to the south, the Farallon Islands to the west, and Bodega Bay to the north the "Red Triangle" or the "Farallon Triangle." Great Whites live here year round, feeding on abundant populations of sea lions and sea elephants.

A Great White tagging program was directed at the Farallon Islands by Peter Klimley of Scripps Institute. He tagged several sharks, including two seventeen-footers, in a 45-minute span. As many as thirteen or fourteen of this size have been documented at one time.

When sharks like these—sharks that weigh 3,500 or 4,000 pounds—decide to eat, they eat. And they are not always picky. In fact, Klimley's Zodiac rubber boat was bit and sunk by a Great White. At the time of the attack, nobody was in the boat, which had been used to shuttle scientists from the island to research vessels. "I'm thankful for that," he told me.

"More adult white sharks are documented (in the Triangle) than in any other location on the West Coast," Klimley said. "I am a believer. That was my rubber boat that got sunk."

Two Great White sharks were tagged with electronic instruments, allowing the man-eaters to be monitored for daily behavior, traveling range, and how they are affected by various environmental factors. Tracking instruments were embedded in big hunks of meat, which the sharks swallowed. The instruments then transmitted ultrasonic "pingers," tracked by the scientists, until the ultrasonic pings suddenly disappeared. The scientists never picked up the sound wave again and they never knew what happened.

The key to the expanding population of Great Whites is the Marine Mammal Protection Act of 1974. Since sea lions and elephant seals have been protected, they have provided a much larger food source for Great Whites. In turn, baby Great Whites started having much higher survival rates in the early 1980s. Now in the '90s there are so many Great Whites that someone gets bit nearly every year, usually a surfer dressed up to look just like shark food.

The type of fishing you do depends on the season (summer is best). The salmon season runs from mid-February through mid-November; rock cod and bass fish all year. Rock cod provides the biggest catches and will take you the farthest out on the Pacific—about 32 miles, to the Farallon Islands. Salmon fishing is done about 15 miles outside the Golden Gate, and bass fishing is done in the San Francisco Bay.

—Stephen Jay Hansen,
The Other Guide to San Francisco

Considerable dispute rages over the size of the largest Great White in history. A 36-footer in England and a 29-footer in the Azores are the largest documented. The largest Great White ever weighed was 7,300 pounds and measured 21 feet, 3 inches long. It was snarled in a net off Cuba in the 1930s. However, there are tales of 40- and 50-footers.

"No doubt larger ones have been seen," said scientist McCosker. "We may have a few off our own coast…It can give you the chills."

The abundance of Great White sharks off the Bay Area has become critical to keep the marine ecosystem in balance. This is how the chain works: because sharks eat sea lions, and sea lions eat fish, more sharks mean fewer sea lions and more fish. Marine mammals, such as sea lions, eat five times as many fish as are taken by sport and commercial fishermen put together. Thus, if you remove the sharks, the sea lions have no enemies—and, ultimately, fisheries can be damaged by increased sea lion predation.

That is why it is illegal to kill sharks. As scary as they appear, their survival is vital. But you won't find me dangling my legs from a surfboard.

The idea that "I might just get eaten today" sat in the back of my mind every time we went fishing for Great White sharks. For good reason. We had seen sharks big enough to eat a person in one bite, with mouths the size of a barrel, huge chainsaw-like teeth and awesome bodies. But there we were again, cruising out from San Francisco to the Gulf of the Farallones in relatively tiny Boston Whaler skiffs, driven by the fascination and excitement that comes with Great White encounters.

We'd been close before. One day, as the boat cruised at trolling speed, Angelo's rod suddenly stopped cold, like he'd snagged bottom. Then the snag moved.

"I think I got the big guy," Angelo said.

The "big guy" is Mr. You Know Who. Angelo leaned back on the rod with everything he had, and the fish didn't budge an inch. Then it swam a bit, moving the boat. With lingcod gear, that shark did not even know it was hooked—it was like trying to stop a freight train with a roadblock. Then the big shark started to swim off, actually towing the boat at five knots, creating a small wake, an unbelievable sight.

But suddenly, the line went limp. Angelo, his heart still jumping around in his chest, reeled in his line—and found the hook had been straightened.

"You must have snagged him accidentally," Abe shouted from his own boat, "maybe in the back."

How big would a fish have to be to tow an ocean-going boat? How big? It made us tremble.

That fish was never seen. But others have made up for that.

A small Great White, about a 300-pounder, came up and swiped a lingcod right off the line just as Angelo was about to bring it aboard.

"It was so close I could have touched him with my hands," Angelo said. "I looked him right in the eye. I think my heart skipped a beat. I just about went into shock."

A much bigger one also stole a lingcod off Abe's line, also just under the boat. This shark was gigantic, about a seventeen-footer—which is about the size of the Great White in the movie *Jaws*. Through the clear water, the shark was spinning and chewing the fish.

"They're getting bolder," said Abe, with a strange mix of nervous laughter, fear, and excitement in his voice.

In another episode the same week, a Great White hammered a sea lion right on the surface, completely ravaging the 650-pound mammal in less than two minutes. Just as Abe was cruising up, the tip of the shark's dorsal fin disappeared below the surface. Another time, a Great White plucked a sea lion right out of the rolling surf, then disappeared. Only a reddish tint in the water was left behind, and that, too, quickly vanished.

The biggest surprise was that getting Great Whites to strike our bait was a mysterious and elusive gamble. Because the water is so clear this far out to sea, our chain may have been spooking them. We tried painting it black to reduce any glare, which seemed to help.

Crazy? Yeah, we were a little crazy. But we weren't crazy enough to go out without the know-how to accomplish our goal. We wanted to fight them. It is the ultimate in the world of fishing—playing a 4,000-pound fish that can eat you, then cutting it free.

Fast forward to Bodega Bay.

Jim Siegle hadn't said a word for twenty minutes. Alongside, Dick Pool stared ahead across miles of open ocean, looking toward Tomales Point.

The big Wellcraft was cutting a clean wake across the open ocean, and with the throttle at cruise speed, I pointed the boat to where we hoped to hook a Great White. The wind was light, not more than five knots, with only a few murres and cormorants sprinkled about the sea, a flawless calm.

"Everything seems perfect," said Siegle.

"That's what scares me," I answered. "Sometimes when everything seems perfect, you're about ready to take a fall."

"I'd thought about that myself," noted Dick Pool.

The three of us had planned this trip for a long time: Great White sharks had been spotted at the mouth of Tomales Bay. We were heading out hoping to tangle with one.

Siegle, who passed away in late 1993, started with a curious fascination about what he called "Nature's perfect eating machines," and then developed a system that has become the standard for shark fishing along the West Coast. Pool is the renowned underwater TV master, who has perfected filming fish striking baits, and in the process has been able to invent new techniques for salmon and albacore fishing.

The three of us, longtime friends from many expeditions, suddenly realized one day that each of us shared the same fixation about catching a Great White. We then spent hours and hours talking strategy, developing rigs, and ultimately, fishing together on the most exhilarating fishing trips imaginable.

"Great White sharks aren't really such bad fellows," Siegle said, "except that they eat people now and then."

It was no accident that the mouth of Tomales Bay was our destination. It was here that a giant Great White came up behind the boat and breached like a whale, then with its head out of the water, began barking like a dog at us as it gulped air. I guess it wanted a bone. "Lunch served yet?"

When we reached the spot, Siegle opened one of four rubber garbage cans; each was filled to the brim with all matter of fish carcasses, obtained from a commercial fish buyer. Siegle then started laying a chum line, feeding the carcasses into a grinder, which leaves a trail of fish bits and chunks in the water, along with a light floating slick from the fish oil.

"The smell is unbelievable!" he shouted.

"Ooh, how about those three- and four-day-old mushy ones," said Pool. The smell of rotten fish is so wicked that after a full whiff, you might find yourself doing some chumming from a five-point stance.

As the chum line was being laid, I reviewed our equipment. For tackle, we used heavy, world-class rods, reels, and line, most of which was supplied by Siegle. He obtained the heaviest rod Sabre makes, rated at 130-pound test and equipped with giant roller guides, and with Penn's largest reel, a size 16/0 (nearly 10 inches across). It was loaded with 700 yards of 130-pound Ande monofilament, the standard for world-class line. The rig was so heavy you practically needed a hoist to strap it on. To support it, you needed a full shoulder and back harness, to which the rod and reel were connected. We also used Penn International reels set up on heavy tuna rods, 80-pound class, which were a lot easier to handle.

The shoulder harness represents a touch of danger when shark fishing. If you hook the Big Guy, get a backlash in the reel, and then the shark takes off on a power run, you could be pulled right into the water because you are connected to the rod by the harness. That is why we always kept a knife at the ready.

Pool always made sure the knife was sharp. "Now if I start getting pulled into the water, one of you guys had better cut the line," he ordered. "Imagine hooking up with a 5,000-pounder, getting pulled into the water, then having him turn around and come for you."

The terminal rigging was an awesome sight. We used giant hooks, 18/0 when we could get them, with chain and five-strand wires. Siegle designed the rigging, using no knots for connectors, but only wire clamps that could take 10,000 pounds of stress.

For bait, we used whatever was available for each trip. As on my trips with the Cuanang brothers, we sometimes used a live lingcod, about a 15- or 20-pounder. Another very good bait was a ray in the 40- to 50-pound class. At times, we also used two or three stickle-back sharks (dogfish), or combinations of small sharks and rockfish.

But on this escapade, we had a different strategy. Pool made a trip to a rural tallow works, where a fellow named Jake was fascinated with our adventure. He gave us several bags of dried blood to feed our chum line, and also a stillborn calf for bait. Jake must have been a little crazy, just like us.

After the bait plopped in the water, Pool rigged his underwater camera from a downrigger, so we could watch everything that happened down there. The picture came in quite clear, thanks to the calm day. The calm was a prerequisite to the trip, we had all agreed. "First, we must have a calm ocean," Siegle said. "Imagine a rough ocean. You lose your balance and then fall in by accident. All Whitey would see would be your legs kicking back and forth as he came up the chum line. It gives me nightmares."

We also worked out precise emergency teamwork maneuvers: keeping a knife nearby at all times if cutting the line is necessary, having the boat prepared to get the heck out of there if the shark attacks and tries to ramrod us, and having a shotgun aboard with deer slugs at the ready.

"Let's keep the chum line going," Siegle directed, and this time it was Pool's turn to hold his nose and reach into the mushy pot of deteriorating carcasses.

So we chummed and we waited. You might think that sharks of all kinds would respond instantly to the chum line. That just plain never happens. Only rarely in the fall when blue sharks are more common has there been even a tremor of visible response. Regardless, we kept at it, because we had learned that a Great White works on instinct, and we hoped to inspire his predatory instinct with the smell of blood.

"The hope is that if a shark is in the area, the chum line may get him in the biting mood," Siegle said. "We could always dangle our feet in the water to do the same, of course, but for now I have decided against that strategy."

The amount of waiting can be agonizing, especially for people who are accustomed to quick results. But wait you must, knowing all the while that a typical Great White off California is a 12-footer that weighs about 1,500 to 1,700 pounds. You also realize that there are several 15- to 17-footers in the 2,500- to 3,000-pound class, and that there is the remote possibility that a 19- or 20-footer weighing perhaps 5,000 pounds will be the next fish swimming under your small boat.

"We know they're here," Siegle said. "The question is, do they know that we're here, too?"

The answer came immediately. A dark shadow appeared on one side of the TV screen, then vanished.

"Look! Did you see that?" Pool asked.

We were tense, too tense to talk. Without a word, Siegle grabbed the big game rod, hoping for a chance to set the hook. Pool and I stared into the TV screen, and then again, on the left side of the screen, a blurred grayish shadow moved across.

"I wish I could focus it, but with this underwater camera, the focal point is fixed. There's no way to tell how big it is until he gets close to the bait. Then he'll be in focus."

The next half hour was the most excruciating I can remember spending on a boat. We knew there was something down there, something big. We knew our bait was waiting for it, that our chum line was now dispersing fish scent for miles.

But at the rod, there was no tug, no nibble, just silence.

"He doesn't want to bite," Siegle said eventually, shaking his head, exasperated that the showdown had come to this.

"Even though everything is giant, it's still fishing," Pool answered. "Giant tackle, giant hook, giant bait, giant sharks, but just like fishing for anything, you can't always get them to bite."

"Maybe he's full," I said with a laugh.

Maybe not.

A few weeks later, Pool heard a bizarre story about a fellow named Hank who had been salmon fishing near the same spot. He called Siegle and me together to share the story with us.

Hank hooked what he figured was the biggest salmon of his life off Tomales Point when a Great White came up and bit it in half. The half of fish that Hank reeled in weighed 25 pounds.

"He was enraged," Pool said, "and the next day returned to the same spot."

Hank poured all matter of fish carcasses in the water, and after an hour, Whitey returned to the scene of the crime. Hank responded by tossing out the remaining half salmon on a giant hook—which was connected by cable to a power winch he'd taken from his four-wheel drive. Well, sure enough, the shark took the bait, and Hank winched the shark right up to the back of the boat, and then started firing at it with a deer rifle. The shark responded by swimming away, actually reversing the direction of the power winch, then pulled the winch right off the floorboard of the boat and into the water.

"Whitey wasn't done yet," Pool said, "He returned and bit the guy's propeller right off."

At last report, Hank had moved to the mountains, renamed his boat the *Mackinaw King,* and was fishing at Lake Tahoe.

Only rarely has anybody tried fishing for Great White sharks. Regardless, it is now illegal to do so. Hopefully, this will ensure the species' survival. Great Whites have roamed the open ocean without fear since prehistoric times. The next time you gaze across the open waters of the Pacific, you can be assured that the Big Guy is out there, never sleeping, always on the hunt, searching for where he can get his next bite.

Tom Stienstra is an avid adventurer who searches for incredible expeditions and secret spots that involve camping, backpacking, and fishing. As a nationally acclaimed outdoors writer, he has a column in the San Francisco Examiner *and has published eight books, including* Epic Trips of the West: Tom Stienstra's Ten Best, *from which this piece was excerpted. He is currently serving as the director of the Outdoor Writers Association of America.*

✳

It is little realized that for more than a quarter century—from 1882 to 1908—San Francisco was the whaling capital of the world, sending out more whalers each year than the traditional New England whaling port of New Bedford. Legendary old blubber hunters like the *Charles W. Morgan* (which still survives, restored, at Mystic, Connecticut) and the bark *Wandered,* among dozens of others, made San Francisco their home port. Dickie Brothers built a series of successful whaling barks with a steam engine as auxiliary power for use in the Arctic Ocean. The venerable builder of whaleboats, J. C. Beetle, shifted his boatbuilding shop from New Bedford to Alameda during these years.

The reason for San Francisco's prominence was proximity to the Arctic Ocean and its bowhead whales. The bowhead, in addition to oil, provided a springy substance, found in the whale's mouth, called "whalebone." In the Victorian era, whalebone was the source of the nation's hoop skirts, buggy whips, corset stays, fishing rods, etc. Whale oil began to lose its importance with the invention of kerosene in 1857; whalebone, which sustained the fleet of old whaling barks into the twentieth century, was superceded by the invention of a light spring steel and the passing of the fashionable "wasp waist."

The ancient barks *John & Winthrop* and *Gay Head* made the last old fashioned whaling voyages out of San Francisco in 1912 and 1914 respectively.

—Gladys Hansen, *San Francisco Almanac: Everything You Want to Know About Everyone's Favorite City*

J. KINGSTON PIERCE

Lotta's Legacy

*A gift from one of America's first stage millionaires
is in need of its own patron.*

LOTTA'S *WHAT?*" RETORTS THE WOMAN FROM THE CITY'S Department of Public Works, distinctly impatient with my questions, sounding convinced that she can't answer them even before she tries. "You say it was commissioned by Lotta *who?*"

Lotta Crabtree, I explain again—"The California Diamond." She was a vivacious, redheaded comedienne of the 19th century, a protégée of stage rage Lola Montez, who charmed embryonic San Francisco with her songs and her dancing and her infectious laugh. She went on to enchant the rest of the nation and the world with her bounteous talents, but never forgot this place that had helped make her a child star right after the Gold Rush, this town that had first loved her. And so in 1875, when Crabtree was famous and wealthy, she had a fancy cast-iron, lions-headed drinking fountain made in Philadelphia and shipped all the way out to

Lotta Crabtree

303

the Bay Area as a token of her gratitude. That tall, spindly, some might even say "homely" pillar still rises from a cement delta at the convergence of Market, Geary, and Kearny streets, diagonally across from the Palace Hotel. But it's been dry for years now.

All I want to know from Public Works is whether water pipes run anymore out to Lotta's Fountain, pipes that might someday again bring refreshment to the frenzied hordes of San Francisco's Financial District. But none of the people in that office seem able to help me. Nor can they recommend another city bureau with better information. The more I dig for leads, the more frustrated they become, until finally the woman who's been trying to guide me through the bureaucratic morass throws up her hands and insists that nobody in town—*probably nobody on the entire planet!*—is actually responsible for the monument in question.

"Are you sure this fountain of yours exists any longer?" she says, eyeing me suddenly as a troublemaker. "I don't think I've ever even *seen* it."

If so, she's certainly not alone.

Every day tens of thousands of workers and probably thousands more tourists scurry by the actress's commemorative column without giving it a moment's recognition. Since the thing no longer serves a purpose other than as street sculpture—and it's dirty, graffiti-marred, newspaper-strewn street sculpture at that—most folks treat it as nothing more than an impediment to their travel. Only on the anniversary of the 1906 earthquake and fire, every April 18th, when the last San Franciscans who lived through that quake gather about this inanimate survivor of the same disaster, does Crabtree's gift receive much respect.

That's a shame. Because Lotta's Fountain is all that remains essentially intact from this crossroads' glory days, when the city's media elites concentrated their power here, and when people gathered at this broad juncture to celebrate their present. Or to renew their fragile faith in the future.

I lean on a lion's noggin and survey the streetscape from Lotta's Fountain. A Muni bus roars west along Market, belching a miasma of pollutants, vying with cars and cabs and careening bicycle messengers for control of the lanes. A pair of teenagers, the skinny boy sporting camouflage wear, his girlfriend in a scarlet tube-top so snug that she must have to cut it off at night like a bandage, huddle on a dirty, striped blanket nearby, sticking out their paws occasionally for spare change. "We took the bus in from Missoula," they mumble to passersby. "We have no place to stay." Absurdly, the folks most likely to help are those who appear least able to afford the gesture.

Two women in polished business armor, clutching full paper lunch sacks, bring traffic to a halt on Kearny as they use the crosswalk, their raven manes billowing in a rampant wind. I'm reminded of what locals called this intersection during the Gilded Age: "Cape Horn," named in dubious honor of the hazardous, blustery headland around which so many Forty-Niners sailed in search of California riches. "Here, on breezy afternoons," wrote Evelyn Wells in her spirited primer *Champagne Days of San Francisco*, "young men and old gathered to watch the girls trip past, clutching at many-gored skirts and flounced petticoats that would not stay down."

Even today, it's best to keep a firm grip on your hairpiece near Lotta's Fountain. But in our more permissive age, when Americans can scoop topless pics of Michelle Pfeiffer off the Internet and screen X-rated videos over Thanksgiving dinner, the most interesting attractions at this gusty corner may be historical and architectural rather than anatomical.

Almost everything was different here on September 9, 1875, as politicians and respectable citizens, along with more than an ample sampling of hellions from the Barbary Coast, assembled to dedicate San Francisco's new public drinking fountain. The very sky seemed larger then, if only because most of the surrounding edifices hadn't yet climbed beyond a few floors. The notable exception lay half a block to the east: the original Palace Hotel, which had opened mere weeks before and on this afternoon hung profusely with guests anxious to view the festivities. Two and a half acres in size, with 800 rooms and six of its seven gold-and-white stories decorated in parallel banks of bay windows, the Palace was this boom-town's pride and joy. But its inauguration had followed too closely the swimming death of its honored developer, William Ralston, and the temporary closing of Ralston's once-invincible Bank of California. Locals were desperately in need of a boost, and the un-veiling of Lotta Crabtree's present promised them just that.

So whilst armed soldiers enforced order among the spectators, Mayor James Otis joined popular actor Harry Edwards beside this cast-iron landmark to laud the California Diamond for her achievements and generosity. Unfortunately, Crabtree herself was touring in the East and couldn't attend the ceremony, but her el-derly aunt, a Mrs. Vernon, graciously sampled the font's first water before allowing the masses their fill. Apparently only the ruffians went away dissatisfied, grousing that there were no spigots labeled either WHISKEY or BEER.

Within another twenty years the neighborhood girding Lotta's Fountain had changed dramatically. The Palace now competed for attention with three other elaborate erections, each housing one of the city's premier newspapers. In their midst, Crabtree's gift ap-peared shrunken, a quaint relic from some pioneer era.

Perhaps the most significant of these new giants was the *San Francisco Chronicle* tower (690 Market Street), an 1890 work by Chicago master architects Daniel H. Burnham and John Wellborn Root. There was a time when strollers along Market could hear the *Chron*'s presses rumbling in the basement of that skyscraper, while ten stories above, a clock (bearing what was supposedly the world's largest lighted face) ticked off the hours. A bulletin screen spanned the structure's lower facade, keeping locals apprised of breaking news. It was in front of that screen, on St. Patrick's Day of 1897, where San Franciscans crowded to read that local boy "Gentleman" Jim Corbett, for more than half a decade the world's boxing champ, had finally been laid flat in Nevada after fourteen grueling rounds against New Zealander Bob Fitzsimmons. Until the earthquake nine years later, few events had more of an impact on more people in this burg than did the downing of that hand-some, dark-haired Irishman.

Kitty-corner from the *Chronicle* stood the shorter, but nonetheless imposing headquarters of William Randolph Hearst's *San Francisco Examiner* (691-9 Market Street). And on the other side of Third Street (at 703 Market), choleric Sugar King Claus Spreckels had created a home for his daily *San Francisco Call* that was every inch an exclamation point on his long capitalistic career.

Designed in the late 1890s by James and Merritt Reid (who went on to create the Fairmont Hotel), the eighteen-story Spreckels Building was a confection of architectural genius and whimsy, with a classical entrance but a heavily embellished dome anchored by turrets. Spreckels was proud enough of this construction that he went to extraordinary and sometimes expensive lengths to protect it. In 1899, for instance, after spending two frustrating years complaining to the San Francisco Gas and Electric Company about how the coal smoke from its nearby plants was smudging his beautiful building, Spreckels decided to take revenge. He started a competing utility with the express purpose of driving SFG&E out of business. And he almost succeeded, before agreeing finally in 1903 to sell his independent power enterprise to SFG&E for a profit of more than $1.2 million—not bad recompense for his trouble.

But all of the Sugar King's money and temporal influence couldn't save the Spreckels Building on that devastating Wednesday in April 1906, which marked the end of the beginning of local history.

The morning's two earthquake tremors pretty much spared the Cape Horn neighborhood. Its principal affect had been to frighten Palace Hotel tenants—among them Italian opera singer Enrico Caruso, who was staying in the hotel during a scheduled weeklong engagement at the Grand Opera House. After the second temblor, the tempermental Caruso was sure he stood on the brink of death. Worse, he feared that he'd lost his voice. *His incredible voice!* It wasn't until he stumbled to an open window and tried to sing—at the top of his lungs, at the top of his form—that Caruso was reassured.

One can only imagine what scared San Franciscans, resting at Lotta's Fountain in their desperate rush over rubble-strewn streets toward the waterfront and bay-going ferries, thought when they heard the world's greatest living tenor bellowing lines from *Carmen* out a fifth-floor window of the Palace.

Not that they had long to ponder it, mind you, for fires that had been ignited by broken power lines and dry debris south of Market soon began licking north. They engulfed the *Call* building, sending temperatures inside as high as 2,000 degrees Farenheit and blowing glass free of melting window frames. From there the inferno stormed Hearst's offices, melting type fonts and typewriters into a mephitic mass unrecognizable as the machinery of a free press.

> *E*ach time I had a walk along Market Street, from the beginning near the Ferry Building to the Civic Center or vice versa, I was reminded of the famous Chinese proverb "Fire melts gold and gold melts man."
>
> —Chiang Yee, *The Silent Traveller in San Francisco*

Across the way, *Chronicle* publisher Michael Harry de Young had marshalled his reporting staff early and kept them on duty until the last possible minute, compiling stories for a special edition. He even persuaded his managing editor to pen an editorial putting the most optimistic spin on the mounting disaster. It never saw print. Neither did any of the *Chronicle*'s other copy that day, for in the middle of production, fire damage severed the building's water supply, forcing its basement presses to shut down and its occupants finally to flee.

Until the afternoon, it looked as if the Palace—well armed with fire hoses and some 760,000 gallons of water stored in subterranean and rooftop tanks—would withstand the conflagration. But when the water ran out, it too succumbed. Around Cape Horn, only Crabtree's rococo monument, on which there was nothing to burn, came through the debacle virtually unscathed.

No wonder Lotta's Fountain became a rallying point for survivors of the Great Fire. And no wonder it was chosen in 1910 as the appropriate site for a Christmas Eve concert intended both to recapture the excitement of old San Francisco and reward locals for their diligent efforts in rebuilding the city. Singing would be Italian soprano Luisa Tetrazzini, who had been a favorite of San Franciscans ever since her first visit in 1905 and was expected to draw a large crowd on December 31.

"Large" was an understatement. Approximately 250,000 people came to see Tetrazzini mount the open-air stage at Market and Kearny, dressed in a rose-pink cloak, a white ostrich boa and gown, and a big translucent hat. After a lengthy ovation, she began to sing, and suddenly every other sound, every other thought was irrelevant. Those who heard her that night, enthused the *Chronicle*, "now know something of the songs the angels sing." And when, in a voice that was more comfortable with Italian than English, she broke into a rendition of "Auld Lang Syne," it seemed that every man, woman, and child in her audience lifted up their voice to meet hers. This city that had so recently climbed from its own ashes was remembering its past but gazing confidently toward its future. No other New Year's Eve ever seemed so magical.

As I stand now beside Lotta's Fountain, sucking exhaust fumes and watching a young office drone scamper after some papers he's lost to the wind, I try to envision this place as it was in 1910. But I can't. Nor can I imagine how it appeared in the summer of 1923, when President Warren G. Harding was dying in Suite 8064 at the Palace, and Mayor James Rolph ordered streetcars passing in the vicinity of Lotta's Fountain to quiet their bells in order that Harding could rest. And no amount of fantasizing gives me a sharp picture of the bizarre goings-on here during the Great Depression, when bankrupted millionaires stood beside this waterworks in three-piece suits to peddle apples for a living.

Too much has changed at this corner. The *Chronicle* building was restored after the Great Fire, but its Romanesque details were hidden in 1962 behind ugly white metal panels. Both the *Chron* and the *Examiner* long ago vacated the financial district. If you look closely at what's now called the Central Tower, at Third and Market, you might still discern the outlines of Claus Spreckels's beloved skyscraper, but a 1938 "modernizing" stripped it of its dome and most of its eccentric fenestration.

Even Crabtree's column hasn't been completely untouched by time. In 1916, it was raised eight feet to match the height of new street lamps along Market. Its horse-watering trough has been removed, and in 1974, during a $25,000 refurbishment, the whole thing was moved ten feet from where it once stood. It's a marvel that this landmark, abused and ill cared for as it seems to be, hasn't been banished from downtown. Not that some people haven't tried. In 1928, there was talk of relocating Lotta's Fountain to Golden Gate Park, but that campaign kicked up such a torrent of nostalgic protest that its supporters eventually backed down.

So Lotta Crabtree's gift to the city she loved remains. With luck, it will still be here a hundred years hence. Even if nobody notices it in all that time. Maybe especially then.

J. Kingston Pierce, a Seattle writer specializing in history, travel, and politics, is the author of San Francisco, You're History!

★

Greatest of the magnificoes of his time was William C. Ralston whose estate at Belmont has never been appraised in dollars but which was admittedly the most princely mansion and grounds in the United States when it was opened for the entertainment of Ralston's friends. It had an air-conditioning plant some seventy years before its time, its own gas works and water works to activate fountains that compared favorably with those at Versailles, and a formidable entrance gate of gilded bronze which anticipated the electric eye of today by rising when a coach drove over a concealed mechanism in the road. Dinner for 200 off silver or gold services, as the spirit moved the owner, was a commonplace: there was a chef ravished from Foyot's in Paris, and stables that would have aroused envy in Napoleon III who was inordinately fond of horseflesh. When he drove home from the Bank of California in the afternoon, there were changes of horses at five private post houses along the Camino and Ralston prided himself on beating the train.

—Lucius Beebe and Charles Clegg, *San Francisco's Golden Era: A Picture of San Francisco Before the Fire*

JOSEPH DIEDRICH

The First Negroni in the No Name Bar

One man's fight for justice, equality, and the American Way.

TOWARDS THE NORTH END OF BRIDGEWAY STREET, WHICH RUNS along the waterfront in Sausalito, there is a bar with a Steam Beer sign over the door. The bar has no name so, inevitably, it has come to be known as the No Name Bar. Like Harry's Bar in Venice, Bricktop's in Rome, and the Butterfly in Wanchai, the No Name Bar is known all over the world by those who pay attention to such things.

How I came to be the person who integrated the No Name Bar (in a certain sense of the word) was decided—as so many things in life are decided—by pure chance. Back in 1968, after seven years of flying around Europe with Pan Am, I wanted a change of scene and transferred to San Francisco to fly the Pacific. I found an old house that I wanted to buy in Sausalito, just across the Golden Gate Bridge. I also found that I needed a mortgage to be able to buy it.

The prospect of asking for a loan made me nervous. I had never applied for a loan before; I had been away from the States for so long that I had no credit history and the only person I knew at the local bank was the girl who had opened my checking account.

311

My Consenting Adult looked me over as I started out the door for my mortgage interview.

"You can't go to a bank looking like that," she announced. "No one would loan you fifteen cents."

Bowing to superior wisdom, I shucked my jeans and topsiders, found a seersucker suit in the closet that I had lugged all over the world and never worn, put on a necktie and lace-up shoes, and left for my appointment at the bank. I had just had a haircut which was too short. I looked like a used car salesman in August.

Getting the loan turned out to be simple and easy. Afterwards, as I came out of the bank onto Bridgeway, I was feeling relieved and happy. I decided to have a drink to celebrate. I saw the Steam Beer sign up the street and headed for the place.

I had never been in the No Name Bar before. It was only the middle of the afternoon, but already there were a lot of people in the place. The bar was crowded with standees and most of the tables were occupied by couples playing chess or backgammon.

I could see at a glance that this was a bar frequented by liberated, free-thinking, individualistic people. I could tell by the uniforms they wore.

The men were in jeans or chinos and tweed jackets with leather patches at the elbows. Hair was medium length and carefully tousled, mustaches were much in evidence as were pipes, some of which were being smoked upside down, thus indicating the nautical propensities of the smoker. (When you are battling the helm in the wind and the rain a pipe will stay lit upside down.) The ladies wore baggy sweaters and jeans, the jeans spotted with paint. Oil paint, not house paint. Female hair was long and ponytailed. Topsiders were unisex.

A hum of conversation was in the air when I came in from the street. A few people glanced at me, then more, then nearly everyone in the place was staring at the Displaced Person in the seersucker suit. Conversation died away.

In silence I marched over to the bar. The group in front of it parted for me like the Red Sea before Moses. The bartender, a pleasant-looking fellow wearing a bartender adaptation of the individualist uniform, glanced at me, did a classic double take, then picked up a towel and began carefully wiping down the bar in the direction away from where I stood. Conversation picked up again. Pipes were chewed and fondled. Chessmen clacked on chessboards. Drinkers crowded the bar.

Except for the yard of vacant space on either side of the jerk in the seersucker suit. Me. I felt like the first African in the lunch counter at the Tupelo Mississippi bus depot.

For a moment I was taken aback. Then I began to get angry. After the bartender passed me for the third time without looking at me, serving drinks to everyone else, I slammed my hand down on the bar and said, loud and clear, "Hey! You! Bartender!"

There was a shocked silence. The bartender turned, looked at me, waited an insolent ten seconds, and then said, "Yes?"

"Is this a public bar?" I demanded.

Slowly the bartender walked over to where I stood, isolated in seersucker. He stopped in front of me.

"This is a public bar," he said.

"Then I want a drink."

He considered this for a moment, then shrugged and said, "All right. What would you like?"

God knows why I asked for it. It is a drink I have never ordered and don't like at all.

"I'll have a Negroni," I said.

The bartender stared at me. A murmur went round the room. "He wants a Negroni!"

"That's an Italian drink," the bartender blurted out, rather inanely I thought.

"I'll have a Negroni," I repeated.

He made me one. The crowd at the bar watched in silence as I drank it, left some money on the bar, and walked out of the place.

At first I laughed when I told friends about it. Then, the more I thought about it, I began to get angry again. I never went into the No Name Bar after that except on the rare occasions, maybe two or three times a year when I happened to be in the right frame of mind to put on my seersucker suit and go pay them a visit.

Sterling Hayden, the actor, may end up as only a footnote in future film encyclopedias, but I firmly believe that Hayden's book Wanderer *will last as long as people care about adventures at sea and soul-searching autobiography. Here is a portion of the last page of that fine book. "He" is himself, of course, and he is in Sausalito saying a final good-bye to his beloved schooner, which he must sell.*

Grabbing his bag, he slips over the bulwarks and down to the heaving logs where, under the tall ship's lee, he turns and stares at the legend:

Wanderer

San Francisco

With his back to the wind he plows up the dock and reaching the land turns left. He corners the squat brown bank, crosses the Bridgeway Road, turns right past The Tides bookstore, and steps from the storm to the warmth of the No Name Bar. He buys a drink and turns to a ship lost in the night and drinks to a life that was.
He turns to stare at a face in the back-bar mirror: a vague face with bleak and querulous eyes. The eyes lock and he drinks to himself alone.
Vale! Wanderer.

—Barnaby Conrad, *Name Dropping: Tales from My Barbary Coast Saloon*

It was pretty much the same each time. The silence. The stares. The parting of the waters. The isolation at the bar. The deliberately slow and insolent service.

I always ordered a Negroni. I was beginning to enjoy the drink.

Then after two years of Pacific flying, suffering with terminal jet lag from shuttling back and forth to Australia, Vietnam, Thailand, and points beyond, I arranged for a transfer back to Europe where the flights were shorter and where I could feel like a human being again. The day before I was to leave I went down to the bank on Bridgeway to close my account, this time I was wearing topsiders, jeans, and an old sweatshirt.

As I came out of the bank someone called my name: an old friend from former days in West Berlin. He had moved to Sausalito a few months back and hadn't known I was there.

"Let's have a drink at the No Name," he suggested.

"I don't like the No Name."

"How come? It's a great place. Home away from home. Don't you know Charlie?"

"Charlie who?"

"Charlie the bartender at the No Name. He's a pal of mine

from way back. I used to live here before I went to Berlin. Come on, I'll introduce you to everybody."

He was an old friend so I went. Inside the No Name he knew everybody, just as he said. I was introduced as an old sidekick from Berlin. Everyone was friendly. A few of the women indicated that they could be more than that, under the right conditions. Then we went over to the bar and I met Charlie. He looked at me a bit oddly, I thought, then shook my hand and asked me what I would like to drink. I smiled at him.

"I'll have a Negroni," I replied.

It was wonderful.

Joseph Diedrich has lived all over the world. Being a pilot (Navy, oil company, Pan Am) made it possible. He is a wandering soul by nature and tends to float downstream rather than struggle against the current.

★

Charles Haid was the brash but vulnerable cop Andy Renko for many years on *Hill Street Blues*. He grew up in Palo Alto and proudly claims to be a product of San Francisco. "For people who remember, I'm the grandson of Roy S. Folger, a well-known and somewhat eccentric San Franciscan," he says. "He was a founder of the Bohemian Club back when it was for businessmen to go sit out in the redwoods."

"I learned at a very young age, through my grandfather, who took me to the city, that San Francisco was a town that tolerated eccentricity, that loved art, that loved color. I was tremendously stimulated by that environment. You could be Emperor Norton. You could be kind of crazy, and that added a great deal. Maybe it still does."

Singer Johnny Mathis remembers a different sort of tolerance from the city's tavern owners—a tolerance that helped his career. During the war the Mathis family bunked with cousins—"twelve of us in five rooms"— in a basement flat on Post Street between Baker and Lyon. Later they moved to 346 32nd Avenue. "We called it the rich section of town," he says.

As a youngster, Mathis haunted North Beach watering holes with Italian track-team buddies. "They were tiny, walk-in saloons, no bigger than most people's living rooms," he recalls. "But people are very festive in San Francisco. My buddies knew the owners of the nightclubs and I'd go with them to have a beer and sing a song. The owners would say, 'If you come back tomorrow, we'll give you five bucks to sing.' That's how I started. I was maybe sixteen."

—Michael Muzell, "Home of the Stars," *San Francisco Focus*

HAROLD GILLIAM

The Specter of Grand View Peak

Nature is full of surprises in San Francisco.

GRAND VIEW PEAK, WHICH HAS A RESIDENT GHOST, IS VIRTUALLY unknown except to people who live nearby, yet it is in some ways the most remarkable of all the hills of San Francisco.

It lies about a mile west of Twin Peaks and is the northernmost high point of the north–south ridge known as Sunset Heights or Golden Gate Heights. It commands a sweeping panorama including Montara Mountain down the peninsula, immense expanses of the ocean, the Farallones, Point Reyes, Tamalpais, the Golden Gate, and large parts of downtown San Francisco and the East Bay.

California poppy

Owing to its strategic location between the ocean and the bay, it is sometimes a meeting place of inland and marine weather conditions, and it is under these circumstances that I have occasionally seen the colossal spook. But more of that in a moment.

317

The hill itself is a rare phenomenon geologically. It is the highest point in the great sand drift that swept in from the ocean, blanketed the western portions of the city, and flowed through the passes to the bay over a period of several thousand years. This drift, unparalleled elsewhere in the United States, rose here some seven hundred feet above its origin at Ocean Beach and flowed around outcrops of Franciscan bedrock, the tops of which are still visible—dark red chert in opulently sculptured layers and volcanic greenstone that erupted millions of years ago when this region was the bottom of an ancient sea.

Botanically, too, this hill is extraordinary. It is the last sizable location where you can see native dune plants of the kind that once covered the land on which the city was built. In early spring there are fragrant beds of sweet alyssum and luminous stalks of Franciscan wallflower, a cream-colored blossom that grows only here and in southern Marin, across the Golden Gate. Later you can begin to see the bright gold of California poppies, followed in turn by blue lupine and then by the spectacular tree lupine with its immense stalks of yellow bloom. In early fall will come goldenrod, Indian paintbrush, and dozens of other varieties, spreading color down these slopes.

Wildlife driven from other areas by the advance of the subdivisions has found refuge here and on the slopes below. Often in the early morning you can see intricate tracings on the damp sand, indicating the presence of small animals. The mellifluous meadowlarks, almost unknown elsewhere in the city, can be heard here. There are quail, red-shafted flickers, woodpeckers, and white-crowned sparrows. Doves and a pair of red-tailed hawks roost in the eucalyptus and Monterey cypresses at the summit.

With the exception of some houses built in an old quarry on the south side of the hill, Grand View Peak has survived as a natural enclave in this densely populated urban area. Plans to build on the rest of the hill were frustrated in 1975 when, after a determined campaign by environmentalists, the city bought the remaining slopes. The hill is to be maintained as a nature preserve where visitors can see what the tip of this peninsula looked like in the days of the first settlers, observe the native plant and animal life and contemplate the creation of the peninsula with all of the elements in plain view—the ocean, the bay, the islands, the Golden Gate, and the central ridge of the city from Mount Davidson to the Presidio.

Or if the day is foggy and the visitors come at the right time, they might even catch a glimpse of the resident ghost.

I first saw it early one winter morning. The air was clear overhead and the sun was about to come up just south of Twin Peaks, but an impenetrable bank of tule fog was drifting from east to west through the valley occupied by Golden Gate Park. As I walked around the north end of the ridge I could see that the rest of the city, except for the highest hilltops, was wrapped in the fog, and the area where I was standing was clear only because it was in the lee of Twin Peaks and Mount Sutro.

I looked west and was surprised to see the shadow of the peak on which I was standing outlined clearly on the fog bank

Sometime around 1966, our Parkside neighborhood buzzed with the story: some kids up on Mount Davidson had been accosted by a naked purple man. We all went back, looking for this prodigy, but he was never seen again. Ten or fifteen years later, when I happened to tell the story of this erstwhile Sasquatch to my wife Christina, she burst out: "That was my grandfather!"

She had heard the story from the other side. He'd been out in nothing but his shorts and shoes picking blackberries. Hearing some kids coming, he'd smeared berries all over his face and chest and jumped out of the bushes with his knife between his teeth. A crusty old sort, Lloyd Berendsen delighted in practical jokes, and would have loved that he became, if only for a short while, an urban legend.

—Tim O'Reilly,
"All St. Cecilia's Children"

over the Sunset District. As I climbed to the summit, the scene began to change. The fog was not only flowing west, it was rising like a tide and soon began to wash against the lower slopes of the peak where I was standing. The air turned cold, and I realized I would soon be enveloped in the fog masses. Then, suddenly, as I was about to leave, I saw the ghost. It appeared to the northwest, a shadowy human form of incredible size. Its legs seemed more than a mile long. They stretched from the hilltop to the point on the fog bank a mile west where the shadow of the peak was projected. Above that point the giant form—trunk, head, and arms—seemed to extend out toward the ocean for a couple of more miles.

Startled, I jumped back. At the same instant the ghost jumped. Then, as I moved again, I grasped the truth: I was looking at my own shadow projected on the fog. I pulled off my sweater and waved it back and forth over my head. Incredulously I watched as the shadow seemed to sweep across the top of the fog in a vast arc over half the city, from the Sunset District, across Golden Gate Park and the outer Richmond District to the vicinity of the Cliff House. With a euphoric feeling of omnipotence I jumped and waved my arms, enjoying myself immensely for about five minutes. Then the rising fog bank enveloped the peak completely, and the stupendous show dissolved into the cold mists.

The experience stirred a vague memory, and when I got home I thumbed through the writings of John Muir until I found his description of a similar incident. In November of 1875, after a fresh snowfall, Muir made his first ascent of Half Dome. As he stood on the summit looking down on the valley nearly a mile below, a flock of small clouds gathered below him.

"Then the sun shone free," he wrote, "lighting the pearly gray surface of the cloudlike sea and making it glow. Gazing, admiring, I was startled to see for the first time the rare optical phenomenon of the 'Specter of the Brocken.' My shadow, clearly outlined, about half a mile long, lay upon this glorious white surface with startling effect. I walked back and forth, waved my arms and struck all sorts of attitudes, to see every slightest movement enormously exaggerated. Considering that I have looked down so many times from mountaintops on seas of all sorts of clouds, it seems strange that I should have seen the 'Brocken Specter' only this once."

Clearly it was the Specter of the Brocken I had seen on Grand View Peak. Turning to the encyclopedia, I learned that the Brocken is a peak in the Harz Mountains of northern Germany where this phenomenon was first observed. The peasants attributed the ghostly figures in the sky to supernatural causes, and it may be for this reason that the Brocken is a mountain of ancient legend.

It is the site of Walpurgis Night in German folklore, when the witches gleefully hold their saturnalian sabbath. The scene appears in Goethe's *Faust* and has raised the hackles of several generations of moviegoers in Disney's *Fantasia* to the diabolic music of Moussorgsky's *Night on Bald Mountain*.

If there are any witches on Grand View Peak, I have failed to see them, perhaps because I have never arrived at the right moment. But I have seen the Specter of the Brocken a few more times, in various forms, when weather conditions were precisely right. And I have learned that the giant ghost has occasionally been observed at other points in the Bay Area—from the summit of Mount Diablo and from the ridge east of Muir Woods, when a summer fog bank in the canyon below creates a similar screen at sunrise. At the latter location, the shadows were surrounded by rainbowlike haloes, known as Brocken bows.

The scientific explanation for the Specter of the Brocken, I find, is that the phenomenon is the result of what artists call a *trompe l'oeil*. It is an illusion caused by the eye's error in estimating the distance of the fog or cloud screen. But I find this explanation highly unsatisfactory. I

Not far to the south of Grand View Peak and Golden Gate Park is another wonderful sylvan retreat: Sigmund Stern Grove, made possible by Rosalie Meyer Stern, a descendant of Levi Strauss and his blue jeans fortune. Free first-class concerts are offered here every Sunday from June through August.

I spent countless happy hours in the Grove as a child, fishing on Pine Lake, building tree forts and exploring nastursia-scented trails. Yet for all its beauty, the Grove is a chasm, a wound in the flesh of the city. There is something mournful and dark about it, even on the sunniest days. Excepting the summer concert season, there are seldom many people here, so be watchful—the morally disordered make it less safe than it was in days gone by. Nonetheless, a walk in the Grove on a clear day will leave you with a sense of that unusual fusion of mankind and nature that is such an essential part of San Francisco.

—Sean O'Reilly,
"Lady of the Avenues"

prefer to believe that for a few unforgettable moments I was a giant three miles tall.

Harold Gilliam also contributed "The Lost Roman Baths of Adolph Sutro" in Part II. Both stories were excerpted from his book The San Francisco Experience: The Romantic Lore Behind the Fabulous Facade of the Bay Area.

★

Wild in the City, a map by Berkeley artist Nancy Morita, recreates the San Francisco known by the Miwoks and Ohlones, in the long centuries before even the Spanish arrived.

This was a peninsula laced with rivers, covered with shifting dunes, quilted with grasslands grazed by elk and deer. Ohlone children ran naked through the Mission, splashing in the small waterfall on what is now the corner of 18th and Valencia streets. Bald eagles cast their slow shadows over Potrero Hill, hunting dusky-footed woodrats hiding in groves of yellow monkey flower. The eastern shore of the peninsula was an amorphous network of marshes and lagoons: a vast sanctuary for migratory birds.

Wild in the City is actually a double map; for alongside her idyllic image, Morita has drawn its modern counterpart: San Francisco today. Here the salt water marshes have been filled, the sand dunes leveled and irrigated. El Polin Creek lies somewhere beneath the Exploratorium, its brackish estuary now a duck-filled lagoon. The rough northern and eastern shorelines of the peninsula have been spackled with landfill, and jigsawed into geometric piers. The skyscrapers of the Financial District stand on the site of Ohlone sweat lodges, and fishing streams have disappeared below a filigree of roads....

Our gaze jumps between the two maps, unsure which one to trust. For a moment we are seized by a terrible nostalgia—for something lost forever. But the feeling passes quickly. The real San Francisco, we realize at last, is the one on the left: that watercolor world of gooseberries and fur seals, kingfishers and ferns, herrings and mint. This is the City in its eternal form. That maze of boulevards, bridges, and sushi bars to the right is nothing more than a thumbnail sketch, useful for a mere decade or two.

We have settled ourselves on our cluttered new map, spread it like a picnic blanket over the rough textures of a once wild land. Someday, though, the wind will shift; the sky will threaten rain. The blanket that we rest on will be rolled up. The long grasses will unbend, streams will trickle in, and steam will pour from the sweat lodges again....

—Jeff Greenwald, "A Meditation on Maps"

* * *

Through the Golden Gate

Swimming the Gate is San Francisco's ultimate rite of passage.

TOWARDS THE END OF SUMMER I REALIZED THAT DARLENE HAD achieved a great deal. She had been afraid of the water since childhood and now was in her 50s. She had never really explained the source of her fear or how it had developed but she wanted to overcome it and learn to swim.

When I first started teaching Darlene to swim, she fought the water. Her petite body stiffened and her brown eyes filled with terror even when she just put her face in the water. But Darlene was determined. She said she had two grandsons who didn't know how to swim and she had a backyard pool. She didn't want anything to happen to them.

During the course of only one summer, Darlene mastered not only the mechanics of swimming, but also learned to breathe, relax, and balance herself and even how to play. During her last lesson, I told her I was very proud of her. And then, to reinforce this accomplishment, I told her about my friend Phillip.

Phillip had contacted me some time ago and asked if I would coach him to swim across the Golden Gate. He told me he had a lot of fear about swimming in the open water. That was normal. Swimming in open water could be dangerous. You had to contend with treacherous currents, frigid waters, and unforeseen obstacles. But Phillip told me he really wanted to; he simply had to swim across the Golden Gate. I knew the feeling. In our very first meeting, I saw that Phillip had the qualities he would need to complete the swim.

Phillip was in his early 30s and had that perfect ice cream cone-shaped swimmer's body, sun- and salt-bleached hair and intense blue eyes that implied intelligence. He was an international banker who was creative and could adapt to changing situations. Mostly he was driven.

Taking Phillip on as a student, though, was a tremendous responsibility. I was tentative about it. He had seriously injured his right shoulder in a workout while training too hard. He admitted that he had been stupid, overriding his body's warning signs. I knew that could be dangerous. One of my friends had almost died from overexposure to the cold when he ignored his body's warnings. But in long-distance swimming there is always that fine line between overdoing it and getting across, and overdoing it and dying.

My trepidation, however, was not only about Phillip, it was about me. I had swum across the Golden Gate at the end of a series of swims around the world, including the English Channel, Bering Strait, and Lake Baikal. I had chosen the swim because I wanted to immerse myself in the bay, to see San Francisco from a different perspective. I thought swimming across the Golden Gate would be a symbolic finish. I didn't expect that it would be very challenging. I was wrong. It was the first time I ever felt completely out of control during a swim. And I had been terrified.

Sailors had warned me. They told me that the Golden Gate Bridge is where the massive Pacific Ocean gushes at up to six knots, through a narrow one-mile opening between the Presidio Headlands. They told me that when the tide changes, the combined waters of the Petaluma, Napa, San Joaquin, and Sacramento Rivers, along with the Delta waters and Suisuin Bay flush back out at up to six knots under the Golden Gate Bridge. They warned me of strong tidal rips at either side of the bridge and they admitted that they had had hair-raising times escaping them.

They also told me that the middle of the bridge, where the water deepens, could be just as dangerous. Here they said, is where you could get run over by a ship.

I had heard stories like these before and while I respected these sailors, and the ocean, I knew I was a strong swimmer. The distance across the Golden Gate was only one mile. I didn't expect to have any problems.

> *Bay swimmers are a different breed of humans in that they are truly conscious and are connected with the elements. That may give greater authenticity to the rest of their lives—perhaps a greater daring, also.*
>
> —Klement Jesck, quoted by Peggy Knickerbocker in "Taking the Waters," *San Francisco Focus*

Just as the sun broke through a low-rolling fog bank, and rays of light lit Alcatraz, Angel Island, Tiburon, and the city of San Francisco as if they were on an enormous outdoor movie screen, I adjusted my swimsuit, cap, and goggles and left Presidio Shoal on the bay side of the bridge. Slowly, I immersed myself in the chilly 53-degree water and felt my toes going numb. I took three steps and the current seized me as if I were a mouse in a boa constrictor's coil.

In a split second, the coiling water dragged me toward the main support structure of the bridge. Here the cement piling was covered with skin-shredding barnacles and mussels. I struggled to pull myself away from the piling. I didn't want to get cut. I didn't want to get blood in the water. Blood could attract sharks.

The support crew on the escort boat was shouting to me to move away from the bridge. Now, the razor-sharp mussels were inches from my face and the water was propelling me toward them. I tried to move to one side to break free from the current but I scraped across the mussels. Pain shot through my arm. I pushed off, turned away from the piling, and with all my strength sprinted parallel to the shore. The coiling current held me in place. I pulled harder. My chest was forcing air in and out of my lungs and my heart was pounding. Slowly, I could feel my body tearing out of the rip current's deadly coil.

When I looked back, I was 100 meters from the bridge. This is a safe distance, I told myself and I turned and faced the opposite shore. Less than a minute later, a second rip caught me. This one was stronger than the first. And it was eerie. I could not hold onto the water. At one moment, I would be swimming through the water and the next moment, the water would drop out from under me. There was nothing to pull but air. Suddenly a surging wave would sweep over me, press me down and spin me around. Fighting for the surface, I'd gasp for air and try to find a horizon. It was like swimming through a washing machine on full cycle.

I was out of control. No matter how hard I swam, I couldn't break free. I was getting scared. I kept trying to move my arms faster, to find a way out, but I didn't have any power. Nothing was working. There was no escape. Then I did something that frightened me beyond words. I stopped fighting. And I just let go. I let the water carry me where it wanted. Then the current released me.

In letting go, I gained control. I swam back under the Golden Gate and gauged my progress by counting the support cables on the bridge. Before I knew it, I could see the Lime Point lighthouse towering above me. And I knew that any moment the rip current would snag me again. And so it did. But this time, I let the rip pull me sideways until I felt it weakening, then I began swimming until the next current pulled me to within a meter of the piling and released me. I sprinted toward shore and felt the warm soft sand beneath my feet, and the arms of friends around my shoulders.

My swim across the Golden Gate had only taken me 40 minutes but I had used every skill I knew and more to get across. And now Phillip was asking if I would take him across. He had much less experience than I had so I hesitated. But he said that swimming across the Golden Gate was his childhood dream. I didn't want to dissuade him but I wanted him to understand what he would have to do to prepare. He was willing to let me guide him through his training and I put him into every difficult situation I could find. Everything that would simulate what he would face when he attempted his crossing. He had to be in top shape physically and mentally. If he wasn't, this childhood dream would turn into a nightmare for both of us.

What Phillip didn't tell me until he had been training with me for three months was that he had grown up in Marin County with his parents and younger brother. His father had been an airline executive based in San Francisco. When Phillip was nine years old, the company moved back East and they insisted that his father and family join them.

"But," Phillip said, looking at me, then looking away and back into memory, "my father didn't want to give up the City. He was very depressed. One night he got drunk and he slipped and fell off a pier or he committed suicide in the bay. I'm not sure. They found his body near the Golden Gate."

He drew in a deep breath and looked at me imploringly. "I want to swim across the Golden Gate to get rid of my father's ghost."

I didn't say anything for a moment; in truth, I didn't know what to say, so I just nodded and encouraged him to keep talking while I decided how I could help him and if I felt strong enough to take this on. Phillip looked down and his voice became high and shaky as he said, "When I was a kid, every time I crossed the Golden Gate in a car my hands got all sweaty. I even got vertigo when I thought that this is where my father died."

Phillip told me that he would understand if I decided to walk away from coaching him. He hadn't exactly been up front with me. I told him that I was with him all the way, but inside I was thinking, I'm not a therapist, how am I going to deal with this?

> *It is a city poised at the end of the continent, civilization's last fling before the land plunges into the Pacific. Perhaps this is why visitors demand something memorable from San Francisco. People expect the city to resonate along a personal wavelength, speak to them, fulfill some ineffable desire at the center of the soul.*
>
> *There is a terrible beauty at the edge of America: the dream begins here, or ends. The Golden Gate Bridge, that arching portal to infinite horizons, is also a suicide gangplank for hundreds of ill-starred dreamers. Throughout American history, those who crossed the country in search of destiny ultimately found it here or turned back to the continent and their own past.*
>
> —Ray Riegert, *Hidden San Francisco and Northern California*

During the last week of his training, I suggested that he move to San Francisco to train on his own in the bay. It was a very tough week for him. The weather was terribly cold and rainy and the bay was a mess. Phillip told me he went to bed every night crying from exhaustion. Two days before his attempt, he decided to swim halfway across the Golden Gate. The current was so strong that it swept him past Ghirardelli Square and all the way to Pier 39.

When he called that night he was very discouraged, but I told him that he'd gotten a great coastal tour of the city. And now he had a sense of how strong the current could be. It made him realize that making the attempt at the right time was critical.

Even though I joked with him, I wondered what would happen if he failed in his attempt. Would his father's ghost haunt him the rest of his life?

Phillip said he had decided that the moment he stepped into the water, he had won. He didn't have to complete the swim to succeed. I hoped this was true.

The night before he swam, Phillip said he realized he had done everything he could to prepare for the crossing and then he prayed like he had never prayed before. He said, "God, whatever happens, happens. I'm in your hands." He let go, and in letting go he was ready.

On the morning of his attempt, the bay was completely calm— no wind, no waves, no fog. Warm light was radiating across the rust-colored bridge, around the entire bay, and upon Phillip's face. He looked so excited.

Cheers and applause from friends on the beach and on board the tug boat broke the morning stillness as Phillip charged into the water. He made a mistake. He was supposed to get in slowly. Cold water ripped his breath away and Phillip stopped short, gasping for air. He treaded water until his breathing evened out and then he began swimming.

I watched him closely from the tug. I wanted to see his face, but he was turning away from me when he breathed. I needed to see his face to see if he was all right. He didn't turn toward me. I wondered if something was wrong.

Unconsciously, I held my breath and waited. When he finally turned toward me, there was a blank expression on his face. He was somewhere deep inside himself. And now the current had pulled him to the Pacific side of the Golden Gate Bridge. We moved the boat near him and I stared at him, hoping he would see me and snap out of his trance. He needed to be aware of where he was. When he finally turned toward me, his eyes were completely vacant.

He turned his head back down into the dark blue water and conjured up his father's ghost. He spoke to him, saying, "Dad, you end here; I start here."

Then Phillip cut back under the bridge and breathed toward me. He blinked. Our eyes locked. The light was back on in his eyes. He was back again. Phillip smiled and laughed heartily. His father's ghost was gone.

An electric charge flowed from Phillip to me and back again. He shouted joyfully and relaxed. He lengthened his arm strokes and he moved into the flow, that perfect place in the universe when everything comes together effortlessly and you know you are in the right place at the right moment.

When I was recovering from a bypass in 1976, I got back in the water gradually—five strokes the first day, then eight. I've been counting ever since. The Golden Gate is 1,445 strokes. Alcatraz is 1,820, depending on the tide.

—J. B. Sullivan, quoted by Peggy Knickerbocker in "Taking the Waters," *San Francisco Focus*

Suddenly a current grabbed him and swung him around. But before I could give him any direction, he turned away from the current, paralleled the shore for 100 meters and returned to his course. He was doing everything right and he knew it. He was flying across the water. Strong, buoyant, fluid. He felt as if nothing could stop him now. He shouted happily to the crew and started playing around. Phillip was letting up. Much too soon, I thought.

At any moment, something could go wrong. If he fell off pace when the tide changed, it would blast him through the Golden Gate and cast him out to sea. And there was also the question of sharks. Phillip was terrified of them. Although no swimmers had been attacked in the area, there had been shark attacks in the region and when you were swimming in deep dark waters, sometimes you had to fight yourself not to think about them.

What Phillip hadn't told me was that he had two friends who were sharpshooters positioned on the bridge and on shore. Phillip instructed them to shoot if they saw a fin heading toward him. Had I known this, there was no way I would have accompanied him on the swim. There was too much of a chance that someone would hit him, the crew, or me.

And then it happened. When we were 300 meters from the finish. A gray form shot like a torpedo across our bow and under Phillip. In a split second Phillip moved from horizontal to vertical backpeddling with his arms. One of the sharpshooters had his sights trained on the water.

The form popped up right beside Phillip and squeaked.

"It's a dolphin, Phillip," I shouted.

Phillip looked down with utter disbelief and shouted without looking up, "Are you certain?" He was very upset and pulling himself rapidly toward the boat.

"Yes," I reassured him. I told him that the dolphin was a good omen. Mariners believed dolphins are escorts sent by the gods. The dolphin would keep the sharks away. Phillip was visibly rattled. Adrenaline was pumping through his body at full speed and he was breathing rapidly. But he managed to regain his concentration and he put his head down and began swimming. The dolphin stayed beside Phillip until he reached the shore.

When Phillip climbed out of the water onto Horseshoe Cove he was laughing and crying, feeling a million things at once, too emotional to speak.

We threw blankets over his shoulders and hugged him and laughed and cried with him. He had made it across the Golden Gate.

I told this whole story to Darlene as we stood in her backyard swimming pool. It was then that Darlene told me that there was another reason she had been afraid of the water. She said her mother had drowned herself in this pool.

Darlene said her mother's health had been deteriorating and she had been depressed by the physical decline. In the middle of the night, Darlene had heard the back screen door open but her dog didn't bark so she rolled over and went back to sleep. In the morning when Darlene woke up she sensed something was wrong. She went downstairs to check on her mother and found her floating in the shallow end of the pool. I took a breath and couldn't speak.

Darlene paused for a moment and let me absorb what she had told me. It must have taken monumental courage for her to learn to swim, I told her. Darlene smiled gently and said she was pleased with her progress and she was happy that I had taught her grandsons.

"They have become very strong swimmers," Darlene said proudly. "Maybe someday, like Phillip, they will swim across the Golden Gate."

At age fifteen, Lynne Cox shattered the men's and women's world records for swimming the English Channel. Years later, after a historic swim across the Bering Strait (chronicled in Travelers' Tales: A Woman's World*), Presidents Reagan and Gorbachev toasted her at the signing of the first INF Treaty. She recently completed a book,* Beyond Borders, *about her life in the water. She lives in Southern California.*

★

Long after the war, Zenji Orita, a retired submarine commander, posed a question to me when I was interviewing him in Tokyo. It was Christmas Eve 1941, he said, and he was executive officer of a submarine lying three miles off San Francisco. He looked at the Golden Gate Bridge through the periscope and gasped at the bright lights of all the traffic.

"What target do you think I would have chosen?" he asked. I replied that fuel tanks along the coast seemed most obvious.

"No, you are mistaken," he replied.

That night Commander Orita informed Tokyo that he was about to give the city and America a Christmas present—fifteen rounds of gunfire directed at the famous bridge.

Shocked, the Japanese navy general staff in Tokyo ordered him to abandon the plan. Didn't he know that Christmas was a great international Christian festival and that Japan had Christian allies in Germany, Italy, and elsewhere?

—Denis Warner, "A Curious War Beneath the Waves,"
International Herald Tribune

* * *

Seeing Stars

Don't you want somebody to love?

"CARE FOR ANOTHER?" QUERIES THE WAITER, HOMING IN ON MY nearly empty Campari glass.

"Not one of these," I answer darkly, "Just bring me some water. Maybe I'll order something else later."

I'm in San Francisco with a couple of early evening hours to kill, so I'm experimenting with a solo visit to Stars, Jeremiah Tower's casually swank restaurant near the Opera House. I fell in love with the jaunty glamour of the place the first time I saw it, and have always reserved visits to Stars for festive occasions. But on this more ordinary evening I'm nestled alone at a table near the baby grand, with a silvery view of high windows, splashy European prints, and the gigantic mirrored bar, attempting to linger over a drink.

I initially ordered Campari and soda, which I hate, because I thought I'd sip it slowly. But my plan has backfired: the glass was tiny, less than half the size I expected, and therefore the ratio of Campari to water was twice as strong. Intending to displace some of the nasty bittersweet stuff to make room for more soda, I'd downed it like medicine before I could spot my waiter's post-modern haircut, with the result that I'm feeling slightly tipsy without having had any fun yet. Hence my dilemma: what to order next that I can savor languorously and still be able to function in an hour or so, when I return to real life.

Musing about just what comprises real life permeates my thoughts tonight. For the past year, I've been re-inventing my livelihood, breaking away from a secure but soul-destroying desk job, and discovering a more serendipitous mode of breadwinning. Real life for me is beginning to take on considerably more color and texture, but is somewhat precarious financially, and has not yet assumed an enduring definition.

I have to confess to some apprehension about hanging out alone in a place like Stars, given the generally high tariff and chic atmosphere. Leaning back in my chair, I survey the room through the eyes of one of those tough-talking female private investigators in mystery novels, a persona I adopt when I anticipate feeling vulnerable. But so far the scene echoes my most vivid memory from past visits: I find myself disarmingly at ease amidst all this breezy *vie-en-rose* grandeur. In spite of my indecision over what to drink, I'm beginning to relax and have a very good time.

Tony cafes and bars have always held a special fascination for me. I'm mesmerized by the seductive array of tinted bottles, the glistening glassware, the bowls of cherries and olives and citrus twists. I want to smell and taste everything; brandies and armagnacs, cognacs and eaus de vie, to drink and toast and philosophize until dawn like the famously dissolute expatriate writers in the Parisian *boites* of the 1920s.

But I don't spend much time at this, for the following reason: in spite of my fondness for impersonating savvy, world-weary types, I'm really sort of a homebody, and I've never understood how a person can last in a cafe for more than, say, fifteen minutes. Drinking alcohol usually makes me sleepy, and drinking coffee makes me nervous; imbibing one to counteract the other generally starts me wondering frantically if my checking account's overdrawn, or whether I remembered to turn off the iron.

I survey the list of drinks printed in white boldface across the floor-to-ceiling mirror behind the bar. What, I wonder, is a Puntegroni? Or a Racquet Club Pink Gin? Mark's Silk Pyjamas? I decide on a globe of garnet Zinfandel, like the one floating by on a tray of highballs suddenly backlit against the cool grey window across the long room, which, as it fills, is beginning to take on an aura of surreal splendor, like some opulently decorated film set.

Quaffing water between sips of wine, I try to imagine how the designer knew these eclectic elements would work together: pale yellow walls with fluted white moldings under an awesomely high ceiling, big bright posters, lots of cognac-colored wood and wine-red leather. The chair I'm sitting in is a provincial jade and cream wicker; the forest green carpet is strewn with golden stars. A chorus line of copper pots swings pertly above the open kitchen, stained-glass baskets hover as chandeliers. Crouched like gargoyles on ledges high above the bar, huge, painted porcelain Chinese vases explode with tall sprays of flowers. This would be an exciting, if apocalyptic, place to be stranded during an earthquake, providing one could avoid the falling pottery.

Other tables are filling with a gorgeous assortment of sleekly coiffured, mostly black-and-white-clad humans. Who are these people, anyway? Wielding his cutlery European style over a plate of gravlax, the delicately natty old gent in the cream-colored three-piece suit really is wearing spats, and patent leather shoes. The sun-bleached hillbilly near the piano, tanned and rock-star beautiful, really is shirtless under his tattered denim overalls. The stylish silver-haired woman intently sipping soup and white wine at the oyster bar, the t-shirted and black-jeaned Generation X foursome discussing a business plan in French over tall amber beer glasses; do they come here often? What sort of wonderful lives do they lead?

Draining the last of my wine, I shift my gaze to the bartender, who looks like a Chinese movie star: shaved head, with a dark burr just on top, a slender bead-braided queue in the back, drop-dead cheekbones, red suspenders. Even the busboy folds napkins with panache. As the pianist slips into place, and begins a poignant cascade of Gershwin tunes, I suddenly understand the allure of this restaurant: it is a film set, and the staff and patrons are the cast; the decor and the lighting are designed to show us all to our best advantage. Here, we are all a little lovelier than life. We are the stars.

When I was a child, my mother sometimes let me stay up to watch old movies with her: films from the '30s, so removed from life as I knew it. Actresses and producers; playboys, and heiresses; smart private eyes and world-weary dames: I remember thinking those lacquered and marcelled figures, with their polished profiles, their dazzling eyelashes and painted lips and eyebrows, their swirling satin gowns and tailored tuxedos, were not people at all, but some exquisite species of moth or butterfly, tamed and taught to flutter about in the glass TV screen. My mother explained to me that times were very hard during the Depression, and that filmmakers thought they should provide some distraction from real life by depicting impossibly rich people engaged in extravagant, frivolous pastimes. Stars reminds me of those movies, come gloriously to life, in 1990s costumery, with 1990s issues lurking in the wings.

It is above that you
and I shall go;
Along the Milky Way you
and I shall go;
It is above that you and I shall go;
Along the Milky Way you
and I shall go;
It is above that you and I shall go;
Along the flower trail you
and I shall go;
Picking flowers on our way you
and I shall go.

—Wintu song, *The Way We Lived:*
California Indian Reminiscences,
Stories and Songs,
edited by Malcolm Margolin

All at once I remember an article I read in the newspaper, written by a real-life female private investigator, about the neighborhood march she led to commemorate the violent deaths of sixteen young people in her neighborhood. She wasn't cynical or hard-boiled. She was sad, but impassioned and eloquent. All in all, I guess I'd rather imagine myself to be like her than like some glamorous character in a movie or novel.

But what of my co-stars' lives? Does anyone here work with the homeless? Does anyone here have AIDS? When they've emptied their frosted glasses glowing with pale yellow liquid, will they leave this magical oasis and go back to hard jobs, to families, to aging parents or children with learning disabilities? Like all movie sets, the sense of unreality can be chilling; in one moment I see limpid faces touched with stardust, in the next I see actors, relentlessly creating a vibrant but ultimately brittle land of make-believe.

I struggle against and then surrender to feeling guilty for enjoying this so: life at its most intoxicating, at its most oblivious. The piano man segues into a weird, jazzy rendition of the Happy Birthday song; faces turn for a moment to search for the recipient, then resume their breathless conversations, like revelers at one of Gatsby's fabled parties.

I'm still fascinated. I could stay all night. I could sit closer to the piano and request my favorite old songs; I'd sing along after another glass of wine. But I have a city to explore, promises to keep, a life to build.

After paying my check and tipping the pianist, I step out of the hubbub onto the quiet, foggy sidewalk. Strolling along in the cool air, I find a dollar in my purse for a man waving an empty paper cup. I look away as he pockets my contribution so that his cup will still be empty for the next passerby, glancing around to make sure he's not about to be popped.

Wending my way towards Union Square, I review my audition as a cafe habitue. I think about the success of a fantasy world like Stars, and concoct a fantasy of my own: that all the local superstar chefs and talented decorators and celebrity architects and artists would work together to open a smashing restaurant, sort of a New Millenium Canteen, where all kinds of folks could work, some for a wage, some as volunteers, with the profits going to house and feed the homeless, or to AIDS research, or to drug education. Then maybe I could go there and play the part of a starstruck waiter, or help make the soup, or just sit at a table by the piano and enjoy a glass of wine, and leave feeling this stimulated, without also feeling so guilty about spending $15 on a couple of drinks, or about being happy drifting for a while in an unreal, enchanted idyll, where life is easy and elegant, where everyone is blessed and beautiful, and no one hurts, or dies too young or ever goes hungry.

Lois MacLean is a freelance writer specializing in food writing, book and restaurant reviews, and personal narratives. She is a regular contributor to the Pacific Sun, *and her work has also appeared in the* San Francisco Chronicle, Veggie Life *magazine, and the* Unofficial Guide to the Bay Area. *She lives in Mill Valley, California.*

*

What is a city anyway—this or any city, small or great? A city, Aristotle tells us, is a place where men and women come together to become more human. A city, Lewis Mumford points out, is both the substance and the symbol of mankind's communal self. We founded cities—Ur, Jerusalem, Athens, Chicago, San Francisco—so that we might fill out for each other what is lacking in each other's lives; as a matter of business and spirit, art and family. We came together in cities—in some dawn time—so that we might cooperate with each other in the work of living, in the joy of creativity, in the struggle for transcendence. No wonder, then, that the great religions of the world so frequently turn to the image of the heavenly city as the symbol par excellence of achieved human felicity.

The heavenly city, the ideal city beyond time, haunts our collective imagination. St. John the Divine saw it, for instance, as "pure gold, like unto clear glass." Our expectations, of course, are less exalted; and yet even the most realistic of us might hope for a renaissance of shared community, for a return to cooperative urbanism. Purely practical struggle, without vision and community, soon descends to fatiguing factionalism, argument and quarrel for their own autistic sake. The present sectionalism of San Francisco, its infinite multiplication of competing interest groups, is valuable as a first stage of consolidation. The next stage—that of cooperation and broad civic concern—is much more interesting and important.

—Kevin Starr, "A Symbol of Civility," *San Francisco*

LARRY HABEGGER

The Art of Lincoln Park

A weekend hacker finds his muse
on the bluffs above the Pacific.

HONNEUR ET PATRIE. HONOR AND COUNTRY. THE WORDS WERE drifting through my mind as I contemplated *The Sculptor and His Muse,* a brilliant and troubling bronze sculpture by Rodin. The poor sculptor (Rodin himself?) was being tormented, or loved, or consoled, it was hard to tell, by a petite and beautiful woman. She stood hard on his thigh, leaned with all her weight on him as he bent away in despair, or longing, or frustration, her flowing hair draping his head while he covered his mouth with one hand.

There were other, more famous, Rodins around me—*The Thinker* contemplated existence in the courtyard I'd just crossed; *The Three Shades* stood tall and powerful before me carrying the weight of this life on their shoulders—but I was transfixed by *The Sculptor.* It spoke to me of pain and agony, of joy and possibility, of the thrills and disappointments of a creative life, of life itself. It was the perfect metaphor for a round of golf.

I had come out to Lincoln Park Golf Course alone, as I often do, to learn that I wouldn't be able to get onto the course for a couple of hours. This wasn't bad news—just the opposite. I had many options: I could take a walk along the cliff-side trails of

340

Land's End, mess around in the ruins of Sutro Baths, stroll the expanse of Ocean Beach, or sip coffee and watch the waves crash in at Louis', the best breakfast joint in town. I went to the museum instead.

Honneur et Patrie. The words are carved in stone above the entrance to the California Palace of the Legion of Honor, a grand replica of the Palais de la Légion d'Honneur in Paris placed in the most striking museum setting in America. It sits high above the sea with views over the Pacific, the Golden Gate, the San Francisco city skyline, surrounded by the rolling green hills and towering cypresses of Lincoln Park Golf Course.

Lincoln Park is one of the country's most beautiful municipal golf courses. It is not beautifully manicured, not a difficult course to play although it has its hazards, but it has a rough and wild grandness that perfectly matches its setting. It has quirky holes that bend and twist, and views that shift from the sea to the skyline to the Golden Gate Bridge, always something dramatic through the trees.

I felt privileged to be inside the museum again. For three years, from 1992 to 1995, it was closed, undergoing seismic retrofitting and expansion. I would play golf, circling the fenced-off museum, and look longingly at the exquisite limestone structure that had become a construction site. Things changed from time to time: signs pointed golfers "this way" around the museum to the sixth tee; a month later the signs directed us the other way; the sixth fairway became an access road and the grass vanished under the weight of sand and heavy vehicles. I wondered if the museum would ever reopen, if the course would ever recover. But now the grass has returned, the fences are down, the museum is back.

Which led me to Rodin. I hadn't noticed *The Sculptor and His Muse* before, but now it supplanted his other works in my mind. I'd never thought of a golfer's muse, but seeing Rodin's work with fresh eyes I saw how the sculptor's relationship with his inspiration mirrored my experience with golf: there were flashes of brilliance, periods of effortless excellence, inevitably followed by a mysterious abandonment of skill. I've always viewed golf as symbolic of life, each round a short life of its own, beginning with promise, dependent on skill, full of hazards and ups and downs, building to success or colossal failure and subject to the whims of fate, luck, or divine intervention. The game could be completely humbling; the muse could torment and flee.

I wandered through several other galleries until it was time to play, and then got matched up with two recent Irish immigrants and a native San Franciscan. They were friendly, easy-going—a good sign, because when you play with strangers you never know what to expect. Over the years I've played with idealists, bigots, saints, and jerks. Often these people have added to the experience, sometimes they've detracted, but never have they ruined it. One of the game's great beauties is that it's both superficially social and deeply private. You can play with others but stay completely within yourself and never suffer an awkward moment, or you can have a party.

We got underway and I made sweet, solid contact, driving the ball straight down the fairway. Usually I take this as a bad omen, figuring I've just hit the best ball of the day and it'll be all downhill from here, but today my swing felt fluid and relaxed.

The Legion of Honor was the brainchild of Alma Spreckels, the descendent of a French general. On a visit to Paris in 1914 she discovered the sculptor Rodin and began collecting art work on a visionary scale. She persuaded her husband, the wealthy sugar baron Adolph Spreckels, to finance a museum based on a copy of the Palais de la Légion d'Honneur in Paris which she had seen at the 1915 International Exhibition. The Palace was opened on November 11, 1924, Armistice Day, and was dedicated to the many California servicemen who gave their lives in France during World War One.

—JO'R, LH, and SO'R

We strolled through the damp grass, hit our shots in turn, smelled the scent of turf and sea. The trees stood by like old friends, silent in the stillness.

After several holes I was still hitting the ball extremely well, better than I'd ever played. Then my mind filled with the face of a beautiful young woman with large eyes and a confident, serene smile. It was the face from the terra-cotta *Portrait Bust of a Young*

Woman by Jean-Jacques Caffieri that I had just seen in the museum's Robert Dollar Gallery. But it was also the face of a woman I knew, a friend who recently had died so young. The face looked at me with comfort and reassurance. It led me forward, looked down through the centuries, through the smell of grass and dew, seeming to say, "It's all right, we're all fine, you're fine."

I hit another perfect shot, not daring to wonder at the miracle of my play today. Maybe this was divine intervention at work.

We made our way up and over the hills, through the trees, along the green fairways beneath the museum that sits on the knoll like a shrine attainable only by circling long enough to prepare our hearts. I remembered images from other times I'd played here. A friend who insisted we start at the crack of dawn one autumn weekday staring into fog so dense we could see only a dozen yards ahead, but we teed off anyway and found our balls through some extrasensory perception; another foggy day on the tenth hole I looked up to see a horseman galloping along the crest of the hill, realizing after a second that it was the statue of Joan of Arc near the museum's entrance and the contour of the hill and the racing fog created the illusion of movement; another dreamy day looking for an errant shot in a grove of trees and discovering for the first time a stone monument that dated back to the time the park was a cemetery for Gold Rush pioneers.

On the third hole I had hit the ball over the cliff into the sea a dozen times (thirty fathoms, we always said), seen a friend hit a hole-in-one on number eight, stumbled upon a marble sculpture in the bushes on number ten. Today I swung easily, the ball flew straight, putts dropped strangely into the cup, and my mind kept flowing back to the museum, now to the haunting eyes of the girl sitting at the well in *The Broken Pitcher* by William Adolphe Bouguereau. She looked at me with a calm forlornness that was chilling. What was she feeling in that moment? That nothing mattered but it all mattered? That there was nothing to be done, so she rested there, staring at strangers without entreaty?

Much as she troubled me, I was more drawn to a painting next to it, *The Bath* by Jean-Léon Gérôme. An alabaster-white woman with black hair was being sponged by a brown woman in a brilliant headdress, cloth wrap, and silver bangles. The light in the room was soft, mystical, washing over the blue Middle Eastern tiles of the bath. The brown hand on the white back, the flow of black hair, the colors of the cloth were stark yet soft, intriguing. It was a simple act full of peace, in a Turkish bath, perhaps, or Moroccan, or Algerian. The tranquility of the light made me want to be there, lose myself there, feel the warm sponge on my own back.

My mind was drifting as we waited on the 14th tee for the group ahead to move on. I thought of the upcoming holes, how I'd played them in the past, how a record score was within reach if I kept shooting par. Thin fog had settled in the tops of the cypresses. The air was cool. Suddenly out of the trees a missile streaked into my vision and a sharp pain zapped in my hand. "Yow!" A ball ricocheted off my thumb and fell at the feet of my companions. I cursed and shook my hand and everybody wondered what was wrong with me.

"I just got hit by a ball," I growled, and slowly it dawned on them as they stared at the inanimate, white sphere lying there in the grass. Of course, this was one of the hazards of the game, but it rarely happened and usually there was some warning, shouts of "Fore!" A moment later the culprit came out of the trees, but what could I do? He couldn't have seen us, couldn't have known we were there. I cursed, he apologized, I shrugged, he shrugged, and we all carried on with our game.

One of the Irish guys hit his ball into the woods, and I was waiting for him to hit his second shot when the ball whacked against a tree and whizzed past me like a rocket, narrowly missing. "Good Lord! Again?" His friend laughed and said, "I'm not getting any closer to you!"

I laughed nervously, somewhat ill at ease. I'd never been hit by a ball before, and now almost twice in five minutes!

We made our way to the green and I was lining up my putt when another ball fell out of the heavens with a thud at my feet. My partners erupted in laughter but for me it was a sign. All I could think of was Rodin and his muse, the torment in the sculptor's face, the heavy weight of that sprightly being's caress.

After that I'm not sure what happened. I began hitting the ball everywhere but the direction I was aiming. On the 15th hole I went into the woods. On the 16th, I went across the road. On the 17th, a long par three that parallels the Pacific's entrance to the Golden Gate with the magnificent bridge in full view, one of the world's most picturesque golf holes, I hit three trees with one shot. Somehow I made it through the 18th, and my miracle of a round had become just another day on the golf course.

Well, not exactly. I'd almost been killed, I'd come to understand Rodin, and I'd seen the game just a little clearer. And perhaps I'd found my muse, for better or worse.

Larry Habegger is co-editor of the Travelers' Tales *series. He is also co-author of "World Travel Watch," a column that appears in newspapers throughout the United States.*

✳

El Camino Del Mar dead ends just north of the California Palace of the Legion of Honor near the Lincoln Park Golf Course. There is parking here and the head of a trail that skirts the rocky edge of Land's End and leads to Merrie Way, a parking lot near the Cliff House and the Sutro Bath ruins. This was once the roadbed of the Ferries and Cliff House Railway, a narrow-gauge steam railroad that ran out California Street and operated here from 1888 to 1906. This scenic trail offers splendid views of the Golden Gate and forests of twisted cypress trees. The wild, broken shore, the booming surf, and the sense of remoteness from the city make this one of the best nature walks in San Francisco. Stay on the trails for the cliffs here are unstable and dangerous.

—Randolph Delehanty, *San Francisco: The Ultimate Guide*

_{★ ★ ★}

Jammin' with Garcia

There was something about the man.

THE MISSION DISTRICT ON A FRIDAY EVENING HAS ALWAYS BEEN an exciting place. The lights of the beer signs blink and spin, shooting neon sparks out into the darkening sky. People have just gotten paid, and no matter how oppressing their lives might feel to them, in fact because of the oppression, they are now ready for fun, and fuck those bills, we'll worry about them tomorrow. The women dress and make-up for action, and the men have also done their homework. Radios snake Latin rhythms. Cars stop in mid-street, while friends and would-be lovers communicate with soul projection, gestures, and words. The psychic pace is hectic, and mostly joyful; there is little trouble this early in the evening. Trouble will come later, when too much alcohol will bring interior frustration to the surface.

The Mission still had lofts in the '60s. Sometimes huge lofts would be partitioned into rooms, and the rooms would be rented by artists. Sometimes they would be left undivided and used as rehearsal halls.

My brother Jerry and Grace and I were going to one of these large lofts now, to a party, we were told, a jam; non-band people would be asked to donate money to something, I think, the Mime Troupe.

We drove through crowds of locals who knew and cared nothing about the loft happenings. Our car stopped repeatedly in the traffic, which was always a sort of mini Mardi Gras. There was seldom only one loud radio playing, although this was mercifully before the boom box's stomach pounding bass. The sound world was a complex and changing mixture of music, car horns, shouts, talking, and laughter, with the obligatory police siren functioning as the lemon rind on the side of the cocktail.

I was excited, inhaling the vibe, along with the smoke from the joint Jerry had just handed me. People and music, dope and celebrity, life was happening. Our local status was such that we were welcomed and helped, given free drugs, invited in, you name it, wherever we went. I was completely unconscious of the way celebrity stroked my ego, and I took it as my birthright, but it, along with the mild paranoia that marijuana inclined me towards, was starting to make me uncomfortable with non-band people; I was starting to walk quickly through a hall or club, and seek, immediately, the musician's room. Even there, I was usually tense, because being there involved talking with musicians from other bands, and managers, photographers, all of the people in the, what was then, little business. Everyone was friendly, but I was tense.

"What's supposed to be happening tonight?" I asked Jerry, who was driving with his usual brake and gas, whiplash technique.

"Shit, I don't know," he said, "they just said come by, if we want, and jam. I don't think anything's really been planned."

"Fuck that," said Grace.

"You could just sing the blues, or something," I said.

"I don't know how to sing the blues," she said.

"What about that Dylan song we've been working on, 'Outlaw Blues?'" I asked.

Grace turned and looked at me with a frowning mouth and big eyes. Her hostility seemed directed as much at herself as at me.

"Shit man," she said, "I don't want to sing with those other guys. I don't know what the fuck they're going to do next, or even when they're going to change chords."

"Just see how it goes," said Jerry, "maybe you'll feel like it at the time."

As we approached the address, we saw the crowd. There were about fifty people talking on the street, and another fifty or so around the doorway making a serious effort to get inside. There were no parking spaces anywhere near, so we continued on in the direction of Potrero Hill for about three blocks, and finally parked the car across the driveway of a cement company that was closed for the night.

Walking back in cold night air that was thick with the smell of roasting coffee from the nearby M.J.B. plant, I shoved my left hand deep in my jeans' pocket, balled my fist, and hunched my shoulders; my right arm I held tight to my side, as I clutched the handle of my guitar case in cold fingers. Some geese flew across the face of the moon, heading south. I kicked at pieces of gravel left by the cement trucks. We walked quickly, Grace drinking her champagne from a small bottle "hidden" in a brown paper bag.

"I wish I'd brought my kick pedal," said Jerry, "I don't mind playing someone else's drums, but I hate like shit to play a different pedal. It's real hard to get a groove going when the throw's all different.

Some of these maverick bohemians lived in a big rooming house at 1090 Page Street, in the Haight-Ashbury. In the spring of 1965, a long-haired Texan named Chet Helms started holding dance parties in the basement there; for 50 cents you could dance to a band that later became Big Brother and the Holding Company. Down in Palo Alto, Ken Kesey and his Merry Pranksters went public with their "acid tests," free-form parties at which the Kool-Aid was spiked with LSD and the house band was the Grateful Dead.

Out of this came the San Francisco Sound, an elusive blend of electric folk, blues, jazz, country, and rock & roll. During the next two years, hundreds of bands formed in the Bay Area. Some of the best were the Charlatans, the Quicksilver Messenger Service, the Jefferson Airplane, the Grateful Dead, the Steve Miller Blues Band, Country Joe and the Fish, Big Brother and the Holding Company, Santana, Creedence Clearwater Revival, and Moby Grape.

—Michael Goldberg, "San Francisco Sound," *Rolling Stone*

"Fuck it," I said, "fuck 'em if they can't take a joke."

As we approached the building, people recognized us, and said hi, and things like that. A young man with jet black hair and blazing blue eyes said, "Take me in with you," to which Grace smiled and laughed in a friendly way. We excused ourselves as we wormed through the crowd on the stairs, and at the top, we were virtually grabbed by the door guard, and pulled inside. The large, hall-sized room was totally packed, standing room only, and in such a tightly packed room, no one would have dared to sit down, even around the edges.

Again, we wormed our way through the crowd towards the three- or four-foot-high stage at the southwest corner of the room. Music filled the air, and I could see Jerry Garcia, and hear his bright, folky, funky, guitar melodies. I felt a little nervous, but intensely happy.

The stage had a back portion to it, behind the amplifiers, though it wasn't an actual separated backstage area; there was no curtain. Someone, I think it was either Danny Rifkin or Rock Scully, was functioning as stage manager in the loose way that the situation called for, just talking to the musicians who might want to jam, and setting it up. My brother and I said, sure we'd love to play, but Grace stuck to her reticence; though improvisation is one of her strongest gifts, she seems to prefer to employ it in the context of known musicians playing known songs. The stage manager said, "Jerry (Garcia) is really hot tonight. He wants to just play and play. Why don't you join him and see what you all can get going?" Bill Kreutzmann was playing drums, and I think Peter Albin was playing bass. Many people cheered when I walked out next to where Jerry Garcia was standing, further inflating my already swollen ego. This scene was just too cool, and I knew it. My brother Jerry joined Bill on a second set of drums, and we all started to jam the blues, almost the only music we could launch into with no more discussion than, "It's in 'A.'" Most of the time, for the next 45 minutes or so, Garcia and I took turns playing solos for a few choruses each, just passing it back and forth like a joint. When he played lead, I put my head down and towards the left, almost like a violinist, and dug into the rhythm. I have always loved playing rhythm guitar, so it was a great pleasure to back him up in that way. Harmonically, I played simple chords, but tried to make powerful and unusual rhythm statements. When I played lead, he smiled and smiled his beautiful smile, even laughing occasionally when I played some particularly dissonant phrase; one of my main goals in music was to break it open and play something really weird that had never been played before, and I was willing to jump off the cliff in order to, hopefully, fly. I was a great admirer of Ornette Coleman, and I wanted my melodies to be quirky like his, but with my own stamp. Few of my attempts to get "outside" made it to disk, but the solo on the Great Society version of "White Rabbit" (Columbia Records) contains examples of this.

Garcia and I played more to each other than to the crowd, communicating with our guitars at least as directly as people ever do with words, and folks loved it; everyone can tell when something real is happening, and though our playing contained elements of showboating, all was done with humor and love. My brother and Bill similarly "talked" to each other and to us, and I could see joy on both their

$ome of the biggest names in music come to Marin to make records. Why? It's not because the county is a music industry center such as New York or Los Angeles, although Marin has some world-class recording facilities and more than its share of rock stars in residence.

It may sound mystical and even a bit silly, but the people in the business say that there's something magical about Marin that comes through in the music that's made here.

"I've been in every recording studio from Europe and Canada to Latin America and I've never found a more beautiful, peaceful place to work than Marin County," says Grammy-winning record producer Walter Afanasieff of San Rafael, who's recorded hit songs in Marin by Michael Bolton, Mariah Carey, Celine Dion, and Peabo Bryson.

"When I offer to go places to work with people, they often say, 'No, no, no, we'll come up there,'" he says. "There's an aesthetic in Marin that brings an artistic spirit out of people."

—Paul Liberatore, "Stars Make Hits in Local Studios," *Marin Independent Journal*

faces. The bass thundered with more bottom than you usually hear nowadays, and the whole thing just seemed to work. When music is really happening, it creates a new world, or even a new universe. Time, in the normal sense, seems to disappear, and the "now" opens up and becomes all pervasive. Notes, riffs, chords, and rhythms become elements that make up the world, and there is acceptance, and even bliss, associated with their position; when I look at a beach, I never say, "This is great, but that piece of driftwood should be a little to the left." Another thing that happens, from the musician's perspective, is that the music seems to play itself. I have marvelled at what I was playing right as I played it, and have even been so detached from it, that I was able to carry on a conversation with someone and simultaneously play far better than I normally do. This was one of those nights: no effort, only ease and a whole range of emotions coming through the music.

Gradually, each of our solos became shorter as we threw phrases back and forth to each other. The mood was building, the intensity increasing. I would "ask" a musical "question," and he would "answer" it. Occasional bits of one-upmanship were not vicious; neither of us tried for a knockout blow, nor even to inflict damage. There was magic in the room that night, and though I have played in many jam sessions through the years, that is the one I remember with the most love, the most respect. When it built to its huge crescendo, and then was over, I felt like a different person than when I started; inner, soul values became more important, and outer, nervous matters, less. I was left with a conviction that Jerry Garcia is a man of great spirit.

Garcia…

His hair was fuzzy and his crooked smile curved up higher on one side. His eyes had sparkles that drugs couldn't extinguish. His commitment to the guitar was big, maybe not total like Jimi's, but big. Of course, I had never heard of Jimi [Hendrix] then. Parapsychotics grew out of his ears, and glands hung hugely down, dripping excesses. His voice was soft, and croaked somewhat, perfectly matching the ironic content it purveyed. His sideburns threatened his large nose. The rabbit seemed ever willing to pop up out of his stovepipe hat, and a little thing like changing one's seat on the train mustn't be allowed to throw one, but somehow it always does, but not him. The barometer was dropping into the sound arena out of the visible light spectrum. How to know what effect not taking drugs would have had on any of us? I hate to blanket a generation, but I can't recall anyone deciding not to take drugs. I remember people refusing specific drugs on specific occasions, most often unknown drugs like, "Here, take this orange and blue one." "What is it?" "Fuck, I don't know." Sometimes, "Okay," sometimes, "Naaah," but everyone I knew took drugs. Frank Zappa wasn't here (it can't happen here). This was our Vietnam, the Battle of the Brain Cells, and drugs were the weapons, the transport ships, the airplanes, and people were the weapons, too. We scraped each other with our knives flat, removing flesh in flakes and chunks, not killing, but only partially dismembering. "Do I contradict myself? Very well, then, I contradict myself." Peace and love.

Some say move on, and we do, what choice have we, but it moves on with us, living still, as history does in Faulkner's south, and maybe everywhere else. The bravery that is required of one, dumped onto this backwater planet with no guarantees, and amidst so much pain! Easier to shut it out, as in Star Trek with the billions of souls marching by, outside of Captain Kirk's luxury window.

Darby Slick was a member of the pioneering San Francisco rock and roll band the Great Society, in which he played lead guitar with Grace Slick on vocals. He later wrote the song "Somebody to Love" which Grace sang with the Jefferson Airplane. He is currently a member of SandOland, a four-piece musical group and has been acclaimed as producing "the newest and most expressive slide sounds of the '90s" using a Slick guitar (designed by Jor Slick), a unique fretless guitar. He is the author of Don't You Want Somebody to Love: Reflections on the San Francisco Sound *from which this piece was excerpted.*

✳

Garcia spoke often of the burden of responsibility the Dead bore for the more wayward members of the flock, and there was at least one lost soul wandering the Haight this weekend who would have clean broken his heart. Empty-eyed, trembling, and nearly naked except for the sleeping bag wrapped around him, the poor guy walked from parking meter to parking meter, confiding to each in a woeful mumble, "Jerry is dead, and I'm all alone."

This was clearly not what the long, strange trip was meant to be about, but then again, who ever said rock 'n' roll was pretty?

The cops, to their credit, did their best to show restraint. One very cool, lighthearted young officer said the gatherings had been generally well behaved, mostly nice folks—not surprising, since the crowds at Dead shows have long been considered the most benign in the business. Generally the bluecoats were only citing for open containers, he said, adding that he had given Just Mark four chances before finally tagging him. Just Mark just shrugged and winked.

Then came a truly Garcian moment. Another graybeard street rabble-rouser began creating a disturbance near the shrine, violently throwing a full plastic bag at the feet of the cop. The guy angrily turned on his heels and began striding away as the cop drew his stick and followed.

"Is there a problem, sir?" the cop asked mildly.

The guy swung around.

"Yeah, there's a problem," he spit savagely. "You're a cop. Can't you show some respect?"

"Why are you doing this?" the cop asked.

"Because I'm a cop, too," the guy screamed, lunging at the shrine to rip off a cloth Grateful Dead emblem. "This is my badge, see?"

"Yeah, I see," said the cop. "Why are you treating me like this? I'm trying to treat you with respect."

"Oh, hell, I'm sorry," said the guy, totally melting, as he rushed over to give the cop a hug. "Jesus, these are hard times, you know?"

"I know," said the cop, patting his back.

—Burr Snider, "Bringing It All Back Home
for Jerry," *San Francisco Examiner*

JUDITH LYNCH

✳ ✳ ✳

Old Growth Houses

The redwood forests live on in San Francisco's unique architectural heritage.

THE DETAILS ATTRACTED ME FIRST, ALL THOSE DOTTY DAFFY
delightful delicious details. I was bewildered by their irresistible
allure. Who designed that plaster face pouting over the portico?
Who concocted that iron handrail disguised as a slack-jawed
dragon, its fangs lovingly whitewashed? Why were these old houses
studded with so much decoration?

Robert Frost said "poetry, like love, should begin
in delight and end in wisdom." My love of San
Francisco's Victorians began in curiosity—who
designed these houses and how and why?—
and ended in a lifelong obsession. I stalked,
counted, and categorized them, then re-
searched their origins. I became a finial
fanatic, taking thousands of slides,
learning more than was sane, and dis-
carding two husbands along the way.

It started in 1973, when I was a city
planner helping a neighborhood coalition develop affordable housing in the
Mission District. While waiting in the

1890s tower house

354

branch library for a perpetually late local leader, I thumbed through a brand new book about historic buildings in the city, *Here Today*. Quickly I turned to the section on the Mission, where the text provided slim pickings indeed. However, the appendix was a neighborhood organizer's dream: more than 230 of the listings in the book were within our planning boundaries. Coalition members invited the owners and tenants of these special buildings to a meeting that later spawned the Victorian Alliance, now a thriving city-wide group.

Along the way, I struggled to satisfy my cravings for insight about these ebullient structures. I learned, for example, that while all the houses were named after Queen Victoria, who ruled the British Empire from 1837 to 1901, the buildings in San Francisco bore little resemblance to their English contemporaries. Also, little was known about the kind and number remaining in the city or about who had designed and built them. A grant from the National Endowment for the Arts enabled me to answer these questions by counting the Victorians and burrowing through obscure and dusty archives on the track of the trade publications that inspired 19th century architects and home builders.

The inventory of San Francisco's Victorian structures was literally a nightmare. Three drivers spelled each other while I hung out the right side of the car with a clipboard, trawling for Victorians

and noting the address, condition, and other significant hallmarks for each one. I used to wake up during the night clammy with sweat: what if I missed one? The results of that ten-month project: San Francisco had an enormous legacy of 19th-century buildings. More than 13,400 survived, half of which were the victims of misguided improvements— attempts by owners to make old houses "modren" or cheaper to maintain. Thousands of homes were shorn of decoratives and smothered with stucco or

1870s bay-windowed house

slathered with textured spray paint. Only the bones of their bays or
false fronts are left as clues to their age, grim reminders of the
decades after the 1906 quake when fancywork fell from favor.

Tallying the survey results clarified doubts about our Victorian
housing stock; however, the mysteries of their origins had yet to be
pieced together. Gleaning information from old builders magazines
meant treks to libraries from Sacramento to Washington D.C., but
what a find when they were finally assembled! Analyzing twenty
years of these publications solved many mysteries about architectural trends; even better, their detailed monthly building activity
columns listed the architects, builders, owners, locations, prices, and
specifications of thousands of hitherto anonymous structures.

Sleuthing for Victorians in San Francisco is as addictive as birding, but you don't need binoculars, and the houses tend to stay put.
Note a few style cues and memorize the markings of a couple of
the most prolific builders. Learn to see and soon you will seek out
and love these giddy whimsical remains from a time when embell-
ishment was cause for celebration, not for embarrassment.

You can discover more than 3100 examples from the 1870s,
when builders began to mass produce housing in San Francisco.
More than 100 real estate development companies set the stage by
buying large tracts of land from the cash-strapped fledgling city
government. They subdivided the blocks into long narrow lots, in-
advertently influencing Victorian house design in San Francisco.

Those skinny lots became the sites for
tall narrow buildings, delirious with
detail fore and plain with clapboard
aft, also known as "Queen Anne
front, Mary Ann behind."

Woodworkers used simple hand-
or horse-powered machinery to turn
cheap and plentiful redwood into
replicas of classical details. To make the
cramped narrow buildings more impressive, iron cresting crowned their

1870s flat-fronted house

false fronts. The Real Estate Associates were major builders during that decade; their offerings can be found at 120-126 Guerrero Street near 14th Street and around the corner at 226-36 Clinton Park. The homes in this stately group sold originally for $800 to $2600.

Two major forces shaped construction in San Francisco during the 1880s, the city's steep terrain and the development of automated milling machinery. Earlier builders located their houses in the flats, serviced by horse drawn street car lines. Then Andrew Hallidie's cable cars tamed the hills. On their tracks went especially designed cars that transported construction crews and building materials up to the very tops of San Francisco's heretofore unbuildable peaks.

Automated woodworking machinery was introduced to Americans at the 1876 Centennial Exposition in Philadelphia. These power-driven machines spurred the establishment of more than 1900 millworks across the country. Their trade catalogues offered inexpensive standardized embellishments never before used as home decoration. No more did millwrights make careful replicas of ancient details; rather the decorative potential of redwood was released in a riot of the "stuff" so characteristic of our Victorians.

The Victorian era has been described as buoyantly optimistic, and to me the abundantly embellished homes of the 1880s best express this hopeful time. More than 3600 are left, happy examples of how our hundreds of architects, contractors and builders chose from a bewitching and bewildering assortment of faces, sunbursts, swags, cartouches, strips, flowers, waffles, holes...usually lumped under the casual category of "decoratives." You can find an intact cluster in the 1800 block of Laguna between Pine and Bush Streets. These 1889 houses, which showcase the talents of builder William Hinkle, sold originally for about $3500 each.

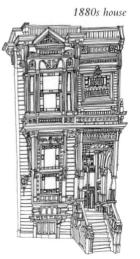

1880s house

The empress of Victorians, the towered redwood castle, is also the rarest; only some 370 remain. The simpler version without the tower abounds; more than 5500 still march up and down the hills, where the relentless zigzag rhythm of their gabled roofs makes them easy to recognize. For a grandstand of 1890s Victorians, visit the cluster built by contractors Cranston and Keenan in the 700 block of Broderick between McAllister and Fulton Streets.

Nothing makes birding more satisfying than identifying a species, and searching for Victorians is no different. Memorize the markings of the homes of Fernando Nelson, one of our most prolific builders, and you will add immensely to your pleasure as you patrol the city.

Nelson's donuts and drips

Nelson is my favorite builder. I spent many delightful hours as his son George recalled the vivid details of life with his father. He also supplied receipt books, house specifications and other family ephemera that reveal much about the work of the turn-of-the-century San Francisco home builder. According to George, Nelson would stroll around well-to-do neighborhoods, gleaning from architect-designed houses ideas to adorn his inexpensive cottages. He scrawled his designs on the back of an envelope, had them milled by the barrelful at Townley Brothers, then hauled out to the jobsite and nailed onto the fronts of his houses.

If you commit Nelson's signature details to memory, you can point out his legacy from Bernal Heights to the Inner Richmond. Two of his favorites were named donuts and drips. Because the frugal Nelson used these details until they were gone, stylish or not, you will find them on his homes dating from the 1870s to the 1910s.

I don't sanction graffiti, but "OPEN YOUR EYES" sprayed on a Haight-Ashbury home made me scramble for my camera. This succinct compelling message expressed what I have spent decades trying to say. Train your eyes to look, and your delight will follow. You too will become one of the loving caretakers of the precious legacy of 19th century San Francisco, our Victorian buildings.

By the way, another bit of Victorian history is out there waiting the patient stalker. These sidewalk calling cards have a less elegant name: sewer vents. Look for these 8-inch square plates near the curb, where they were installed to vent miasmic sewer gas, thought in those days to cause numerous diseases. Whoever claimed the sidewalk first got to install the vent, whether the builder, the plumber, the stove supplier, the furnace installer, or the concrete contractor. Each vent has a round slotted center insert, flanged like the lid of a teapot. Around the edge is the name and address of the

1890s row house

business and sometimes a bit of advertisement. More than 800 have been documented so far, but one of the tastiest has eluded my camera for years. Somewhere in the Mission District it reads "Oil Heat Cooks Good!" If you find it, let me know.

Judith Lynch collaborated on the books A Gift to the Street, Victoria's Legacy, *and* American Victoriana. *She has produced programs about San Francisco history and architecture for public radio and for local cable channels. She founded City Guides, the volunteers who have offered free walking tours of San Francisco since 1978. She is currently teaching first grade at an Alameda public school that is surrounded by Victorian houses.*

San Francisco artist Wendy Wheeler drew the illustrations in this story for the 1978 book Victoria's Legacy.

✳

This is their temple, vaulted high,
And here we pause with reverent eye,
With silent tongue and awe-struck soul;
For here we sense life's proper goal;

To be like these, straight, true and fine,
To make our world, like theirs, a shrine;
Sink down, O traveller, on your knees,
God stands before you in these trees.

—Joseph B. Strauss, Chief Engineer of the Golden Gate Bridge

JIM PAUL

Tennessee Valley Dream

The gods have many representatives
by the Golden Gate, and their language is enigma.

BELIEVING THAT I WAS NOT IN LOVE, THAT I DID NOT WANT TO BE
in love, that I had gotten beyond being in love, I'd begun to believe
I was dying. I had symptoms to prove it, which I compiled as
spring went to cold summer that year. I listed them on a piece of
paper that I kept with me so that each recurrence might—as with
the tolling of a bell—confirm my diagnosis: night sweats, extreme
nervousness, hot and cold flashes, inability to eat, obsessive
thoughts, lassitude, a ringing in my ears, bouts of fear. And whatever it was, it would be fatal.

One day, struggling against it, I decided that a jog in the country would be good for me. I drove up into the Marin Headlands,
into Tennessee Valley. From the parking lot I jogged down the trail
that descends into this deep valley with the sea at its mouth, then
decided to climb one of the steep side trails, heading north up the
ridge. I'd run over toward Green Gulch, I thought, toward the Zen
Center. Just the thought of it was enough to calm me a little. That
afternoon the fog was starting to come in off the ocean, a towering summer fog into which I climbed as I ascended the ridge. Soon
I was in the thick of the clouds that the northwest wind whipped

360

inland—clouds that tumbled across the brush, opening intermittently to show the sky overhead.

It had been warm and sunny when I'd gotten out of the car, and I'd begun running without a shirt. Now, climbing the hill and soaked with sweat, I felt naked, cold, slick, and suddenly full of dread, as if fate were pulling me up this hill to witness something. The fog grew denser as I reached the crest. Then overhead I heard a hoarse cry, like a bark of laughter, and saw a flash of a raven, its black wings outstretched, hovering against the strong wind above the ridge, for an instant distinct and vivid, black as a cutout against the sky, then gone. A Japanese demon. Freezing and wet, I followed the red road as it faded and intensified, feeling the ache in my legs and the dreamy sense of reiteration, of running and running and going nowhere.

I heard the caw again, and again there he was, still for an instant and then lost in the fog. I stepped up the pace. The road turned and started downhill. Suddenly the fog opened and before me was the Abbot's House, a low deserted hut, dark wood and glass, perched on the brow of the ridge with the fog breaking around it. The farmer Wheelwright had built it to give his dying wife a view of the ocean. I came to the gate, barbed wire with tufts of cow hairs on the barbs. It was locked, the house beyond it silent, empty. Shivering, I turned back and ran down the hill to my car, which was by this time completely obscured by fog. Everything, every bit of the hour had seemed personal and symbolic, fateful and mortal. By then I had stopped finding poems. They were finding me.

Jim Paul is a San Francisco poet and author, whose books include Catapult: Harry and I Build a Siege Weapon, Medieval in L.A.: A Weekend on the Edge of the West, *and* What's Called Love: A Real Romance, *from which this piece was excerpted.*

★

I do not think I am qualified to discuss Chinese philosophies, yet I somehow feel that all the three great Chinese philosophies are adhered to in the city of San Francisco, though it would be difficult to say exactly how and where. "Do nothing and all things are done;" that is the keynote of Lao

Tzu's teaching. Therefore, "no teaching but teaching is everywhere," might be an extension, I suppose. At any rate, I feel that something had taught me something in San Francisco each time I returned.

—Chiang Yee, *The Silent Traveller in San Francisco*

DARLA HILLARD

Return to Devil's Gulch

Not too long ago Marin was wild and remote. It still is, if you look for it.

FORGET-ME-NOTS CARPETED THE BANKS OF PAPERMILL CREEK with blue blossoms that March weekend my Aunt Ginny and I spent at Marin County's Samuel P. Taylor State Park. A quarter century divides Ginny and me, but at 71 she looked less like my father's sister and more like my own, in her straight-leg Levis with her close-cropped white hair hidden under a khaki crush hat. Still, the flowers couldn't have been more appropriate. Ginny was determined to find whatever might be left of a secret cabin that my uncle Van and his friends had built in Devil's Gulch, before the park, when a banker's widow held the foreclosed deed to the land.

"I hope I can remember where it was," Ginny had said over the phone. "The shack, as they called it, was barely standing when Van and I last visited the park in the sixties. I don't suppose it would have survived this long."

I thought it both amazing and wonderful that Van and his friends had gotten away with having such a hideaway in the first place, trespassers as they were, and considering how impossible such a thing would be today.

There was no Golden Gate Bridge back then, and only a few people with the foresight to realize the impact that its 1937 opening would have on the bucolic county of Marin. My uncle was one of the innocents. Nearly every weekend he and his beloved Airedale, Pat, would catch the ferry from their home in San Francisco to Sausalito. Dogs might actually have been allowed on the ferry, but they definitely were not allowed on either the electric connector train or on the North Pacific Coast narrow gauge which ran from San Rafael to Tomales Bay. Once smuggled aboard, Pat would lie quietly hiding under the seat until they reached Lagunitas—the countryside, as near to wilderness as anywhere, and heaven for dog and man.

Clyde Polk and Emmet "Shorty" Atkins were two of Van's partners in crime. Clyde lived in Forest Knolls and Shorty in Lagunitas, but the friendship revolved entirely around the shack. No one remembers how they met, or how Clyde and Shorty made a living. Van had never even visited their homes. Van's sister, Virginia, was sixteen when she first visited the shack. She remembers blue-eyed Clyde as a brawny six-footer, and handsome. And though Shorty stood less than five feet tall, he provided big entertainment value. Like the time he fell off his horse. Asked if he was hurt he responded, "Only my dignity—I swallowed my tobacco."

They built the shack out of materials scrounged, scavenged, and packed in by the sweat of their backs. From Virginia: "It was a long hike from the gate at the highway, but the boys were young and strong and they carried all the supplies up the hill as if it were a breeze. They harnessed the little waterfall and generated enough electric power for one light bulb to burn a couple of hours. Believe me, it was a big deal! Sometimes in the early mornings, we would hike up the slopes of Mount Barnabe and gather mushrooms and feast on them that evening. None of us died, so I guess they were o.k." Hot water ran through a system of coiled pipes heated by the fire. They swam and fished for steelhead in Papermill Creek. And—back before *endangered species* became household words—they poached game.

Pat served as messenger. With a note folded into his collar, grinning, panting, and beside himself with happiness, he raced over the ridge, knowing the exact spot below Stairstep Falls where other young men kept a similar cabin. It, however, was in ruins by 1949, the first year Van had shown Ginny the shack.

Dogs, horses, and camping were three vital ingredients in Ginny and Van's forty-one-year marriage. When they gave up horse-pack trips in the Sierra for gentler summer wanderings, Ginny, thirteen years the younger, drove the truck and trailer. They had a circuit from Mount Lassen to Arizona and annual dates with friends at every campground. Finally, Van grew too frail to travel even beyond his bed. Ginny was his nurse, as she had been in the Navy and for two decades at Kaiser. Over two homebound years she tended him, fended off the hospital heroics and machines, and gave him his final wish, at eighty-four, to die at home.

Now, a year later, I was glad that Ginny was free to roam again; even alone, it seemed the surest way to live with grief. That I was to be part of the current adventure was like a bridge to my past, and a chance to rediscover my favorite aunt. The summer I was twelve, she had plucked me out of preteen despondency with a magical pack trip into the mountains. If it had been a short-lived remedy for hormone overload, it was a potent cure for unrequited horse-love, and Van had been the quintessential Marlboro man.

The most exciting memory I have of my long life in San Francisco through all these many changes was the day that the Golden Gate Bridge opened! Actually the celebration started the night before on Chestnut and Polk Streets. There was a lion's cage on the street and the merchants put you in it if you were caught without a beer in your hand. I went with a couple of friends and, with an incentive like that, it wasn't long before we were roaring drunk.

So—I remember a terrible hangover as the beginning of that famous day. Despite this problem I got to the Bridge at about 9 a.m. It was a beautiful and sunny day. You were supposed to dress in frontier style so I had a beard, jacket, and cowboy hat.

When we got to the other side, some people went to Sausalito and took the ferry back. I just rested awhile because I wanted to walk back, too. About halfway back my hangover caught up with me and I threw up—christening the bridge in my own way.

—Adriano Biagiotti with Audry Lynch, "The Day the Golden Gate Bridge Opened"

Van was fifty years old that summer, a man who belonged in the old days. His ample talents as photographer and outdoorsman would never net him the satisfaction of a steady income. Ginny's nursing degree would provide that, and a reversal of roles that was, in the postwar '50s, and for the daughter of a Methodist minister, highly unusual.

I'd always been half afraid of my lanky, brown-haired uncle, who seemed perpetually mad at his horses. Yet here was the man who had rescued the racer Early Dude from the glue factory. Here was a consummate storyteller, in his element in the mountains, camping beside a meadow, fishing for trout in granite-bottomed lakes, and exploring on horseback. I was fully immersed in my cowgirl fantasy, unaware that Ginny was giving me more than just a vacation. And unaware of the conventions she and Van defied for love of each other and a life centered around being in the wilderness.

Not since that summer had Ginny and I spent more than an afternoon together. I had soon been drawn to the urban life of San Francisco and on to foreign lands. Twenty years had passed before I returned to settle near my childhood home.

She drove her newly acquired "micro-mini" motor home, one step up from a camper truck, and just right for her reedy, fit, five-foot two-inch frame. "I wanted something manageable for an old lady," she explained. "And I thought it would be safer to have the cab open to the back, since Matilda and I will be traveling alone a lot."

Matilda, a blue merle Australian shepherd who had escaped the customary tail-chopping, took her place in the passenger seat. Relegated to the back seat, I laughed as we headed out Sir Francis Drake Boulevard toward the ocean.

In the late 1800s, what became Samuel P. Taylor State Park was a thriving mill town producing paper and blasting powder, before dynamite was invented. The Taylor enterprises also included a fur tannery, firewood collection, and the vacation resort known as Camp Taylor. Today, campgrounds occupy the former location of a 100-room hotel, dance hall, bowling alley, saloons, riding stable, grocery store, butcher shop, and laundry. Camp

Taylor drew families from San Francisco to spend whole summers camping by the creek. The men commuted to their city jobs by train and ferry—an hour's journey, free of "traffic updates every ten minutes."

Samuel P. Taylor died in 1886. A nationwide financial panic in 1893 doomed the town and its industries. Taylor's wife and sons were unable to repay a mortgage for mill improvements. The lender foreclosed and then died, leaving the property to his widow, Elizabeth, who soon married Mr. Rodgers, the lender's attorney.

Apparently, the new owners weren't themselves keen on camping, though they tried for a few years to keep the resort open. By 1905 Elizabeth was again a widow, living in San Francisco's Fairmont Hotel. That year she ordered the demolition of all buildings that hadn't already been accidentally burned or otherwise destroyed. She had warning signs posted along the roadway forbidding anyone under penalty of arrest to stop or picnic on the land, and she had it patrolled.

Though the train still ran to Tomales until 1933, ridership declined without the mills and tourists. The streams and woodlands were returned, for a time, to the mountain lion, black bear, quail, deer, bobcat, and coyote. Mrs. Rodgers apparently considered the land so worthless that she stopped paying property taxes. By 1940, she owed Marin County $11,000 in back taxes. But still, acquisition of the park took five years of relentless lobbying and complicated negotiating. The state legislature would have to approve the purchase and the county would have to waive the tax bill. But the hardest part was convincing Mrs. Rodgers to sell. However eccentric she might have been, we can be thankful that she was no more interested in selling to developers than to the state. And finally, after her son-in-law took over her finances, she agreed to the deal.

We arrived at the campground in early afternoon, with time to get settled and take a walk before dinner. Matilda set the pace, half choking herself in her eagerness for the hike and the promise of a wade in the creek. The dog still had a lot to learn. She had been just six weeks old when Van had become bedridden. "Waltzing Matilda" had been one of his favorite shower songs. If his dancing days were over, the puppy would help keep his spirits up. But there had been little time in those two years for training a dog, or for showing her the delights of swimming.

Now, Ginny held tight to the leash, her arm stretched horizontal. "Have I told you the 'Roman Hat Creek Belly Flop' story?" she asked. I replied that she hadn't. "We were at Mount Lassen last fall. Silly me, it never entered my head that Matilda, a water-loving species, had never known a body of water bigger than her bucket. She took to Hat Creek—so suddenly and enthusiastically that I never had time to let go of her leash, so I went flying, literally, and landed flat out in the creek!"

We got up early in the morning, picking a good luck forget-me-not as we left the campground, crossed the highway and entered the shade of Devil's Gulch. We were prepared to bushwhack if Ginny could find where the old trail once led up the gully from the creekside. Our map was out of date, showing a path proposed for 1989 and marked as out of bounds for horses, bikes, and dogs. "Well, it won't be the first time the rules have been bent around here," said Ginny. "If Matilda gets caught we'll just have to throw ourselves on the mercy of the ranger. This quest requires a dog."

We found the right gully, but there was no trail and the place was thick with poison oak. So we retraced our steps downstream and found the trail to Mount Barnabe, crossing over the creek and climbing four or five hundred feet up the steep hillside. Ginny was worried. "I don't think the shack was so high above the creek, and I doubt I'd recognize the setting from above."

The path leveled out and led along the contour. We passed through spreading coast live oak trees, pungent laurel, and orange-trunked madrone. "There was an orchard somewhere up the gulch," Ginny said. "Van and the boys would filch a bucket of apples, and while the others peeled and sliced Van made crusts and did the baking. The pies would be gone as fast as he could get them out of the oven—which was a five-gallon drum."

We had crossed a little side stream and were heading for the next ridge when she stopped—"There's something about this place"—and walked back and stood looking uphill at a tree leaning over the gully. Then she looked down. Fifty feet below the trail lay an old piece of corrugated tin with red paint still showing through the rust. "It's part of the roof!" she exclaimed. "It had a red advertisement painted on it. I remember that madrone, too. Oh goody! We've found it!"

We made our way carefully down the steep bank. Broken boards were nearly obscured by trees and bushes along the shallow stream where Matilda lapped water. Ginny poked in the loose earth and found an S-shaped section of pipe. "It's part of the hot water system. These coils were under the stone fireplace."

"Pancakes for breakfast," I said, picking up a rusted syrup tin. "They must have had good times here."

"Oh, yes," replied Ginny. "You know they came even in winter, rain or shine. They always had a good supply of wood. Shorty composed a poem that they left tacked to the door. It welcomed anyone who happened by and asked that the shack be left as it was found. I never met Shorty, but Van's spirit is sure all around here— I can feel his nearness."

Chickadees chattered in the trees. Strong sun warmed the hillside, and our thoughts turned to lunch and the beers, cool in their newspaper wrappers at the bottom of our daypacks. Ginny snapped the leash onto Matilda's collar and got a free haul back up to the trail.

"I guess it's a good thing that Elizabeth Rodgers's border guard was either incompetent or sympathetic," I pointed out between bites of my sandwich. "Over the years she owned the land, there must have been lots of people who ignored the signs to have a picnic and a swim, not to mention building a cabin."

"It looks like the shack just eventually fell down," Ginny said. "I'm really surprised the park rangers, or somebody, didn't demolish it. But I guess anyone who would wander up there must have loved Devil's Gulch, and Papermill Creek, and the redwoods. Thank goodness it's a state park and not 'Taylor Estates.'"

Just hours ago the forget-me-nots had nodded encouragement as we set out on our quest. Now they seemed to hail our success, dancing in patches of sunlight beneath the creekside trees. The shack had all but returned to the earth, but like the roots of a perennial flower, its place was marked. For me, it would always be a symbol of the legacy that Ginny and Van had passed to me—the awareness of being completely alive in the wilderness.

Darla Hillard wrote Vanishing Tracks: Four Years Among the Snow Leopards of Nepal, *a story of high adventure in a landmark ecological study. She lives with biologist Rodney Jackson in Sonoma. She has written for numerous magazines, but this is her first published work that has nothing whatsoever to do with snow leopards.*

⋆

As a cross-county competition for runners, the 6.8 mile Dipsea Race is one of the more rugged in the country. Each year, on the last Sunday in August, several hundred aspirants of all ages take off from Lytton Square, across from the Mill Valley Bus Depot, sprint up three tall flights of steps, then run as fast as they can over the southwestern flanks of Mount Tamalpais to end by the sea in Stinson Beach. The fastest runners make it in about 48 minutes. Average ones do it in about an hour. The slowpokes struggle in later.

Because of the race and the founding friends who called themselves Dipsea Indians, the route they take is known as the Dipsea Trail. Except for that single race day of the year, as every walker who has discovered the Dipsea knows, it is one of the splendid hiking trails in the Bay Area, winding through ever-changing landscape, offering contrast of woodland and meadow, punctuated with exhilarating views. Best of all, it is convenient to public transportation at either end and in the middle. The race's reputation for ruggedness, however, has put off many tenderfoot hikers, who fail to consider that what may be tough to run in an hour can be exceedingly pleasant to walk in a leisurely half-day. Especially with a jug of wine, a book of verse, and thou.

—Margot Patterson Doss, *Paths of Gold: In and Around
the Golden Gate National Recreation Area*

Driving Your Karma

A cabbie learns a lesson in cosmic balance.

ONE SUNDAY NIGHT SHORTLY AFTER I WAS ISSUED MY CAB DRIVER'S badge, I picked up a young guy at the cable car turnaround near Fisherman's Wharf. I was still green enough to think he might be a tourist, but then he said he was headed to the corner of Griffith and Fitzgerald, out by Candlestick. I used to park my own car near that very same corner to save five bucks during Giants' games, and I knew it was the boundary of one of the city's most pitiful housing projects. Sir Francis Drake was probably Griffith and Fitzgerald's last tourist.

The way this kid started chatting me up made me wary. I'd had a couple of over-friendly fares before, and later, after they'd run on me without paying, I recognized their exuberance as an (effective) attempt to loosen me up, put me off guard. Still, you can't convict someone for being friendly: almost everyone, even chatty people, usually comes up with the fare. You never know until a ride's over.

We talked about Joe Montana the whole way—he'd brought the 49ers from behind in the fourth quarter that day—and by the time we reached Griffith and Fitzgerald there were fifteen dollars on the meter. "I'll be right back," the guy said, and then, leaving the door yawning wide behind him, he dashed off into the projects like Joe Montana himself slipping away from a safety blitz.

Even if you see it coming, and even if you consider that a customer running on you is just part of the territory, (it's called a "no-pay" in the cab world, and I get maybe ten of them a year) it still aggravates when it does happen. And now I was almost too angry to drive.

Fortunately it was 9 o'clock, time for the Sunday night airport rush, and Griffith and Fitzgerald is just ten minutes from SFO. I drove down Highway 101, entered the bowels of the parking garage, took my spot at the end of the cab line, and told my tale of woe to a couple of other drivers I knew. By the time I was called upstairs to take my next fare I was feeling a lot better.

I was driving, no doubt absent-mindedly, in a narrow hotel parking lot in Palo Alto, when I heard the dismaying screech of metal on metal. Sure enough, I had sideswiped a delivery van. I got out to do the insurance shuffle when I was confronted by a white-haired, white-bearded man wearing a purple suit. I waved apologetically at the damage and reached for my wallet but he looked me in the eye and said, "You know...at the end of our lives, I think this will all work out." He took my hand, shook it, and drove off. It's no wonder, I thought, that my children call this place the Holy Land.

*—James O'Reilly,
"San Francisco 2020"*

The new guy was an older, gray-haired, very dignified looking fellow. He wore a suit and said he was going to his home in the Marina District. When I started chatting him up he told me he'd been a lawyer in Atlanta when Jimmy Carter was governor of Georgia. When he was elected President, Carter brought my fare along to Washington to serve in his cabinet. One of my fare's first assignments was to fly to Taiwan to convey the new administration's greeting to the apprehensive Taiwanese government. Chiang Kai-shek's son and a full red-carpet state reception were waiting at the bottom of the airplane steps.

Later during the Carter administration, my fare and Andrew Young went on a three-week tour of Africa aboard Air Force One. Andrew Young had been the first black mayor of Atlanta, and later was the United States' ambassador to the United Nations. Young could have been elected president in a landslide in any one of the dozen or so countries they visited, and everywhere they went the entire entourage was first mobbed and then feted like royalty. For reasons of his own, Andrew Young did not want to sit in the President's seat on Air Force One, so my fare sat there for three heady weeks.

The meter read twenty-five dollars when we reached his house, which looked to be about a two-iron from the looming Golden Gate Bridge. He gave me two twenties, forty bucks, and said keep the change: the biggest tip of my young career.

I drove away almost euphoric, thinking about the two human beings who had most recently warmed an identical spot in my back seat; thinking about the wide gulf separating and coloring their experiences of life; thinking that if lives could somehow be calibrated and assigned spots on a graph, wasn't it quite possible that my life would wind up smack between theirs (the way my apartment in the Haight lay halfway between their homes); thinking about getting a $15 no-pay and a $15 tip back-to-unlikely-back; and thinking that in the cosmic scorebook everything, somehow, added up darn close to perfect.

Brad Newsham has been a San Francisco Yellow Cab driver since 1985. He is the author of All the Right Places: Traveling Light Through China, Japan, and Russia.

*

There are days I wake up feeling oppressed, in that Joycean mood of "exile, cunning, and silence" even though the weather outside is clear, bright, warm, and caressing. The aroma of coffee mixes with a cool breeze that is scented with pine and eucalyptus, yet I feel unable to shake that unseen black cloud that seems to hover over me, bringing forth from me an attitude of mild but persistent misanthropy that has the taste of bitter, black, stale coffee. Then I drag myself to the top of Holy Hill in north Berkeley and gaze out at the city below, the bay beyond, and the Golden Gate Bridge exactly opposite of where I'm standing. And I remind myself that it's a lovely day, that I live in one of the most beautiful spots that

I've seen, and that in my own way, with a little help from my friends, I have found myself a home in the world.

—Rajendra S. Khadka, "A Home in the World"

LAURA MILLER

Is There Really a San Francisco?

The city is both beneficiary and victim
of its own myth-making.

I STILL HAVE A PHOTOGRAPH OF THE REASON WHY I MOVED TO San Francisco, a snapshot taken when I was a child in the late '60s. And it's a good thing, too. My reason—a multicolored Chinese dragon suspended mid-writhe and spitting a mirrored ball covered with paper flames in the lobby of a bank on Grant Avenue—has since vanished.

To a kid from the bland suburbs of Southern California, that dragon stood for everything fantastical and extravagant, everything the big world beyond San Diego promised, finally revealing itself to me in all its glory. It was equal, even, to my own wild imagination. When my family left San Francisco at the end of that visit years ago, I remember thinking: they really know how to do things there.

"The City That Knows How" is what President William Howard Taft called San Francisco in 1911, flushed with delight (and perhaps more than that) during an honorary banquet at the Palace Hotel. No doubt he was impressed with how the city had rebuilt

itself after the earthquake and fire of 1906. The quote usually pro-
vokes grim little smiles and remarks that things certainly aren't
what they used to be—but that ruefulness is probably more San
Franciscan than anything else. "Is there really a San Francisco?" this
story asks, when the more fitting question may be: "Was there ever?"

When Alfred Hitchcock's 1958 masterpiece, *Vertigo,* was re-
released in the 1980s, viewers in San Francisco, where the movie
was filmed, laughed at two points: when the actors drove past a
half-excavated California Street (the street always seemed to be
under reconstruction) and when one character, a shipping magnate,
said "San Francisco's changed. The things that spell San Francisco
to me are disappearing fast."

We laugh because we've all heard it so many times before.
Scottie, the *Vertigo* "hero," fetishizes the doomed and the forever
lost, so Hitchcock picked the perfect setting for his story. San
Francisco's semi-official columnist laureate, Herb Caen, has made a
career out of lamenting a city that he sees as perpetually slipping
away. He's been doing it since 1938.

But, like the dead woman Scottie worships, the lost ideal never
really existed. Caen himself, in the 1948 volume, *The San Francisco
Book,* describes a city full of people, like himself, mourning "the
ghosts of a tradition that died before it was born." San Francisco
has a history of sudden blossomings and just as sudden disappear-
ances, one population displacing another and producing a generation that moons about over the way of life their parents destroyed.
It's as chronic as the earthquakes.

In *The Lure of San Francisco,* a self-published 1915 travelogue by
Elizabeth Gray and Mabel Thayer Potter, the authors' young hero-
ine offers her east coast suitor a tour of the town. The Bostonian
swain declares San Francisco "modern to the core," but the native
insists on taking him to Mission Dolores and passionately describes
herself as filled with "the spirit of the old padres."

There's a Yankee tradition of harking back to the days of
Spanish and Mexican rule (whether by the missionaries or the
rancheros) as California's Golden Age of gracious, elegant living. Of
course, at the time the Americans seized the state, they accused the

rancheros of indolence, waste and lack of progressive zeal. The Mexicans, in other words, weren't fulfilling California's potential—precisely the charges levelled at the Native Americans by the Spaniards.

At one time, even the Native Americans (whose ancestors crossed the Bering Strait from Asia) were newcomers here. Perhaps they descended upon the Bay Area determined to create a better society. San Francisco attracts utopians and idealists, from conquistadors seeking El Dorado to the handful of Yankee cranks leading the Bear Flag Revolt, to the flower children, to the Symbionese Liberation Army and other radical sectarians of the 1970s.

The novelist Frank Norris described San Francisco as "one of America's three storybook cities," a quality which makes it irresistible to people who want to live a fairy tale. The city's ravishing beauty and reputation of social tolerance seem like the ideal petrie dish to those who believe that, with the perfect social structure, we can eliminate human misery. Were the Spanish missionaries—determined to rescue the souls of the Ohlone

On Powell Street one afternoon, I bumped into an old schoolmate who lives in a thriving San Joaquin Valley town. After we'd chatted of this and that, and traded lies on how young we both looked, he said in parting:

"You guys down here had better watch it. Our population is over 400,000 and growing every minute. One of these days we'll be more of a city than San Francisco."

I could have replied, "When you have a million people that'll still be a small town," but you don't say things like that to old schoolmates, so I merely rolled my eyes and looked frightened. Besides, his was a familiar statement that San Franciscans have been hearing for years, and a familiar misconception: people are forever trying to measure cities in terms of population, and it doesn't work.

A city is a state—of mind, of taste, of opportunity. A city is a marketplace—where ideas are traded, opinions clash and eternal conflict may produce eternal truths. A city is wide open—to the winds of freedom, to the bittersweet smell of success and failure, and especially to people, all kinds of people, in their endless search to find (or lose) themselves.

—Herb Caen, "The Scenes, Scents and Sounds of San Francisco"

Indians from the perils of idleness and paganism—all that different from the hippies, intent on saving materialistic American society by insisting on a return to some version of the Ohlone way?

Idealists are impossible to please; their disillusionment is inevitable. The veterans of the Love Generation tend to grumble as they reminisce; they're as nostalgic for their halcyon days as Caen is for his—but often less honest about the accuracy of their memories. The cycle of idealism and nostalgia feels as montonous as a nursery rhyme that keeps repeating: "San Francisco isn't what it used to be"—until you want to scream.

Some people here are satisfied and nostalgia-free. Idris Ackamoor, founder of the theatrical company Cultural Odyssey (whose many activities include The Medea Project and the African-American Performance Festival) sounds as happy as the proverbial clam. A transplant (like most of us), he left the Midwest, drawn by San Francisco's age-old reputation as a "wide-open" town. Here he found the opportunity to connect with audiences and collaborators from many racial and cultural backgrounds. "That diversity really exists here," he assures me. "There's no place like it in the world."

Time changed. It disappeared. Time went away. There isn't as much time as there used to be. I don't know; it's magical, and kind of mystical. What happened to time? Everybody's always looking at a watch and saying, 'I gotta go! Gotta go!' It's all those time-saving devices that are using up all the time. Somewhere, a lot of time is being saved and stashed away, for other people."

—Herb Caen, quoted by Mark Powelson, "Citizen Caen," San Francisco Focus

Comedians tell a dozen variations on the same joke about San Francisco. It goes something like this: here, you might see a man on a street corner wearing nothing but a tutu, a g-string and a purple turban, riding a unicycle and lip-synching Billie Holiday—and the people passing by will give him a quick, appraising glance, and remark, "Nice turban."

Like a lot of jokes about California's "fruits and nuts," this one marvels at San Francisco's tolerance, particularly of those who break the gender molds, meaning gays and lesbians. Armistead Maupin's *Tales of the City* may not have made it onto film until the world could be properly nostalgic over the lost hedonism of the 1970s, but he wrote his serial novel from the very thick of the revels. Gays and lesbians have come here seeking less to change the world, than simply to be themselves.

However often the commentators speak soberly of AIDS, San Francisco remains the place where you can do just that. Gold Rushes and the depressions that follow them, earthquakes, assassinations, viruses—no disaster can permanently dampen the *joie de vivre* that seems to rise out of the very earth beneath us. The Ohlones, the original residents, spent their days dancing and eating shellfish until the Spaniards arrived to break up the party. The conquerors managed to crush the Ohlones before succumbing to the pleasure principle themselves.

"The intensified pursuit of human happiness," is what California historian Kevin Starr calls this impulse. The prequake journal *Annals of San Francisco* described the populace at the turn of the century as "excitement-craving, money-seeking, luxurious-living, reckless, heaven-earth-and-hell-daring citizens." We tempt fate, but when providence strikes back—with temblor or plague—we find ourselves partying in Dolores Park during the black-out or bringing hot lunches to people we never would have met or loved if not for the catastrophe. Some veterans of the 1906 quake didn't mourn the ruined city as much as they rued the day when people took their stoves off the streets and began cooking dinner inside their rebuilt homes.

Sometimes this confederation of misfits gels magnificently. In 1934, the longshoremen's union, under Harry Bridges, called a general strike and virtually shut down the city for four days. The culmination of a violent struggle with their employers, scabs, and the police, the general strike secured San Francisco as a union town with decent wages and working conditions. Only the nationwide crumbling of organized labor has been able to shake that.

We may see ourselves as a city of visionaries, but it often seems like we create the most change when we're merely trying to carve out a space to live as we choose, or coping with the latest disaster. It's when we feel the urge to tell other people how to live and what to think that we start to become the monster we fled, when we're least San Franciscan. They say the Left eats its young, and when it comes to political correctitude, the leftish impulses that helped San Francisco blossom into a citadel of tolerance seem to be intent on destroying one of its most glorious creations.

Amy Scholder, an editor at the publishing division of City Lights, observes that "people come here for more freedom, for personal transformation with less stress on making it." She tells me about a recent queer writing conference at the Women's Building, packed with 400 writers "who were willing to lock themselves up in a dark room for panel discussions on a nice weekend because they care about writing. Aspiring writers here are still willing to contemplate issues of creative expression and finding their voice rather than being immediately caught up in having a career."

The promise of a career may eventually lure some of them away, to New York and Los Angeles. Even Ackamoor, well-funded by various city agencies and popular with local audiences, has to tour. For, despite the fact that San Francisco has the highest percentage of adults who regularly attend live theater, music, dance, and the movies of any U.S. city (well, we're tied with Boston for moviegoers), there just aren't that many adults here. The performing and visual arts sell more tickets in San Francisco than do all the Bay Area's major sports franchises combined, but it's still not that many tickets.

Or is it? Perhaps what the southern and eastern metropoli offer is not so much an audience as the ear of the nation's tastemakers, the chance to rub shoulders with studio executives and national magazine editors. When your career depends on building a reputation, it's probably smart to leave a city full of people trying not to care what other people think.

Nevertheless, the ambitious still build their fortunes (or at least enjoy them) in San Francisco's environs. From silver mines to software, the quest for a bonanza continues. Around South Park, starry-eyed futurists concoct the next manifestation of high-tech, multimedia. Chris Carlson, a founder of *Processed World,* a 'zine for dissident office workers and data slaves has already begun to adapt the medium to his own ends. His project, an "interactive, multimedia excursion through San Francisco's past, present, and future," has as its guide "the next Forty-Niner, from 2049, a radical historian trying to recover the truth about the city's alternative tradition."

A tradition of alternatives, a small city that acts big, a model of racial diversity with a history of vicious anti-Chinese vigilantism, a fleshpot capitol that closes down at 2 a.m., Harvey Milk and ex-mayor Frank Jordan: these are just some of the contradictions that San Francisco contains, and will probably always contain. Is the city as great as it never was or less than what we hoped it could be? My dragon is gone now, but for today's seven-year-old future resident, the strands of red paper lanterns hanging from the pagoda-style eaves of the Mei Wong Trading Company probably serve the same purpose. There's only one correct answer to the question "Is there really a San Francisco?" and that's "Nice turban."

Laura Miller, a native Californian, has lived in San Francisco for fifteen years. In addition to writing for SF Weekly, *the* San Francisco Chronicle, *the* San Francisco Examiner, *and various other national publications, she worked for Good Vibrations, the feminist erotica shop, for seven years. Currently, she is senior editor at* Salon, *a World Wide Web magazine of books, arts, and ideas.*

✳

My parents used to take us to the Presidio as children. I remember always being happy at the thought of going there. The wildness of the place, the stunning views of ocean and headlands, the smell of eucalyptus and wildflowers—it was an intoxicating mix.

There is a bluff we would visit, towards the end of Washington Boulevard; some call it the Washington Bluffs, others Rob Hill, but it really has no name. There at the sweeping curve of the road you will find one of the finest views of the Golden Gate and the Pacific to be had anywhere. I always come back to this place borne by the waves of sun and water that extend far beyond the boundaries of the eye, and reminisce about times long gone, dreams unfulfilled, and visions yet to be explored. An ancient Chinese couplet haunts me here:

The moon in the water resembles
the moon in the sky;
The person in the heart is
the person in front of you.

The sea- and pine-scented air fills me with hope and the belief that all men and women are made better by a visit to this place. The dream of San Francisco is that humanity might live in harmony with nature but at the same time enjoy the benefits of civilization.

Call to yourself down through the centuries and see if it is not here that you will return. San Francisco isn't just a city, it is a jumping-off point to eternity. In an ocean of light, this is the place.

—Sean O'Reilly, "Lady of the Avenues"

PART FOUR

IN THE SHADOWS

The Late Victorians

One man learns to accept death.

ST. AUGUSTINE WRITES FROM HIS COPE OF DUST THAT WE ARE restless hearts, for earth is not our true home. Human unhappiness is evidence of our immortality. Intuition tells us we are meant for some other city.

Elizabeth Taylor, quoted in a magazine article of twenty years ago, spoke of cerulean Richard Burton days on her yacht, days that were nevertheless undermined by the elemental private reflection: This must end.

On a Sunday in summer, ten years ago, I was walking home from the Latin mass at St. Patrick's, the old Irish parish downtown, when I saw thousands of people on Market Street. It was San Francisco's Gay Freedom Day parade—not the first, but the first I ever saw. Private lives were becoming public. There were marching bands. There were floats. Banners blocked single lives thematically into a processional mass, not unlike the consortiums of the blessed in Renaissance paintings, each saint cherishing the apparatus of his martyrdom: GAY DENTISTS. BLACK AND WHITE LOVERS. GAYS FROM BAKERSFIELD. LATINA LESBIANS. From the foot of Market Street they marched, east to west, following the mythic American path toward optimism.

I followed the parade to Civic Center Plaza, where flags of routine nations yielded sovereignty to a multitude. Pastel billows flowed over all.

Five years later, another parade. Politicians waved from white convertibles. Dykes on Bikes revved up, thumbs upped. But now banners bore the acronyms of death. AIDS. ARC. Drums were muffled as passing, plum-spotted young men slid by on motorized cable cars.

Though I am alive now, I do not believe that an old man's pessimism is truer than a young man's optimism simply because it comes after. There are things a young man knows that are true and are not yet in the old man's power to recollect. Spring has its sappy wisdom. Lonely teenagers still arrive in San Francisco aboard Greyhound buses. The city can still seem, I imagine, by comparison to where they came from, paradise.

Four years ago on a Sunday in winter—a brilliant spring afternoon—I was jogging near Fort Point while overhead a young woman was, with difficulty, climbing over the railing of the Golden Gate Bridge. Holding down her skirt with one hand, with the other she waved to a startled spectator (the newspaper next day quoted a workman who was painting the bridge) before she stepped onto the sky.

To land like a spilled purse at my feet.

Serendipity has an eschatological tang here. Always has. Few American cities have had the experience, as we have had, of watching the civic body burn even as we stood, out of body, on a hillside, in a movie theater. Jeanette MacDonald's loony scatting of "San Francisco" has become our go-to-hell anthem. San Francisco has taken some heightened pleasure from the circus of final things. To Atlantis, to Pompeii, to the Pillar of Salt, we add the Golden Gate Bridge, not golden at all but rust red. San Francisco toys with the tragic conclusion.

For most of its brief life, San Francisco has entertained an idea of itself as heaven on earth, whether as Gold Town or City Beautiful or Treasure Island or Haight-Ashbury.

San Francisco can support both comic and tragic conclusions because the city is geographically *in extremis,* a meta-phor for the farthest-flung possibility, a metaphor for the end of the line. Land's end.

To speak of San Francisco as land's end is to read the map from one direction only—as Europeans would read or as the East Coast has always read it. In my lifetime, San Francisco has become an Asian city. To speak, therefore, of San Francisco as land's end is to betray parochial-ism. Before my parents came to California from Mexico, they saw San Francisco as the North. The West was not west for them.

I cannot claim for myself the memory of a skyline such as the one César saw. César came to San Francisco in middle age; César came here as to some final place. He was born in South America; he had grown up in Paris; he had been everywhere, done every-thing; he assumed the world. Yet César was not condescending toward San Francisco, not at all. Here César saw revolution, and he embraced it.

Whereas I live here because I was born here. I grew up 90 miles away, in Sacramento. San Francisco was the nearest, the easiest, the inevitable city, since I

It was Halloween night at the famous Mabuhay Gardens, the punk club of that time. A local group called The Vktms, headed by one of the toughest blonde chicks ever seen and boasting a single, "100% White Girl," were about halfway through their set when Nyna Crawford, the tough blonde chick, said, "Okay, sluts on stage!" Suddenly from out of nowhere, crawling over the tops of speakers, slithering from side stage on all fours and thrusting from behind the band to the front and center came half a dozen of the wildest, skinniest, technicolored, twitching, praying mantis-like, day-glo, matrix-like drag things performing lewd moves, mocking unnatural sex acts, touching their wadded-up-newspaper breasts, and flicking their longer than average tongues at the crowd. This group of dancers was called Sluts A Go Go and little did anyone know that these queens would eventually be-come stars without peer. The Sluts included Doris Fish and Tippi (God rest their souls) and Miss X. They were long San Francisco's reigning drag triptych of talent.

—Don Baird "The King Is Dead… Long Live the Queens: The Fags and Hags of S.F. Rock and Roll," *Monk, the Mobile Magazine*

needed a city. And yet I live here surrounded by people for whom San Francisco is a quest.

I have never looked for utopia on a map. Of course, I believe in human advancement. I believe in medicine, in astrophysics, in washing machines. But my compass takes its cardinal point from tragedy. If I respond to the metaphor of spring, I nevertheless learned, years ago, from my Mexican parents, from my Irish nuns, to count on winter. The point of Eden for me, for us, is not approach but expulsion.

After I met César in 1984, our friendly debate concerning the halcyon properties of San Francisco ranged from restaurant to restaurant. I spoke of limits. César boasted of freedoms.

It was César's conceit to add to the gates of Jerusalem, to add to the soccer fields of Tijuana, one other dreamscape hoped for the world over. It was the view from a hill, through a mesh of electrical tram wires, of an urban neighborhood in a valley. The vision took its name from the protruding wedge of a theater marquee. Here César raised his glass without discretion: to the Castro.

There were times, dear César, when you tried to switch sides if only to scorn American optimism, which, I remind you, had already become your own. At the high school where César taught, teachers and parents had organized a campaign to keep kids from driving themselves to the junior prom in an attempt to forestall liquor and death. Such a scheme momentarily reawakened César's Latin skepticism.

Didn't the Americans know? (His tone exaggerated incredulity.) Teenagers will crash into lampposts on their way home from proms, and there is nothing to be done about it. You cannot forbid tragedy.

By California standards I live in an old house. But not haunted. There are too many tall windows, there is too much salty light, especially in winter, though the windows rattle, rattle in summer when the fog flies overhead, and the house creaks and prowls at night. I feel myself immune to any confidence it seeks to tell.

To grow up homosexual is to live with secrets and within secrets. In no other place are those secrets more closely guarded than within the family home. The grammar of the gay city borrows metaphors from the nineteenth-century house. "Coming out of the closet" is predicated upon family laundry, dirty linen, skeletons.

I live in a tall Victorian house that has been converted to four apartments; four single men....

Architectural historians credit the gay movement of the 1970s with the urban restoration of San Francisco. Twenty years ago this was a borderline neighborhood. This room, like all the rooms of the house, was painted headache green, apple green, boarding-house green. In the 1970s homosexuals moved into black and working-class parts of the city, where they were perceived as pioneers or as blockbusters, depending.

Two decades ago some of the least expensive sections of San Francisco were wooden Victorian sections. It was thus a coincidence of the market that gay men found themselves living with the architectural metaphor for family. No other architecture in the American imagination is more evocative of family than the Victorian house. In those same years—the 1970s—and within those same Victorian houses, homosexuals were living rebellious lives to challenge the foundations of domesticity.

San Francisco seems always to have had some homosexual activity, even as far back as the Gold Rush, when newspapers talked obliquely about the "Lavender Cowboys," a cadre of gay men who traveled on horseback through Northern California's then mostly masculine society. The number of gay men here grew significantly during World War II, when the U.S. military tried its best to muster out homosexual servicemen. A great number of those soldiers were shipped back to the States through San Francisco and many, chary of explaining to their families the precise reason for their discharge, decided to remain in the Bay Area.

—J. Kingston Pierce,
San Francisco, You're History

Was "queer-bashing" as much a manifestation of homophobia as a reaction against gentrification? One heard the complaint, often enough, that gay men were as promiscuous with their capital as otherwise, buying, fixing up, then selling and moving on. Two incomes, no children, described an unfair advantage. No sooner would flower boxes begin to appear than an anonymous reply was smeared on the sidewalk out front: KILL FAGGOTS.

The three- or four-story Victorian house, like the Victorian novel, was built to contain several generations and several classes under one roof, behind a single oaken door. What strikes me is the confidence of Victorian architecture. Stairs, connecting one story with another, describe the confidence that bound generations together through time—confidence that the family would inherit the earth.

If Victorian houses exude a sturdy optimism by day, they are also associated in our imaginations with the Gothic—with shadows and cobwebby gimcrack, long corridors. The nineteenth century was remarkable for escalating optimism even as it excavated the backstairs, the descending architecture of nightmare—Freud's labor and Engels's.

I live on the second story, in rooms that have been rendered as empty as Yorick's skull—gutted, unrattled, in various ways unlocked, added skylights and new windows, new doors. The hallway remains the darkest part of the house.

This winter the hallway and lobby are being repainted to resemble an eighteenth-century French foyer. Of late we had walls and carpet of Sienese red; a baroque mirror hung in an alcove by the stairwell. Now we are to have enlightened austerity of an expensive sort—black-and-white marble floors and faux masonry. A man comes in the afternoons to texture the walls with a sponge and a rag and to paint white mortar lines that create an illusion of permanence, of stone.

The renovation of Victorian San Francisco into dollhouses for libertines may have seemed, in the 1970s, an evasion of what the city was actually becoming. San Francisco's rows of storied houses proclaimed a multigenerational orthodoxy, all the while masking the city's unconventional soul. Elsewhere, meanwhile, domestic America was coming undone.

Suburban Los Angeles, the prototype for a new America, was characterized by a more apparently radical residential architecture.

There was, for example, the work of Frank Gehry. In the 1970s Gehry exploded the nuclear-family house, turning it inside out intellectually and in fact. Though, in a way, Gehry merely completed the logic of the postwar suburban tract house—with its one story, its sliding glass doors, Formica kitchen, two-car garage. The tract house exchanged privacy for mobility. Heterosexuals opted for the one-lifetime house, the freeway, the birth-control pill, minimalist fiction.

The age-old description of homosexuality is of a sin against nature. Moralistic society has always judged emotion literally. The homosexual was sinful because he had no kosher place to stick it. In attempting to drape the architecture of sodomy with art, homosexuals have lived for thousands of years against the expectations of nature. Barren as Shakers and, interestingly, as concerned with the small effect, homosexuals have made a covenant against nature. Homosexual survival lay in artifice, in plumage, in lampshades, sonnets, musical comedy, couture, syntax, religious ceremony, opera, lacquer, irony.

I once asked Enrique, an interior decorator, if he had many homosexual clients. "*Mais non,*" said he, flexing his eyelids. "Queers don't need decorators. They were born knowing how. All this A.S.I.D. [American Society of Interior Designers] stuff—tests and regulations—as if you can confer a homosexual diploma on a suburban housewife by granting her a discount card."

A knack? The genius, we are beginning to fear in an age of AIDS, is irreplaceable—but does it exist? The question is whether the darling affinities are innate to homosexuality or whether they are compensatory. Why have so many homosexuals retired into the small effect, the ineffectual career, the stereotype, the card shop, the florist? *Be gentle with me?* Or do homosexuals know things others do not?

This way power lay: once upon a time the homosexual appropriated to himself a mystical province, that of taste. Taste, which is, after all, the insecurity of the middle class, became the homosexual's licentiate to challenge the rule of nature. (The fairy in his blood, he intimated.)

Deciding how best to stick it may be only an architectural problem or a question of physics or of engineering or of cabinetry. Nevertheless, society's condemnation forced the homosexual to find his redemption outside nature. *We'll put a little skirt here.* The impulse is not to create but to recreate, to sham, to convert, to sauce, to rouge, to fragrance, to prettify. No effect is too small or too ephemeral to be snatched away from nature, to be ushered toward the perfection of artificiality. *We'll bring out the highlights there.* The homosexual has marshaled the architecture of the straight world to the very gates of Versailles—that great Vatican of fairyland—beyond which power is converted to leisure. In San Francisco in the 1980s the highest form of art became interior decoration. The glory hole was thus converted to an eighteenth-century French foyer.

I live away from the street, in a back apartment, in two rooms. I use my bedroom as a visitor's room—the sleigh bed tricked up with shams into a sofa—whereas I rarely invite anyone into my library, the public room, where I write, the public gesture.

I read in my bedroom in the afternoon because the light is good there, especially now, in winter, when the sun recedes from the earth.

There is a door in the south wall that leads to a balcony. The door was once a window. Inside the door, inside my bedroom, are twin green shutters. They are false shutters, of no function beyond wit. The shutters open into the room; they have the effect of turning my apartment inside out.

A few months ago I hired a man to paint the shutters green. I wanted the green shutters of Manet—you know the ones I mean— I wanted a weathered look, as of verdigris. For several days the painter labored, rubbing his paints into the wood and then wiping them off again. In this way he rehearsed for me decades of the ravages of weather. Yellow enough? Black?

The painter left one afternoon, saying he would return the next day, leaving behind his tubes, his brushes, his sponges and rags. He never returned. Someone told me he has AIDS.

Repainted façades extend now from Jackson Street south into what was once the heart of the black "Mo"—black Fillmore Street. Today there are watercress sandwiches at three o'clock where recently there had been loudmouthed kids, hole-in-the-wall bars, pimps. Now there are tweeds and perambulators, matrons and nannies. Yuppies. And gays.

The gay male revolution had greater influence on San Francisco in the 1970s than did the feminist revolution. Feminists, with whom I include lesbians—such was the inclusiveness of the feminist movement—were preoccupied with career, with escape from the house in order to create a sexually democratic city. Homosexual men sought to reclaim the house, the house that traditionally had been the reward for heterosexuality, with all its selfless tasks and burdens.

Leisure defined the gay male revolution. The gay political movement began, by most accounts, in 1969, with the Stonewall riots in New York City, whereby gay men fought to defend the nonconformity of their leisure.

It was no coincidence that homosexuals migrated to San Francisco in the 1970s, for the city was famed as a playful place, more Catholic than Protestant in its eschatological intuition. In 1975 the state of California legalized consensual homosexuality, and about the same time Castro Street, southwest of downtown, began to eclipse Polk Street as the homosexual address in San Francisco. Polk Street was a string of bars. The Castro was an entire district. The Castro had Victorian houses and churches, bookstores and restaurants, gyms, dry cleaners, supermarkets, and an elected member of the Board of Supervisors. The Castro supported baths and bars, but there was nothing furtive about them. On Castro Street the light of day penetrated gay life through clear plate-glass windows. The light of day discovered a new confidence, a new politics. Also a new look—a noncosmopolitan, Burt Reynolds, butch-kid style: beer, ball games, Levi's, short hair, muscles.

Gay men who lived elsewhere in the city, in Pacific Heights or in the Richmond, often spoke with derision of "Castro Street clones," describing the look, or scorned what they called the

ghettoization of homosexuality. To an older generation of homosexuals, the blatancy of sexuality on Castro Street threatened the
discreet compromise they had
negotiated with a tolerant city.

*Of the brothels, the Nymphia
was the largest and most
imaginative. The U-shaped building was three stories tall and had
150 cubicles on each floor. When
the building opened in 1899, the
owners, the Twinkling Star
Corporation, wanted to call it the
Hotel Nymphomania. The police
said no to that, but Nymphia was
all right. The police were remark-
ably tolerant of the place. Two pa-
trolmen stood outside the front
door every night, not to interfere
with the activity inside but to
watch the street. They would
go inside if there was a shooting
or a serious stabbing, but they
would have nothing to do with
the drunken brawls that were
a nightly occurrence.*

*One floor of the Nymphia was
given over to nymphomaniacs, or
women who advertised themselves
as such, and all the women in the
place were naked while in their
cubicles. And there was no privacy
in their rooms. A tall, narrow window had been cut into every door,
and the shade which covered the
opening raised automatically for a
few moments when a dime was
put into a nearby slot.*

—Charles Lockwood, *Suddenly
San Francisco: The Early Years
of an Instant City*

As the Castro district thrived,
Folsom Street, south of Market,
also began to thrive, as if in
counterdistinction to the utopian
Castro. The Folsom Street area
was a warehouse district of pud-
dled alleys and deserted streets.
Folsom Street offered an assortment of leather bars, an evening's
regress to the outlaw sexuality of
the Fifties, the Forties, the nineteenth century, and so on—an
eroticism of the dark, of the
Reeperbahn, or of the guards-
man's barracks.

The Castro district implied
that sexuality was more crucial,
that homosexuality was the central fact of identity. The Castro
district, with its ice-cream parlors
and hardware stores, was the
revolutionary place.

Into which carloads of vacant-
eyed teenagers from other districts or from middle-class
suburbs would drive after dark,
cruising the neighborhood for
solitary victims.

The ultimate gay basher was a
city supervisor named Dan
White, ex-cop, ex-boxer, ex-
fireman, ex-altar boy. Dan

White had grown up in the Castro district; he recognized the Castro revolution for what it was. Gays had achieved power over him. He murdered the mayor and he murdered the homosexual member of the Board of Supervisors.

Katherine, a sophisticate if ever there was one, nevertheless dismisses the two men descending the aisle at the Opera House: "All so sleek and smooth-jowled and silver-haired—they don't seem real, poor darlings. It must be because they don't have children."

Lodged within Katherine's complaint is the perennial heterosexual annoyance with the homosexual's freedom from child-rearing, which places the homosexual not so much beyond the pale as it relegates the homosexual outside "responsible" life.

It was the glamour of gay life, after all, as much as it was the feminist call to career, that encouraged heterosexuals in the 1970s to excuse themselves from nature, to swallow the birth control pill. Who needs children? The gay bar became the paradigm for the single's bar. The gay couple became the paradigm for the selfish couple—all dressed up and everywhere to go. And there was the example of the gay house in illustrated lifestyle magazines. At the same time that suburban housewives were looking outside home for fulfillment, gay men were reintroducing a new generation in the city—heterosexual men and women—to the complacencies of the barren house.

Puritanical America dismissed gay camp followers as Yuppies; the term means to suggest infantility. Yuppies were obsessive and awkward in their materialism. Whereas gays arranged a decorative life against a barren state, Yuppies sought early returns—lives that were not to be all toil and spin. Yuppies, trained to careerism from the cradle, wavered in their pursuit of the northern European ethic—indeed, we might now call it the Pan-Pacific ethic—in favor of the Mediterranean, the Latin, the Catholic, the Castro, the Gay.

The international architectural idioms of Skidmore, Owings & Merrill, which defined the city's skyline in the 1970s, betrayed no awareness of any street-level debate concerning the primacy of play in San Francisco nor of any human dramas resulting from urban redevelopment. The repellent office tower was a fortress raised against the sky, against the street, against the idea of a city. Offices were hives where money was made, and damn all.

In the 1970s San Francisco was divided between the interests of downtown and the pleasures of the neighborhoods. Neighborhoods asserted idiosyncrasy, human scale, light. San Francisco neighborhoods perceived downtown as working against their influence in determining what the city should be. Thus neighborhoods seceded from the idea of a city.

The gay movement rejected downtown as representing "straight" conformity. But was it possible that heterosexual Union Street was related to Castro Street? Was it possible that either was related to the Latino Mission district? Or to the Sino-Russian Richmond? San Francisco, though complimented worldwide for holding its center, was in fact without a vision of itself entire.

In the 1980s, in deference to the neighborhoods, City Hall would attempt a counter-reformation of downtown, forbidding "Manhattanization." Shadows were legislated away from parks and playgrounds. Height restrictions were lowered beneath an existing skyline. Design, too, fell under the retrojurisdiction of the city planner's office. The Victorian house was presented to architects as a model of what the city wanted to uphold and to become. In heterosexual neighborhoods, one saw newly built Victorians. Downtown, postmodernist prescriptions for playfulness advised skyscrapers to wear party hats, buttons, comic mustaches. Philip Johnson yielded to the dollhouse impulse to perch angels atop one of his skyscrapers.

In the 1970s, like a lot of men and women in this city, I joined a gym. My club, I've even caught myself calling it.

In the gay city of the 1970s, bodybuilding became an architectural preoccupation of the upper middle class. Bodybuilding is a parody of labor, a useless accumulation of the laborer's bulk and strength. No useful task is accomplished. And yet there is something businesslike about the habitués, and the gym is filled with the punch-clock logic of the workplace. Machines clank and hum. Needles on gauges toll spent calories.

The gym is at once a closet of privacy and an exhibition gallery. All four walls are mirrored.

I study my body in the mirror. Physical revelation—nakedness—is no longer possible, cannot be desired, for the body is shrouded in meat and wears itself.

The intent is some merciless press of body against a standard, perfect mold. Bodies are "cut" or "pumped" or "buffed" as on an assembly line in Turin. A body becomes so many extrovert parts. Delts, pecs, lats.

I harness myself in a Nautilus cage.

Lats become wings. For the gym is nothing if not the occasion for transcendence. From homosexual to autosexual...

I lift weights over my head, baring my teeth like an animal with the strain.

...to nonsexual. The effect of the overdeveloped body is the miniaturization of the sexual organs—of no function beyond wit. Behold the ape become the Blakean angel, revolving in an empyrean of mirrors.

The nineteenth-century mirror over the fireplace in my bedroom was purchsed by a decorator from the estate of a man who died last year of AIDS. It is a top-heavy piece, confusing styles. Two ebony-painted columns support a frieze of painted glass above the mirror. The frieze depicts three bourgeois Graces and a couple of free-range cherubs. The lake of the mirror has formed a cataract, and at its edges it is beginning to corrode.

Thus the mirror that now draws upon my room owns some bright curse, maybe—some memory not mine.

As I regard this mirror, I imagine St. Augustine's meditation slowly hardening into syllogism, passing down through centuries to confound us: evil is the absence of good.

We have become accustomed to figures disappearing from our landscape. Does this not lead us to interrogate the landscape?

With reason do we invest mirrors with the superstition of

memory, for they, though glass, though liquid captured in a bay, are so often less fragile than we are. They—bright ovals or rectangles or rounds—bump down unscathed, unspilled through centuries, whereas we...

The man in the red baseball cap used to jog so religiously on Marina Green. By the time it occurs to me that I have not seen him for months, I realize he may be dead—not lapsed, not moved away. People come and go in the city, it's true. But in San Francisco in the nineties, death has become as routine an explanation for disappearance as Allied Van Lines.

AIDS, it has been discovered, is a plague of absence. Absence opened in the blood. Absence condensed into the fluid of passing emotion. Absence shot through opalescent tugs of semen to deflower the city.

And then AIDS, it was discovered, is a nonmetaphorical disease, a disease like any other. Absence sprang from substance—a virus, a hairy bubble perched upon a needle, a platter of no intention served round: fever, blisters, a death sentence.

In the Eighties San Francisco led the way again in the fight against AIDS, as the back side of sexual liberation reared its ugly head. Long before President Reagan could even say the word "AIDS," San Francisco's gay and lesbian community was heroically reaching out to those in need, creating hospices, meal programs, and persuasive pamphlets that quickly and effectively taught the how's and why's of safer sex. Those men and women were models of bodhisattva compassion, yet to this day they have not received their due in the nation's press, even though their pioneering work has saved thousands of lives, from all races and sexual orientations.

—Jim Crotty, "San Francisco: What the Hell Did You Do to Your Hair," *Monk, The Mobile Magazine*

At first I heard only a few names—names connected, perhaps, with the right faces, perhaps not. People vaguely remembered, as through the cataract of this mirror, from dinner parties or from intermissions. A few articles in the press. The rumored celebrities. But within months the slow beating of the blood had found its bay.

One of San Francisco's gay newspapers, the *Bay Area Reporter*, began to accept advertisements from funeral parlors and casket makers, inserting them between the randy ads for leather bars and tanning salons. The *Reporter* invited homemade obituaries—lovers writing of lovers, friends remembering friends and the blessings of unexceptional life.

Peter. Carlos. Gary. Asel. Perry. Nikos.

Healthy snapshots accompany each annal. At the Russian River. By the Christmas tree. Lifting a beer. In uniform. A dinner jacket. A satin gown.

He was born in Puerto La Libertad, El Salvador.

He attended Apple Valley High School, where he was their first male cheerleader.

From El Paso. From Medford. From Germany. From Long Island.

I moved back to San Francisco in 1979. Oh, I had had some salad days elsewhere, but by 1979 I was a wintry man. I came here in order not to be distracted by the ambitions or, for that matter, the pleasures of others but to pursue my own ambition. Once here, though, I found the company of men who pursued an earthly paradise charming. Skepticism became my demeanor toward them— I was the dinner-party skeptic, a firm believer in Original Sin and in the limits of possibility.

Which charmed them.

He was a dancer.

He settled into the interior-design department of Gump's, where he worked until his illness.

He was a teacher.

César, for example.

César could shave the rind from any assertion to expose its pulp and jelly. But César was otherwise ruled by pulp. César loved everything that ripened in time. Freshmen. Bordeaux. César could fashion liturgy from an artichoke. Yesterday it was not ready (cocking his head, rotating the artichoke in his hand over a pot of cold water). Tomorrow will be too late (Yorick's skull). Today it is perfect (as he lit the fire beneath the pot). We will eat it now.

If he's lucky, he's got a year, a doctor told me. If not, he's got two.

The phone rang. AIDS had tagged a friend. And then the phone rang again. And then the phone rang again. Michael had tested positive. Adrian, well, what he had assumed were shingles...Paul was back in the hospital. And César, dammit, César, even César, especially César.

That winter before his death César traveled back to South America. On his return to San Francisco he described to me how he had walked with his mother in her garden—his mother chafing her hands as if she were cold. But it was not cold, he said. They moved slowly. Her summer garden was prolonging itself this year, she said. The cicadas will not stop singing.

When he lay on his deathbed, César said everyone else he knew might get AIDS and die. He said I would be the only one spared—"spared" was supposed to have been chased with irony, I knew, but his voice was too weak to do the job. "You are too circumspect," he said then, wagging his finger upon the coverlet.

So I was going to live to see that the garden of earthly delights was, after all, only wallpaper—was that it, César? Hadn't I always said so? It was then I saw that the greater sin against heaven was my unwillingness to embrace life.

It was not as in some Victorian novel—the curtains drawn, the pillows plumped, the streets strewn with sawdust. It was not to be a matter of custards in covered dishes, steaming possets, *Try a little of this, my dear.* Or gathering up the issues of *Architectural Digest* strewn about the bed. Closing the biography of Diana Cooper and marking its place. Or the unfolding of discretionary screens, morphine, parrots, pavilions.

César experienced agony.

Four of his high school students sawed through a Vivaldi quartet in the corridor outside his hospital room, prolonging the hideous garden.

In the presence of his lover Gregory and friends, Scott passed from this life...

He died peacefully at home in his lover Ron's arms.

Immediately after a friend led a prayer for him to be taken home and while his dear mother was reciting the Twenty-third Psalm, Bill peacefully took his last breath.

I stood aloof at César's memorial, the kind of party he would enjoy, everyone said. And so for a time César lay improperly buried, unconvincingly resurrected in the conditional: would enjoy. What else could they say? César had no religion beyond aesthetic bravery.

Sunlight remains. Traffic remains. Nocturnal chic attaches to some discovered restaurant. A new novel is reviewed in the *New York Times*. And the mirror rasps on its hook. The mirror is lifted down.

A priest friend, a good friend, who out of naïveté plays the cynic, tells me—this is on a bright, billowy day; we are standing outside—"It's not as sad as you may think. There is at least spectacle in the death of the young. Come to the funeral of an old lady sometime if you want to feel an empty church."

I will grant my priest friend this much: that it is easier, easier on me, to sit with gay men in hospitals than with the staring old. Young men talk as much as they are able.

But those who gather around the young man's bed do not see spectacle. This doll is Death. I have seen people caressing it, staring Death down. I have seen people wipe its tears, wipe its ass; I have seen people kiss Death on his lips, where once there were lips.

Chris was inspired after his own diagnosis in July 1987 with the truth and reality of how such a terri-

You are dead.
   You will go above
      there to the trail.
      That is the spirit trail.
   Go there to the beautiful trail.
   May it please you not to walk
         about where I am.
         You are dead.
      Go there to the beautiful
            trail above.
         That is your way.
Look at the place where you used
            to wander.
   The north trail, the mountains
      where you used to wander,
            you are leaving.
      Listen to me: go there!

—Wintu burial oration, *The Way We Lived: California Indian Reminiscences, Stories and Songs*, edited by Malcolm Margolin

ble disease could bring out the love, warmth, and support of so many friends and family.

Sometimes no family came. If there was family, it was usually mother. Mom. With her suitcase and with the torn flap of an envelope in her hand.

Brenda. Pat. Connie. Toni. Soledad.

Or parents came but then left without reconciliation, some preferring to say cancer.

But others came. Sissies were not, after all, afraid of Death. They walked his dog. They washed his dishes. They bought his groceries. They massaged his poor back. They changed his bandages. They emptied his bedpan.

Men who sought the aesthetic ordering of existence were recalled to nature. Men who aspired to the mock-angelic settled for the shirt of hair. The gay community of San Francisco, having found freedom, consented to necessity—to all that the proud world had for so long held up to them, withheld from them, as "real humanity."

And if gays took care of their own, they were not alone. AIDS was a disease of the entire city; its victims were as often black, Hispanic, straight. Neither were Charity and Mercy only white, only male, only gay. Others came. There were nurses and nuns and the couple from next door, coworkers, strangers, teenagers, corporations, pensioners. A community was forming over the city.

Cary and Rick's friends and family wish to thank the many people who provided both small and great kindnesses.

He was attended to and lovingly cared for by the staff at Coming Home Hospice.

And the saints of this city have names listed in the phone book, names I heard called through a microphone one cold Sunday in Advent as I sat in Most Holy Redeemer Church. It might have been any of the churches or community centers in the Castro district, but it happened at Most Holy Redeemer at a time in the history of the world when the Roman Catholic Church still pronounced the homosexual a sinner.

A woman at the microphone called upon volunteers from the AIDS Support Group to come forward. One by one, in twos and threes, throughout the church, people stood up, young men and women, and middle-aged and old, straight, gay, and all of them shy at being called. Yet they came forward and assembled in the sanctuary, facing the congregation, grinning self-consciously at one another, their hands hidden behind them.

I am preoccupied by the fussing of a man sitting in the pew directly in front of me—in his seventies, frail, his iodine-colored hair combed forward and pasted upon his forehead. Fingers of porcelain clutch the pearly beads of what must have been his mother's rosary. He is not the sort of man any gay man would have chosen to become in the 1970s. He is probably not what he himself expected to become. Something of the old dear about him, wizened butterfly, powdered old pouf. Certainly he is what I fear becoming. And then he rises, this old monkey, with the most beatific dignity, in answer to the microphone, and he strides into the sanctuary to take his place in the company of the Blessed.

So this is it—this, what looks like a Christmas party in an insurance office and not as in Renaissance paintings, and not as we had always thought, not some flower-strewn, some sequined curtain call of grease-painted heroes gesturing to the stalls. A lady with a plastic candy cane pinned to her lapel. A Castro clone with a red bandanna exploding from his hip pocket. A perfume-counter lady with an Hermès scarf mantled upon her left shoulder. A black man in a checkered sports coat. The pink-haired punkess with a jewel in her nose. Here, too, is the gay couple in middle age, wearing interchangeable plaid shirts and corduroy pants. Blood and shit and Mr. Happy Face. These know the weight of bodies.

Bill died.

…Passed on to heaven.

…Turning over in his bed one night and then gone.

These learned to love what is corruptible, while I, barren skeptic, reader of St. Augustine, curator of the earthly paradise, inheritor of the empty mirror, I shift my tailbone upon the cold, hard pew.

Richard Rodriguez is an editor at Pacific News Service, an essayist on the MacNeil/Lehrer NewsHour, *and the author of* Hunger of Memory:

The Education of Richard Rodriguez, *and* Days of Obligation: An Argument with My Mexican Father. *He lives in San Francisco.*

★

Humans first trickled into California 15,000, 20,000, or perhaps 30,000 or more years ago. They hunted with spears, for the bow and arrow had not yet been invented. Without knowing how to make mortars and pestles they could not grind seeds or acorns, but survived by gathering roots, greens, and berries. We know almost nothing about how they lived or what languages they spoke. Yet it is quite probable that many of their stories featured the "Trickster."

The trickster figure was widespread throughout North America and the Old World, ancient beyond calculation and enormously complex. He is at the same time good and evil, crafty and foolish, godlike and scroungy. He is both the prankster and the dupe. He seems to exist in the free and wild area of the mind beyond duality—beyond the trick of intellect that divides things into good or bad, smart or stupid, winner or loser, allowable or forbidden. The trickster is everything at once. He dies, is dismembered, decays, and then is pulled back together again to continue his journey. He exists in an undifferentiated, boundless, intensely creative world.

The specific embodiment of the trickster varies from people to people across North America. Sometimes he is human, sometimes animal, often both at once. He was variously called Manabozho, The Foolish One, The Great Rabbit, Glooscap, Sweet-Medicine, Wakdjunkaga, Hare, or Raven. In California, the Southwest, and in much of Mexico the trickster generally took his name from the sly doglike animal who skulked around the outskirts of villages, hunting gophers, scavenging the refuse piles, and occasionally stealing salmon and deer meat from the drying racks.

In a typical Coyote story the "hero" sets off on a foolish mission and gets into trouble, as he falls victim to his own irrepressible curiosity and compulsions.

—Malcolm Margolin, *The Way We Lived: California Indian Reminiscences, Stories and Songs*

BETTY ANN WEBSTER

Rocking the Cradle

Intimations of mortality are frequent by the Golden Gate.

THE BABY FINALLY FELL ASLEEP. I LAID HIM ON MY BED AND collapsed on the chaise longue on the deck just outside my room. The time was 5:04 p.m. on October 17, 1989. The place, Berkeley, California.

Life suddenly lost all stability. The earth shook, heaved, roared. Objects on the moldings around my room fell clattering to the floor and the desk. The baby woke screaming. My heart dropped into my shoes as I leapt for the door, ran to the bed, grabbed the baby, and ran out onto the deck, frantically trying to think what I should do. I felt as though I were shaking as badly as the earth. No doubt the baby thought so, too. We endured hours of pure terror in fifteen seconds.

Three-month-old Tomas's parents were celebrating their very first outing since his birth. John had bought tickets to the Giants-A's World Series game at Candlestick Park in San Francisco and they had left on BART an hour earlier, anxious about leaving their son for the first time. But they assured me that they wouldn't worry; there was no one else they'd leave him with this soon. Emmanuelle was still nursing him; she had pumped enough milk to last until their return.

Fortunately Berkeley's electricity survived the earthquake. Far into the night, walking the still-wailing baby, I watched TV, horrified at the sight of the collapsed Cypress Freeway, trapped cars, the view of the fallen section of the Bay Bridge with a car toppling over the edge, raging fires in the Marina. Where were John and Emmanuelle? Were they safe? When would I hear from them? When and how would they get back?

At 11 p.m. the phone rang. At last! It was John; they had been on BART when the quake hit, hadn't yet reached Candlestick Park. The car stopped, of course; underground, they weren't quite sure what had happened, the lights went out. But there was no panic, people rallied, the train was manually towed to the nearest station and they were able to leave it walking out into a dark city not knowing how much damage the earthquake had caused, what they were going to do, or how they would get home. Generous strangers on the train, in the manner of people everywhere during disasters, offered to take them home for the night and they thankfully, though reluctantly, accepted when it became clear that they had no chance of getting home that night. Surprisingly some phones still worked. They wouldn't be able to get back to Berkeley until the next day, but they would come as soon as they could, however they could. We hung up with mutual sighs of relief and thanks to whatever powers there be.

The baby finally cried himself to sleep. As I lay awake much of that night apprehensively anticipating yet another aftershock, I thought of the stories about the Great Earthquake and Fire of 1906 told to me years before by survivors of that catastrophe. I had tape recorded the life histories of three such survivors as part of an oral history project. The next day I resurrected those tapes and listened again to how it had been for them in that earlier but similar time.

Alma W., the oldest of the three, was born in San Francisco, in 1885. I had known Alma for years; she was the mother of a friend. In her 94th year Alma looked like a benign witch, tall, gaunt, gnarled hands leaning on a cane, long nose and chin inclining toward one another. Her mind and memory were as sharp as her nose. Alma was born in San Francisco of German immigrant parents. Her father was a musician, a coronet player who once played in Sousa's band. He traveled with various bands, was seldom home, and, Alma indicated delicately, was clearly a woman-izer. When Alma was four-teen her father was shot to death in Los Angeles by his mistress.

"All my mother ever said was 'Well, Alma, thank God now I know where he is.'"

On the day of the earthquake Alma was 21 years old, working in Carmel as a waitress at the Pine Inn hotel. She thought she was in heaven; prior to coming to Carmel she had never even eaten in a restaurant. Carmel was badly shaken by the earthquake and Alma was frantically worried about her mother in San Francisco. Somehow she man-aged to get to the city the next day, how she could no longer re-member. "It was lucky I did," she added, "or I wouldn't have been able to get into the city, oh, it was awful! Everything came down, there was rubble everywhere. And, you know, there was this man there who had a big dairy farm in Carmel. He said it was a funny thing, he'd never seen it before, but all the cattle went down on their knees before the earthquake came. They sense it, you know.

It was my first visit to Santa Cruz, where my cousin was working toward her Ph.D. She'd only recently come to California from Ireland via Vancouver. We were waiting in the supermarket checkout line when she said, "Paula, tell me about earth-quakes. I'm a bit nervous about the whole idea of being in California."

"Oh, they're no big deal," I replied. "The ground rocks and rolls for a few seconds, you ride the waves, and it's over. It's kind of fun, really."

At that instant the floor began to tremble and she grabbed my arm.

"Don't worry," I said. "It's noth-ing. It'll be over in a second." But I was wrong. The shaking got stronger, the floor began to buckle, stuff flew off the shelves and racks collapsed in heaps. Everyone ran out the door and it looked like the world was falling down. A little boy went by on a skateboard and shouted, "Wow, that was the coolest earthquake I've ever felt in my whole life!" When it finally stopped we were so terrified we were afraid to drive home. I've never felt the same about earthquakes since.

—Paula Mc Cabe,
"Last Visit to Santa Cruz"

"Anyway, I got up there, everything was in the streets; you couldn't get through. I went to live with this friend of mine, she'd just gotten married not too long before. That's the way you did it, everybody stayed wherever you could. We had to put our stoves out in the street, all the chimneys had fallen down, you can imagine what a catastrophe it was. And the panic and the looting? We were under martial law.

"My money was running out. I went to the Standard Shirt Company where I'd worked to see what they were doing. The factory was gone, just piles of rubble. But the company sent me to Portland to their factory up there. There was no such thing as welfare. Your welfare was right among your friends.

"All the big stores, Emporium, White House, all that, of course they were in the center of town, they were just rubble. They put up temporary stores on Fillmore Street. I remember one store so vividly, Weinstein's. He bought anything people would need in a hurry, he found this building on Fillmore Street and just put big crates of stuff in there—that's how they got started again."

George B., a handsome, articulate man of 83, was born in 1898 in San Francisco. He was 8 years old in 1906 and remembered the earthquake this way:

"It so happens on the morning of the earthquake my Uncle Joe and his wife Gussie were visiting from Los Angeles. Uncle Joe occupied the best room in our house which resulted in my brother and I being thrown out of our room. I was put in a bed someone got out of the basement, in my mother and father's room. On this particular morning at 5 a.m. I was awakened by the bed rocking as if I were on a train. It was common in these bedrooms to have a little wash basin in a corner of the room and up on a high shelf to have glasses to brush your teeth. I looked up there and these glasses were teetering and finally one of these glasses teetered to the edge of the shelf, off the shelf, down to the floor and shattered. The second, down it came, the third glass, down it came. There was screaming and hollering from down in Aunt Gussie's room—she had gone into hysterics. No one knew what had happened.

"Well, someone got me out of bed and told me to get dressed. Everyone went out on the street. The chimneys weren't reinforced so they all collapsed—there were plenty of bricks so we carried them out to the curb and made little ovens so we could cook outside—you couldn't cook inside. This was Boy Scouting such as we'd never enjoyed. We'd never known our neighbors before but now everyone was running up and down the streets, you knew what everyone was eating, and we were having a great time. You had to queue up for food and water. We soon found, my brother and I (he was 9 or 10 and I was 8), when children queued up in line they got better treatment than the adults and we just queued up one place and another and brought food back to the whole block. And the bigger boys brought the water, which they probably had to get from two or three blocks away. All the mains and sewers were pretty well destroyed. Military law was declared—you couldn't go downtown, all the windows were broken, looting was taking place, people were going out to Golden Gate Park and pitching tents if they could

All the shrewd contrivances and safeguards of man had been thrown out of gear by thirty seconds' twitching of the earth-crust.

By Wednesday afternoon, inside of twelve hours, half the heart of the city was gone. At that time I watched the vast conflagration from out on the bay. It was dead calm. Not a flicker of wind stirred. Yet from every side wind was pouring in upon the city. East, west, north, and south, strong winds were blowing upon the doomed city. The heated air rising made an enormous suck. Thus did the fire of itself build its own colossal chimney through the atmosphere. Day and night this dead calm continued, and yet, near to the flames, the wind was often half a gale, so mighty was the suck.

Wednesday night saw the destruction of the very heart of the city. Dynamite was lavishly used, and many of San Francisco's proudest structures were crumbled by man himself into ruins, but there was no withstanding the onrush of the flames.

—Jack London, "Jack London's Eyewitness Account," *Collier's*

find one, sleeping out in the open. This was the condition until the ground stabilized and the fire was brought under control. Until they knew the Van Ness Avenue dynamiting was successful they didn't know whether the whole city was going to be wiped out. We used to walk up Webster Street hill at night to the park on Jackson and Octavia and look down below there just to see the flames; it was unbelievable—the panorama you looked at was just fire unchecked, because the water mains had been depleted, no way to check it whatever. It was a pretty horrible time for people. But for kids it was exciting and fun—we didn't realize the seriousness of the situation.

"The one aim of everyone was to get out of San Francisco, but how? We had a horse and wagon, which was practically like having a gold mine. People would pay any price to get that horse and wagon of ours to take them down to the ferry when there was a resumption of some transportation, to get them across the bay to Oakland and get them going on the railroads or whatever. So in the destitute condition we were in, why, obviously my brother and the family were just waiting feverishly for martial law to be lifted so they would be permitted to do this.

"Well, the day finally arrived, probably a week or more from the time all these groceries had been brought in and martial law had been declared. So, bring the horse out and attach him to the buggy which was in the stable. But lo and behold, when it came to bringing the horse out—the horse had been back there in our backyard eating for a week and doing no exercising—for the life of us we couldn't get that horse out of that cabbage patch in the backyard. The space between those houses on the Avenues is narrow, you know. Now this may seem comical but it was tragic! They had to diet or starve that horse for four or five days before they could get him out of there and by that time some of the gold was out of the mine! Nobody realized he was getting so fat—they had too many other things to worry about. A bonanza at their door and this poor family couldn't collect on it…"

Marie R., another friend's mother, was born in 1886 in San Francisco, to French parents. A short, pretty woman, Marie at 93 had smooth, fair skin and her face was practically unlined. Her mind was as sharp as her wit. Marie and her family lived on Hudson Avenue in south San Francisco. She finished the eighth grade and then was withdrawn from school.

When she was an adolescent, Marie was severely anemic. Nothing the doctor prescribed seemed to help. Finally her father, who worked at the slaughterhouse as a butcher, took her to the kosher slaughterhouse where she was given warm, fresh blood from just slaughtered cattle and made to drink it. Apparently it cured her.

Marie was an exquisite seamstress; even at 93 she sewed beautifully. It was work she had done most of her life, often for very wealthy families. She liked to work and remarked that after the

Will Irwin, a respected observer who knew the pre-fire quake city as well as anybody, insisted to his death that something intangible, some mystical quality, vanished in the flames of 1906. "There was only one San Francisco," he often said. "The city that arose after the quake was quite another thing."

—Herb Caen,
One Man's San Francisco

earthquake she got very tired of staying home, so she went out and applied for a job as a maid but was hired as a governess to teach French to the children of a wealthy family. She married in 1907 at 21. Her first husband, a Mexican, was murdered by his mistress. Marie was reluctant to talk about him. She married George R. in 1927.

When Marie described the 1906 quake she, too, mentioned the devastation and the horrifying fires, the collapsed chimneys and cooking in the street, but the area in which her family lived was a long way from the epicenter of the earthquake.

"My father was in the hospital, French Hospital, when the earthquake happened. We were worried about him, of course. Nothing happened to the house, just the chimney toppled. My uncle and aunt lived next door. We didn't know what was happening downtown. There were policemen on horseback then, one was very infatuated with my cousin next door so he came to see how we were. My uncle drove a big four-horse team to deliver meat to San Francisco. And, you know, the slaughterhouse toppled into the bay; it was right on the water and I can just see those horses swimming and my uncle in this little rowboat saving them, grabbing the horses and trying to get them out of the water. My father was brought home from the hospital in a laundry wagon after the earthquake.

"The first time I saw the fire I cried. We were on top of a hill and I couldn't believe it—we didn't know. Luckily we had all the supplies we wanted. My mother said to me, 'Go down in the road and if you see a poor family who needs help, bring them home.' We had a good basement, all cement floor and clean. I brought home a family: father, mother, and two kids; they had this little wagon, I remember. They were running away from the city. And then we thought we'd never get them out! They stayed about six weeks I think."

Alma W. lived to be 102 years old. Marie R. died at age 97. I met George B. only once on the occasion of the taping.

Alma and Marie were exceptional; hardy, self-confident women who enjoyed working and valued themselves, their lives, and their work. And that despite the fact that one's philandering father and one's philandering husband had been murdered by their lovers. It seems to me an additional extraordinary coincidence that the earthquake of 1989 occurred on October 17th. Alma W. was born on October 17th. Marie R. died on October 17th. Perhaps I should take up astrology.

Back to 1989. John and Emmanuelle finally made it back to Berkeley at eleven on the morning of October 18th. Tomas, a perfectly contented infant after a good night's sleep, was happy to see them. But not nearly as happy as I was.

Betty Ann Webster is a clinical social worker, freelance writer, oral historian, and a committed traveler. She has lived and worked in India, returning to visit eight times. She currently resides in Berkeley, California, and travels wherever and whenever possible.

＊

Insouciance served San Francisco's citizens well when the great earthquake of 1906 struck. Alice B. Toklas, who was born and raised in the city, wrote in her memoir, *What is Remembered:*

> Life went on calmly until one morning we and our home were violently shaken by an earthquake. Gas was escaping. I hurried to my father's bedroom, pulled up the shades, pulled back the curtains and opened the windows. My father was apparently asleep. Do get up, I said to him. The city is on fire. That, said he with his usual calm, will give us a black eye in the East.

Toklas walked up the hill to the Presidio, and her father, finally risen, "walked down to the business quarter to see if the vaults of his bank were holding."

—Luree Miller, *Literary Hills of San Francisco*

⋆ ⋆ ⋆

Mean Streets

A mother weighs the benefits and risks of
raising her children in an urban environment.

THIS HOW IT USUALLY STARTS: I SEE A HEADLINE IN THE PAPER OR one of our cars gets broken into or I'm in bed overhearing an argument on the street and wondering whether or when to call 911. Then my throat constricts and the thought erupts: I want to move away from here, and then I'm moving all right, off and running.

This is how it started this morning: the kids and I walked together to the Ashby BART station, them to take the Fremont train to school; me to board the San Francisco train I take every day to work. Inside the station, two BART cops are talking to a boy twelve or thirteen, about Peter's age. The boy is crying and covering one eye with his hand. He looks as embarrassed to be crying in public as Peter or Jesse would be, all the briefcase people staring as they herd themselves through the turnstiles.

"He got beat up," Peter says flatly, slicing through my denial of that same thought. I see that he's got that studied "Shit Happens" look on his downy little face. Jesse's big brown eyes get bigger; he gives me one of those surreptitious sidelooks that says, simultaneously, "Don't get overprotective; I'm eleven years old; don't embarrass me," and, "Are you my mother? Are you protecting me?"

The cops take notes as the kid talks in bursts through the sobs that keep collapsing his swollen face.

"At eight o'clock in the morning," I mutter, and immediately regret my words. Peter exhales loudly, shakes his flat-topped head, and gives me a long-suffering frown. "Mom," he begins, and I know I'm in for it. "People get beat up here all the time. Teenagers hang around in the parking lot and wait for younger kids to beat up on. We're used to it. Why do you make such a big deal out of every little thing?"

My heart aches. I'm torn, as always in these interactions, between hanging on to my self, whether my kids like her responses or not ("My babies! This world is too harsh for my babies...") and the cool, detached, streetwise Mom who mimics, and therefore is acceptable to, my children ("Shit Happens").

I try for a compromise between the two. "What do you guys do to protect yourselves?" I don't know why I always say "you guys;" it's Peter, the shop steward for the younger half of our family, who invariably provides the answer, while Jesse silently and attentively fact-checks his brother's response. "Run," Peter says without hesitation, the tightening around his downcast eyes the only hint of emotion. Jesse focuses on me intently, then quickly looks away.

This is how it starts, the self-berating that builds on its own momentum. I can't believe I'm raising my kids like this. How can I call myself a mother when I can't even keep my kids safe? How can they turn out to be the sweet, sensitive men I promised myself I'd produce when the life I've given them requires such callousness, such denial, such smooth detached responses to fear? I moved to California to raise my kids so they wouldn't grow up to be crime-glazed New Yorkers. Now they're more jaded than I am. How did I let this happen—to them, to me?

The kids' train pulls in. I squeeze Jesse's arm good-bye, the most affection I am permitted to display in public, and look longingly down the platform where Peter stands (so as not to be seen in the presence of his mother). I'm in luck today: graced with a glance from my firstborn son. Peter's curt nod in my general direction satisfies me, because it has to. Jesse lets his hand graze mine as he steps away from me into the crowd. They do love me.

I watch my children whiz by me in the silver train: Jesse looking young and tall and innocent; two cars back Peter looking nearly man-sized and bored. All that work, all their lives, to teach them to know their own feelings. Will I ever again be allowed to know what they feel?

If I'd raised them on a farm in Petaluma, a hilltop in Marin, in a commune in North Berkeley, would they be as open with me on a subway platform as they are in their bedrooms in the dark, way past their bedtimes when they keep me up way past mine, so I can scratch their velvety backs and inhale their puppy scents while they talk to me for hours about making out with girls at parties, and how outraged and afraid they were after the Rodney King verdict, and whether it's entrepreneurial or unethical that Peter rents out his "Fuck Authority" button for a dollar a period at school, and the likelihood of Jesse's making a living someday as a comic-book artist, and—nine years after the fact—why their dad and I got a divorce?

A small man in a Chevron cap hoses off the sidewalk of the Rincon Center, checking you out for a millisecond. At the Spear Tower, a blazered guard sits in an ergonomic office chair in an empty, polished lobby. He looks at you and picks his ear. On Market Street, a man in a suit rests on a bench, smoking a cigarette as if it were filled with essential vitamins. A girl walks briskly past, carrying a canvas shoulder bag and an Evian bottle. Two cable cars sit idle on California Street, their operators reading quietly. Figures stagger out of the office towers in trench coats and carrying umbrellas, lugging big briefcases of paperwork back to their homes. Their gaunt faces and slumped posture suggest a thorough and recent horsewhipping, and it all starts up again tomorrow morning.

"Shit man, goin' mumble mumble, gotta help with a little change?" slurs a wild-eyed bum at Union Square, extending a beat-up cup. "Shit man, mumble slur mumble, fucking corporations."

Which corporations? you ask.

"All of 'em!" hollers the bum. "Now gimme some change!"

—Jack Boulware, "Night and the City," *San Francisco Weekly*

If I'd sent them to private school? If they were girls? If I wasn't a lesbian? If the women's movement had succeeded?

Moments later I embark on the San Francisco train, alone.

When I get like this, the world around me tends to cooperate. Today's morning newspaper headline announces: "Seven Murders in 24 Hours Jolt Oakland." Oakland, I remind myself needlessly, is where I have entrenched myself—where I own a house and pay taxes and send my children to school. I imagine my richer, wiser, and infinitely more fortunate friends in Mill Valley, Menlo Park, North Berkeley reading that headline and wondering what Meredith's problem is, anyway. When will she ever get over that outdated commitment to raising her kids in a "mixed" (meaning: mostly black and poor) neighborhood and move somewhere safe, already?…

Since the 1989 earthquake, since the week after it when I moved with my lover and my children into our still-shuddering dream house on the fault line, every moment of stillness has felt to me like a warning, a gathering of the forces of disaster preparing for the next strike: a brief cease-fire between the sounds of over-powered undermuffled American cars screaming through the streets with cop cars in hot pursuit; between diagnoses of AIDS and cancer in people I count on for my happiness; between dark rainy nights when my kids come home a few minutes late to find me shaking with terror and rage, between earthquakes and firestorms.

This is how it goes on from here: "I've got to get away from Oakland, get safe. I'll put the kids in private school, convince their father to move to New Mexico, Vermont, Marin…"

Eight years ago I uprooted my children, and eventually my joint-custodial ex-husband, from suburban San Jose, where we never locked our doors and a car break-in was a gossip-worthy neighbor-hood event. I wanted to raise my kids in what I then referred to as "the real world." I wanted them to know people who weren't white. I wanted neighbors who didn't wear bras. I wanted to walk to demonstrations at Sproul Plaza and Mime Troupe plays in the park.

And so, after five years of sociopolitical deprivation and emo-tional isolation in the stucco tracts of San Jose, I put my $10,000 divorce settlement down on an $80,000 cottage on the Berkeley-Oakland border and hurtled myself and my kids into the closest thing to a sixties life I could construct.

I put Peter and Jesse in an Oakland public school and went to endless meetings to make sure their education was politically, if not academically, correct. I rode my bicycle to the market and rode home with my backpack full of exotic lettuces and tomato-basil baguettes. I helped organize our Neighborhood Watch Association. I took my kids to puppet shows about Nicaragua at the neighborhood community center, whose walls were papered with flyers announcing solidarity marches, multicultural day care centers, and incest survivor support groups.

I got to know my neighbors, the mix I'd dreamed of: longhaired carpenter guys and shorthaired carpenter gals. Friendly Southern black men whose grandchildren played double Dutch on the sidewalk. A coven of pagans who danced with flutes in their adjoining backyards. A couple of lesbian chiropractors, and never mind about the crack house up the block and the speed freaks across the street and the unemployed young man next door who rattled my house and my brain with pounding rap music all day while I sat at my computer trying to earn a living as a freelance journalist.

I slept with a crowbar next to my bed for the first few months and installed a burglar alarm in my house, but for the first time since I'd left the Haight-Ashbury in 1972 and embarked on a course that led me, eventually, to Marxism and ten years of factory organizing and living among white working-class people who'd never met a Jew, let alone a communist, and believed (correctly, based on their own empirical experience) that there was no difference between the two—I felt again that I was living among my people.

Five years later I sold the first house I'd ever lived in without parents or a man, the nest from which I'd launched my brave new life, for $185,000—an inadvertent beneficiary of the Bay Area real estate boom—and bought a three-story Victorian a few blocks away, big enough so that after six years together my lover, Ann, and I could live under the same roof, and Peter and Jesse would each have his own door to shut.

Now I find myself poised for what must honestly be named white flight, bound to my urban life not by principles but by the geographic restrictions imposed by joint custody—and by profound ambivalence.

As my parents did, as I scorned my parents for doing, I find myself yearning for the good and safe old days, when the drugs being bought and sold on my block were pot and peyote, when the absence of children in my life kept my lofty child-rearing principles untested and unshakable, when I never leashed my dog, locked my car, hesitated to take a walk alone at night.

As my parents did, as I came of age swearing I would never do, I find myself worrying about who my children's role models and friends are, and why my children choose them, and what these strangers might teach or convince my children to do.

As my parents did, as I never could imagine myself doing, I find myself turning to money as the balm for my fears, and I resolve to earn or somehow acquire more of it: money to move into a neighborhood or, better yet, a town, in which beepers are worn by pediatricians, not twelve-year-olds; in which the silence of night is not shattered by gunfire or the rattling of shopping carts filled with rags and bottles being pushed down the street; in which bicycles are left unchained outside shops without cast-iron bars on their windows, and teenagers speak politely to each other's parents on the telephone.

As my parents did, twice each month I tell Peter and Jesse that tomorrow the housecleaner is coming, and I want them to clean their rooms, so she can clean their rooms. And, just as I did 30 years ago, my sons stall and argue and invoke their right to privacy and constitutional amendments not yet written, until I glower and growl and threaten to withhold their allowances and inevitably end the evening sulking in my room, blaming myself for spoiling these boys who will someday, I am certain, leave wet towels and underwear on the floors of their own houses, and will therefore be divorced by their feminist wives and separated from their own children—all because their mother, who could afford to hire a house-cleaner, trained them to expect a woman to swab out their dirty toilets, change their flannel sheets, and pick up their smelly socks.

As my parents were, I am called to parent conferences three, six, eleven times in each school year, and confronted with relentless rows of F's in Citizenship, which causes me to bemoan my child-hood, the sixties, my own and my children's laziness, everything that has caused me to fail so miserably as a disciplinarian. And yes, I have uttered aloud on several occasions the two words I swore I'd never say—"private school"—and my politically correct commit-ment to "fighting to make the public schools work" has been re-placed by the indignation of a property-tax payer at the failure of the schools to make their own damn selves work.

How have I come to these transgressions?

Is it that my kids have graduated from the safe if underfunded elementary school that I used to complain about having to drive them to and from every day, and they now take public transporta-tion to a junior high school where young men twice my weight punch and kick the flesh of my flesh and steal the Chicago Bulls caps off their stylish shorn heads?

Is it that life in the city—any city, but most certainly the one I live in, whose very name, to those who don't live here and many who do, evokes all that is terror-provoking in modern urban life—has simply gotten exponentially worse (along with my fear level) since I lived here happily eight years ago?

Is it that, despite all I'd sworn would never happen to me, the upper-middle-class values I ingested along with formula from ster-ilized bottles have curdled and congealed in my middle-aged soul?

And whatever the source of these twin fears—of the dangers in my life, and of a solution that contradicts all I've believed in—what can I do about it now?

What should I do about it now?

Would I be happier, would I feel like a better mother, would I be a better mother if I sent my kids off on mountain bikes to the very nearly all-white school I used to pass every morning on my way to work in Mill Valley, where the blond kids dress the way my kids dress, but without benefit of proximity to the culture whose style they're emulating, whose overheard conversations once jolted me into a rare moment of perspective: Meredith, you'd be kicking yourself every day if you'd brought your kids up in a place like this.

Would my kids be happier?

Driving through a small California town one night on our way to a weekend at our cabin in the woods, I dreamily ask Peter and Jesse, "Wouldn't you love to move to the country? Where people are friendly and we wouldn't have to be afraid all the time?"

"Yeah, right, Mom," answers Jesse, rolling his eyes in the rearview mirror. "Then we could hang out in the 7-Eleven parking lot every Friday night and smoke cigarettes. Sounds really great."

"But what's so much better about living where we live?" I persist. "What do you do on Friday nights that's so exciting?"

"I couldn't live without Telegraph," says Jesse of the Berkeley avenue on which the People's Park war was waged, where his father was shot while throwing tear gas grenades back at the National Guardsmen who'd fired them at him, where today homeless panhandlers extend their begging cups from sleeping bags stretched across the sidewalk, and Jesse is regularly threatened and occasionally robbed by the boys he beats at video games.

During a family trip to New York last summer, Peter overheard me muttering to myself that I could have chose a worse place than Oakland to raise my kids. "I'm glad I grew up in Oakland, Mom," he said. "Now I'm prepared for anything. If I decide I want to live in New York someday, I know I'll be able to handle myself."

I'm anchored now in the city I chose, the life I chose, the life I chose all those years and decisions ago, because it's not just me, not just my lover and me, who live in it. This is the place and the life, the streets and the people, my children know and therefore is the place and the life they want to be in, and are old enough to say they don't want to be wrenched away from. Backed into a nineties corner by my sixties politics—and by my sons, whose childhoods and values reflect those politics—I am forced to confront the most difficult decision of all. Can I carry on the struggle to overcome what's wrong in the world, while keeping my children, my family, myself safe and sane within it?

I remember the night a year ago when Peter, at age twelve, requested (and was denied) the right to carry a knife, for self-protection, to junior high school. "I didn't raise you guys to believe in violence," I declared.

"Make up your mind, Mom," replied my clear-eyed son. "If you didn't want us to grow up this way, you shouldn't have raised us in this neighborhood."

Make up my mind, indeed.

Meredith Maran started her journalistic career as co-publisher of the nation's first high school underground newspaper at the "prestigious" Bronx High School of Science (circa '67). Since then she has lived life as a back-to-the-land hippie in Taos, a union organizer on Bay Area assembly lines, a suburban wife and mother, a freelance journalist for magazines ranging from Bride's *to* Mother Jones; *from* Parenting *to* New Age Journal, *an urban lesbian mother, and editor/creative vice-president/creative consultant to a host of socially responsible companies including Banana Republic, Smith & Hawken, Working Assets, and Ben & Jerry's Homemade.*

★

I live in a sunny, picturesque neighborhood of San Francisco called Noe (Noh-ee) Valley. It has quiet streets, magnificent views, four coffee bars, three bookstores, two bakeries, two parks, a half-dozen fine restaurants, the church featured in the Whoopi Goldberg movie *Sister Act,* and lovingly restored Victorian and Edwardian homes. In many ways, Noe Valley is an urban oasis where people of astonishingly diverse backgrounds live shoulder-to-shoulder in surprising harmony: owners and renters; young and old; families and childless; straight and gay/lesbian; Catholic, Protestant, and Jewish; and white, Asian, and African-American, including recent immigrants from France, Thailand, China, and the Philippines.

The neighborhood's popularity and tranquility have driven housing prices sky-high, but many residents choking on rent or mortgage payments believe that they have purchased reasonable safety from crime. As I overheard one woman say to another outside our local coffee shop recently, Noe Valley is a place where a single woman can feel safe going out alone after dark for a decaf latte. It's a good place, she added, to raise a family.

I agree—my little corner of the cosmos is a reasonably decent place to raise a family. But anyone who calles Noe Valley "safe" is living in a day-dream. I know because I'm a devoted reader of the police column in our monthly neighborhood newspaper, the *Noe Valley Voice*. In a typical month, our 100-block neighborhood experiences a few burglaries and car thefts, one or two muggings or sexual assaults, and a half-dozen acts of vandalism. (Actual neighborhood crime figures are undoubtedly higher; the police column covers only reported crimes.)

—Michael Castleman, "Opportunity Knocks," *Mother Jones*

✦ ✦ ✦

Sharing the Pain

A sometime voyeur searches for creatures of the night.

AS THE HINDUS AND BUDDHISTS KNOW ONLY TOO WELL, IN THE beginning was Desire, rather than the Word, as the Christians would say. Having heard whisperings about a dark and mysterious sado-masochistic-bondage *Scene* in San Francisco, and being a good Hindu, I acted upon my whimsical desire and made my way to a sado-parlor of some renown.

The bouncer/gate boy, pale white but in black leather, motorcycle garb, a fuzz of vertical hair running from the lower lip to the chin, is from Alabama. Guarding the entrance to the sado parlor is his full-time job. He is affable and chatty, and is occasionally joined by an SP (sado parlor) gal, all hugs and girlish giggles as she mingles and mushes with the bouncer boy. Intricate, colorful tattoos are visible wherever her flesh shows; a sparkling metallic loop pierces her belly-button; more metal loops between her nostrils and drips below her nose, the kind of nose ring one sees among the cattle of India and Nepal. They are both young and hip, on the cutting edge, if not in the "pierced zone." The bouncer boy sounds uncharacteristically optimistic and bourgeois. Says he, "My father, back home, he approves! I have a steady job, a car, and a motorcycle. I'm looking into going to college soon." No nihilism here, for sure.

"When does the club close?" I ask.

"Three in the morning, but most start leaving around one-thirty, last call. So the less intelligent ones drift off to other bars where they can drink. The club has really been supported by rockers and others who like to come here and hang out after hours."

I like the way he said, "The less intelligent ones." The boy will go far, I know.

Another black leathered male joins him. He has a braided goatee. The bouncer boy laughs wildly. Stroking his thin, vertical, faux goatee, he gloats, "Man, I almost braided my goatee too, but I'm really glad I didn't. I shaved it off. Most of it."

The gal with the cattle nose ring now throws herself into the arms of the newcomer with the braided goatee. Hugs and mushes make me think there is more "touchy feely" here than rage and despair.

Inside, I pay a five dollar entry fee. The back of my wrist is stamped so I have "in-out privi-

> *It is the paradise of ignorance, anarchy, and general yellowness.*
>
> *It needs another quake, another whiff of fire, and more than all else, a steady tradewind of grape-shot.*
>
> *It is a moral penal colony. It is the worst of all the Sodom and Gommorrahs in our modern world.*
>
> —Ambrose Bierce, *Letters of Ambrose Bierce* (1922)

leges." Loud, thumping, lyricless industrial music reverberates throughout the cavernous space. Some clean-cut college kids wearing jeans and button-down shirts are playing pool and drinking bottled beer, swaggering as only college kids can do. The bar, the cavernous dance floor, the entire club is almost empty. Above the dance floor hang slowly revolving "disco balls" the likes of which I haven't seen since my own undergraduate days when the crowd would go wild when some sort of mist rose from the dance floor. Looks as if things haven't changed much in two decades.

Next to the entrance, opposite the pool tables, two chic underdressed young girls in stockings, very short skirts, hair streaked in henna, rings and bracelets all over fingers and wrists, high heels, are selling rings, playing cards that have anti-drugs and anti-smoking messages (is there irony in these messages, I wonder? humor macabre?), and t-shirts with logos of "Bondage a Go Go" around a picture of a bound woman—fifteen bucks, thank you.

I go upstairs to another bar where a woman who appears to be of mixed race—a blonde black woman—is selling more stuff: incense, candles, massage oils in tiny bottles, colorful salt crystals in plastic bags, fragrant bubble bath items. I'm beginning to feel that the club is a meeting ground of the new-agers and the leather-clad, tattooed, body-parts-pierced "rough crowd," with both displaying the aggressive spirit of fin-de-siecle capitalism.

I order a beer. No one is handcuffed to the bar. I ask the bartender about it and he says that that specific bondage item has been taken off the menu. Diagonally across the bar, there is a corral where a few young men and women mill about, the main attraction, as it turned out. The girls look suspiciously under-age, precocious even as they look tough, very under-dressed, all black clothing that stretches when even a muscle (or in most cases, fat) moves. A girl with long, thick, puffy hair has a black t-shirt on that says on the front "Fuck Me" and on the back "Then Leave." Some whips with stripped leather are on display on the wall above a sign that says, "Toys 4 Sale." There it is again, this optimistic spirit of the entrepreneur in this cavern of delinquency.

Food is also available, and near the kitchen, a notice of health again: "No smoking near the kitchen area and condiments."

Meanwhile, the patrons are arriving. It's a mixed crowd: college kids, 9-5 working folks, Generation X-ers. Dress ranges from t-shirts and jeans to bondage gear. Lots of silver jewelry and tattoos on much exposed flesh. There are many bondage wanna-bes, especially pre-pubescent suburban girls, many wearing slips and bra, and a coat to throw over when they step out to catch some fresh air, for the air is getting thick as the bodies begin to arrive and the action on the dance floor and in the corral begins in earnest.

I meet a couple who tell me their names are Daphne and Master Dick. Daphne is a young woman dressed all in black; Dick is thin-lipped, hooded-eyed, and apparently twice her age. She is getting an "electric" caress by a short, tubby, sweaty but very pleasant man who has some sort of a drill-like instrument, wired and connected to a socket and from which bluish sparks fly. He runs his nails all over her, her fishnet, crotchless stockings, black vinyl skirt, false eyelashes, magenta-black lipstick and eyeshades, black nails, but *false* nose ring, just as Master Dick has a *false* ear ring. One can tell these are not serious disciples of the diabolical Marquis de Sade, may the Devil torture his soul. This false note is especially jarring when one sees women stick out their pierced tongues!

Daphne shudders and sometimes squeals as the sweaty, tubby electric caresser runs his nails over her bare arms and runs his tongue over that exposed flesh. He moves his hands in and around the fish-netted legs, as Master Dick glares. Daphne shudders with delight. The Hindu licks his suddenly dry lips.

Soon, there are butts upturned on a carpenter's horse. Fat butts, skinny butts, bikinied butts, tattooed butts: they are stroked, swished, smacked. Girls' arms are spread and clamped to an overhanging bar; they're blindfolded with a fancy accessory that looks like aviator sunglasses. Then they are stroked with feathers, furs, whips, tassels; a lone woman—hands bound—is kissed, stroked, licked, and tantalized by a half-dozen men and women. The bound woman squirms.

*S*HE SAYS: *I sat on the rack behind the harness swing and slowly adjusted to the environment. I was beneath ground. The bottom floor. In a swirl of confused emotions, my curiousity at war with the sleaziness of this sex parlor, I watched the voyeurs across from us. Two men in their forties or fifties, quietly peeked through a window and watched the two young lesbians play their game of tease and torture. This was seedy, and digusted me. I was lost in a sea of contemptibility.*

HE SAYS: *As we contemplated the suspension harness hanging from the ceiling, a weird device that wrapped a wide leather strap around the chest and held the ankles in loops at the ends of a spreader bar, a softspoken, nice looking young man in his skivvies appeared at the door and introduced himself as Ted.*

"I was wondering," he said, "If you would care to suspend me and, well, whatever."

—Dick Silver and Daphne Cole, "Love Hurts"

On a sawhorse, a small, thin young woman is bound upturned, her naked upper body exposed; she is only wearing a leather bikini bottom. Her Master (Pleasure-Giver) works on her like a dedicated artist, using a shining hunter's knife (no doubt dull-edged) and a small, curved scythe where the sharpened blade shines like a crescent moon. The master is using both knives all over her body. The girl has her eyes closed. Her high-heeled feet tremble occasionally. Her lips, like the Hovering Hindu's, are dry. She doesn't lick them, unlike the Hindu.

I overhear a thick frat boy say in bewildered joy, "You mean these dudes get paid to whip those chicks?"

Two suburban post-pubescent gals, blonde and brave, stand behind me watching the master do his thing with the knives. One says to the other, "The first drop of blood and I'm out the friggin' door."

And so the action continues. The dance floor is full of swaying, whirling bodies; blue, red, green spotlights dance off the revolving disco ball above the dance floor, which is thick with cigarette and incense smoke, as well as body heat. Yet it is all paradoxically unerotic. The body does not respond, the soul remains sacred. Even the voyeur is quickly bored. It is quickly becoming comical. The participants in their S&M acts are young and eager, and drinking from bottles of "Jolt" cola, as if more adrenaline were required to launch their eager bodies and souls.

And as the Hovering Hindu shuffles around, he is thinking of Dostoevsky's *Notes from the Underground,* and he thinks that only a person with a Dostoevskian delirium, with his epileptic seizure, could do an extended riff on the scene around me. But then maybe not. For this rather tame, wanna-be scene lacks even that "fear and loathing" that might attract the latter-day disciple of gonzo journalist Hunter Thompson.

I think of Dostoevsky because he speaks about how when a person is jaded by normal, ordinary pleasure, he seeks to go beyond these normal bounds because the normal is boring. So the Russian writer remembers some historical Queen who had golden needles stuck into the breasts of her slave girls, and got pleasure from watching their pain.

At two a.m., his mind full of tattoos, black leather, silver jewelry, butts, boobs, pubes, and Dostoevsky, the Hovering Hindu decides it is time to return to his hovel. For there he will find peace, and for him, that is bondage enough.

Rajendra S. Khadka was born in Nepal, educated by Jesuits in Kathmandu and Yankees in New England. His desultory career pursuits have included freelance journalism, managing a movie theater during the pre-VCR days, and a chef-on-call. He is now an editor at Travelers' Tales. *When he is not sleeping, he can be found cooking, reading, or practicing zazen by doing nothing in the People's Republic of Berkeley.*

*

We were two inexperienced kids from Indiana, what did we know? The Ford LTD was stuffed and our parents were strong and sweet as we drove away. We were so confident. I can't recall one specific conversation during that drive west, but we talked nonstop during those five days. The high didn't wear off until we spotted the trademark San Francisco skyline for the first time. It was the Emerald City and the thrill of arrival was tinged with dread. We knew no one, had no place to live, no jobs, and small bank accounts to open. The first night we kept driving and stayed at the Travel Lodge near Oakland Stadium.

For days we crossed the bridge in search of a cheap San Francisco apartment. There weren't any. We ended up with a one-bedroom for which we had to pay cash each month. It was on Divisadero and Haight Streets, in a diverse, ethnic neighborhood with a few residents who'd dropped a little too much acid decades ago. The next two weeks were spent job searching during the day and staying in every night. It was a strange city and who knew what would happen out there? We were accustomed to keggers and friendly faces. One teary night we walked to the phone booth down the block and tried not to cry at the sound of Mom and Dad's "Well, how is everything?" They'd been right, it was far away.

There was one guy in the area who I'd known since the second grade. We'd been voted "Most Theatrical" in high school. Since he'd played my father, brother, and husband in school plays, I felt close enough to him. John came down from Sebastopol to take us girls out on the town. And he brought his male lover with him; as he explained it, he wasn't hetero or homosexual, just "sexual." Okay, no problem. My only friend would not be fixing us up with anyone.

The four of us went to Hamburger Mary's, where an animated man in a dress was our waiter. Then to The Stud, where John and I danced next to two men in dresses. Surprisingly, that night set me free. I still decided to keep to men as love interests, but my worldview had been jump-started. I'd finally let loose and was promptly seduced by San Francisco.

—Kay Schaber, "No Turning Back"

WILLIAM PLUMMER

✦ ✦ ✦

A Survivor

On second thought...

He woke on the morning of August 21, 1985, with the certainty that he would be dead by nightfall. It was another routine scorcher in California's San Joaquin Valley, where Kenneth Baldwin lived with his wife, Ellen, both then 28, and their 3-year-old daughter, Catherine. Ken and Ellen had both grown up in the Valley. They liked its dry heat, flat terrain, and rural flavor—so much so that just three years earlier they'd bought their first home, on Almond Blossom Lane in the farming community of Tracy, about 60 miles southeast of San Francisco. Ellen was a graphic designer at nearby Lawrence Livermore National Laboratory, a site for nuclear weapons research. Ken, a $15,000-a-year computer draftsman, worked in an architectural firm 30 miles away in Stockton. Parents, house owners, and a dual career couple, the Baldwins seemed in perfect sync with their times, yet their marriage was divided by a secret. Though he could never bring himself to tell Ellen, Ken was being crushed by a tightening sense of despair.

As the couple walked out to their cars that morning, Baldwin told his wife that he planned to work overtime and would be unable to pick Catherine up from the babysitter.

What Kenneth Baldwin really planned to do was kill himself.

"I had been thinking about suicide for some time," says Ken. "But I don't really know why, on that day, I decided to jump from the bridge. I had been depressed about work for months. I was afraid I was going to be fired. Ellen had supported the family for two years while I went to school to learn drafting. She had really sacrificed for me, and I was going to let her down. I felt incredible pressure. In school I had gotten good grades, but out in the real world I felt I couldn't cut it. Or worse, that my family couldn't depend on me.

"I really believed that killing myself would be an act of love for my family. I imagined Ellen marrying someone who was very responsible, a man who could always make the mortgage payments. But I have to admit that part of my desire to die was selfish. I was in such pain, such anguish, I wanted it to stop. I wanted to escape."

Baldwin chose the Golden Gate Bridge because "it wasn't messy" like some other forms of suicide. "I heard the current in the bay was so strong the bodies were often swept out to sea and sometimes never found. I found that reassuring. I didn't want my family going through a funeral. I just wanted them to forget me, to let me go." And there was something familiar about the bridge. As a boy, he had occasionally walked across it with his parents, even spit over its side with school chums.

On that day, Baldwin drove to work but never arrived at his office, he says. "But I think I wanted to give myself one more chance to do something normal like drive to work, just to see if it would break me out of the depression. But the closer I got to work, the more I wanted to jump." Last minute hesitation is common among those drawn to the bridge for self-destruction. Suicide prevention officials say they log more hotline calls from a pay phone at the bridge's toll plaza than from any phone in the country.

Baldwin never stopped the car on the 90-minute journey. "I just headed for the bridge," he says. Elated that he had finally made up his mind to die, he turned up the radio full blast and sang along with the tunes. The music went out of him, however, when he got out of his car and actually stood on the bridge. He was attacked by misgivings. "I kept thinking of my wife and daughter. I loved them deeply. And I wondered what it would feel like to hit the water. I realized it might hurt. I didn't want to fall on top of a boat. I didn't want anyone standing near me when I jumped. I felt I had been treated badly, and I wanted to tell the world how I felt. No one really noticed me. Well, they were going to notice me now. Suddenly, there were many things to consider...."

Baldwin counted to ten but couldn't jump. When he reached ten the second time, he glanced briefly across the bay at the city of San Francisco and went over the side. "I remember my hands leaving the railing, the sensation of falling. I instantly realized I had made a mistake. I can't tell you how frightening that was. I didn't want to die. Yet here I was heading for certain death. There was nothing I could do about it. I was falling feet first with my legs pulled under me a little. Before I hit, I blacked out from fear, I guess."

After falling for three seconds, Baldwin smashed into the water at 75 miles per hour. The impact subjected parts of his body to pressures of 15,000 pounds per square inch, a power often likened to that of a speeding car hitting a brick wall. Jumpers generally suffer massive internal

Perhaps there is something about water, or anything bridging a body of water, that seems to attract people to jump off out down into it. Very few people jump down into a pit of manure, except by accident, but there is something about a bridge over clear water, no matter how far down (perhaps the farther the better), that does pull people down into it, toward it. I know this pull well, and I have no feeling of impatience or anything but tolerance for the people who jump....

I have not said that the Golden Gate itself had a feeling of evil when I almost jumped off it. Rather, I felt an urging toward oblivion, I suppose, toward peace. I do not believe it was bad. I do feel the Golden Gate Bridge is a place of great beauty, where many people merge with that beauty into a kind of serenity, a compulsion to get out of this world and into a better one. And that is not evil at all. But I do know that there are many evil things that lurk in the minds of all people who are left after the suicide of somebody they love.

—M. F. K. Fisher, *Last House: Reflections, Dreams, and Observations 1943–1991*

injuries, but Baldwin's buttocks and thighs absorbed the worst of the shock. He came to under water, wondering briefly whether he was alive or dead. "When I surfaced I instinctually started swimming and yelling for help," he says. "I remember shouting 'Help me! Help me!' God, I was happy to be alive."

Rescued by the Coast Guard, Baldwin arrived at Letterman Army Medical Center fully conscious, apologetic, and suffering slightly from exposure. He had a bruised lung and a cracked rib.

The damage to his marriage was more severe. When Ellen was first told her husband had leaped from the bridge, she laughed, believing it was a joke. Then she went into shock. "I didn't know what to think," says Ellen. "Generally, when you've been married for a while, you think you know your partner. Kenny always comes across as a fun-loving, outgoing guy and I thought we were the perfect family. The suicide attempt took me completely by surprise. I knew he was unhappy about work. But who is so unhappy that they would kill themselves?"

Ellen felt confused, guilty, angry. At one point, she considered leaving Ken. Both have since been helped by psychological counseling and therapy, but rebuilding trust has not been easy.

"Even today I wonder if Kenny is telling me the truth," says his wife. Still, Ken is learning to be more open, more willing to confess and share his fears. A few weeks ago, for example, Ken, who has found a new drafting job, was worried once more that his boss had found him wanting and was going to get rid of him. Says Ken: "The fear tormented me every day. In fact, I felt so sure this would happen that my productivity actually started to slip. I went to Ellen and told her I thought I was going to get fired and was depressed about it. Her response was, 'So what? You'll get another job. We'll work it out.' That really put things into perspective for me. She was right, of course. Life would go on."

Recently Baldwin heard about another person who jumped off the bridge and survived. He says he was really rooting for her and was saddened when he learned that she had died from her injuries. He says he wished he had been able to talk to her before she made the leap, to tell her his own story, to tell her that suicide is a permanent solution to a temporary problem. And that the Golden Gate Bridge, as alluring as it seems, is merely a way of getting from San Francisco to Marin County, and nowhere else.

William Plummer is an author and former academic with a Ph.D. in English from Rutgers University. He has published two books and has been a book reviewer at Newsweek, *literary editor at* Quest Magazine, *and Contributing Editor to the* Paris Review. *He lives in New Jersey with his family.*

✳

Some ideas for stopping suicides from the Bridge have been downright bizarre. In 1948, for example, after the death of a Hollywood stuntman who had planned on surviving his jump, a law against committing suicide from the bridge was proposed.

Some proposals have incorporated reverse psychology. A Maine woman suggested that a diving board, a hook for hanging one's jacket, and a mailbox for suicide notes would "remove the drama and make bridge suicides look silly."

Over the years, barriers have been tested, but no single design has garnered much support. Generally, economic and aesthetic considerations have trumped public health concerns.

Opponents of barriers (the majority, according to opinion polls) believe that no type of structure would really work, that those deterred from jumping would simply find other means to self-inflicted ends.

—Jeff Stryker, "An Awful Milestone for the Golden Gate Bridge," *The New York Times*

Lost Treasures

Treasure Island was once a celebration of tomorrow.

PEOPLE WHO ARE NEW TO SAN FRANCISCO KNOW THEY ARE entering an enchanted city when they drive across the Bay Bridge. They see it in the signs, especially the one pointing out the "Treasure Island" turnoff.

Treasure Island? The mind fills with images from the days of the Barbary Coast and the Gold Rush.

What few people realize is that in those days, the island never existed. It didn't rise from the San Francisco Bay like some mythical Atlantis-in-reverse. The City built it the old-fashioned way, shovelful by shovelful, scraping the bottom of the bay to dredge it into existence.

Politicians and engineers did this at the strangest possible time—at the height of the Depression, between 1937 and 1939—and for the strangest possible reason—to celebrate. They built the island to celebrate for the Golden Gate International Exposition, a West Coast world's fair (running concurrent with the New York World's Fair) to celebrate the completion of the Bay Bridge and Golden Gate Bridge.

And, for a variety of reasons, people still recall the fair with great nostalgia more than 50 years later. Will people in the year 2024 remember the 1974 World's Fair in Spokane with great fondness? I doubt it.

In short, the fair was important socially, economically, politically, scientifically, and culturally. Just as San Francisco said to the World in its 1915 Panama-Pacific Exposition that it had rebuilt itself from the great earthquake, so too did the people of San Francisco cry out to the world that it was now a world-class city which even in the midst of a depression could build two engineering wonders in its two new bridges.

It was a dream made of plywood and plaster, deliberately built only to last a couple of years. In 1940, after the Navy traded land for it, engineers tore down all but two airplane hangars and the Fair Administration building to make way for a naval base that would run the war in the Pacific. San Franciscans who recall say this era was the best time of their lives, that this fair held for them a kind of magical innocence which they can never recapture, that this fair was the most beautiful thing they had ever seen.

They remember it fondly also because they were involved. From people who donated full-grown trees and the engineers who dredged the Bay to form Treasure Island, to the hundreds of high school bands that marched there, the thousands of people the Fair employed, and the hundreds of thousands who attended the Fair, everyone seemed to have a stake in the Golden Gate International Exhibition.

Just look at the week before the Fair opened. Sister Karen Marie, O.P., former principal of St. Rose Academy, remembers that "just before the Fair opened, the whole city celebrated with an enthusiasm we have never duplicated. The district stores, as well as the big downtown ones, had false fronts, making the whole city look like a mining town. Everyone had something western or Spanish to wear for the fiesta. I can still remember the wonderful smell of a leather holder through which I looped a colorful cowboy bandanna. I wore that with a black Spanish hat with yellow pompoms around the rim. I guess I wanted to be both Spanish and a cowgirl. One day my father arrived home late from work. He had been in the hoosegow. He had grown neither beard nor a mustache for the celebration so he was plucked from the street and put into a cage-like jail cell right out in the open. Although he was guilty of being clean-shaven, he did have the fiesta spirit and enjoyed the whole experience."

From dances, to concerts with Benny Goodman and Tommy Dorsey, to Gayway concessions such as the headless woman, miniature horses, incubator babies, Stella of "Have You Seen Stella?" fame, Sally Rand's Nude Ranch, and Ripley's Believe It or Not, everyone came to the Fair to have a good time. Herb Caen's former assistant, Jerry Bundsen, worked as Press Agent for Sally Rand and her Nude Ranch. He remembers Sally Rand "as being all business. She had her girls all decked out with western outfits without tops and with skimpy bottoms. Sally would get up on the balcony where the patrons couldn't see her or hear her and she'd yell to the girls: 'Come on Nadine. Get over there and jump more, will you? And Helen, for God's sake, get up off your duff and walk over and bend down to pick the basketballs up.' She used to stand there like a maestro running an orchestra."

Retired Admiral James Grealish remembers the dances. "The main attraction for kids my age—nineteen at the time—was not so much the exhibits, but the dancing. It was a big deal to go across the Bay and have a night over there, listening to Benny Goodman or whoever it might be. It wasn't very expensive in those days. That was a typical college or high school approach to the Fair. I was shy, I guess. But there were always plenty of girls, and we'd get courage in numbers."

The Fair was more than fun, though. It was beautiful. The architecture was a mishmash of Pacific Rim styles, some real, some imagined. Michael Crow, founder of the Art Deco Society, praises the art and architecture of the island and points to its origins.

"There was an emphasis on the Pacific Basin at the time the Fair at Treasure Island was being constructed. The Pacific Rim was going to be opened for exploitation, and San Francisco and the Bay Area wanted to be the center for that. So some of the buildings were designed at the Fair to recall the Pacific Basin. But when you look at them in their detailing, you see that many are really Art

Deco, with zig-zags, steps, rays, chevrons, and stylized flower decorations. Flowers were shown as single round circles surrounded by the scalloped edges, very flat, very two-dimensional. The Mayan influence can also be seen in the Fair decorations. There was a very strong Egyptian revival after 1922, and a lot of those kinds of style elements were also used."

For many people, the buildings came alive only at night, when hidden spotlights bathed the strange Art Deco buildings. "There is a misconception that Art Deco is always pastel," Crowe adds. "For the most part there is a strong use of color in Art Deco. This was very much a part of the lighting of the Fair buildings. The idea of using strong color on buildings not only to paint them but also to light them was something that was an outgrowth of German Expressionism. The lights there were hidden in trees and bushes because naked light bulbs were no longer considered attractive. At one time they had been, of course; they were considered wonderful because they were a new invention, so you wanted to see them, to show them off. But by 1939 the movement was to control them a little and to create moods."

Other people only had eyes for the flowers, especially the magic carpet made of multi-colored ice plants. Vivian Girod, the widow of Julius Girod, the chief gardener at the Fair, remembers the great care they took to plant each bulb.

"Everything was planted according to when each flower would bloom. The bulbs, hundreds of thousands of bulbs, were put on ice so they wouldn't bloom too soon. That was quite a thing to figure out—to have everything blooming when the Fair opened. They used electricity, actually heating the soil, with some of the other plants. Each court was planned to highlight one particular color. For the blue court, my husband wanted ceanothus. It grows wild, but it can be cultivated. Everybody said, 'It's too cold here to transplant ceanothus.' My husband figured out that by heating the soil, he could do it."

Finally, people remember the Fair because it taught them how provincial they were. Great art from Europe and Asia came to the city like it never had come before. Katherine Caldwell, a retired art teacher from Mills College, served as director of education at the Fair's Palace of Fine Arts. She recalls the remarkable collections from Europe and Asia.

"This was the first time that a significant amount of material had been gathered in San Francisco for an Asian collection. There were some works of art from The David Collection in London that have not been inside this country before or since. It is a great collection of Chinese ceramics, chiefly Song Dynasty. But people weren't ready for it. People had no idea what they were looking at."

With the closing of the Fair and the bombing of Pearl Harbor one year later, San Franciscans put their memories of the Fair on hold. They didn't have time to think about the Fair, to reflect on the good times they had there.

In 1989, they had a chance to recall those glory days in a 50th anniversary celebration on the island, through television specials and in *The San Francisco Fair: Treasure Island 1939–1940,* from which the above recollections were taken.

San Franciscans fell in love with the Fair because it reflected our past and promised our future. It showed San Franciscans that all along they had been part of a Pacific Rim culture. And it heralded a future filled with robots such as Westinghouse's Voder, which could actually speak, and a new-fangled device called a television. You could walk in front of a camera in one room and your friends could actually see you on a television tube in the next room.

The Fair, too, was a kind of utopia. Overseas, Germany warred with France and Japan was occupying China. But on the island, the Chinese and Japanese exhibits coexisted peacefully. In most of the U.S., unemployment still made bread lines long. But on Treasure Island, they were giving away food from shiny aluminum booths. The Fair promised what life could be: peaceful, prosperous, and happy.

That's why people remember the island. It was a place where we all wanted to live.

Paul Totah is a San Francisco native who teaches English at St. Ignatius College Preparatory School. He is the editor of San Francisco Fair 1939-

1940 *and* Genesis III, *an alumni magazine for St. Ignatius. He feels he has reached suburban bliss with the acquisition of a mini-van and a cat, bringing his family dependents to 2.3.*

✳

Returning to San Francisco after a long stay in France, I was startled by a harangue about Treasure Island from a friend who is a cab driver, gardener, San Francisco historian and native, Vietnam vet, royalty watcher, and Victorian-architecture advocate—in short a typically unique San Franciscan. That fine afternoon in North Beach, G. K. had a lot to say about the future of the island, which he looks at every day and night from his Telegraph Hill garden.

G. K.'s plan, which he acknowledges to be quixotic, is for the island to become an "Isle de France," a working showcase of French language, cuisine, technology, and culture—in short, a Gallic counterpoint to Eurodisney in America's most European city. He reminded me of the long history (by American standards) of the French in San Francisco, from the Gold Rush, to the Palace of the Legion of Honor, to late-twentieth-century high-tech links with Silicon Valley and wine connections with Napa Valley. *If* the French, he argued, are serious about combatting American cultural imperialism, *if* they want Mitterand's Grand Biblioteque to be more than just a monument to a dead man and a dying way of life, they must take the fight to the Golden State—and specifically, to the city by the Golden Gate.

What's in it for San Francisco? G. K. envisions French culinary academies and markets, French language schools and cafes, fashion, science and wine institutes, all on a Nice-like promenade just a ferryboat ride from downtown San Francisco. It would be, he said, a celebration of France for those who cannot afford a trip to the real thing. After all, years ago San Francisco abandoned shipping and committed itself lock, stock, and barrel to tourism; France is the biggest tourism destination in the world: why not marry the two? This is the vision of someone whose first remembered dream was of France, who attended the Sorbonne at nineteen in fulfillment of that dream.

Later that afternoon, at another cafe on Washington Square, as I eavesdropped on two French women and watched an old man in a black beret sip Pernod, I wondered if G. K. might not be right. I thought of the words of another man who had marvelous dreams for San Francisco at a prior century mark, architect Daniel H. Burnham: "Make no little plans. They have no magic to stir men's blood and probably will not be realized. Make big plans."

Willie Brown, Dianne Feinstein, Jacques Chirac—are you listening?

—James O'Reilly, "San Francisco 2020"

PART FIVE

THE LAST WORD

Footprints in the Sand

*Mister San Francisco reflects on the
passage of friends, and the inadequacies of Heaven.*

"A QUINTESSENTIAL SAN FRANCISCAN." A SPLENDID PHRASE THAT
rolls trippingly off the tongue, as it did all through the long, dark
rainy weekend. A religious person said "The heavens are crying."
I looked at her, but if it made her feel better to say so, fair enough.
We all have our own ways of trying to cope with the loss of dear
ones, beloved friends and enemies, or people we scarcely knew
and yet recognize as irreplaceable pieces in the mosaic of San
Francisco life.

"A quintessential San Franciscan." The rhythmic orotund phrase
was applied for days to Edmund G. "Pat" Brown, to Prentis Cobb
Hale, to Rhoda (Mrs. Richard) Goldman, to Scott Beach, these
memorable, colorful, important-to-the-city people who died
within days or hours of one another as, yes, the heavens wept and
their survivors had to think about the unthinkable.

Quintessential, "the pure, highly concentrated essence of something," as one famous dictionary puts it in a strangely offhand way.
The "something" in this case is the San Francisconess of the departed. How define that? A respect for the history and traditions
of the city. A certain modesty of demeanor, a dislike of showiness,

an eye for phoniness. A truly democratic spirit of accepting people on their own terms. A high tolerance for eccentrics and ec-
centricities, an all-out appreciation of talent and artistry.

Most of all, the quintessential San Franciscan is not *impressed*. Let
other cities and their people brag and boast. The QSFan sits back
with an amused smile, secure in the knowledge that binds us all
together: we live in a unique place. We've seen it rise and fall,
sometimes literally, and no, it isn't perfect. There are a lot of things
that need fixing and we'll get around to fixing them. All in due
time. Meanwhile, let us mix a martini (easy on the vermouth),
admire the view and talk at length about our good fortune.

Pat Brown was as QSF as they come, a plainspoken guy who
just plain loved his fellow man. To some, this made him "a back-
slapper and handshaker," as though those were bad things. There
was warmth in his handshake and he didn't slap your back to pinch
your wallet. Not only a quintessential San Franciscan but its corol-
lary in the higher reaches of the cliché, a consummate politician.

And yet there was nothing devious about him. He was a
"gee/golly" kind of guy. "Gee, I don't know," he'd say when hit
with a tough question, "but I'll sure as heck find out." When he
won his first race, to become district attorney, he was moved to
a loud "Golly!" The local press had backed him 100 percent
because he hung out at the old Press Club at Powell and Sutter,
drinking with "the boys" and playing the slot machines that paid
the club's bills, and then some. When he became D.A., he immediately ordered the slot machines confiscated. "Before I was
elected, they weren't illegal," he explained, "but now they are."

Pat was naive, sweet, honest and unguarded. "Bumbling Pat" was
one of the nicknames his detractors hung on him. When riots
broke out on the Cal campus, he said "Golly, this is the worst
thing to happen to California since I was elected." His reluctance
to crack down made him "a tower of Jell-O." A sample of his
humor: after duck hunting with Earl Warren, he returned from
the blinds with four ducks, whereas the chief justice had five, the
legal limit. "I commuted one," Pat explained with a laugh.

Too bad he didn't do the same for Caryl Chessman.

Prentis Cobb Hale was born into a life of privilege but there wasn't a pretentious bone in his body. Their mutual love for the city made Prentis and Pat good friends, though I doubt Prentis ever voted for him. Unlike Pat, Prentis was tough. Like Pat, he had no use for fancy clothes or fancy cars but had friends in all walks of life. "I can't stand phonies," he said many times, and he could spot one, unerringly, at 100 feet. Non-phonies were never a problem. Prentis was either the worst or the best driver I ever rode with. He had a beat up old Buick he'd drive to Opera openings, while the phonies arrived in their rented limos, and this was when he was president of the Opera. With his beloved wife, Denise, screaming in terror, he'd drive the wrong way up Franklin to his parking space behind the Opera House. "I'm the president," he'd say. "I can go in either direction." Police officers would siren him down, take a look at that familiar tough/handsome face and say "Oh, good evening, Mr. Hale. Need an escort?"

The women in their lives: Pat's Brown's wife, Bernice, was and is one of the most beautiful and gracious of women. "My greatest asset," Pat would say. Prentis' first wife, Pat, was every-

Edmund G. "Pat" Brown—governor of California from 1959 to 1967, and father of Jerry Brown, who was California governor from 1975 to 1983.

Prentis Cobb Hale—business and civic leader who served many years as president of the San Francisco Opera and director of the San Francisco Symphony and War Memorial Board.

Rhoda Haas Goldman— philanthropist who established the Richard and Rhoda Goldman Fund and created the Goldman Environmental Prize. She was a member of the Haas family, descendants of Levi Strauss, and owners of the jean company that bears his name.

Scott Beach—Renaissance man with a thundering voice who was known for his comic genius, knowledge of serious music, his work in radio and film, and as a popular M.C. for fund-raising events.

Caryl Chessman—convicted kidnapper who died in the gas chamber in 1960. Governor Brown, who was deeply opposed to capital punishment, allowed him to be executed because his oath of office bound him to enforce the law.

—JO'R, LH, and SO'R

body's sweetheart, warm, delightful and a hard worker for city causes. His widow, Denise, brought sophistication, wit and glamour into his life. Which brings us to Rhoda Goldman, who died unexpectedly at 71. Like all members of the amazing Haas family, she was quintessentially San Franciscan, a striking woman of means and dignity who was also shy and even plain in her resolute eschewing of fine feathers. Quality without glitz—the entire Haas family has it, a tribute to the founding fathers, who must have instilled a sense of modesty from the very beginning. As for their sense of public duty and generosity, they are unsurpassed.

Death, the final frontier, the last taboo. We don't want our friends to die. As quintessential San Franciscans, they are doomed to be eternally unhappy. Even if they go to heaven, a place that is said to resemble Sonoma in the spring, they'll say "It's nice but it isn't San Francisco."

Herb Caen was the ultimate quintessential San Franciscan. He wrote his daily newspaper column about the city from 1938 until his death on February 1, 1997, and was one of San Francisco's most beloved citizens. The San Francisco Chronicle *columnist was awarded a special Pulitzer Prize in 1996 shortly after his 80th birthday, with the Pulitzer board citing his "extraordinary and continuing contribution as a voice and a conscience of his city." His wit and charm are sorely missed.*

⋆

Books for Further Reading

We hope *Travelers' Tales San Francisco* has inspired you to read on. A good place to start is the books from which we've made selections, and these are listed below along with other books that we have found to be valuable. Some of these may be out of print but are well worth hunting down. General guidebooks are also worth reading, and the best have annotated bibliographies or sections on recommended books and maps.

Barron, Cheryll Aimee. *Dreamers of the Valley of Plenty.* New York: Scribner, 1995.

Barton, Bruce Walter. *The Tree at the Center of the World: A Story of the California Missions.* Santa Barbara, California: Ross-Erikson Publishers, 1980.

Bean, Walton. *Boss Ruef's San Francisco: The Story of the Union Labor Party, Big Business, and the Graft Prosecution.* Berkeley: University of California Press, 1952.

Beebe, Lucius and Charles Clegg. *San Francisco's Golden Era: A Picture Story of San Francisco Before the Fire.* Berkeley: Howell-North Books, 1960.

Beebe, Morton. *San Francisco.* New York: Harry N. Abrams, Inc., 1995.

Brammer, Alex. *Victorian Classics of San Francisco.* Sausalito, California: Windgate Press, 1987.

Bronson, William. *The Earth Shook, The Sky Burned.* Garden City, New York: Doubleday and Company, Inc. 1959.

Bruce, J. Campbell. *Escape from Alcatraz.* San Francisco: Comstock Editions, 1986.

Caen, Herb. *One Man's San Francisco: A Continuing Love Affair with The City.* New York: Doubleday & Company, Inc., 1976.

Conaway, James. *Napa: The Story of an American Eden.* New York: Richard Todd Books (a division of Houghton Mifflin Company), 1990.

Conrad, Barnaby. *Name Dropping: Tales from My Barbary Coast Saloon.* New York: HarperCollins West, 1994.

Conrad III, Barnaby. *The Martini: An Illustrated History of an American Classic.* San Francisco: Chronicle Books, 1995.

Corbett, Michael, R. and Charles Hall Page & Associates, Inc. *Splendid Survivors: San Francisco's Downtown Architectural Heritage.* San Francisco: California Living Books, 1979

Daniels, Douglas Henry. *Pioneer Urbanites: A Social and Cultural History of Black San Francisco.* Berkeley: University of California Press, 1990.

Delehanty, Randolph. *In the Victorian Style.* San Francisco: Chronicle Books, 1991.

Delehanty, Randolph. *San Francisco: The Ultimate Guide.* San Francisco: Chronicle Books, 1995.

Dillon, Richard H. *The Hatchet Men: The Story of the Tong Wars in San Francisco's Chinatown.* San Francisco: Comstock Editions, 1962.

Doss, Margot Patterson. *Paths of Gold: In and Around the Golden Gate National Recreation Area.* San Francisco: Chronicle Books, 1974.

Farnetano, Bernardino. *Saint Francis of Assisi.* Italy: Casa Editrice Francescana, 1984.

Ferlinghetti, Lawrence. *A Coney Island of the Mind.* New York: New Directions Publishing Corp., 1958.

Ferlinghetti, Lawrence and Nancy J. Peters. *Literary San Francisco: A Pictorial History from Its Beginnings to the Present Day.* San Francisco: City Lights Books and Harper & Row, Publishers, 1980.

Fisher, M.F.K. *Last House: Reflections, Dreams, and Observations 1943-1991.* New York: Pantheon Books, 1995.

Fong-Torres, Shirley. *San Francisco: A Walking Tour.* Berkeley: Pacific View Press, 1991.

Gentry, Curt. *The Madams of San Francisco.* Sausalito, California: Comstock Editions, Inc., 1964.

Gilliam, Harold. *The San Francisco Experience: The Romantic Lore Behind the Fabulous Facade of the Bay Area.* New York: Doubleday, 1972.

Ginsberg, Allen. *Howl and Other Poems.* San Francisco: City Lights Books, 1959.

Gold, Herbert. *Bohemia: Where Art, Angst, Love and Strong Coffee Meet.* New York: Simon & Schuster, Inc., 1993.

Gold, Herbert. *Travels in San Francisco*. New York: Arcade Publishing, Inc., 1990.

Hammett, Dashiell. *The Maltese Falcon*. New York: Vintage Books, 1972.

Hansen, Gladys. *San Francisco Almanac: Everything You Want to Know About Everyone's Favorite City*. San Francisco: Chronicle Books, 1995.

Hansen, Stephen Jay. *The Other Guide to San Francisco*. San Francisco: Chronicle Books, 1980.

Hart, James, D. *A Companion to California*. New York: Oxford University Press, 1978.

Holliday, J.S. *The World Rushed In: The California Gold Rush Experience*. New York: Simon and Schuster, 1981.

Levy, JoAnn. *They Saw the Elephant: Women in the California Gold Rush*. Hamden, Connecticut: Archon Books, 1990.

Lewis, Oscar. *Bay Window Bohemia: An Account of the Brilliant Artistic World of Gaslit San Francisco*. Garden City, New York: Doubleday and Company, Inc. 1956.

Lewis, Oscar. *This Was San Francisco: Being First Hand Accounts of the Evolution of One of America's Favorite Cities*. New York: David McKay Company, 1962.

Lockwood, Charles. *Suddenly San Francisco: The Early Years of an Instant City*. San Francisco: California Living Books, 1978.

London, Jack. *The Valley of the Moon*. California: David Rejl, 1988.

Maran, Meredith. *What It's Like to Live Now*. New York: Bantam Books, 1995.

Margolin, Malcolm. *The Way We Lived: California Indian Reminiscences, Stories & Songs*. Berkeley: Heydey Books, 1981.

Margolin, Malcolm. *The Ohlone Way: Indian Life in the San Francisco-Monterey Bay Area*. Berkeley: Heydey Books, 1978.

McKinney, John. *A Walk Along Land's End: Discovering California's Unknown Coast*. New York: HarperCollins West, 1995.

Miller, John. *San Francisco Stories: Great Writers on the City*. San Francisco: Chronicle Books, 1990.

Miller, Luree. *Literary Hills of San Francisco*. Washington, D.C.: Starhill Press, 1992.

Miloscz, Czeslaw, translated by Richard Lourie. *Visions from San Francisco Bay*. New York: Farrar, Straus, Giroux, 1982.

Paul, Jim. *What's Called Love: A Real Romance.* New York: Villard Books, 1993.

Pierce, J. Kingston. *San Francisco, You're History.* Seattle: Sasquatch Books, 1995.

Pitcher, Don. *Berkeley Inside/Out.* Berkeley: Heydey Books, 1989.

Quiett, Glenn C. *They Built the West: An Epic of Rails and Cities.* Los Angeles: D. Appleton-Century, 1934.

Richards, Rand. *Historic San Francisco: A Concise History and Guide.* San Francisco: Heritage House Publishers, 1995.

Riegert, Ray. *Hidden San Francisco and Northern California.* Berkeley: Ulysses Press, 1996.

Rogers, Susan Fox. *Another Wilderness: New Outdoor Writing by Women.* Seattle: Seal Press, 1994.

Setterberg, Fred. *The Roads Taken: Travels through America's Literary Landscapes.* Athens, Georgia: The University of Georgia Press, 1993.

Siefkin, David. *The City at the End of the Rainbow: San Francisco and Its Grand Hotels.* New York: G. P. Putnam's Sons, 1976.

Slick, Darby. *Don't You Want Somebody to Love: Reflections on the San Francisco Sound.* Berkeley: SLG Books, 1991.

Stienstra, Tom. *Epic Trips of the West: Tom Stienstra's Ten Best.* San Francisco: Foghorn Press, 1994.

Theriault, Reg. *How to Tell When You're Tired: A Brief Examination of Work.* New York: W.W. Norton & Co., Inc., 1995.

Unterman, Patricia. *Patricia Unterman's Food Lover's Guide to San Francisco.* San Francisco: Chronicle Books, 1995.

Weirde, Dr. *Dr. Weirde's Weirde Tours: A Guide to Mysterious San Francisco.* San Francisco: Barrett-James Books, 1994.

Williams, Mary Ada. *More Parkside Pranks and Sunset Stunts.* San Francisco: The North Scale Institute, 1990.

Wollenberg, Charles. *Golden Gate Metropolis: Perspectives on Bay Area History.* Berkeley: Institute of Governmental Studies, 1985.

Yee, Chiang. *The Silent Traveller in San Francisco.* New York: W. W. Norton & Co., Inc., 1964.

Index

Index of Contributors

Acknowledgements

Heartfelt thanks to Wenda Brewster O'Reilly, Andrea, Noelle, and Mariele O'Reilly, Paula McCabe, Brenda O'Reilly, Clement, Seumas, and Liam O'Reilly, Timothy O'Reilly, Susan Brady, Raj Khadka, Cindy Collins, Maureen and Kerry Kravitz, Judy Anderson. Special thanks also to Gary Kray, Keith Granger, David White, Cynthia Lamb, Steve Anderson, Deborah Greco, Trisha Schwartz, Jennifer Leo, Patty Holden, Jeff Davis, George Lau, Him Mark Lai, Irene Bricca, Garrett Meyers, Bob Holmes, George V. Wright, Judith Lynch, Lorraine June, Helen Chang and Cynthia Westerbrook of the San Francisco Convention and Visitors Bureau, and Janet Dustin of *National Geographic Traveler.*

"Pearl Necklace" by Steve Van Beek reprinted by permission of the author. Copyright © 1996 by Steve Van Beek.

"Wild Light" by Andrei Codrescu reprinted from the September 1995 issue of *Southwest Airlines Spirit Magazine.* Reprinted by permission of the author. Copyright © 1995 by Andrei Codrescu.

"Pacific World" by George Vincent Wright reprinted by permission of the author. Copyright © 1996 by George Vincent Wright.

"What You See is Who You Are" by Mark Childress reprinted from the April 1992 issue of *San Francisco Focus.* Reprinted by permission of the author. Copyright © 1992 by Mark Childress.

"When San Francisco Was Cool" by Herbert Gold excerpted from *Bohemia: Where Art, Angst, Love and Strong Coffee Meet* by Herbert Gold. Reprinted by permission of the author. Copyright © 1993 by Herbert Gold.

"I Was a Teenage Yogi" by James O'Reilly reprinted by permission of the author. Copyright © 1996 by James O'Reilly.

"The Real Mission" by John Krich reprinted from the October 1,

1989 issue of *The New York Times Magazine*. Copyright © 1989 by the New York Times Company. Reprinted by permission.

"Circle of Gold" by Michele Anna Jordan originally appeared as "Yellow and Gold" in the March 4, 1993 issue of the *Sonoma County Independent*. Reprinted by permission of the author. Copyright © 1993 by Michele Anna Jordan.

"Freakin' in Frisco" by Michael Lane and Jim Crotty (The Monks) reprinted from *Monk, The Mobile Magazine*. Reprinted by permission of the authors. Copyright © 1995 by Michael Lane and Jim Crotty (The Monks).

"North Beach at Twilight" by Gary Kamiya reprinted from the June 27, 1993 issue of *Image Magazine*. Reprinted by permission of the *San Francisco Examiner* and the author. Copyright © 1993 by the *San Francisco Examiner*.

"City Perched on a Frontier" by Tom Cole reprinted from *San Francisco,* Photographs by Morton Beebe, Essays by Various Authors. Reprinted by permission of the author and Morton Beebe. Copyright © 1985 by Tom Cole.

"Glide and the Family Church" by Sean O'Reilly reprinted by permission of the author. Copyright © 1996 by Sean O'Reilly.

"The Heavenly Gates" by Chiang Yee excerpted from *The Silent Traveller in San Francisco* by Chiang Yee. Copyright © 1964 by W. W. Norton & Company, Inc. Reprinted by permission of W. W. Norton & Company, Inc. and Methuen.

"Dreaming of Muir Woods" by Mary Tolaro Noyes reprinted by permission of the author. Copyright © 1996 by Mary Tolaro Noyes.

"My Father's Jack London" by Fred Setterberg excerpted from *The Roads Taken: Travels Through America's Literary Landscapes* by Fred Setterberg. Reprinted by permission of The University of Georgia Press and the author. Copyright © 1993, 1995 by Fred Setterberg.

"Night Skates" by Susanna Levin reprinted from *Another Wilderness: New Outdoor Writing by Women* edited by Susan Fox Rogers (Seal Press, Seattle, WA). Reprinted by permission. Copyright © 1994 by Susan Fox Rogers.

"The Lost Roman Baths of Adolph Sutro" and "The Specter of Grand View Peak" by Harold Gilliam excerpted from *The San Francisco Experience: The Romantic Lore Behind the Fabulous Facade*

Additional Credits (arranged alphabetically by title)

Reprinted by permission of *Discover Magazine.* Copyright ©
1993 by The Walt Disney Co.

Selection from "Beat San Francisco" reprinted from the November
1990 issue of *Sunset.* Reprinted by permission of Sunset
Publishing Corp. Copyright © 1990 by Sunset Publishing
Corp.

Selection from Historical Introduction by Malcolm Margolin to
Berkeley Inside/Out by Don Pitcher reprinted by permission of
Heydey Books. Historical introduction copyright © 1989 by
Malcolm Margolin, text copyright © 1989 by Don Pitcher.

Selection from "The Best Place to Pee in the Mission" reprinted from
the July 26, 1995 issue of the *San Francisco Bay Guardian.*
Reprinted by permission. Copyright © 1995 by the *San Francisco
Bay Guardian.*

Selections from "Boys in the Avenues" by James, Sean, and Tim
O'Reilly reprinted by permission of the authors. Copyright ©
1996 by James, Sean, and Tim O'Reilly.

Selection from "Bringing It All Back Home for Jerry" by Burr Snider
reprinted from the August 13, 1995 issue of the *San Francisco
Examiner.* Reprinted by permission of the author. Copyright ©
1995 by Burr Snider.

Selection from "Californian Idolatry" reprinted from the February
10, 1990 issue of *The Economist.* Reprinted by permission of
The Economist. Copyright © 1990 by The Economist
Newspaper Group, Inc.

Selection from "Call me 'Dude" by Kathryn Marshall reprinted from
the December 1995 issue of *Southwest Airlines Spirit Magazine.*
Reprinted by permission of the author. Copyright © 1995 by
Kathryn Marshall.

Selection from "Citizen Caen, An Interview with Herb Caen" by
Mark Powelson reprinted from the December 1995 issue of *San
Francisco Focus.* Reprinted by permission of *San Francisco Focus.*
Copyright © 1995 by *San Francisco Focus.*

Selections from *The City at the End of the Rainbow: San Francisco and
Its Grand Hotels* by David Siefkin reprinted by permission of
Putnum Publishing Group. Copyright © 1976 by David Siefkin.

Selection from "A City-State of Mind" by William Rusher reprinted
from the February 19, 1990 issue of the *National Review.*
Reprinted by permission of the *National Review.* Copyright ©

Selection from *Historic San Francisco: A Concise History and Guide* by Rand Richards reprinted by permission of Heritage House Publishers and the author. Copyright © 1995 by Rand Richards.

Selection from "A Home in the World" by Rajendra S. Khadka reprinted by permission of the author. Copyright © 1996 by Rajendra S. Khadka.

Selection from "Home of the Stars" by Michael Muzell reprinted from the June 1992 issue of *San Francisco Focus.* Reprinted by permission of the author. Copyright © 1992 by Michael Muzell.

Selection from "House of Cards on the Barbary Coast" by James O'Reilly and Larry Habegger reprinted by permission of the authors. Copyright © 1996 by James O'Reilly and Larry Habegger.

Selection from *How to Tell When You're Tired: A Brief Examination of Work* by Reg Theriault copyright © 1995 by Reg Theriault. Reprinted by permission of W. W. Norton & Company, Inc.

Selection from "Howl" by Allen Ginsberg excerpted from *Howl and Other Poems* by Allen Ginsberg. Copyright © 1956, 1959 by Allen Ginsberg. Reprinted by permission of HarperCollins Publisher, Inc.

Selection from "In Golden Gate Park That Day…" by Lawrence Ferlinghetti excerpted from *A Coney Island of the Mind* by Lawrence Ferlinghetti. Reprinted by permission of New Directions Publishing Corp. Copyright © 1958 by Lawrence Ferlinghetti.

Selection from "Inner Sunset" by Lisa Meltzer reprinted by permission of the author. Copyright © 1996 by Lisa Meltzer.

Selection from "Jack London's Eyewitness Account" by Jack London reprinted from *Collier's.* Reprinted by permission of Time-Life Books. Copyright © Time-Life Books.

Selection from "The King is Dead…Long Live the Queens: The Fags and Hags of SF Rock & Roll" by Don Baird reprinted from *Monk, The Mobile Magazine.* Reprinted by permission of *Monk, The Mobile Magazine.* Copyright © 1995 by *Monk, The Mobile Magazine.*

Selections from "Lady of the Avenues" by Sean O'Reilly reprinted by permission of the author. Copyright © 1996 by Sean O'Reilly.

Selection from "The Last Chants" by Richard Rodriguez reprinted

Selection from "Napa Valley Wine Train" by Patricia Unterman reprinted from the August 22, 1993 issue of the *San Francisco Chronicle.* Reprinted by permisison of the *San Francisco Chronicle.* Copyright © 1993 by the *San Francisco Chronicle.*

Selection from "Night and the City" by Jack Boulware reprinted from the March 20, 1996 issue of the *San Francisco Weekly.* Reprinted by permission of the author. Copyright © 1996 by Jack Boulware.

Selection from "No Turning Back" by Kay Schaber reprinted by permission of the author. Copyright © 1996 by Kay Schaber.

Selection from *The Ohlone Way: Indian Life in the San Francisco-Monterey Bay Area* by Malcolm Margolin reprinted by permission of Heydey Books. Copyright © 1978 by Malcolm Margolin.

Selections from *One Man's San Francisco: A Continuing Love Affair with The City* by Herb Caen. Copyright © 1976 by Herb Caen. Used by permission of Doubleday, a division of Bantam Doubleday Dell Publishing Group, Inc.

Selection from "Opportunity Knocks" by Michael Castleman reprinted from the May/June 1995 issue of *Mother Jones.* Reprinted by permission of *Mother Jones.* Copyright © 1995 by Foundation for National Progress.

Selections from *The Other Guide to San Francisco* by Stephen Jay Hansen reprinted by permission of Chronicle Books. Copyright © 1980 by Stephen Jay Hansen.

Selection from *Paths of Gold: In and Around the Golden Gate National Recreation Area* by Margot Patterson Doss reprinted by permission of Chronicle Books. Copyright © 1974 by Margot Patterson Doss.

Selection from "Pet Cemetery" by Lucy McCauley reprinted by permission of the author. Copyright © 1996 by Lucy McCauley.

Selections from *Pioneer Urbanites: A Social and Cultural History of Black San Francisco* edited by Douglas Henry Daniels reprinted by permission of University of California Press. Copyright © 1990 by the Regents of the University of California.

Selections from "A Poet Visits the New Main Library" by Robert Hass reprinted from the April 14, 1996 issue of the *San Francisco Examiner.* Reprinted by permission of the author. Copyright © 1996 by Robert Hass.

Selections from *San Francisco's Golden Era: A Picture Story of San Francisco Before the Fire* by Lucius Beebe and Charles Clegg. Copyright © 1960 by Howell-North Books.

Selection from "The Scenes, Scents and Sounds of San Francisco" by Herb Caen reprinted by permission of the author. Copyright © by Herb Caen.

Selection from "Secret Swell" by David Batstone reprinted from the August 10, 1994 issue of the *San Francisco Bay Guardian*. Reprinted by permission of the author. Copyright © 1994 by David Batstone.

Selection from "See It at Its Best" by Diane Johnson reprinted from the November 1989 issue of *Condé Nast Traveler*. Reprinted by permission of the author. Copyright © 1989 by Diane Johnson.

Selection from "Shark Fishing: Lots of Sport, Beginners Welcome" reprinted from the October 1991 issue of *Sunset*. Reprinted by permission of Sunset Publishing Corp. Copyright © 1991 by Sunset Publishing Corp.

Selections from *The Silent Traveller in San Francisco* by Chiang Yee. Copyright © 1964 by W. W. Norton & Company, Inc. Reprinted by permission of W. W. Norton Company, Inc. and Methuen.

Selection from "Stars Make Hits in Local Studios" by Paul Liberatore reprinted from the March 20, 1994 issue of the *Marin Independent Journal*. Reprinted by permission of the *Marin Independent Journal*. Copyright © 1994 by the *Marin Independent Journal*.

Selection from *Suddenly San Francisco: The Early Years of an Instant City* by Charles Lockwood reprinted by permission of the author. Copyright © 1978 by Charles Lockwood.

Selection from "Sunday Morning Improv" reprinted from the July 1995 issue of *Psychology Today*. Copyright © 1995 by Sussex Publishers, Inc. Reprinted by permission.

Selection from "A Symbol of Civility" by Kevin Starr excerpted from *San Francisco,* Photographs by Morton Beebe, Essays by Various Authors. Reprinted by permission of the author and Morton Beebe. Copyright © 1985 by Kevin Starr.

Selections from "Taking the Waters" by Peggy Knickerbocker reprinted from the February 1994 issue of *San Francisco Focus*. Reprinted by permission of the author. Copyright © 1994 by Peggy Knickerbocker.

About the Editors

James O'Reilly and Larry Habegger first worked together as late night disc jockeys at Dartmouth College in New Hampshire. They wrote mystery serials for the *San Francisco Examiner* in the early 1980s before turning to travel writing. Since 1983, their travel features and self-syndicated column, "World Travel Watch," have appeared in magazines and newspapers in the United States and other countries. James was born in Oxford, England, raised in San Francisco, and lives with his family in Leavenworth, Washington and France; Larry was born and raised in Minnesota and lives on Telegraph Hill in San Francisco.

Sean O'Reilly is a former seminarian, stockbroker, and bank slave who lives in Arizona with his wife Brenda and their four small boys. Widely traveled in Europe, he most recently spent time roaming East Africa and the Indian Ocean. He is also at work on a book called *Politics and the Soul: The River of Gold,* which he describes as a "re-examination of classic Greek, Roman, and Christian philosophies as tools for moral excellence in modern society."

TRAVELERS' TALES

LOOK FOR THESE TITLES IN THE SERIES

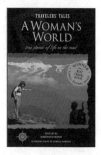

"I loved this book! From the very first story, I had the feeling that I'd been waiting to read these women's tales for years. I also had the sense that I'd met these women before. I hadn't, of course, but as a woman and a traveler I felt an instant connection with them. What a rare pleasure."

—Kimberly Brown, *Travel & Leisure*

TRAVELERS' TALES: A WOMAN'S WORLD
Edited by Marybeth Bond
1st Edition June 1995, ISBN 1-885211-06-6

A WOMAN'S WORLD and THAILAND,
Winners of the Lowell Thomas Award for
BEST TRAVEL BOOK
Society of American Travel Writers

"This is the best background reading I've ever seen on Thailand!"

—Carl Parkes, author of *Thailand Handbook, Southeast Asia Handbook* by Moon Publications

TRAVELERS' TALES THAILAND
Edited by James O'Reilly & Larry Habegger
1st Edition December 1993, ISBN 1-885211-05-8

"If Paris is the main dish, here is a rich and fascinating assortment of hors d'oeuvres. *Bon appetit et bon voyage!*"

—Peter Mayle, author of *A Year in Provence* and *Toujours Provence*

TRAVELERS' TALES PARIS
Edited by James O'Reilly, Larry Habegger & Sean O'Reilly
1st Edition March 1997, ISBN 1-885211-10-4

Check with your local bookstore for these titles or call O'Reilly to order:
800-889-8969 (credit cards only-Weekdays 6 AM -5 PM PST)
707-829-0515, 800-998-9938 (inquiries), or email to: order@ora.com

"*Travelers' Tales Hong Kong* is a most elegant, entertaining, and reliable way of getting to grips with the conundrum that is Hong Kong."

—Jan Morris, author of *Journeys, Locations*, and *Hong Kong*

TRAVELERS' TALES HONG KONG

Edited by James O'Reilly, Larry Habegger & Sean O'Reilly
1st Edition January 1996, ISBN 1-885211-03-1

"Only the lowest wattage dimbulb would visit Brazil without reading this book."

—Tim Cahill, author of *Jaguars Ripped My Flesh* and *Pecked to Death by Ducks*

TRAVELERS' TALES BRAZIL

Edited by Annette Haddad & Scott Doggett
1st Edition January 1997, ISBN 1-885211-11-2

"Sterling's themes are nothing less than human universality, passion and necessity, all told in stories straight from the gut."

—Maxine Hong Kingston, author of *Woman Warrior* and *China Men*

TRAVELERS' TALES FOOD

Edited by Richard Sterling
1st Edition November 1996, ISBN 1-885211-09-0

The first smaller format, "tips" book in the Travelers' Tales series, Gutsy Women is an indispensable pocket guide with travel tips for women on the road. It offers a wealth of fresh ideas on how to travel safely, comfortably, within your budget, alone, with your mother or children. It's packed with instructive and inspiring travel vignettes— a must-have for novice as well as experienced travelers.

TRAVELERS' TALES: GUTSY WOMEN
TRAVEL TIPS AND WISDOM FOR THE ROAD

By Marybeth Bond
1st Edition October 1996, ISBN 1-885211-15-5

"A superb, eclectic collection that reeks wonderfully of gazpacho and paella, and resonates with sounds of heel-clicking and flamenco singing—and makes you feel that you are actually in that amazing state of mind called Iberia."

—Barnaby Conrad, author of *Matador* and *Name Dropping*

TRAVELERS' TALES SPAIN
Edited by Lucy McCauley
1st Edition November 1995, ISBN 1-885211-07-4

"All you always wanted to know about the French but were afraid to ask! Explore the country and its people in a unique and personal way even before getting there. Travelers' Tales: your best passport to France and the French!"

—Anne Sengés, *Journal Français d'Amérique*

TRAVELERS' TALES FRANCE
Edited by James O'Reilly, Larry Habegger & Sean O'Reilly
1st Edition June 1995, ISBN 1-885211-02-3

"The essays are lyrical, magical and evocative: some of the images make you want to rinse your mouth out to clear the dust."

—Karen Troianello, *Yakima Herald-Republic*

TRAVELERS' TALES INDIA
Edited by James O'Reilly & Larry Habegger
1st Edition January 1995, ISBN 1-885211-01-5

"*Travelers' Tales Mexico* opens a window on the beauties and mysteries of Mexico and the Mexicans. It's entertaining, intriguing, baffling, instructive, insightful, inspiring and hilarious—just like Mexico."

—Tom Brosnahan, co-author of Lonely Planet's *Mexico—a travel survival kit*

TRAVELERS' TALES MEXICO
Edited by James O'Reilly & Larry Habegger
1st Edition September 1994, ISBN 1-885211-00-7

VISIT TRAVELERS' TALES ON THE INTERNET

READ A STORY. ENTER A CONTEST. PLAN A TRIP.

Way back in 1993, we were the first travel book publisher on the World Wide Web, and our site has been growing ever since. Point your Web browser to **http://www.ora.com/ttales** and you'll discover which books we're working on, how to submit your own story, the latest writing contests you can enter, and the location of the next author event. We offer sample chapters from all of our books, as well as the occasional trip report and photo essay from our hard-working editors. Be sure to take one of our Webtours, an exhaustive list of Internet resources for each of our titles, and begin planning your own journey.

SUBMIT YOUR OWN TRAVEL TALE

Do you have a tale of your own that you would like to submit to Travelers' Tales? We highly recommend that you first read one or more of our books to get a feel for the kind of story we're looking for. For submission guidelines and a list of titles in the works, send a SASE to:

Travelers' Tales Submission Guidelines
101 Morris Street, Sebastopol, CA 95472

or send email to *ttguidelines@online.ora.com*
or check out our website at **www.ora.com/ttales**

You can send your story to the address above or via email to *ttsubmit@ora.com*. On the outside of the envelope, *please indicate what country/topic your story is about*. If your story is selected for one of our titles, we will contact you about rights and payment.

We hope to hear from you. In the meantime, enjoy the stories!